The Expanding City

JEAN GOTTMANN, 1983

[Photograph by Hazel Rossotti
Fellow of St Anne's College
Oxford

The Expanding City

ESSAYS IN HONOUR OF PROFESSOR JEAN GOTTMANN

---

edited by

JOHN PATTEN

Hertford College
Oxford

1983

ACADEMIC PRESS

A Subsidiary of Harcourt Brace Jovanovich, Publishers

LONDON   NEW YORK
PARIS   SAN DIEGO   SAN FRANCISCO   SÃO PAULO
SYDNEY   TOKYO   TORONTO

ACADEMIC PRESS INC. (LONDON) LTD.
24/28 Oval Road
London NW1

United States Edition published by
ACADEMIC PRESS INC.
111 Fifth Avenue
New York, New York 10003

British Library Cataloguing in Publication Data

The Expanding city.
1. Gottmann Jean   2. Cities and towns — Growth —
Addresses, essays, lectures
I. Patten, John   II. Gottmann, Jean
307.7'6   HT371

ISBN 0-12-547250-1

LCCCN 82-074351

Phototypeset by Dobbie Typesetting Service, Plymouth, Devon
Printed in Great Britain by Galliard (Printers) Ltd, Great Yarmouth

Contributors

Professor Y. Ben-Arieh
Department of Geography
The Hebrew University of Jerusalem
Jerusalem
Israel

Professor M. Chisholm
Department of Geography
University of Cambridge
Downing Place
Cambridge
CB2 3EN
UK

Professor W. B. Fisher
Department of Geography
Science Laboratories
University of Durham
South Road
Durham City DH1 3LE
UK

Professor J. B. Goddard
Department of Geography
Daysh Building
The University
Newcastle upon Tyne
NE1 7RU
UK

Professor P. Hall
Department of Geography
University of Reading
Whiteknights
Reading RG6 2AF
UK

Professor D. Hooson
Dean, College of Letters and Science
University of California, Berkeley
201 Campbell Hall
Berkeley
California 94720
USA

Professor R. Lawton
Department of Geography
University of Liverpool
Rosby Building
PO Box 147
Liverpool L69 3BX
UK

Professor David Lowenthal
Department of Geography
University College London
University of London
Gower Street
London WC1E 6BT
UK

John Patten
Hertford College
Oxford

Dr D. I. Scargill
School of Geography
Oxford
OX1 3TB

Dr David Ward
Department of Geography
University of Wisconsin-Madison
324 Science Hall
Madison
WI 53706
USA

Dr C. Peach
St. Catherine's College
University of Oxford
Oxford

Professor P. Pinchemel
Institut de Geographie
Université de Paris I
191 rue Saint-Jacques
75005, Paris
France

Professor J. Wreford Watson
Department of Geography
University of Edinburgh
High School Yards
Edinburgh
EH1 1NR

Preface

Some years ago one of the contributors to this book, Dr Ian Scargill, first aired the idea that a volume such as this should be produced. I am grateful to him and to my old friend and colleague Dr Andrew Goudie —like Jean Gottmann and myself a Fellow of Hertford College—for their kind encouragement and help in the task of editing at a time when my own interests were not academic full-time.

My thanks are also due to a number of others in London and in Oxford. My private secretary, Alexandra Loyd, gave invaluable secretarial assistance, and Mrs Mary Fargher was good enough to provide a translation of the contribution by Professor and Mrs Pinchemel.

I am deeply indebted in particular to Miss Sheila O'Clarey who, throughout the whole process of the production of this book, acted as a clearing house for manuscripts, typed the select bibliography of Professor Gottmann's work which Dr Goudie had revised most kindly, and ensured that total secrecy obtained. This last was no easy task, as she was Professor Gottmann's private secretary for a lengthy period, right until his retirement: I trust he will forgive her the mild deception that was involved from time to time.

Of course, I am most grateful to the thirteen distinguished contributors themselves, for the speed, efficiency and secrecy with which they worked, completing the manuscript in time to ensure publication of this book near to the time of Professor Gottmann's retirement. Editing such contributions was indeed an easy task; references are given at the end of each chapter, although slightly different reference systems are used within some of the chapters themselves, in keeping with their different aims and styles. The contributors come from universities almost entirely British or American. They wrote originally almost entirely in English; the one notable and happy exception is that of Professor and Mrs Pinchemel from Paris. Equally happily, Professor Ben-Arieh represents scholarship in the Eastern Mediterranean.

All of us join in hoping that Jean Gottmann will enjoy the result, offered to him with our good wishes. Those of us who have contributed to this volume are happy to take the opportunity to mark the milestone in his career that is his retirement. In the varied pages of this volume a number of readers, and perhaps Professor Gottmann himself, will recognize the influence that his work has had on geographical ideas and writing in the mid and later twentieth century.

John Patten
Hertford College
Oxford
May 1983

Contents

Jean Gottmann: an Appreciation

This collection of essays, entitled *The Expanding City* has been written by thirteen geographical scholars of varied interests but of international standing in honour of Professor Jean Gottmann. Professor Gottmann retired in 1983 at the University of Oxford, aged sixty-seven, from an academic career which had begun as a Research Assistant in Human Geography at the Sorbonne in 1937. Thus, Gottmann's professional career in Geography has spanned forty-six years in all.

There is perhaps no single English word that sums up what these essays and their authors have set out to do in quite the same sense as the German term, *Festschrift*, does; but *Essays in Honour of . . .*, though less succinct, does convey exactly the spirit in which the contributors to this volume have written. It is fashionable, perhaps understandable, for reviewers of such volumes to say that they are often "disparate", or "varied" or whatever. This, however, may simply reflect their expected and natural state, and indeed it is hard to imagine how such a set of essays could be otherwise. For those writing while the honorand is still alive, to criticize his work or to attempt to evaluate it in a historical context would to some extent defeat the purposes of the volume, and furthermore proper critical evaluation of the whole lifetime's writing of any scholar is not normally possible, or even a fruitful exercise, until a good many years after it is completed.

So, these thirteen essays, some of which are themselves inspired or influenced by Gottmann's work, are loosely grouped around the theme of the expanding city. Urban growth, urban expansion, the meaning of urbanism, and communications between and centrality within cities have indeed always been his interest.

They have not been his only interests, however, and it would be surprising if the academic concerns of one of the olympian figures of mid twentieth century geography should have been so restricted. His career has been international in style and standing. He has ended his working academic life in the University of Oxford, but his migratory way of life and formidable scholarly achievements certainly cannot be encapsulated in some such term as "Geography at Oxford" alone. His life has involved a myriad of academic appointments in France, the United States, and England, but political appointments were also combined with academic posts in earlier days, as was his administrative role at the United Nations in its formative years. Any one of these three avenues—academic, political, administrative—might have been pursued by him; eventually he chose to follow the academic path which he had set out on at the Sorbonne before World War Two. However, his governmental and international administrative experience served to strengthen and deepen his perspective on political geography and the world's great urban problems. These were to become his consuming academic passions in the post-war world of the French, American and English universities which were his milieu and between which he was constantly travelling.

His transhumant life began early. Born of prosperous parents in pre-revolutionary Kharkov, he was to be on the move almost at once. Both his parents were killed in the troubled year of 1917, and at the age of two Gottmann was taken by his uncle, Michel Berchin, on a journey of escape which ended in Paris. There he joined the growing colony of Russian emigrés who formed such a vigorous community in the city; his aunt and uncle brought him up in a home that was the epitome of an emigré circle. His uncle became the art and music critic of a Russian newspaper produced there by exiles and drew around him a number of expatriate intellectuals, such as the historian Milhiukov; others like the artist Chagall were visitors to their home. Cosmopolitan, travelled and talkative was the household in which Gottmann spent his formative years; the influence of his childhood surroundings on his intellectual development must have been profound.

He studied first at the Lycée Montaigne and then the Lycée St-Louis. After entering the Sorbonne, he began to study law, but like so many scholars his first interest did not turn out to be his eventual love and he soon changed to geography, becoming immersed in the vibrant geographical life of academic Paris in the 1930s. As a student at the Sorbonne from 1932, he was particularly influenced by the distinguished geographer Albert Demangeon; E. F. Gautier and André Siegfried also taught and influenced him. Particularly interested then in geography, history and great cities of the world, and their influence, he specialized early in economic and political geography, especially of Western Europe and the Mediterranean countries.

The intellectual environment in which he studied was one where academic boundaries of the time, in the English sense, were neither as clearly demarcated nor as closely guarded and cherished. Political science and philosophy were a pervasive part of the atmosphere; the frontiers between geography and history, for long rigid in the English-speaking world in the nineteenth and early twentieth centuries, were practically non-existent in the French universities. Gottmann's Diplome d'Etudes Supérieures, taken in 1934, and his Licencié ès Lettres, taken in 1937, were both in "Histoire et Geographie". His early work under Demangeon was concerned, however, as it always was to be, with strictly contemporary geographical matters and problems; he began with both irrigation in arid countries and the expansion of the Paris region.

Gottmann's early academic career was cut short by the Nazi occupation of France. He was deprived of his university post by them in 1940 and in 1942 he fled south to Montpellier and, via the Iberian Peninsula, reached the United States on the day of the Japanese attack on Pearl Harbor. He was fascinated by New York and its surrounding urban region and was forcibly struck by the growth and development of the United States; it made an instant impact. His first job in the United States was at the Institute for Advanced Study in Princetown; he combined this with teaching at Johns Hopkins University with war service as a consultant with the US Board of Economic Warfare and other agencies. Afflicted since his youth with a number of what cumulatively have seemed sometimes to be near-crippling illnesses, he was unable to see active service, although this did not prevent him being a member of De Gaulle's Fighting French Organization. So, while on the Faculty of the Johns Hopkins University between 1943 and 1948 he was often away. Yet his output of published work continued apace, as the bibliography of his major published literature that follows shows. In 1944 he was sent on a cultural inspection mission to the French West Indies, and early in 1945 he returned to Paris and served on the staff of the Minister of National Economy. At once he was given a political opening as Chargé de Mission au Cabinet of Pierre Mendès France. There he was involved in the planning of post-war reconstruction in France. After serving in Paris throughout 1946 he was seconded to become Director of Studies and Research in the United Nations Secretariat, servicing the Economic and Social Council in New York.

However, the prospect of developing his academic life was stronger than the joys of international administration or of French domestic politics, and it was to France in particular that he returned to answer the call of academic life. From the 1940s to the 1960s he held chairs in Paris and North American concurrently with each other and with continuing membership of the Institute at Princetown, this last an association which he greatly valued. Boats and then aeroplanes became much part of his life, as his love affair continued with the United States, the home country of his wife.

It was a most fruitful period. He wrote a great deal and published a dozen books on both sides of the Atlantic, some in English, some in French, and some in both languages. First, in 1949, came Le Amerique, swiftly followed by A Geography of Europe published in 1950; both had a great influence on the teaching of geography on both sides of the Atlantic. French students had their perceptions of American moulded by his views in the same way that American students learnt of the geographical problems of Europe through his writing.

Nineteen fifty-two saw his small treatise on political geography, La Politique des Etats et Leur Geographie, which was followed by a volume on resources published in 1956. This was a most significant year for Gottmann: during it he was asked by the Old Dominion Foundation of Washington to undertake a study of the State of Virginia. This led him to take a new interest in regional studies in America and, most significantly, to concentrate his attentions on the role of large urban areas within them. None the less, more than any other of his prodigious list of publications the resultant volume was in the style of the classic French regional monograph. There was a long preparation for Virginia at Mid-Century, published in 1955, and indeed many of the ideas were conceived during one of his unfortunately lengthy stays in hospital.

The book had a notable impact, and a year later in 1956, while in Paris, Gottmann was invited to study the large-scale metropolitan problems of the United States of America; the driving force behind this invitation was Robert Oppenheimer, a Director of Twentieth Century Fund. Since his arrival as a refugee from war-torn Europe in 1942 Gottmann had been fascinated by the long string of large cities and urbanized areas that stretches from Boston to Washington, with New York City in its centre. The lengthy preparation for his book on Virginia was repeated once again, and Megalopolis, perhaps his most seminal work, was the result. It saw publication in 1961. This book, and its concepts, has had a worldwide effect on urban studies. It was a monumental achievement and ranks as one of the most important single geographical ideas of the mid twentieth century.

Megalopolis and the concept of the very large urbanized region considered as one entity attracted deep interest. The original insight he bought to bear on the analysis of the Eastern Seaboard of the United States was repeated time and time again in the ideas expressed in his other published works; for instance in the field of political geography in his *The Significance of Territory* and in his involvement with Constantine Doxiadias and the Ekistics movement. A bibliography of Gottmann's major published work between 1933 and 1983 is to be found in this volume (p.xvii) and reflects in particular his Franco-American transhumance and the effects this had on his perceptions of geography in the 1950s and 1960s. The international background to, and flavour of, his work was not merely confined to the Franco-American axis in this period: during the 1950s and 1960s he frequently lectured on and studied largely urban problems in many other countries, in particular Great Britain, the Netherlands, Belgium, Israel, Switzerland and Italy, as well as Central and Southern America. Relatively late on in the 1970s his links with Japan grew stronger and stronger.

While an evaluation of his work listed in this bibliography must of course await the more leisurely attentions of later scholars, a bald statement of some of honours paid to him can at least now show the standing in which he is held by his contemporaries. There are the honorary degrees from the University of Wisconsin and from Southern Illinois in the United States of America. There are the Palmes Academiques Chevalier de la Legion d'Honneur of France and the Victoria Medal and Vice-Presidency of the Royal Geographical Society in the United Kingdom. There is his Honorary Membership of the American Academy of Arts and Sciences, of the American Geographical Society, and of the Société Royale Néerlandaise de Geographie. Of course, he is also a Fellow of the British Academy. His Japanese interests are acknowledged in his Honorary Citizenship of Yokohama. He remains a Fellow of Hertford College, University of Oxford, which was his first collegiate home during his long and successful tenure of the Professorship of Geography in the School of Geography at the University of Oxford, which ran from 1968 to 1983.

His life has taken him from pre-revolutionary Russian via many stops and side tracks to Oxford; his academic career has spanned much of the mid-twentieth century over its forty-six years and undoubtedly is not ended.

Jean Gottmann: Bibliography of Major Published Literature, 1933 to 1983

1933

La première année du second plan quinquennal de l'U.R.S.S. *Annales de Géographie* **42**, 551-552.

1934

Une nouvelle route au Turkestan russe. *Annales de Géographie* **43**, 336.
La situation économique de l'Uzbekistan. *Annales de Géographie* **43**, 444-445.
Un nouveau centre industriel en Sibérie Orientale. ibid., 445-446.
La colonisation russe en Asie. ibid., 446.

1935

L'irrigation en Palestine. *Annales de Géographie (Paris)* **44**, 143-161.
La situation économique de l'U.R.S.S. *Annales de Géographie* **44**, 649-652.

1936

L'agriculture suédoise. *Annales de Géographie* **45**, 333-335.
Un annuaire de l'économie palestinienne. ibid., 335-336.
Orient et Occident: Problèmes Palestiniens. *L'Information Géographique* **1**, (1), 5-12.
Une carte de l'aridité en Palestine. *Annales de Géographie* **45**, 430-433.
Le Tricentenaire des Antilles et de la Guyane. ibid., 536-538.
L'Institut Panamèricain de Géographie et d'Histoire. ibid., 557.
La production agricole et industrielle de l'Australie en 1929-1934. ibid., 557-560.
Le nomadisme en Arabie septentrionale. *Annales de Géographie* **45**, 664-665.
Au Paraguay: l'immigration russe et la situation économique. ibid., 665-667.
Libres reçus. ibid., 209-216, 322-329, 433-441, 545-550 [unsigned].

Collaboration in *Bibliographie Géographique Internationale 1935.* XLVe Bibliographie annuelle, Paris.

1937

Un ouvrage sur la Pologne. *Annales de Géographie* **46**, 83-84.

Une géographie nouvelle de l'U.R.S.S. ibid., 209-210.

Tendances du commerce extérieur de l'U.R.S.S. ibid., 210-212.

Mémoire sur l'Approvisionnement de la France en matières premières et grandes denrées alimentaires. Conférence Générale d'Etudes sur le Reglement Pacifique des problèmes internationaux, Mèmoire Français No. 7 (Conférence Permanente des Hautes Etudes Internationales Xe Session), Paris, Institut International de Coopération Intellectuelle, Avril 1937, 57pp.

La Maison Rurale en France. [Collaboration in] Catalogue-Guide illustré Exposition Internationale de 1937, Groupe I, Classe 3, Musées et Exposition, Edité par L'Amour de l'Art, Paris, Edit. Denvel, 1937, 20pp.

The Pioneer Fringe in Palestine Settlement Possibilities South and East of the Holy Land. *The Geographical Review* **27**, 550-565. [Reproduced in Readings in *The Geography of the Mediterranean Region* **14**, 1948, 377-392.]

Contributions recentes à la géographie humaine de Levant. *Annales de Géographie* **46**, 629-632.

Livres reçus. ibid., 94-100, 196-203, 312-320, 411-419, 520-526, 632-639 [unsigned].

Collaboration in *Bibliographie Géographique Internationale 1936*: XLVIe Bibliographie annuelle, Paris.

1938

Le problème Palestinien et le projet de partage du pays. *Annales de Géographie* **47**, 101-104. [Reprinted in *Etudes sur l'Etat de Israel*, 1959.]

Demographie juive en Palestine. ibid., 104-105.

Le developpement du port de Beyrouth. ibid., 105-106.

Le developpement économique de l'Iran. ibid., 106-107.

La géographie en U.R.S.S. ibid., 207-208.

La situation économique de la Transcaucasie. ibid., 208-209.

Les grands travaux en U.R.S.S. ibid., 209-210.

Le problème des matières premières: L'approvisionnement de la France. *L'Information Géographique (Paris)* **2** (4), 155-157.

La capacité de peuplement de la Palestine: Aspects géographiques du problème, *Comptes-Rendus de Congrès International de Géographie*, Amsterdam, Tome II, Sections A-F, 91-97. [Reprinted in *Etudes sur Etat d'Israel*, 1959.]

Presentation d'une planche de l'Atlas de France with A. Libault. *Comptes-rendus de Congrès International de Géographie*, Amsterdam, Tome I, Commission du Peuplement et de l'Habitat rural, 554-557.

L'Homme, la route et l'eau en Asie Sud-Occidentale. *Annales de Géographie*, **47**, 575-601. [Reprinted in *Etudes sur Etat Israel*, 1959.]
Population industrielle. *In* "Atlas de France". Paris, Comité National de Géographie, Planche No. 47.
Livres reçus. *Annales de Géographie* **47**, 78-86, 195-198, 306-313, 410-416, 514-521, 640-643 [unsigned].
Collaboration in *Bibliographie Géographique Internationale, 1937*. XLVIIe Bibliographie annuelle, Paris.

1939

Le chemin de fer transiranien, *Annales de Géographie* **48**, 106-107.
Les villes de Palestine, *Bulletin de l'Association de Géographes Français* No. 119, 41-47. [Reprinted in *Etudes sur Etat d'Israel*, 1959.]
Le réchauffement de l'Arctique, *Annales de Géographie* **48**, 206-207.
Les relations commerciales de l'U.R.S.S. avec ses voisines l'Asie. ibid., 207-208.
Au pays de Saba. ibid., 209-212.
Le commerce extérieur de l'Irak. ibid., 212-214.
L'Irrigation, *L'Information Géographique* **3** (4), 153-157.
Tendances de l'economie australienne. *L'Information Géographique* **3** (5), 214-217.
Agricultural possibilities of the desert of Sinai [Review of C. S. Jarvis, "Desert and Delta"]. *Geographical Review* **29**, 514-515.
Le revitaillement en matières premières des grandes puissances européenes. *Bulletin de l'Association de Géographes Français* No. 125, 167-175.
Livres reçus. *Annales de Géographie* **48**, 75-78, 191-193, 302-312, 416-423, 523-528.
Le problème des matières premiers (in collaboration with Etienne Dennery, M. Chezeau, E. Mantoux, J. Sirol). *Conférence Permanentes des Hautes Etudes Internationales, Paris, Institut International de Co-operation Intellectuelle*, 246pp.
Collaboration in *Bibliographie Geographique Internationale, 1938*. XLVIIIe Bibliographie annuelle, Paris.
Les progrès de l'irrigation autour de la Mediterranéean AFAS, 63e session, Liège 1939. *Congres de l'eau — Séances des Sections*, Paris 1038-1045.

1940–41

Revision and update of "Les Grands Marchés des Matières Premières" by F. Maurette (8e edition). Paris, Collection Armand Colin. (Préface de A. Demangeon.)
L'evolution économique de l'U.R.S.S. *Annales de Géographie* **49**, 73-80.
L'evolution economique de la Grande-Bretagne. *L'Information Geographique* **4** (3), 49-57.

Jules Sion (Obituary). *Geographical Review* **30**, 691.
Introduction to "Sur la Civilisation agraire Mediterranéean. Oeuvres Posthumes de Jules Sion". *Bulletin de la Société Languedocienne de Géographie*, 2nd Series, **11**, Montpellier, 1940, 18-19.
Le petrole en Asie Occidentale. *Annales de Geographie* **49**, 154-157.
Livres reçus. ibid., 60-64, 145-151.
"Le Grand Atlas Soviétique du Monde", 221-223.
[Avec Pierre Gourou] Albert Demangeon (1872-1940). *Bulletin de la Société Languedocienne de Géographie*, 2ᵉ Serie, Tôme XII, premier fascicule, Montpellier, 1941, 1-15.
Nouvelle carte mondiale de l'indice d'aridité (in collaboration with Emm. de Martonne). *Annales de Géographie et La Météorologie*.

1942

Laterization in Africa: Scaëtta's work on its cause and cure. *Geographical Review* **32**, 319-321.
New facts and some reflections on the Sahara. ibid., **32**, 659-662.
The Caucasian borderland. ibid., 671-672.
"Les Relations Commerciales de la France" (Vol. I de la Collection *France Forever*). Préface du Prof. Henri Langier, Montréal, Les Editions de l'Arbre, 1942, 213pp.
The background of geopolitics. *Military Affairs, Journal of the American Military Institute*, **6**, (4), 197-206, Reprinted in "Studies on War", a Military Affairs Reader (Fighting Forces Series). Washington Infantry Journal, 1943, pp.56-66.

1943

A review: The Ukraine. A history: Soviet Asia: Democracy's first line of defense. *Geographical Review* **33**, 161-163.
Nature and men in French North Africa. *The Yale Review* **32** (3), 474-492.
Economic Problems of French North Africa. *Geographical Review* **33**, 175-196.
A review: North Africa. *Geographical Review* **33**, 336.
A review: Europe and Italy's acquisition of Libya, 1911-1911. ibid., 522.
France and Europe's Economic Reconstruction. *New Europe* **3** (9), 16-18.
The Italo-Yugoslav frontier region. *Geographical Review* **33**, 668-669.
Bugeaud, Galliém, Lyautey: The Development of French Colonial Warfare. *In:* "Makers of Modern Strategy, Military Thought from Machiavelli to Hitler" (ed. E. M. Earle). Princeton, Princeton University Press, 234-259.

1944

Vauban and Modern Geography. *Geographical Review* **34**, 120-128.
Recent contributions to the Geography of the Sahara. ibid., **34**, 147-150.
A review: La Tunisie Orientale: Sahel et Basse Steppe. ibid., **34**, 166-167.
A quarter of a century of the Earth Sciences in the Soviet Union. ibid., **34**, 496.
A review: Strany Tikhovo Okeana. ibid., **34**, 691.

1945

Raw materials in the Western Pacific. *Ninth Conference of the Institute of Pacific Relations*, Hot Springs, Virginia, January 1945, French Paper No. 1, 15pp. (mimeo.).
Vegetation of the French Niger Colony. *Geographical Review* **35**, 149.
Progress in the Chad and other areas of French Africa. ibid., **35**, 149-151.
The Isles of Guadeloupe. ibid., **35**, 182-203 (4 figs).
A review: Osnovy Kartovedemya Istoricheskaya Chast. ibid., **35**, 510.
Les Etats-Unis et le Monde Mediterranéen. *Politique Etrangère (Paris)* **10** (1), 19-32.
"La Federation Française" (in collaboration with Jean de la Roche). Montréal, Editions de l'Arbre, 1945, 642pp.
A review: Compass of the World. A symposium on Political Geography. *Pacific Affairs* **18** (4), 398-399.
La Géographie aux Etats-Unis pendant la guerre. *Bulletin de l'Assoc. de Géographes Français* No. 171-172, 76-83.

1946

French colonial records — a review. *The Yale Review* **35** (2), 370-372.
French geography in wartime. *Geographical Review* **36**, 80-91.
Soviet geography at war. ibid., 161-163.
Tin under control — a review, ibid., 166-168.
Les Services de l'Agriculture du Gouvernement Americain (in collaboration with James C. Foster). *In:* "Etudes et Documents." Paris (Centre de Coordination et de Synthèse des Etudes sur la Reconstruction), **2**, (13-14), 119-133.
A Review: Osnovy Kartovedemiya *Geographical Review* **36**, 695.
L'Essor des Etats Unis et l'économie d'après-guerre. *Annales Economies, Sociétés, Civilisations (Paris)*. **1** (2), 97-115 (introduction by Ch. Morazé).

1947

A review: Vue Générale de la Mediterranée. *Geographical Review* **37**, 173-174.

Doctrines Géographiques en Politique. *Les Doctrines Politiques Modernes,* Brentano's, New York. 1947 (322pp.), 17-40.

De la methode d'analyse en géographie humaine. *Annales de Géographie (Paris)* **56**, 1-12.

Jacques Weulerosse: Obituary. *Geographical Review* **37**, 507.

Review of "La France Economique et Humaine" 1^{repartie}. ibid., 682-684.

Grandeur et problèmes des transport aériens. *Annales de Géographie* **56**, 206-209.

La position du Canada en Amérique. ibid., 235-236.

La consommation de la houille aux Etats-Unis. ibid., 237-238.

1948

Review of "Pâtres et paysans de la Sardaigne." *Geographical Review* **38**, 161-162.

Changements de structure dans la géographie humaine des Etats Unis. *Annales de Géographie* **57**, 131-145, and 219-226.

Les tendances d'evolution des Amériques. *Politique Etrangère* **13** (4), 315-328.

De l'organisation de l'espace aérien [review of John C. Cooper, "The Right to Fly"]. *Annales Economies, Sociétés, Civilisation* **3** (3), 371-373.

A new periodical on the psychology of nations. *Geographical Review* **38**, 676-677.

La voie maritime du Saint-Laurent. *Annales de Géographie* **57** (307), 282-283.

Vues sur les tendances regionalistes dans le Nouveau Monde. *Bull. de l'Assoc. de Géographes Français* No. 196-197, 119-126.

Une Commission Internationale pour l'Etude des Ports. *Annales de Géographie* **57**, (308), 372.

1949

New French Periodicals on human and economic Geography. *Geographical Review* **39**, 330-331.

L'organisation rurale sioniste d'après M. Reutt. *Annales de Géographie (Paris)* **58** (309), 60-62.

Baltimore: un grand port industrial. *Revue de La Porte Océane* **5**, (52-53), 11-16.

Mer et terre esquisse de géographie politique. *Annales Economies, Sociétés, Civilisations* **4** (1), 10-22.

"L'Amérique" [Vol. I of the collection "Les Cinq Parties du Monde"]. Paris, Hachette, 451pp.

Reviews of "La Civilisation du Désert" and "Géographie Humaine du Fezzân" (1944-1945). *Geographical Review* **39**, 687-688.

Les Grandes Régions Economiques des Etats-Unis. *Journal des Professeurs (Paris)* **3**, (6), 192.

1950

Social Motives in Geographical Analysis. *Geographical Review* **40**, 146-148.
Review of "Les Fondements de la Géographie Humaine" Vol. 2. ibid., 159-160.
Elicio Colin: an obituary. ibid., 334.
"A Geography of Europe." New York, Henry Holt. ix + 688pp.
De l'organisation de l'espace: considerations de géographie et d'économie. *Revue Economique (Paris)* **1**, (1), 60-71.
La politique de conservation des eaux du Gouvernement Federal aux Etats Unis. *Bull. de l'Association de Géographes Français* No. 210-211, 105-115.
Review of "La France Economique et Humaine" 2ᵉ partie. *Geographical Review* **40**, 499-500.
Geography and the United Nations. *Scottish Geographical Magazine* **66**, (3-4), 129-134.

1951

Geography and international relations. *World Politics* (New Haven) **3**, (2), 153-173.
Une economie nationale au berceau: Notes sur l'Etat d'Israel' *Revue Economique* **2** (1), 77-92.
La Région Charnière de l'économie américaine, *Revue de la Porte Océane* (Le Havre) **7**, (71 + 72), 9-14 (No. 73 and 74), 11-20.
L'Histoire de la cartographie d'après Mr Lloyd Brown. *Annales de Géographie* **50**, (318), 50-52.
Le creuset des populations en Israel. *Politique Etrangère* **16**, (2), 109-118. [Reprinted in *Etudes sur Israel*, 1959.]
La vie politique dans l'Etat d'Israel (in collaboration with Michel Berchin). In: *Revue Française de Science Politique* **1**, (1-2), 156-166. [Reprinted in *Etudes sur Israel*, 1959.]
Vues américaines sur les problèmes français. *Politique Etrangère* **16**, (3), 279-284.
"A Geography of Europe" (2nd printing, with revisions). Henry Holt, New York, 699pp.
De la doctrine de Monroe au Pacte Atlantique. *Le Monde*, Paris, 27 December, p.3.
Organisation Internationale et Géographie Régionale. In: *Evidences*, Paris, December, 19-22.

1952

"La Politique des Etats et leur Géographie" (Coll. Sciences Politiques). Librarie Armand Colin, Paris, 1952, xi + 228pp.

"L'Aménagement de l'Espace: Planification Régionale et Géographie" (Cahiers de la Fondation Nationale des Sciences Politiques, No. 32) (in collaboration with A. Sestini, O. Tulippe, E. C. Wittatts and M. A. Vila). Paris, Librarie Armand Colin, 140pp.
The political partitioning of our world: an attempt at analysis. *World Politics* (*Princeton*) **4**, (4), 512-519.
La contribution de la géographie humaine et des études économiques aux area studies. *Bulletin International des Sciences Sociales, Area Studies* **4**, (4), UNESCO, Paris, 694-703.

1953

La Compagne Présidentielle de 1952 aux Etats Unis. *Revue Française de Science Politique (Paris)* **3**, (1), 108-140.
Ebauche d'un portrait d'Israel. *Evidences (Paris)* **5**, (31), 1-9. [Reprinted in *Etudes sur Israel*, 1959.]
Matières Premières et Echanges Internationaux. Paris, *Les Cours de Droit*, 1952-53 (Cours de l'Institut d'Etudes Politiques), 3 Fascicules, 450pp.

1954

"A Geography of Europe" (revised edition). New York, Henry Holt. xii + 724pp.
"L'Amérique" (2ᵉ editions revue et augmentié). Paris, Hachette, 470pp.
Review of "Varia Politica" (by W. E. Rappard). *Kyklos (Bâle)* 191-193.
Compte-Rendu de "Pionniers et Planteurs de Sao-Paulo" (by P. Monbeig). *Revue Française de Science Politique (Paris)* **4**, 901-904.

1955

Problèmes d'Israel. *Geographia (Paris)* 32-38.
Elements de Géographie Politique (Cours de l'Institut d'Etudes Politiques, 1954-55). Paris, *Les Cours de Droit*, 2 fascicules, April/May 1955, 303pp.
Le rôle des Capitaux dans la vie régionale. [Review of *"Les Capitaux et la Région"*, by Jean Labasse]. *Le Monde*, Paris, 16 July 1955, 10.
La ville américaine. *Geographia (Paris)* **48**, 9-14.
"Virginia at Mid-Century." Henry Holt, New York. viii + 584.

1956

Review of "The Future of Underdeveloped Countries" (by E. Staley). *Economic Geography* **32**, (1), 88-89.
Obituary: Emmanuel de Martonne. *Geographical Review* **46**, (2), 277-279.
Metamorphoses: L'adolescence d'un jeune Etat. *La Revue de FSJU* **5**, (17), 43-45. [Reprinted in *Etudes sur Israel* 1959.]

1957

"Les Marchés des Matières Premières" (Coll. Sciences Politiques). Paris, Librarie Armand Colin, 435pp.

Expansion urbaine et mouvements de population, *REMP Bulletin* (Le Haye, Pays-Bas) **5**, (2), 53-61.

Megalopolis, or the urbanization of the Northeastern Seaboard. *Economic Geography* **33**, (3), 189-200.

Locale and architecture. *Landscape* (Santa Fé, NM) **7**, (1), 17-26.

Megalopolis: The super-city [an interview]. *Challenge* (New York) **5**, (11-12), 54-59.

Discussion of P. E. James's paper "Man-Land relations in the Caribbean Area". *In:* "Caribbean Studies: A Symposium." Jamaica, W.I., University College of West Indies, 20-21 (ed. Vera Rubin).

1958

Regional planning in France: A review, *Geographical Review* **48**, (2), 257-261.

Megalopolis: some lessons from a study of the urbanization of the Northeastern Seaboard. Insert in "Annual Report, 1957". The Twentieth Century Fund, New York. 8pp. [Reprinted with The "Sou'eastern". Southeastern Chapter Bulletin of American Institute of Planners, July 1958, Decatur, Ga.]

La nation Israélienne. *Evidences* **10**, (74), 10-16.

1959

Revolution in land use. *Landscape* (Santa Fé, NM) **8**, (2), 15-21.

"Etudes sur l'Etat d'Israel et le Moyen Orient." Paris, Librairie A. Colin, 176pp.

Notes sur la géographie appliquée. *Cahiers de Géographie de Québec (Canada)* **3**, (5). Historique de la géographie appliquée: une définition, les premières réalisations, 8-12. La géographie et les affaires: quelques exemples, 28-30. Géographie et planification régionale, 36-39. Géographie et urbanisme: le cas de Mégalopolis, 48-50.

Megalopolis or the urbanization of the Northeastern seaboard. (*Economic Geography*, 1957) Reprinted in "Readings in Urban Geography" (ed. Harold H. Mayer and Clyde F. Kohn). Chicago, Chicago University Press. 46-56.

Plans de villes des deux cotés de l'Atlantique. *Cahiers de Géographie de Québec* **3**, (6). (Melanges géographiques canadiens offerts à Raoul Blanchard, 237-242.)

1960

The impact of urbanization. In: *"The Nation's Children"* (ed. Eli Ginzberg). Vol. I: "The Family and Social Change" Golden Anniversary White House Conference on Children and Youth. New York, Columbia University Press. 180-208. [Reprinted in "Health and the Community (ed. Albert Katz and J. S. Felton). New York, Free Press. 1965.]

Le problème Européen: le problème géographique. In: "L'Europe du XIXe et du XXe siècle I." Milan, Marzorati. Tome I, 1-30.
"L'Amérique" (3e edition, revue et augmentée). Paris, Hachette, 470pp. Water quality and water consciousness. [Reprinted from "The Water of New York State: A Symposium of the State University of New York", 1960.]

1961

L'urbanisation dans le monde contemporain et ses conséquences politiques. *Politique Etrangère* **6**, 1960, 557-571 (published February 1961).
"De Dynamiek der Gronstofmarkten" (translated and revised by John J. Hanrath). Amsterdam-Antwerpen, Wereld-Bibliothek. 376pp.
Review of "Niveaux Optimas des Villes", "Champagnole" and "Lyon: Ville industrielle". *Economic Geography* **37**, (4), 371-373.
"Megalopolis: The Urbanized Northeastern Seaboard of the United States." New York, The Twentieth Century Fund, xi + 810.

1962

"A Geography of Europe" (3rd edition). New York, Holt, Rinehart and Winston, xii + 788.
Review of "New York Metropolitan Region Survey" (by R. Vernon *et al.*). *Geographical Review* **52**, (2), 312-314.
Megalopolis: Région laboratoire de l'urbanisation moderne. *Cahiers de la République* (*Paris*) **7**, (46), 590-597.
"Economics, Esthetics and Ethics in Modern Urbanization." New York, The Twentieth Century Fund, 37pp.
"Géographia de Europa" [translation from the English]. Barcelona, Ed. Omega.
"A Geography of Europe." Colombo, Sri Lanka [translation into Singhalese].

1963

Urban growth and planning in Europe. In: "Newsletter". Twentieth Century Fund, New York, No. 46, 4.
Megalopolis. In: "The Book of Knowledge Annual 1963". New York and Toronto, Groher, 144-153.
Economics, esthetics and ethics in modern urbanization [summarized from pamphlet]. *Ekistics* (*Athens*) **15**, (89), 197-204.
L'Amérique de Kennedy. *Bulletin 1963 de l'Association des Anciens Elèves de la Rue St-Guillaume* (Paris). 95-109.
Max Sorre: An obituary. *Geographical Review* **53**, (3), 464-465.
L'Urbanisation en Amérique du Nord et en Europe Occidentale: Notes comparatives. In: "Information sur les Sciences Sociales". Paris-La Haye,

Mouton pour le Conseil International des Sciénces Sociales, *2*, No. 3, September 1963, 33-52. [Translated into Italian in *Nord e Sud*, Napoli, March 1964.]

Henri Baulig: An obituary. *Geographical Review* **53**, (4), 611-612.

La politique et le concret. *Politique Etrangère* **28**, (4-5), 273-302.

1964

Great capitals in evolution. *Geographical Review* **54**, 124-127.

Mankind is reshaping its habitat. In: "Metropolis: Values in Conflict" (ed. C. E. Elias, Jr, James Gillies, and Svend Riemer). Belmont, California, Wadsworth Publishing Co. Inc. 3-8. [Reprinted from "Economics, Esthetics and Ethics in Modern Urbanization" 1962.]

"Documents pour servir à l'étude de la Structure Agraire dans la Moitié Occidentale de la France" (Etudes et Mémoires du Centre d'Etude Economiques, No. 58). Paris, Armand Colin, 347pp.

Incidences politiques de l'évolution agricole modern. *Politique Etrangère* **29**, (2), 181-192.

De la ville d'aujourd'hui à la ville de domain: la transition vers la cité nouvelle. In: "Prospective, No. 11, L'Urbanisation". Paris, Presses Universitaires de France. 171-180.

Destin de Paris: Remarques de conclusion. *Urbanisme* **33**, (84), 66-68.

Charles Robequain: Obituary. *Geographical Review* **54**, (4), 594-595.

Problems e promesse dell'urbanizazione. *Mercurio (Rome)* **7**, (10), 41-45.

Civilisation des Etats Unis. "Encyclopedie Visuelle". Paris, Armand Colin-Verenèse.

Paris. In: "Collier's Encyclopedia". New York, Crowell and Collier Co., **18**, 443-449 [and articles on other cities, including Besançon, Bordeaux, and Caen].

1965

The Future by Design of New York City — An Interpretive Summary', In: "The Future by Design — Transcript". New York, City Planning Commission, October 14, 15, 16, 1964 (publ. 1965), pp.156-163.

La Géographie Politique, *Die Moderna Wissenschaften und die Aufgaben der Diplomatie*, Wien, Verlag Styria, 1965, pp.141-160. (Conférance faite au Seminar Diplomatique de Klessheim bei Salzburg, 1962.)

Grandeur et Misères de l'Urbanisation Moderne. *Urbanisme*, Paris, No. 88, Juin 1965, pp.40-50.

1966

Review of "Economic Geography of Canada" (by Camu, Weeks and Sametz). *Geographical Review* **56**, 131-133.

The ethics of living at high densities. *Ekistics* **21**, (123), 141-145.

Megalopolis: The main street of the nation [reprinted from "Megalopolis", 1961, 3-16]. In: "Perspectives on the American Community: A book of readings" (ed. Roland L. Warren). Chicago, Rand McNally. 117-129.

Why the Skyscraper? *Geographical Review* **54**, 190-212. [Reprinted in "Taming Megalopolis" Anchor Pub.]

Géographie politique. In: "Géographie Générale — Encyclopedia de la Pléiade". NRF Gallimard, Paris. 1749-1765.

"Essais sur l'Aménagement de l'Espace habité" (Ecole Pratique des Hautes Etudes-Sorbonne). Paris. Laye, Mouton and Co. 347pp.

La création de villes neuves. *Revue Economique et Sociale* **24**, (2), 111-123.

The corrupt and creative city. In: "Center Diary: 14". Center for the Study of Democratic Institutions, Santa Barbara. September/October, 34-37.

Emerging problems of growth and development. In: "International Conference on Regional Development and Economic Change 1965" Toronto. 186-194 (mimeograph).

Morphologie et Modes de vie des villes de demain. In: "Commerce et Urbanisme: Rapports introductifs". Bruxelles, Fédération belge pour l'urbanisme et l'habitation, le developpement et l'aménagement du territoire. 4th Part, Chapter I, 12pp.

The rising demand for urban amenities. "Planning for a Nation of Cities" (ed. Sam B. Warner, Jr). Cambridge, Mass. and London, The MIT Press (MIT 54), 163-178.

Environment and ways of life in the modern metropolis. *Northern Geographical Essays in honour of G. H. J. Daysh* (ed. J. W. House), Department of Geography, The University, Newcastle upon Tyne. 3-13.

1967

"Metropolis on the Move: geographers look at urban sprawl" (ed. Jean Gottmann and Robert Harper). New York, London and Sidney, John Wiley. 203pp.

Que seront les villes de demain? *Revue Générale Belge (Bruxelles)* Jan. 11-25.

Water quality and water consciousness. "The Fresh Water of New York State: its Conservation and Use" A Symposium held at the State University of New York, at Buffalo (ed. by Lauren B. Hitchcock). Dubuque, Iowa, Wm. C. Brown Book Cy. 235-240.

Warum Wolkenkratzer? *Der Monat (Berlin)*. April, Heft 223, 55-65 [translation of "Why the Skyscraper?"].

"América" (translated by Francisco Payarols). Barcelona, Editorian Labor, S.A. 435pp.

Communication au Colloque sur L'Organization Départementale et Communale à l'épreuve du XXe siècle. *Administration* (Revue d'information du Corps Préfectoral, Paris, Ministère de l'Interieur) **21**, (59), 181-183.

Review of "American City: An Urban Geography" by Raymond Murphy. *Geographical Review* **57**, (4), 588-589.

Megalopolis revisited—Exclusive interview with Jean Gottmann. *Railway Age* New York, November, **6**, 18-23.

Urbanization and the American landscape: The concept of Megalopolis. In: "Problems and Trends in American Geography" (ed. Saul B. Cohen). New York, Basic Books. 37-46.

1968

The growing city as a social and political process. *Transactions of the Bartlett Society* (London, University College) **5**, 11-46.

A vision of the future of the urban environment. In: "The Papers and Proceedings of the International Symposium on Regional Development." Japan Center for Area Development Research, Tokyo (1967-68), 49-64 [summarized in *Ekistics*, May 1968].

Preface to Dov Nir, "La Ville de Beth-Chéani" (Etudes et Mémoires du Centre d'Etudes Economiques). Paris, Librairie A. Colin, 9-10.

1969

"Virginia in our Century." Charlottesville, University Press of Virginia, xii + 656pp.

Evolution des villes et avenir de la civilisation urbaine. *Revue Générale Belge (Bruxelles)* Jan., 161-177.

"The Renewal of the Geographic Environment." An Inaugural Lecture delivered before the University of Oxford on 11th February, 1969. Oxford, Clarendon Press. 35pp.

Environment and ways of life in the modern metropolis [reprint of 1966, plus discussion with editors Warner Bloomberg and Henry J. Schmandt]. In: "Urban Affairs Annual Reviews, Vol. 3, The Quality of Urban Life". Beverly Hills, California, SAGE Publication, 61-94.

"A Geography of Europe" (Fourth Edition). New York, Holt, Rinehart and Winston, xii + 866pp.

The Redcliffe-Maud Report. An international comparative view. *Area* **4**, 4-5.

Prospecting future trends of human settlements. *Ekistics* **28**, (167), 281-282.

The growing city as a political process. *Southeastern Geographer* **9**, (2), Chapel Hill, NC. 4-16.

1970

The green areas of Megalopolis. In: "Challenge for Survival: Land, Air and Water for Man in Megalopolis" (ed. Pierre Dansereau). New York, Columbia University Press. 61-65.

Introduction to "Il mezzogio no nella politica scientifica" (by Guiseppe Sacco) (nuova collana di saggi 35). Milan, Etas-Kompass. 5-8.

Urban centrality and the interweaving of quarternary activities. *Ekistics* **29**, 322-331.

"Megalopoli" (edizione italiana a cura di Lucio-Gambi, Guilo Einauli, editore). Torino, 2 vol., **37**, 952pp.

"Expanding Metropolis." [Review of "Chicago: Growth of a Metropolis" (by Harold M. Mayer and Richard C. Wade, with the assistance of Glen E. Holt) Chicago and London, The University of Chicago Press, 1969. ix + 511pp.]. *Geographical Journal* **136**, (4), 600-602.

1971

Office growth and decentralization: the Case of London. *Geographical Review* **61**, (1), 136-138.

Forme, funzione composizioni della città contemporanea. In: "Enciclopedia de la Scienza della Tecnica, Annuario della EST 71". Milan, Mondadori. 457-468.

Pour une géographie des centres transactionnels, *Bull. de l'Association Géographes Français* No. 385-86, 41-49.

Urbanization: Planning human environment in Europe. In: "Citizen and City in the Year 2000" (European Cultural Foundation). Deventer, Kluiver. 82-84.

The urbanization phenomenon and its implications. In *Plan* (Toronto) *The Town Planning Institute of Canada* Special issue, 15-24.

Grandeur et misères de l'urbanisation aux Etats-Unis. *KNAG Geografish Tijdschrift* **4**, (4), 511-516.

1972

Review of "Milan" by Dalmasso. *Geographical Journal* **138**, (1), 78-79.

Nuovo caracter de la centralization urbana. *Eidos (Madrid)* No. 35, 61-84.

L'Utilisation de l'Espace Européen. In: "L'Europe en l'An 2000" (Fondation Européenne de la Culture). Paris, Fayard. 139-167.

Comments on a design for Japan in the 21st century. In "The 4th International Symposium on Regional Development", Tokyo, Japan Center for Area Development Research. 228-235, 181-183, 198-200.

The city is a crossroads. *Ekistics* **204**, 308-309.

Future use of space in Europe (Offprint from "The Future is To-morrow— 17 Prospective Studies"). The Hague, Martinus Nijhoff. 238-267.

1973

Review of "History in Geographic Perspective—The Other France" by E. W. Fox. *Geographical Review* **58**, (1), 128-129.

"The Significance of Territory." Charlottesville, The University Press of Virginia, x + 169pp.

Review of "Suburban land conversion in the United States" by Marion Clawson. *Economic Geography* **49**, 86-88.

The Hong-Kong Experiment (Pamphlet of *Ecology Poster Exhibition*). Hong Kong, The Hong Kong Arts Centre. 4-5.

Papers in "Seminar on the International Comparative Study of Megalopolises". Tokyo, Japan Center for Area Development Research, June 25-28. 27-43, 205-207, etc.

1974

Appollonion: its significance for Ekistics, In: *D. A. Review* (Athens) **10**, (87), 18-20. [Also published as "Plato, Aristotle and Alexander." *Ekistics* **37**, (219), 146-148.]

The evolution of urban centrality—orientations for research. *(Research Papers), Oxford, School of Geography*, No. 8, 44pp.

The need of an international policy for the sciences, In: "Co-ordination in the Field of Science and Technology—Nobel Symposium 26" (ed. A. Schon and Finn Sollte). Oslo, Universitetsforlaget. 7-13.

Review of "All Possible Worlds" by P. E. James. *The Australian Geographer* **12**, (5), 469-470.

Dynamics of large cities and planning policies. In "Symposium on Urban Development". Rio de Janeiro, BNH. 125-128.

The dynamics of large cities. *Geographical Journal* **140**, (2), 254-261.

Foreword to "Population and Urbanized Area Growth in Megalopolis" (ed. Clyde E. Browning). University of North Carolina, Department of Geography, *Studies in Geography No. 7*, Chapel Hill, NC. 1-11.

1975

The centrality of Oxford. In: "Oxford and its Region: Geographical Essays" (ed. C. G. Smith and D. I. Scargill). Oxford, Oxford University Press. 44-47.

The agglomerations of the East. *Times Literary Supplement* (London) No. 3802, 58.

The evolution of urban centrality. *Ekistics* **40**, No. 233, 220-228.

When in Milwaukee. . . . (Change in American Cities). *New York Times*, 2 June, 1975, p.25.

The evolution of the concept of territory. *Social Science Information* (*Paris*) **14**, (3/4), 29-47.

1976

Megalopolitan systems around the world. *Ekistics* **41**, (243), 109-113.

Paris transformed—a review. *Geographical Journal* **142** (1), 132-135.

The present renewal of mankind's habitat: an overview of present trends of urbanization around the world, In: "Towards a Better Habitat for the 21st Century, Report of Nagoya Habitat Conference". Nagoya, Chuba Region Development Research Center. 42-49.

The ekistics philosophy of C. A. Doxiadis. *Ekistics* **41**, (247), 383-385.

Les poussées megalopolitaines dans le monde. *2000* (DATAR) (Paris) No. 35, 3-6.

Pogovori z delosovei (Dialogues with the Delians. Jean Gottmann interviewed by Milos R. Perovic). *Sinteza* (Ljubljana) Nos. 36-37, June 1976. 57-77 [in English and Slovenian].

Urban geography and the human condition. In: "Man in Urban Environments" (ed. G. A. Harrison and J. B. Gibson). Oxford, Oxford University Press, 6-24.

Şehirsel Merkeziyetín gelişmesi. Istanbul Üniversitesi yayin No. 2087; Cografya Enstitüsü yayin No. 80, 1-50.

The urban quest for a better life. In: "Improving Urban Settlements" (ed. H. P. Oberlander). Vancouver, U.B.C. Press. 1-16.

Megalopolitan systems around the world, *Geografski Glasnik* No. 38, 103-111.

A dinamica das grandes cidades (La dynamique des grandes villes), *Bol. geogr. brasil (Brés.)* **34**, No. 251, 5-14. Bibliogr. (18 réf.) [Translation of the article published in *Geographical Journal*, **140**, (2), London, 1974.]

1977

Megalopolis and antipolis: the telephone and the structure of the city. In "The Social Impact of the Telephone" (ed. Ithiel de Sola Pool), Cambridge, Mass. and London, MIT Press. 303-317.

I limiti dello sviluppo urbano. *Scienza e Tecnica 77, Annuario della EST*. Milan, Mondadori. 265-278.

The American quest for a New World, In: "Three Europeans look at America" (with Wilhelm Nöllig and Oliver Franks). Berkeley, Institute of Governmental Studies, University of California. 21-36.

Articles "Geography", "Density", "Megalopolis", "Urbanization", etc. In: "The Fontana Dictionary of Modern Thought". (ed. A. Bullock and O. Stallybrass). London, Fontana.

The rôle of capital cities, *Ekistics* **44**, (264), 240-243.

Il territorio: un concetto in evoluzione (traduzione di Martin Hérisson). Estratto da *Nord e Sud*, Anno XXIV, Terza Serie, February, N. 25 (267), Naples, 41-63.

1978

Verso una megalopoli della Pianura Padana? In: "Megalopoli Mediterranea (ed. C. Muscarà). Milan, Franco Angeli, 19-31.

The mutation of the American city: a review of the comparative Metropolitan Analysis Project. *Geographical Review* **68**, (2), 201-208.

Urbanization and employment: towards a general theory, *Town Planning Review* **49**, (3), 393-401.

How the Central City works: the case of New York, *Geographical Journal* **144**, (2), 301-304.

Originalités apportées dans la croissance par la présence du pouvoir politique, 3rd theme in *Colloque sur les Capitales et Metropoles méditerranéeunes, Bulletin de l'Association de Géographes Français*, No. 454, 239-245.

New avenues for urban geography. *Herbo News*, Oxford, School of Geography, No. 20, 2-6.

Forces shaping cities. The University of Newcastle upon Tyne, Fiftieth Anniversary Jubilee Lecture, Department of Geography. 14pp.

How large can cities grow? *Revista da Universidade de Coimbra* **26**, 3-14.

Terms of employment and urban concentration. In: "Questions for Debate". "Confronto a pui voce", *Isveimer Bulletin*, Naples, No. 7, 15-30 and 51-58.

La personalita dell' Europa, *L'Europa* (acura di Eug. Turri). Novara, Istituto Géografico de Agostini. 2-9.

The child in a moving, quaternary-oriented society. *Ekistics* **45**, (272), 348-350.

1979

World cities and their present problems. In: "Survival Strategies: Paris and New York" (ed. George G. Wynne) International Urban Reports, 2/79. New York, The French-American Foundation and the Council for International Urban Liaison (Transaction Books), 75-80.

Office work and the evolution of cities. *Ekistics* **46**, (274), 4-7.

The recent evolution of Oxford. *Ekistics* **46**, 33-36.

1980

Interview with Gottmann by S. Kiuchi, *Chiri*, Tokyo, Vol. 25, No. 1, 58-71 [in Japanese].

"Centre and Periphery: Spatial Variation in Politics" (ed. J. Gottmann) (a SAGE Focus Edition), Beverly Hills and London, SAGE Publications. 226pp. (Includes: Preface (7-9); Confronting centre and periphery (11-25); Organizing and reorganizing space (217-224).)

Review of "Elisée Reclus: Historian of Nature" by Gary Dunbar. *Journal of Historical Geography* **6**, (2), 228-229.

Planning and Metamorphosis in Japan: a Note. *Town Planning Review* **51**, (2), 171-176.

Organiser l'espace japonais pour l'avenir. *L'Espace Géographique* **9**, (2), 162-164.

Spatial partitioning and the politician's wisdom. *International Political Science Review*, SAGE, Beverly Hills, **1**, (4), 432-455.

A message of greetings to the geographers in Virginia. *The Virginia Geographer*, George Mason University, Fairfax, Va., Fall/Winter.

Les frontières et les marches: Cloisonnement et dynamique du monde. In: "Geography and its Frontiers: in memory of Hans Boesch" (ed. H. Kishimoto). Berne, Kummerly and Frei. 53-58.

The City and the University in the 1980's, In: "CUIUA, Selected Papers from the 1980 Meeting of the Council of University Institute of Urban Affairs" Washington, (Harvey K. Newman, ed.). Atlanta, Ga. 3-17.

1981

Managing Megalopolis in Europe. *Geographical Journal* **147**, (1), 85-87.

From brawn to brains. *PHP Magazine*, Tokyo, July 6-12 and 77-81.*

Book Notes on "Villes Françaises", "L'Espace Urbain", "Le Grand Paris", and "L'Hôpital et la ville". *Town Planning Review* **52**, (3), 260-226.

Japan's organization of space: fluidity and stability in a changing habitat. *Ekistics* **48**, (289), 258-265.

Review of "Planning Smaller Cities" by H. J. Bryce, *Town Planning Review*, **52**, (4), 480-481.

Basic Principles for Improvement of the Environment towards the 21st Century *1980 International Conference on Human Values*, Tokyo, 51-54.

1982

Review of "Le Grand Paris" by Michael Carmona. *Geographical Journal* **148**, 80-82.

Review of "L'Espace Urbain" by J. Bastié and B. Dèzert. *Geographical Journal*, ibid., 104-105.

The metamorphosis of the modern metropolis, *Ekistics* **49**, 7-11. Italian translation: Le Metamorfosi della Megalopoli moderna. *Nord e Sud* **29**, (19-20), 332-337.

PHP Magazine is produced by the PHP (Peace, Happiness, Prosperity for All) Institute International, Inc., Tokyo, Japan.

The basic problem of political geography: the organization of space and the search for stability. *Tijdschrift voor Economische en Sociale Geografie* **73**, (No. 6), 340-349.

1983

The bounty of the tropics. Review of P. Gourou "Terres de Bonne Espérance". *Times Literary Supplement*, (4163) 14th January, 41.

Chapter One

Urban Development in the Holy Land, 1800-1914

Y. BEN-ARIEH

More than forty years ago Jean Gottmann published in the *Bulletin de l'Association de Géographes Français* a short article on the towns of Palestine (Gottmann, 1939). In it he claimed that although there was an extensive literature on the towns of Eretz-Israel, written by both historians and archaeologists, the study of these urban centres had been neglected by geographers. He suggested that the wealth of historical evidence that filled the country might have hampered geographical studies of these urban settlements.

Since the publication of that article there has been an impressive urban development in the country and a general revolution in its settlement. Israeli geographers have produced many studies on the development of the Israeli cities, participated in planning them, and summed up this urban development in many published works. This chapter will concentrate on studying and analysing only one phase in the history of the urban development of the country during a period which hitherto has not been sufficiently examined—the early period of the modern era, which started in 1799, the year of Napoleon's invasion of this area, and ended in 1914 with the outbreak of the First World War. This period will be generally referred to, for brevity, as the nineteenth century period. Its importance stems from the fact that at the beginning of the period the towns of Eretz-Israel had not changed for hundreds of years and during the period they started to undergo an urban transformation. The main purpose of this chapter is to examine to what extent the historical

THE EXPANDING CITY
ISBN 0 12 547250 1

heritage of these cities until the beginning of the modern era, and the
early urban developments during the period under investigation, have
together influenced the general urban development in the country during
modern times.

To achieve this I shall reconstruct in detail the urban geography as it
was at the beginning of the nineteenth century and the principal early
developments concerning them which occurred during that century. The
discussion will be pursued in the following order: first, the most
important city—Jerusalem; second, six inland cities—Beit-Lehem and
Nazareth, Safed and Tiberias, Hebron and Shechem; thirdly, the six
coastal towns—Acre and Haifa, Jaffa and Gaza, Ramla and Lod (Fig. 1). In
conclusion, I shall attempt to trace the historical heritage of the cities of
Eretz-Israel at the beginning of the modern era, determine the nature of

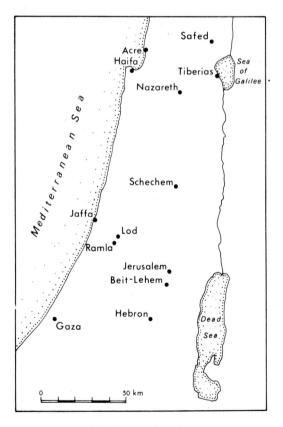

Fig. 1   Location Map

the early urban changes which occurred in these cities, and examine change against continuity in the development of these cities during the nineteenth century.

JERUSALEM

Jerusalem was the largest and the most important city in Eretz-Israel during the nineteenth century. In 1799 the city was just a provincial centre for its immediate surroundings, with no special governmental or administrative status; its main significance lay in its historical value and in the fact that it was sacred to the Moslems, the Christians and the Jews.

During the nineteenth century the administrative status of the city gradually changed and it began to acquire increasing importance as a ruling centre for almost the entire area of southern and central Palestine. The city had also become a centre for Western activity, with a growing number of foreign consulates. These developments resulted from reforms in the Ottoman constitution (*Tanzimat*), including the re-establishment of the Law of Capitulations, from the increased interest taken by Christian Churches and European Powers in this city, and from the improved means of transportation and traffic which had made the city much more accessible.

The population of Jerusalem in 1799 was approximately 9000, consisting of 4000 Moslems, 3000 Christians, and 2000 Jews. The Christians were divided into three large communities (1400 Greek Orthodox, 800 Latins (Catholics), and 500 Armenians) and three smaller communities, Copts, Ethiopians and Syrians, with a few dozen members each. The Jewish community was composed almost entirely of Sephardi Jews (Jews whose ancestors had come from Spain); officially there was no Ashkenazi (Jews whose ancestors had come from eastern and other western European countries) community in Jerusalem at this time.

During the nineteenth century, even before the beginning of Zionist settlement, the population of Jerusalem—particularly the Jewish community—grew considerably. The 1820s saw the Ashkenazi community re-established. In the 1830s, under Egyptian rule, conditions improved, and the Jews were granted licences to repair and renovate the old Sephardi synagogues and started building the first Ashkenazi synagogues.

During the 1840s, after the Ottomans had regained power, the Jewish immigration began in earnest, its main stream turning toward Jerusalem. The growth of the Jewish population between 1840 and 1880 was spectacular—from about 5000 to some 18 000. The Old City remained the centre of the Jewish community, while the Jewish Quarter was growing and spreading in all directions, with a large number of Jews even moving into Moslem areas. Another outcome of this growth was the division of the community into various groups and congregations. First the Sephardi and Ashkenazi Jews split, then various groups detached themselves from the Sephardi community and formed separate congregations, such as the Mugrabis (North African Jews), the Georgians, and the Kurds. The Ashkenazi Jews divided into *Hassidim* (followers of a sect founded by the famous Rabbi Israel Ba'al Shem Tov, who stressed joyful observance of the precepts of religion and humane morality), and their opponents, the *Prushim* (followers of a sect founded by the celebrated Rabbi Eliyahu Ha'Gaon of Vilna, who attached more significance to serious study of the Law of Moses). These divided further into many *Kollelim* (organizations of sections within the Jewish community), mostly according to countries and towns of origin. Between 1840 and 1880 there developed in Jerusalem what came to be known as the Old Yishuv (Yishuv—Jewish population before the establishment of the State of Israel), which led separately its special way of life.

The Christian and Moslem populations also grew during the nineteenth century, prior to the early 1880s. The most important development among the Christians was the beginning of Protestant activity in the city. The first Protestant missions began their activity in the city officially during the 1830s under Egyptian rule. In 1841 a joint Bishop was appointed for the Anglican and the Lutheran Churches. Later a small Protestant congregation was formed; it consisted of two parts, Anglican and Lutheran. The Greek Patriarch returned to Jerusalem in the 1840s, the Latin Patriarchate also resumed its place, and various Catholic Orders began to be active in the city.

The different Christian congregations started to build public structures: churches, monasteries, hospitals, school-houses and institutions of health, education and charity. The Jews also built new institutions of this kind, and the Ottoman authorities started to take part in public building and made improvements in the city's sanitation arrangements and general conditions of life.

The Jewish community of Jerusalem continued to grow impressively —from 18 000 in 1880 to some 45 000 by 1914. Jerusalem held in those days the largest concentration of Jews in Eretz-Israel, about 50% of the total Jewish population. The Christian and the Moslem populations also grew, and by 1914 the total population of Jerusalem was more than 70 000. The city, which in 1800 had had the same population as several other cities in the country, including Acre, Gaza, and to some extent Shechem (Nablus), became by 1914 the largest in the country, followed by Yaffo-Tel-Aviv with a population of some 42 500 and Haifa with 22 500.

The location of Old Jerusalem, its built-up area and its geographic layout derived from developments that had taken place over many centuries. The outlines of the wall surrounding the city and its geographic layout originated in the Roman city, Aelia Capitolina, and subsequently underwent changes and adjustments; the present wall was built in the sixteenth century by the Turkish Sultan, Suleiman the Magnificent, who based it on the alignment of walls from earlier periods.

Until the middle of the nineteenth century Jerusalem had been confined within the limited area enclosed by the walls of the Old City. Even this area was not entirely built up, and some of the vacant spaces were cultivated as vegetable gardens (Fig. 2).

The Jewish inhabitants of the Old City clustered around the Sephardi synagogues and the courtyard of Hurbat Rabbi Yehuda Hassid synagogue, forming a Jewish quarter. The two large Christian congregations, the Greek Orthodox and the Latins (Roman Catholics), with the two smaller congregations, the Copts and the Ethiopians, concentrated in the Christian Quarter around the Holy Sepulchre. The Armenians were in a separate quarter, around St James's church; this quarter, which was smaller than it is at present, was surrounded by a wall with gates in it. The small Syrian congregation lived close to their church, St Mark's, between the Jewish Quarter and the Armenian Quarter.

The Moslems clung to the Temple Mount. Until after the Crimean War (1856) non-Moslems had been strictly banned from entering the limits of the Temple Mount. The Temple Mount/Haram-Esh-Sharif area was generally empty, and the Moslem population was concentrated in the adjacent area, between that area and the city wall in the north, and between it and the Christian and Jewish Quarters in the west.

Hygiene, sanitation, housing and the general standard of living were very bad, as indeed they were in great European cities. One of the most acute problems was that of water, which came from water-cisterns and also from the Gihon spring, the Siloam pool, or the Well of Ein Rogel. The water from the cisterns was polluted and, together with famine and general hardship, this contributed to epidemics and the spread of many diseases.

From the end of the sixteenth century until the early 1830s practically no new buildings were built in Jerusalem. The period of Egyptian rule (1831-1840) was marked by a renewal of building activity in the city, particularly that of public building. This became even more intensive after the Turks regained power in 1840, and a great number of public

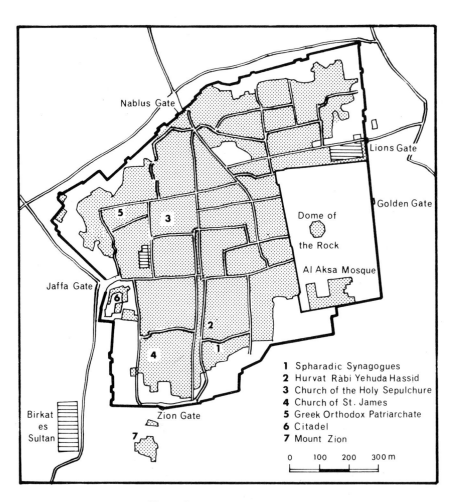

Fig. 2   Jerusalem 1841 (Alderson)

buildings were built in the city, especially by Christians and Jews. Between 1840 and 1880 there was an intensive building activity in the Old City, filling it up with new structures.

Until the early 1870s the city gates were closed at nightfall, and no-one was allowed in or out. The gate-keepers also closed them at noon on Fridays in order to attend the service in Al-Aksa Mosque. Until the middle of the nineteenth century usually only four gates were left open during the day-time. From the 1850s onwards several other gates began to be left open regularly during the day-time. A new gate was installed in the wall at the end of the 1880s, and a breach by Jaffa-Gate was made on the occasion of the visit of Kaiser Wilhelm in 1898. From the early 1870s the gates were left open constantly even at night.

The first buildings outside the walls were built in the 1850s. At first only private houses were built; then came larger building projects, such as the Russian Compound, the Schneller Orphans' School, and Mishkenot Sha'ananim (the first Jewish neighbourhood outside the walls). By the early 1880s the built-up area outside the walls included nine Jewish neighbourhoods, several private houses belonging to Moslems, local Christians and Europeans, and a large number of Christian-European public structures.

The new city reached its outermost growth at the end of the nineteenth century and the beginning of the twentieth. The exceedingly rapid building activity outside the walls had created by 1914 a built-up area that was much larger than the Old City. A new city was springing up in Jerusalem.

The Jewish community of Jerusalem lived primarily on *Hallukah* (money donations received from abroad for distribution among the Jewish population). A small minority were engaged in trading or crafts, and a few provided services to the rest of the Jewish population. Following the growth of the Jewish population during the nineteenth century, the number of Jews who earned their living by trading, craftsmanship, or services grew, but there was also an increase in the number dependent on *Hallukah*, which continued to constitute the basis for the subsistence of the Jewish community in Jerusalem.

The Christian congregations were also financially supported by considerable sums received from abroad; they had also amassed considerable property. This was the case with the Roman Catholic community, which was headed by the Franciscan Order and supported by the Catholic European countries. Many other Catholic Orders began to operate in Jerusalem during the century. The Greek Orthodox community was headed by the Greek Patriarchate and the Great Greek Monastery, which depended on Greek monks who had come from the Greek mainland and islands. They were also supported by Russia in its capacity as an Orthodox Christian country. The Armenian community, too, had ties with members in other countries. Armenians living in Jerusalem were engaged in trade and services and owned much property. The thousands of Christian pilgrims to Jerusalem—Catholics, Greeks, and Armenians—constituted an important source of income for its inhabitants. The Christian European activity, which increased during the century, led to the construction of many public structures funded by money from abroad, thus contributing a great deal to the city's economy.

The Moslem community, unlike the Christian and the Jewish communities, apparently did not enjoy great financial support from outside sources. Most of its members were engaged in various crafts and services within the city. Some earned their living by cultivating fields in the vicinity of the city, producing olives, wheat and barley. Intensive cultivation of fruit-trees and vegetables was practised in the Kidron Valley.

The main industries in the city were soap making, indigo dye-making, and tanning. An important handicraft, mainly practised by Christians, but also by Jews and Moslems was making souvenirs. The city's artisans were mostly goldsmiths, silversmiths, coppersmiths, masons, blacksmiths, potters, carpenters, tailors, shoemakers and food producers. Many worked in the flour-mills. The market-places served as trading and servicing centres for the surrounding rural population as well as for the Bedouin tribes who came into town to trade. The spread of building not only provided work for builders but increased the number of people engaged in services and various public institutions.

However, Jerusalem still continued to rely on external sources of income. Its growth during the nineteenth century, particularly the growth in population, had not strengthened its economic foundation, and it had developed no industry or any other sources that could support its large population. This continuing weakness led during the First World War— when financial aid from outside had been cut off—to a grave economic crisis. The Jewish population suffered the most, because it had been most dependent on financial assistance from abroad. Emigration and mortality drastically reduced the Jewish population of Jerusalem, which started to recover from this severe blow only after the war, with the British occupation of the city.

THE INLAND CITIES

Within Eretz-Israel there were six other places outside Jerusalem which were important enough to be considered as towns. I shall treat them here as three pairs: Beit-Lehem and Nazareth, holy Christian towns; Safed and Tiberias, holy Jewish towns; and Hebron and Shechem (Nablus), inland provincial towns.

Beit-Lehem and Nazareth: Holy Christian Towns

Beit-Lehem and Nazareth were very similar in their growth and development during the nineteenth century; there was also some similarity between their development and that of Jerusalem, owing to the Christian element shared by all three. However, the Jewish element, which was very influential in Jerusalem, was entirely absent in the other two cities.

Beit-Lehem and Nazareth at the beginning of the nineteenth century each had a population of no more than 1500 to 2000. By 1914 this had reached 8000 to 10 000. Neither contained any Jews, and in both the Christians outnumbered the Moslems. In Beit-Lehem the Christian majority was overwhelming, the Moslems forming only one-tenth of the population; in Nazareth, however, Moslems formed one-third of the population.

In Beit-Lehem the Christian community consisted mainly of Latins (Roman Catholics) and Greek Orthodox in almost equal proportions (the Catholics having a small advantage) and a very small Armenian minority. In the course of the century the Protestants (Lutherans and Anglicans) entered the city.

In Nazareth, the largest Christian congregation were the Greek Orthodox, followed by the Roman Catholics; the proportion between the two congregations was two to one. Besides these were two small minorities, Greek Catholics and Maronites. Here, too, the Protestants settled during the century.

The area of the towns was very limited at the beginning of the century, each containing no more than 100 to 300 houses. Beit-Lehem was built on two hills linked by a narrow saddle, having thus an elongated shape with an east-west direction. The western hill, which was the higher, carried the compact centre of the city. On the eastern hill stood as a secluded fortress, the monastery of the Church of the Nativity (Fig. 3).

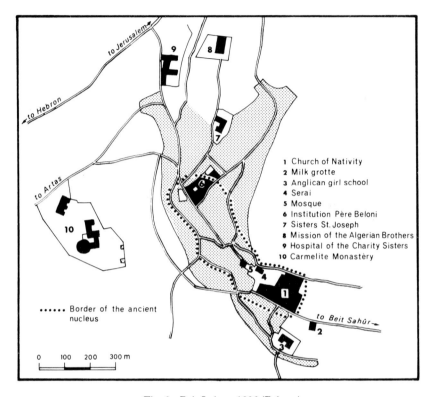

1 Church of Nativity
2 Milk grotte
3 Anglican girl school
4 Serai
5 Mosque
6 Institution Père Beloni
7 Sisters St. Joseph
8 Mission of the Algerian Brothers
9 Hospital of the Charity Sisters
10 Carmelite Monastéry

••••• Border of the ancient
       nucleus

0   100   200   300 m

Fig. 3   Beit-Lehem 1893 (Palmer)

Nazareth was situated on the side of a steep mountain with its houses
built on the lower part of the slope. Being built on a slope it had the
shape of an amphitheatre, with its houses clinging to the rock in rows
that ran one above the other. Starting from the middle of the century
both towns witnessed an awakening in the building activity; more
new houses were added with the years, and new building elements
were introduced. According to contemporary sources, over the century
the number of houses in the town had multiplied by three or four
(Fig. 4).

Both towns were divided into quarters. Sources from the beginning of
the century mention the presence of four quarters in Beit-Lehem: Latin,
Greek, Armenian and Moslem. At the close of the century eight quarters,
which were not divided exclusively according to religious affiliations, are
mentioned. In Nazareth there is mention at the beginning of the century
of three quarters: Greek Orthodox in the north, Roman Catholic in the
south-west, and Moslem in the east. Here, too, maps from the end of the

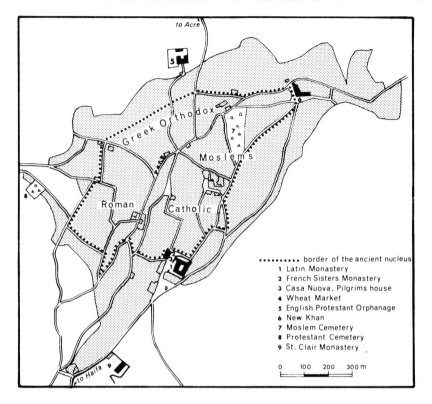

Fig. 4   Nazareth 1890 (Schumacher)

century show a much larger number of quarters or neighbourhoods. Large structures stood out at central points in both towns. These were generally the products of religious denominations: monasteries and churches, together with the schools, hospitals and homes connected with the religious communities.

The inhabitants of both towns supported themselves mainly by cultivating the lands around their cities. The valleys around Beit-Lehem are described as being well-tended, with terraced slopes on which grew various crops: olives, grapes, fruit, grains, beans and vegetables. Watchtowers rose up in the fields and plantations, and vegetables and fruit were supplied to the growing population of Jerusalem.

The fields cultivated by the farmers of Nazareth lay on the hills and along the surrounding mountain sides and even in the Valley of Yizre'el, and the main crops were similar to those grown in Beit-Lehem. A prominent industry was grazing, and many inhabitants raised cattle and sheep and goats for milk and meat.

Nazareth was an important centre of trading and road-traffic. Shipments of wheat passed through on their way to Haifa and Acre, and fine fabrics on their way to Damascus. The merchants of Nazareth had links with tradesmen from east of the Jordan River, for instance from As-Salt. There were granaries in the town, and some of the citizens earned their living from transporting grain loads by camel. The market-place with its numerous shops played an important role in the town's economy, receiving agricultural produce from neighbouring villages and supplying the villagers with all their needs. Most of the villagers from the vicinity, as well as Bedouins from the Valley of Yizre'el and the Jordan Valley, came here to buy and sell.

Some of Beit-Lehem's citizens also lived on trade and supplying services to the neighbouring villages and to the Bedouins who were scattered in large numbers in the Dead Sea area, but it could not match Nazareth, because nearby Jerusalem took over most of these functions. Beit-Lehem concentrated on the manufacturing of religious souvenirs for the pilgrims: crosses, prayer-beads, models of the Church of the Nativity and other places sacred to Christians, figurines of Christ, the Virgin Mary and saints. These were sold to the numerous pilgrims who swarmed in to visit the city and the Church of the Nativity and were also exported to Jerusalem and even to Europe, particularly to its Catholic countries.

In addition, the town had developed crafts connected with the building trade: stone-masonry and quarrying. These were boosted by the increased building activity throughout the country as a whole and around Jerusalem and Beit-Lehem in particular. In Jerusalem the most active element in this field were the Christian communities, who preferred to employ Christian Arabs, most of whom came from Beit-Lehem, thus contributing a great deal to the development of Beit-Lehem itself.

Craftsmanship also developed in Nazareth in the nineteenth century, but the manufacture of religious souvenirs was not so widespread there. The industry of Nazareth was mainly associated with handicraft, agriculture, trade and the demands of the local market.

The main difference between the development of the two towns was that Nazareth retained to a greater extent its agricultural nature: unlike Beit-Lehem it was not close to an important expanding city like Jerusalem. Nazareth grew mainly by its own strength and because of its function as a link between the coastal towns of Acre and Haifa, and the southern and eastern regions of Transjordan, Hauran, and Damascus.

Beit-Lehem, on the other hand, benefited from its proximity to Jerusalem and from its great religious significance as the birthplace of Christ.

Safed and Tiberias: Jewish Holy Cities

During the nineteenth century two other inland towns were important in the Holy Land—Safed and Tiberias, both sacred in Jewish tradition and containing large Jewish communities which constituted at times an overwhelming majority of their populations. Very few Christians, if any, resided in these towns. Tiberias and Safed differ outstandingly in their respective geographical locations and sites, but they had developed along similar lines, and both served as regional centres for the numerous settlements around them. Their Moslem population maintained close connections with those of the neighbouring villages.

Safed and Tiberias suffered grave damage in an earthquake in 1837; a considerable portion of the built-up area in these towns was ruined, and a great many people killed, most of them members of the Jewish community. The population of Safed at the beginning of the century was around 5000 to 6000, about half Jews and half Moslems; there were apparently no Christians in the city. By 1914 the population had reached about 13 000 to 14 000, about two-thirds Jews and one-third Moslems. The Jewish community of Safed was severely affected by the war; and it became a minority that constituted only one-third of the general population. Its decline in comparison to other cities continued throughout the period of the British Mandate, until 1948.

The general population of Tiberias at the beginning of the century is estimated at only 2000, half of whom were Jews. The Jewish population increased during the century, reaching 6000 by 1914 and forming three-quarters of the population; the rest were Moslems. This Jewish majority was retained and even strengthened throughout the time of the British Mandate.

The built-up area of Safed concentrated, at the beginning of the century, on the mountain slopes; on top of the mountain rose the city's citadel. The town consisted of three residential quarters. Two were inhabited by Moslems, one on the slopes east of the citadel and the other on the highest part of a col, south of the citadel. The Jewish quarter was located on the steep western slope of the same col. Between these two areas lay the market-place.

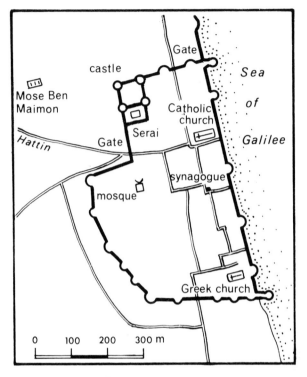

Fig. 5   Tiberias 1885

Tiberias at the beginning of the century was a small, shabby town confined within turretted walls, which enclosed the town on its three landward sides, the coast of the Sea of Galilee forming its borderline on the east (Fig. 5). The houses within the walls were scattered sparsely and randomly. Contemporary reports, from the beginning of the century, tell of new buildings in the town, mostly belonging to Jews, and of progress and development in the building activity. This became even more noticeable at the close of the century and the beginning of the twentieth century.

As for the sources of income, a distinction must be made between the Jewish and Moslem populations. The majority of the Jews in both towns were supported by *Hallukah* funds. A small number, mainly Sephardim, were engaged in crafts and services in the market-places, including even a few tradesmen, but most devoted their time to learning Torah (the Law of Moses) in the religious schools and Yeshivas.

The position of the Moslem population was similar to that prevailing in Nazareth and Beit-Lehem. Most Moslems maintained themselves from agricultural work in the countryside outside their towns. According to contemporary sources, Safed was surrounded by large olive groves, vineyards and orchards of assorted fruit-trees. Large fields of wheat and other cereals were cultivated on the mountain slopes and on terraces. The warm climate of Tiberias enabled the cultivation of sub-tropical crops. The speciality of Tiberias was fishing; the number of boats sailing on the Sea of Galilee grew towards the end of the century, and the catches were marketed to Safed, Nazareth, and even to Jerusalem.

The citizens of Safed engaged in small-scale manufacturing: olive-oil production (some was exported), wine production, indigo dyeing, and olive-wood handicrafts. The town was famous also for its special brand of cheese. Its markets served the neighbouring villages and every Friday a fair was held and various products were traded. Tiberias also traded with neighbouring villages and with the Bedouins who came in from the Jordan Valley. There were beginnings of road construction from the city towards the end of the Ottoman reign. These were westward towards Acre and Jaffa and southward to the hot springs of Tiberias and to the railway station in Samakh. The hot baths near Tiberias were developed, and communication services, both mail and telegraph, banks and travelling agencies were opened in the city.

Both towns were small during most of the nineteenth century. Toward the close of the century both started to grow and develop, the rate of growth and development in Tiberias being by far the greater. There were two causes: first, Tiberias was on a crossroads of geographical regions that were the most developed in Palestine in the modern era—the Northern Valleys and Lower Galilee; Safed was located in the middle of Upper Galilee mountainous region that had hardly developed. The second reason involved the change in the Jewish population of Tiberias, as elements connected with the Zionist new *Yishuv* started to establish themselves in the city, making it a centre for the numerous Jewish settlements around it and giving rise to the first signs of urban development.

Hebron and Shechem: Inland Provincial Towns

The other two important inland towns in nineteenth century Palestine were Hebron and Shechem (Nablus) which were located in the Central Hills Region. Their geographical position and function were similar;

both were situated in valleys between mountains, both functioned primarily as marketing centres for the large rural areas surrounding them. Neither held any religious significance for the Christians, and their Christian population was scanty or non-existent.

Although Hebron is one of the four Holy Jewish Cities in the Holy Land (Jerusalem, Safed, Tiberias and Hebron), its Jewish community in the nineteenth century was small and its contribution to the development of the city insignificant. The Jewish community of Shechem consisted of merely few families; its Samaritan community was larger. A comparison can be drawn between the position of the Jewish community of Hebron and that of the Samaritan community of Shechem: both constituted minority groups in the midst of an overwhelming majority of Moslems who ruled these towns and determined their character.

Hebron's population was estimated at the beginning of the century at 6000, the great majority of whom were Moslems, with only about 300 Jews. By 1914 the population had increased to about 15 000. The Jewish population was about 10% of the total and consisted of Orthodox Jews from the Old Yishuv, living on allowances granted to them from the *Hallukah* funds. Few Jews were engaged in trading and services.

The population of Shechem was somewhat bigger than that of Hebron at the beginning of the century, numbering around 7500. By 1914 it had almost doubled, reaching about 15 000. Throughout the century this population was practically all Moslem, with tiny minorities of 100 to 200 Samaritans, 150 to 500 Christians, and 30 to 50 Jews.

The major source of income of both towns was agriculture; both were situated in valleys that were among the most fertile in the country. The cultivated lands around the towns were planted with vineyards and grew several other crops. The main difference between the towns was that Hebron grew chiefly vines, with the important addition of olive groves, whereas the orchards of Shechem were much more diversified, and many other crops—including irrigated varieties—made up an important part of its agriculture. This stemmed mainly from the difference in their water sources. The land around Hebron was saturated by rain during the winter, but its other water sources were quite scarce, and the farmers practised only dry-farming. Shechem, on the other hand, is described as having an abundant water supply, and its farmers were able to irrigate some crops, using springs, water cisterns, water canals, and streams which collected the flow of rain-water and water streaming down from the mountains.

Both towns were engaged in manufacturing and commerce. The main industry in Hebron was glass blowing. The glass products, which were sold all over the country and even exported, particularly to Egypt, included bottles, glasses, jars, lamps, bracelets, rings, ear-rings, and beads. Some of the products were dyed.

In Shechem the major industry was soap manufacturing. Contemporary sources mention 15 to 20 soap factories using olive oil as their raw material, and the soap was exported in large quantities to Egypt and other countries. Shechem also exported olive-oil.

Shechem's other industries were tanning and manufacturing, especially water-bags made of goat and sheep skins. There was also some wool-trading, and the town played an important commercial role, acting mainly as an intermediary between Jaffa and Damascus (Shechem was a major stopping-point for caravans).

The built-up areas of the two cities were very similar. Hebron was an elongated, narrow city, stretching for about three-quarters of a mile in a narrow valley surrounded by mountains. Travellers approaching the city from the direction of Jerusalem could not see it until they were very close. Part of the town was built on the slopes of the surrounding hills, particularly towards a hill on its south-east, where the citadel and the chief mosque of the city—the Cave of the Patriarchs—were located. The city was divided into several quarters. Hart-el-Kal'a was the Citadel quarter, also called Hart-el-Haram, because the great mosque of Hart-el-Halil (Cave of the Patriarchs) was located in it, and sometimes called Hart-el-Kadim (the Old Quarter). Down from this quarter, towards the valley, lay the quarter that contained the town's markets (the bazaars); some of the shops sold cotton and silk fabrics. A section of this quarter, known as Ksasy, contained glass works. Nearby was the Jewish quarter. On the other side of town, in the north-west, was Hart-el-Sheikh, the quarter reached first when coming from the direction of Jerusalem. Inside this quarter was a mosque, above which towered a minaret that could be seen from a distance (Fig. 6).

Here and there, between the residential quarters, were cultivated areas, mainly orchards; but on the whole it was a compact area, forming an urban unit that stretched along the main road going in a north–south direction.

Shechem was also an elongated, narrow town, at the foot of Mount Gerizim. It was approximately one mile long, and its compact inner part was only 100 to 200 yards wide. A single main street, bifurcating half-

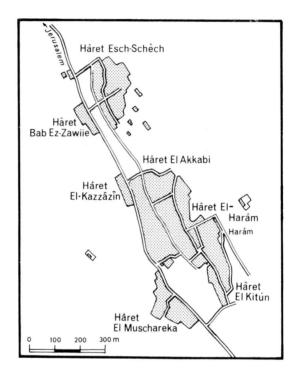

Fig. 6   Hebron 1851 (Saulcy)

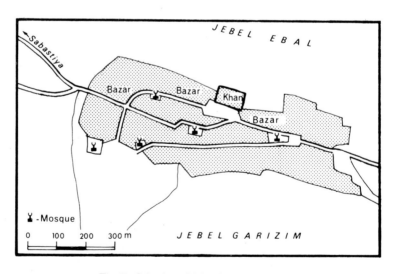

Fig. 7   Schechem (Nablus) 1858 (Murray)

way through, crossed the city in an almost straight direction, from east to
west. A gate was installed at the eastern side of town. The main street
contained the major religious structures and the many shops and stores
that formed a large central market-place (Fig. 7).

Shechem, like Hebron, was on an important road. Moreover, it was at
a most important cross-roads from which roads ran west to Jaffa and the
sea-coast, north-west to Nazareth, Haifa and Acre, north-east and east to
the Jordan Valley, the Dead Sea and Transjordan, and south to Jerusalem.
A large khan (or caravanserai) accommodated the numerous caravans that
passed through Shechem.

The most prominent central structure was the chief mosque, the
entrance to which was decorated and ornamented richly. Some nineteenth century travellers said that this entrance resembled the entrance to
the Holy Sepulchre, and others claimed that an important Christian
church had been standing on the same spot. The place was held sacred by
various traditions. There were also several other mosques which were
associated with biblical traditions, as well as other public buildings, such
as sheikhs' tombs, school houses, and sebils (drinking fountains).

Despite the great geographical distance between them, Hebron and
Shechem were outstandingly similar. Both were situated on main roads,
in narrow valleys, and were built around ancient important structures
associated with old traditions. They were similar in area and size of
population, and the same kinds of trades were pursued. The reason for
this similarity lies in their functions as traffic and trading centres, but
also in their role as market-towns serving the surrounding countryside.

THE COASTAL TOWNS

Haifa and Acre: Ports of the North

Apart from the inland towns there were also important coastal towns in
nineteenth century Palestine, such as Haifa and Acre.

At the beginning of the century Acre ranked among the most important
towns in the country; it was the seat of the Pasha and the centre of
government. Haifa, on the other hand, was small and insignificant. In the
course of the century the situation was completely reversed: Acre's
development came to a standstill and the town lost much of its
importance, whereas Haifa rose to become one of the three greatest cities
in the country.

Haifa's population was estimated at the beginning of the century at a mere 1000 to 1500, all of them Moslems. By 1914 it had reached 22-23 000. About 3000 were Jews, and the rest were Moslems and Christians in almost equal proportions. A prominent group among the Christians were the German Templars, who numbered a few hundreds.

The decline of Acre began in the second half of the century and was particularly marked towards its close. Its population had ceased to grow, and even showed signs of a slight decline. At the beginning of the century the estimated population was 8000 to 10 000; by 1914 it had declined to about 7000 to 8000. About 80% were Moslems, and the rest Christians. The two largest Christian communities were the Greek Orthodox and the Greek Catholic; there were also a few Latins (Roman Catholics) and Maronites. There was a small Baha'i community but practically no Jews.

The built-up area of Haifa was, at the beginning of the century, a tiny settlement surrounded by a trapezoid wall built in 1761 by the Bedouin ruler of Galilee, Dahr el Omar. The wall had two gates, one in the east (Acre Gate) and one in the west, which were closed at nightfall. A road linked the two gates, crossing the whole length of the city, and consti- tuted a section of the main road from Acre to Jaffa (Fig. 8). By 1914 the

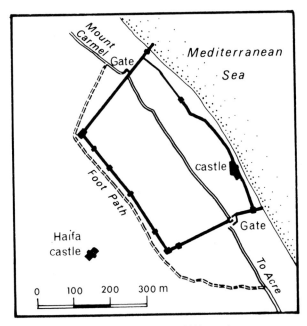

Fig. 8   Haifa 1841 (Alderson)

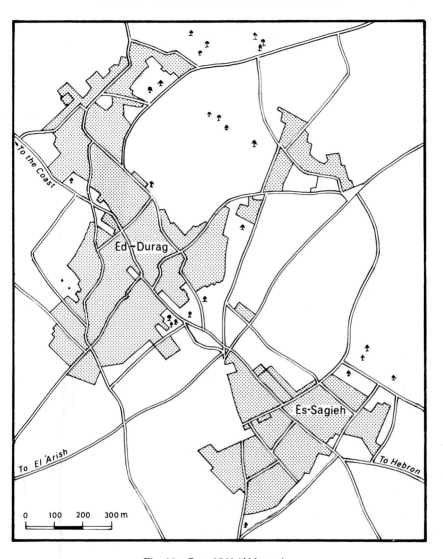

Fig. 10 Gaza 1841 (Alderson)

During the nineteenth century Gaza did not have a real port. There was an open harbour near the shore but no adjacent settlement, not even warehouses, and the building of a port started only at the beginning of the twentieth century.

Gaza was an important town throughout the nineteenth century. Compared to other towns in the country its position was relatively higher during the first half of the century. However, in the second half, when European influences and technological changes started to infiltrate the country, their greatest impact was felt in Jerusalem, Jaffa and Haifa, which became the three largest cities. Gaza was only slightly affected by these changes and continued to develop as a typical desert-border city, an inland gateway to Egypt, and a centre for the surrounding rural population and the Bedouins.

Jaffa: Gate to Jerusalem and Chief Port of the Country

At the beginning of the nineteenth century Jaffa was insignificant compared to the other main coastal towns, Acre and Gaza. During the century it began to develop and became the major port along the entire coast of the country. It occupied second place after Jerusalem, with which it maintained close links. The beginning of the town's development and growth were linked with those of Jerusalem, but Jaffa began gradually to detach itself and develop by its own power. At the end of the nineteenth century and the beginning of the twentieth, development and growth in Jaffa seem to have been even more rapid than in Jerusalem.

At the beginning of the century Jaffa was a small port-town, situated on top of a low hill. It was surrounded by a wall (double in places) with towers and an encircling protective ditch and was fortified with guns. Only one gate, locked nightly, opened landwards, to the east. Within the walled area were open lots on which tobacco was sometimes grown. Public structures consisted of three mosques, three monasteries and churches, market-places, and cafés (Fig. 11).

Under Egyptian rule (1831-1840) several Egyptian villages, called *sakhnat*, grew up around the city. These eventually became urban neighbourhoods within Jaffa. From the second half of the nineteenth century houses and neighbourhoods were built outside the city walls. This included an attempt by two American mystical groups to establish agricultural settlements there, and in 1869 the first arrivals of the German Templars, who built two colonies near Jaffa. In 1869 a second gateway was broken through the eastern wall, and in the 1870s the wall and its surrounding ditch were reported as falling into ruin, and stones from the crumbling wall were taken for building houses outside it. By the beginning of the 1880s khans, shops and warehouses had been built outside the city, alongside the main roads emerging from it, and

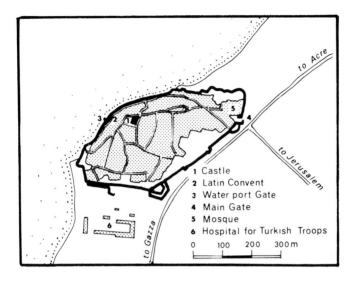

Fig. 11   Jaffa 1841 (Alderson)

residential buildings had appeared, especially north and south of the city. During the 1880s the Jews became involved in building, and Jewish neighbourhoods began to spring up on the fringes of Jaffa. At the end of the century the pace of building accelerated, and all three large communities, Moslems, Jews and Christians, were involved. At the beginning of the twentieth century the Jews began to play a central role in the city's development, and a new suburb, Tel-Aviv, arose by the side of the old town.

Jaffa's population at the beginning of the nineteenth was estimated at only 2500 to 3000. It grew comparatively slowly, reaching an estimated 5000 in 1840. The Jewish population was still only 200. From the middle of the century the growth of the population quickened, reaching 10 000 in 1880, 1000 of whom were Jews. By 1914 the population had reached more than 40 000, one quarter of whom were Jews.

Agriculture was probably Jaffa's main source of income at the beginning of the nineteenth century. Contemporary visitors described the surrounding gardens. They were irrigated by water-wheels and con-tained citrus groves, orchards of assorted fruit-trees and vegetable gardens. Watermelons, sugar-cane and tobacco were grown. Jaffa's citrus fruits had a good reputation and were exported. With the introduction of steam-boats into the eastern Mediterranean in the 1840s citrus exports increased.

There were two main causes for the beginning of Jaffa's growth and development. First, it was the closest and most direct link between Jerusalem and the world, so when Jerusalem began to grow in the 1840s Jaffa grew with it. The second cause was its fertile countryside, its abundance of water, and its mild climate, which attracted newcomers, including Europeans, to settle and engage in agriculture or trade.

Throughout the first half of the century Jaffa's port was small and, for some of the year, inactive. It exported agricultural products, such as dried fruit, sesame, olive-oil, cereals, some citrus fruit, raw cotton, and soap. It also imported rice from Egypt and a few consumer goods from Europe.

Several changes in the middle of the nineteenth century greatly influenced the development of ports along the eastern shore of the Mediterranean, including Jaffa. The first was the introduction of steamboats carrying cargo and passengers to and from the region; Jaffa became a port-of-call for the liners of the great shipping companies on their way to the East. Secondly, political and constitutional changes in the Ottoman Empire, strengthened the position of the Western Powers in the country, especially in Jerusalem. This encouraged pilgrim traffic to the Holy Land and Jerusalem and from the 1840s onwards helped to intensify the commercial ties between Europe and Eretz-Israel, through Jaffa. Thirdly, the construction of the Suez Canal (1869) added to the increase in the general shipping traffic in the region, and this, too, benefited Jaffa.

Jaffa was also a centre of home-trade. The city's markets and fairs served as places where farmers, Bedouins, and people who came in from other settlements to offer their merchandise, met with the citizens of Jaffa, particularly with its artisans, who supplied them with the goods they required and provided road services.

After the Crimean War (1856) there was a great expansion of trades and crafts in Jaffa. Some contemporary sources mention an influx of tradesmen and artisans into the city, which offered them opportunities to earn a good living. The German Templars contributed greatly by introducing new crafts, some of which were connected with passengers and cargo transportation, for instance, the manufacturing, assemblage and repairing of carriages.

By the end of the nineteenth century the first signs of industrial growth could be detected. The progress of trade and crafts, particularly among the Jewish population of Jaffa, had been greatly boosted by the establishment of the Jewish settlements in its vicinity.

The peak of Jaffa's growth was reached at the beginning of the twentieth century, when it became the centre of the new Jewish population. From Jaffa sprang the first modern Jewish town, Tel-Aviv. The first signs of the rise of the new city of Jaffa-Tel-Aviv to the position of principal city of Eretz-Israel could be detected by the end of the Ottoman Empire.

SUMMARY AND CONCLUSIONS

Historical Heritage: Traditional Towns

At the beginning of the nineteenth century, when the modern era started in Eretz-Israel, there were thirteen settlements that could be considered towns. Their population was very small: the largest had less than 10 000 people and more than half had a population of less than 3000.

However, as Gottmann (1936) pointed out, their composition was highly and unusually diversified. He emphasized the fact that every town in Eretz-Israel had its own unique and indefinable ethnic composition. He tried to explain this by the intensive influx of people which had been a characteristic feature of the Holy Land's history and which was responsible not only for the creation of many towns in it but also for the formation of an extremely mixed population within those towns. The rural population remained basically unaffected, but the urban population had been stamped by every wave of immigration and every conquest of the country.

This view of the expanding city is substantiated by the reconstruction of the nineteenth century urban population in the Holy Land in this chapter. However, war and immigration were not the only causes for the unique ethnic composition of that urban population. The special religio-cultural past of the cities of the Holy Land attracted visitors and settlers from all over the world.

Not only was the population of the traditional towns of nineteenth century Eretz-Israel small; their built-up areas were also small. At the beginning of the century five of the eleven towns discussed here were still confined within fortified walls with closing gates: Jerusalem, Acre, Haifa, Jaffa, and Tiberias. Five other towns — Shechem, Safed, Hebron, Beit-Lehem and Gaza — had remnants of walls with gates which had delineated the boundaries of the compact blocks of their respective built-up areas. Only Nazareth had a comparatively dispersed layout and was in that sense, more of a dispersed agricultural village than an agglomerated urban settlement. The built-up area of the largest city—Jerusalem—amounted to no more than a square kilometre, and that of the other towns was even much smaller. (See Figs 2–11; all to the same scale.)

Urban conditions were poor. The streets of the traditional towns were usually narrow, winding lanes with archways only wide enough for the passage of animals. In the middle of the lanes ran ditches which drained rain water and sewage water. There were no active underground sewers or any other arrangements for drainage and sanitation. Garbage was not cleared from the streets or public places, ruins were common, and the towns were generally filthy.

In hilly regions houses were generally built of stone; on the plain there were many mud-houses as well. Stone houses were built in the traditional style of the Orient, with arched windows and doorways forming part of an arched roof which created a dome. Buildings in the hilly region and stone structures elsewhere usually had dome-shaped roofs; those of mud-houses were flat. On mountain slopes the houses were built in terraces, with the courtyards of one row of houses forming the roof level of the other. In crowded, built-up blocks there were sometimes two or more such floor-levels.

The residential areas were usually divided into quarters and neighbourhoods of specific communities according to the religious affiliations: Moslems, Christians and Jews, with further subdivisions according to groups and sects. Inside the urban quarters important public buildings stood out: mosques, palaces, military-camps (*serrais*), khans, monasteries, churches, synagogues, and ancient ruins. These were usually the main landmarks of the cities and largely dominated their skylines.

Between the residential quarters were oriental-style market-places. In these the various communities mixed, the numerous small shops selling foodstuffs were located, services were provided, trade was handled, and cafés and *sebils* (drinking-fountains) could be found. Most of the settlements were located along central route-lines and on cross-roads, so trade and the provision of services were major functions.

In most of the towns discussed in this chapter the inhabitants maintained themselves partly from agriculture; in this sense they were rather large villages. Dry-farming of plantations, orchards and annual crops was the common practice, but many farmers also had plots under intensive cultivation by irrigation from spring-water, wells, or rain-water canals.

Almost all of the settlements serviced the rural population in their vicinity. Usually they contained market-places which served the towns and their adjacent villages, including the Bedouin tribes, who often pitched their tents close to those settlements. Villages in the nineteenth century did not contain shops or provide services, and the villagers got supplies and services in the central towns.

Most of the towns had an important commercial position owing to their location beside central route-lines that crossed the country. Many fulfilled commercial and intermediary functions for the whole country and were the homes of merchants who traded with distant parts of the country, as well as with overseas countries. In the coastal towns, particularly Acre, Haifa and Jaffa, the port played an important role, and any changes to the port also affected the growth and development of the adjoining town.

In the larger settlements there were also some handicraft and manufacturing. Manufacturing included soap making, oil-pressing, weaving and dyeing fabrics, tanning, pottery and ceramic making, glass-blowing, manufacture of souvenirs from olive-wood and other materials, food production, and flour-milling.

Beginning of Modern Era: First Urban Changes

From the beginning of the nineteenth century until 1914, the traditional towns of Eretz-Israel were affected by the first modern developments; their population grew, and they underwent a complete hierarchial change.

At the beginning of the century the cities were divided into four main groups. First were three towns of national importance, each with a population of some 8000 to 9000: Jerusalem, which was sacred to Judaism, Christianity and Islam; Acre, the major town of the Ottoman government within the boundaries of Eretz-Israel; and Gaza, the city on the fringes of the desert which served as a departure-station on the way to Egypt. Secondly were three towns which can be referred to as provincial capitals: Shechem, the central town in the Samarian Hills; Hebron, the central town of the Hebron mountain region; and Safed, the central town of Galilee. Each had a population of between 5500 and 7500. Thirdly were towns with a population of 2000 to 3000 and with an important historical background: Jaffa, Ramla and Tiberias. Fourthly were towns with a population between 1000 and 2000 which could hardly be considered as towns; these were typified by Haifa, Nazareth, Beit-Lehem and Lod.

Between 1799 and 1914 the sizes of these towns underwent a revolutionary transformation. The oustanding changes were: (1) the rise of Jerusalem to the position of primary and central city in the entire area of Eretz-Israel; (2) Jaffa's leap to the position of the second large city in the country, with a rate of growth that was, at the end of that period, even faster than that of Jerusalem; (3) Haifa's rise to challenge Gaza as the third largest city in the country (the considerable growth which occurred in Haifa toward the end of the Ottoman period was a sure indication of future developments); (4) a rapid growth of Moslem towns such as Ramla, mainly after 1880, and a comparative growth of their inland counterparts such as Shechem and Hebron; (5) a relatively growth of the Jewish towns, Safed and Tiberias, which was slight until 1880 and increased toward the end of the Ottoman period, particularly in Tiberias; (6) a complete halt in the development of Acre and a slight growth in Gaza (see Table 1). The composition of population in most of the towns (except for the three which were in process of becoming the largest: Jerusalem, Jaffa and Haifa) did not undergo significant changes. Beit-Lehem and Nazareth retained their Christian character; in Safed and Tiberias the Jewish basis was strengthened. In the others — Shechem and

Table 1 Population of the towns of Eretz-Israel during the nineteenth century

	Year		
	1799	1880	1914
JERUSALEM	9 000	31 500	70 000
INLAND TOWNS			
Beit-Lehem	1 600	5 000	8 500
Nazareth	1 750	6 000	9 000
Safed	5 500	8 300	13 500
Tiberias	2 000	4 000	8 000
Hebron	6 000	10 000	18 000
Shechem	7 500	11 500	15 750
COASTAL TOWNS			
Acre	8 000	9 000	8 000
Haifa	1 250	6 500	22 500
Gaza	8 000	18 000	25 000
Jaffa	2 750	10 000	42 500

Hebron in the centre of the country, and Acre and Gaza in the Coastal Plain — the Moslem element remained predominant. The Jewish community of Hebron had in fact grown slightly, and a few Jewish families settled in other towns as well; the Christians had gained two Protestant extensions — the Lutheran and Anglican, who conducted missionary and philanthropic work, and the Catholic community increased its strength. However, none of these was sufficient to alter the basic predominance of the Moslem population in those towns.

The main changes took place in the three major cities. In Jerusalem the Orthodox Jewish population, known as the Old Yishuv grew stronger, eventually forming two-thirds of the entire population of this city. Jaffa and Haifa turned into centres of the "New" Zionist Jewish population which had embarked upon the settlement in Eretz-Israel toward the end of the Ottoman period. The coastal towns, Jaffa and Haifa, experienced an economic development which was associated with the growing importance of their respective ports. Commerce expanded, and the first signs of modern industry began to appear in those cities.

The physical layout of those settlements also underwent an impressive transformation. For the first time new structures were built within the compact built-up area; soon the settlements outgrew their old boundaries, and the new additions were built, mainly in the vacant areas at the outskirts. As this new building activity became more intensive, it broke out of the confines of the walled area. The gates were left open, and the walls themselves began to be pulled down. In Haifa, Jaffa and Tiberias they were completely or partly destroyed and the stones used for new houses. In Acre the wall remained the boundary of the urban built-up area almost to the end of the Ottoman period, largely because of the stagnation in the town's development. In Jerusalem, however, the large-scale development and emergence from the enclosed area to build a new city put an end to the closing of the city-gates; new breaches were made in the wall. The massive structure of the wall and the strict policy of conservation enforced by the British authorities at the beginning of the Mandate period saved the wall from total destruction.

The new building spread especially along the roads radiating from the old nucleus. It was characterized, particularly in its earlier phases, by building promoted by consuls and other European representatives. Contemporary accounts emphasized the magnificence and whiteness of the houses, which usually had glass windows. These houses were very often associated with the expansion of agricultural gardens and the spread of rural suburbs, where the growing of new crops and tree plantations symbolized the intrusion of modern European influence. At the same time, the effects of change within the older nuclei of the settlements were demonstrated in the completion of new houses, street-paving, drainage and sewage installation. The port-towns built and developed new harbours.

The inhabitants' occupational patterns also underwent changes, although these were quantitative rather than qualitative. In most towns the citizens continued in traditional occupations. Notwithstanding population growth and the development of the built-up area, these remained mainly agriculture and local trade, combined with light industry, which intensified towards the close of the nineteenth century.

Change and Continuity: Beginning of Urban Growth

In the nineteenth century the towns of Eretz-Israel fulfilled three main functions: they were centres of trade and road-traffic, they served as market-towns for the surrounding rural areas, and they were historical towns of religio-cultural significance. The relative importance of these functions varied from town to town, and each had its own unique character.

The relative importance of these functions started to alter with the beginning of urban development. The first change occurred in transportation. Until the beginning of the modern era there was only internal transportation, using mainly land-routes. When maritime links started to develop, the inland towns began to lose their importance, and the coastal towns, which linked the country with the West, grew in importance. New means of transport, such as carriages, trains and cars, appeared, and the new roads did not always follow the path of the historical ones. The use of modern means of transport shortened distances and reduced the need for stops and internal crossroads. The main crossroads shifted from the heart of the country to the coast.

There were also changes in the size of the areas served by the towns. The situation at the beginning of the century was static, with each of the towns serving the countryside surrounding it. During the century changes occurred, particularly in the Coastal Plain, the Northern Valleys and the Lower Galilee, where new Jewish settlements were established. Consequently, the functions of Jaffa and Haifa (the coastal towns) and those of Tiberias (the inland town providing services to the Northern Valleys and the Lower Galilee) expanded.

A factor that had a great impact on the continuity in the towns of nineteenth century Eretz-Israel was their religio-cultural aspect. The development of certain towns was still greatly influenced by their historical-cultural importance and by the presence of sacred religious sites in or near them. This was especially true of Jerusalem, the city sacred to the three universal religions of Judaism, Christianity and Islam, but was also felt in Beit-Lehem and Nazareth, which were sacred to the Christians, and to a great extent in Safed and Tiberias, which were sacred to the Jews.

Another factor affecting continuity in the urban development of the settlements was inertia. The very fact that these towns — small as they were — existed as important settlements in Eretz-Israel at the beginning of the nineteenth century, had made them the main basis for the new urban concentrations which grew up in the country in modern times. The eleven towns discussed in this chapter are still, to a great extent, the most important towns of Eretz-Israel. Towards the end of the Ottoman period, and later, during the British Mandate, new urban centres appeared in Eretz-Israel, but until 1948 their development was limited. The general revolution in the situation of settlement in Eretz-Israel occurred in 1948 with the establishment of the state of Israel, when a large number of Arabs left the area of the new state and were replaced by a large Jewish population. Nevertheless, even today the dominance of the towns discussed in this chapter can be perceived very clearly.

The pattern of three large urban concentrations, which is so prominent on the urban map of Eretz-Israel, stems from developments that occurred during the nineteenth century. A significant change did occur during the British Mandate, when the second largest city, Jaffa–Tel-Aviv, surpassed the formerly largest city, Jerusalem, but the distribution pattern of the important towns in Eretz-Israel remained very much the same as during the nineteenth century, and to a great extent the same as earlier times.

Eretz-Israel and the state of Israel are often given as examples of a region that has undergone revolutionary changes in modern times. Although in many respects it is true that the rate of development and change has been extremely rapid in Eretz-Israel, the powerful influence of historical continuity on the urban development of the towns of this country is an interesting aspect that should not be ignored. The cities and towns may have changed and expanded, but the basic pattern has altered little.

Note

This chapter is based on a detailed study now being conducted by the author, on the "Settlement Geography of Palestine Eretz-Israel in the Nineteenth Century", with the aid of research funds of the Hebrew University. The sources can be found in a much more detailed work published in Hebrew (Ben-Arieh, 1981). The select bibliography that follows refers only to the English edition.

SELECT BIBLIOGRAPHY

Alderson, C. R. (1844). "Notes on Acre — Papers on Subjects connected with the duties of the Corps of the Royal Engineers VII." London.

Avissar, O. (ed.) (1970). *The Book of Tiberias* (Hebrew) Jerusalem 1970; *The Book of Hebron* (Hebrew) Jerusalem 1973.

Baedeker, K. (1876). "Palestine and Syria, Handbook for Travellers" (First Edition). Leipzig.

Barron, J. B. (1923). *Palestine Report and General Abstracts of the Census of 1922.* Jerusalem.

Ben-Arieh, Y. (1975). The population of the large towns in Palestine during the first eighty years of the nineteenth century According to Western sources. *In* M. Ma'oz (ed.) "Studies on Palestine during the Ottoman Period." Jerusalem. pp.32-49.

Ben-Arieh, Y. (1975). The growth of Jerusalem in the nineteenth century. *Annals of the Association of American Geographers* **65**, 252-269.

Ben-Arieh, Y. (1981). The development of twelve major settlements in nineteenth century Palestine. *Cathedra for the History of Eretz-Israel and its Yishuv* **19**, 83-144 (in Hebrew).

Carmel, A. (1977). "The History of Haifa under Turkish Rule." Jerusalem (in Hebrew).

Conder, C. R. and Kitchener, H. H. (1881-1883). "The Survey of Western Palestine, Memoirs" (3 vols.). London.

Cuinet, V. (1896). "Syrie, Liban et Palestine." Paris.

Ewing, E. (1913). "The Holy Land and Glasgow, Our Jewish Mission." Edinburgh.

Guerin, V. (1868-1875). "Description de la Palestine." 7 Tomes, Paris.

Gatt, G. (1888). Legende zum plane von Gaza. *Zeitschrift des Deutschen Palästina Vereins (ZDPV)* **XI**, 149-150.

Gottmann, J. (1939). "Les villes de Palestine." *Bulletin de l'Association de Géographes Français* **119**, 41-47.

Hamilton, R. W. (1939). "A Guide to Bethlehem." Jerusalem.

Hyamson, A. M. (1939-1941). "The British Consulate in Jerusalem in Relation to the Jews of Palestine 1838-1914" (2 vols.). London.

Kark, R. (1976). *The Development of the Cities Jerusalem and Jaffa, 1840 up to the First World War*, Ph.D. Thesis (Hebrew), Jerusalem.

de Hamme le Frére, Lievin (1869). "Guide Indicateur des Sanctuaries et Lieus Historiques . . ." (First Edition). Jerusalem.

Mansell, A. L. (1863). "Coast Survey of Palestine." London.

Makhouly, N. and Jones, E. N. (1946). "Guide to Acre." Jerusalem.

Murray, J. (1858). *Handbook for Travellers in Syria and Palestine* (First Edition). London.

Oliphant, L. (1887). "Haifa or Life in Modern Palestine." London.

Palmer, L. P. (1894). Das jestige Bethlehem. *ZDPV* **XVII**, 89-97.

Palestine Exploration Fund Quarterly Statements (1869 onwards). London.

Perowne, S. (1965). "Jerusalem and Bethlehem." London.

Range, P. (1913). "Nazareth." Leipzig.

Robinson, E. and Smith, E. (1841). *Biblical Researches in Palestine* (3 vols). London.

Rustum, A. J. (1926). "Notes on Akka and its Defences under Ibrahim Pasha." Beirut.

de Sauldy, F. (1854). "Narrative of a Journey around the Dead Sea." London.

Schumacher, G. (1890). Das jestige Nazareth. *ZDPV* **XIII**, 235-246.

Scrimgeour, F. J. (1913). *Nazareth of Today*, Edinburgh and London.

Seetzen, U. J. (1854-1859). "Reisen durch Syrien, Palästina." (4 vols). Berlin.

Schwarz, G. (1880). Jaffa und Umgebung. *ZDPV* **III**, 44-51.

Tobler, T. (1858). *"Denkblätter aus Jerusalem."* Konstanz.

Tobler, T. (1868). "Nazareth in Palästina nebst Anhang d. vierten wanderung." Berlin.

Williams, G. (1849). "The Holy City." London.

Chapter Two

City, Region, and— What Kind of Problem?

MICHAEL CHISHOLM

> There is a recurrent tendency in economics for important new ideas to ossify into dogma, which lacks the breadth of vision of the original ideas, fails to re-interpret unchanging objectives in the light of changing conditions, and possesses less and less relevance to current problems (Hallett, 1981, p.59).

The year 1981 proved eventful in the history of Britain's larger cities, and especially their inner areas. Preliminary results of the 1981 census of population show a massive loss of population in the preceding decade; 10·1% for Greater London and 4·6% for the metropolitan districts in England, representing an acceleration in the rate of loss compared with 1961-71. In August 1981, at the time of completing this chapter, the Secretary of State for the Environment announced proposals for job creation and environmental improvement in Merseyside and had prepared more general proposals for urban regeneration to be considered by the Cabinet, and in September 1981, *The Guardian* and Gulbenkian Foundation jointly sponsored a conference on "What's gone wrong?" in the inner cities.

Table 1 summarizes recent population changes in England and Wales. The general picture of rapid and accelerating decline for the bigger cities

THE EXPANDING CITY
ISBN 0 12 547250 1

Table 1 Population change for different categories of district, 1971–81

Category of district	Number of districts	Population present on census night 1981 (thousands)	1971-81 population change		1961-71 population change (percentage)
			Thousands	Percentage	
ENGLAND AND WALES	403	49 011	262	0·5	5·7
GREATER LONDON BOROUGHS	33	6696	−756	−10·1	−6·8
1 Inner London	14	2497	−535	−17·7	−13·2
2 Outer London	19	4199	−221	−5·0	−1·8
METROPOLITAN DISTRICTS	36	11 235	−546	−4·6	0·5
3 The principal cities[a]	6	3486	−386	−10·0	−8·4
4 Others	30	7749	−160	−2·0	5·5
NON-METROPOLITAN DISTRICTS	334	31 080	1564	5·3	11·8
5 Large cities (over 175 000 population in 1971)	11	2763	−149	−5·1	−1·4
6 Smaller cities	16	1687	−55	−3·2	2·2
7 Industrial districts					
(a) Wales and the three northern regions of England	39	3348	42	1·3	3·7
(b) Rest of England	34	3320	158	5·0	12·1
8 Districts that include new towns	21	2165	283	15·1	21·8
9 Resort and seaside retirement districts	36	3335	156	4·9	12·2
10 Other urban, mixed urban-rural and more accessible rural districts					
(a) Outside South East	42	3793	307	8·8	21·9
(b) In South East	57	5656	354	6·7	22·1
11 Remoter, largely rural, districts	78	5013	468	10·3	9·7

[a]Birmingham, Leeds, Liverpool, Manchester, Newcastle upon Tyne and Sheffield.
Source: Office of Population Censuses and Surveys (1981) p.5

approximately one-fifth of the national total in 1951.[34] Also, together with Birmingham, it is the city to which regional policy has been the most strongly applied in an effort to divert growth to the assisted regions. Until 1961, aggregate industrial employment in what is now the GLC area was rising, albeit at a slower rate than in the country as a whole, and substantially more slowly than in the South East region outside London. Although the GLC area as a whole was continuing to attract additional industrial employment during the 1950s, inner areas were experiencing net decline.[18] Annual figures for Greater London show that early in the 1960s the upward trend was reversed: according to Weatheritt and Lovett,[50] the year of peak employment was 1961; Foster and Richardson[12] give it as 1962. Between 1961 and 1971, the decline was general to all the Main Order industries, although the rate of decline varied considerably.

The single most important study of the mechanisms involved in the falling level of industrial employment in London is that carried out by Dennis in 1978 (see also Gripaios).[15] By whatever criteria one might choose, the period of Dennis's study (1966-1974) would be described as being one in which regional policy was "active". During that period, Greater London saw 390 100 jobs in manufacturing disappear, representing 27% of the total. This was substantially more than one half of the 703 000 manufacturing jobs that ceased to exist nationally, this national decine being 8·4%. Shift-share analysis shows that by far the greater part of London's loss of industrial employment was due to local factors, i.e. it was *not* primarily due to the mix of industries in London being particularly unfavourable (see also Danson *et al.*[6]). To determine exactly what was going on, Dennis examined changes on a plant-by-plant basis; his findings are summarized in Table 5.

Two facts stand out with startling clarity. First, planned moves, to the assisted areas and to overspill towns, account for a mere 16% of the total number of jobs lost; clearly, regional policy has not been responsible for the decline in employment in Greater London through its impact on mobility. Secondly, almost half the total decline in jobs was caused by the excess of "deaths" of old firms over the "births" of new ones, and almost one-third is attributed to reduced payrolls of firms that remained in existence. Neither of these effects is an intended outcome of regional policy.

Attention appears to have focused much more on the "deaths" of firms and the factors that might be responsible for this process, rather than

Table 5 The composition of the decline in industrial employment in Greater London, 1966-1974

	Number of jobs	Percentage
Move to assisted area	36 200	9
Move to overspill towns	26 000	7
"Unplanned" movement	43 100	11
Net decline due to the difference between openings and *complete* closure not associated with a move	170 300	44
Estimated decline in firms employing fewer than 20 people	26 000	7
Residual shrinkage	88 500	23
Total	390 100	

Source: Dennis (1978) p.68

upon the lack of "births" and *in situ* expansion. Whether the "deaths" are due to the restructuring of companies in a context of mergers and rationalization of production processes is a matter of less importance than to enquire why new enterprises shun the capital.

Other recent studies indicate that the processes at work in London are general to the major cities, although the precise balance of forces varies. Danson *et al.*[6] have shown that the poor employment performance of the conurbations cannot be attributed to the excessive concentration of slowly growing and/or quickly declining industries. Furthermore, in the case of both inner Merseyside and Manchester, the period 1966-75 saw a substantial excess of firm "deaths" over "births" that is not attributable to relocation across the boundaries of the study areas.[31,35]

A conclusion of major importance may be drawn from the preceding discussion. Employment decline has become general to all the conurbations. Sixty per cent of this decline is attributable to London and the West Midlands, with London alone accounting for about one half. Very little of the loss from these two conurbations has been due to the diversion of employment to the assisted regions. Together, London and Birmingham account for a very substantial part of Britain's industrial employment. Therefore, the behaviour of their industries has a significant impact on the national employment trends. Now, in the methodology adopted by Moore and Rhodes, and other workers, the national rate of employment change for each industry is applied to the employment structure of the assisted regions. If the national growth is depressed, or decline accelerated, because of the impact of local (conurbation) factors in the non-assisted regions, then the relatively good performance of the assisted regions is due less to the success of regional policies than to the failure of the urban, especially metropolitan, economies. This in turn, may be due to general changes in firms' location requirements, or to policies pursued within the conurbations themselves, or to some combination of both.

Clear recognition that something was drastically wrong with the economies of the conurbations, and the policy of dispersal that had been followed hitherto, came in 1977. The Location of Offices Bureau was instructed to seek to attract office employment into major cities, especially the central areas, instead of encouraging dispersal from London, in an attempt to replace at least some of the jobs lost in manufacturing. As part of this new remit, attempts are being made to attract international investment which might otherwise go to continental centres, such as Paris and Brussels. Given the seriousness of the recession which has affected the British economy, the recession experienced by other leading industrial economies, and the short period of time since the reversal of office location policy occurred, it is too early to assess the success of the Bureau in its new role. However, it is abundantly clear that were the employment needs of the larger cities to be met by the growth of office employment, this would imply a massive further shift of the national economy away from manufacturing and toward the tertiary sector, contributing yet another major twist to the downward spiral of "de-industrialization". It seems more than somewhat implausible to suppose that there is a sufficient demand for *export* services (banking, insurance, offices for multinational corporations, etc.) to ensure that the expansion of office jobs could occur on anything approaching the necessary scale. This being the case, attention must continue to focus on industrial occupations, though not exclusively.

What are the lessons that can be learned from the experience over two decades of regional policy? The formal analytical approach to the economies of the less prosperous areas treats each region as an economic unit, distinguishable from national economies mainly by the existence of a unified currency (therefore no regional exchange re-valuation is possible) and the absence of import and export controls. Viewed as a balance-of-payments problem (Thirlwall),[47] the management of regional economies requires that some substitute for currency revaluation must be found; the Regional Employment Premium was justified on these grounds, among others. As a direct consequence of the structural view of the origins of unemployment in the assisted areas in combination with the treatment of regions as if they were national economies in microcosm, both the causes of the problems and the solutions thereto have been regarded as essentially exogenous. It is the exogenous deficiency of demand that is blamed for the fall in employment; it is the exogenous supply of mobile firms, drawn from London and Birmingham in particular, that has been regarded as the source of salvation. An important aspect of this demand-orientated approach was the phenomenon of low unemployment in the Midlands and South-East relative to most of the rest of the country. In this context, it was plausible to argue the need to encourage firms to establish and/or expand in the assisted areas. The pressure of demand on scarce labour resources in the prosperous regions would be reduced thereby, and hence the pressure of inflationary national wage settlements lessened. Simultaneously, people who would otherwise be unemployed are gainfully occupied in the assisted regions, thereby adding to the national income. The plausibility of this argument depends on low rates of unemployment in the more prosperous regions, a condition which has not been fulfilled for a considerable number of years.[5] However, there are two other aspects of this demand management approach which deserve particular attention.

A regional economy is much more "open" than the nation of which the region is a constituent. In general, the smaller the geographical area, the greater is the trade across its boundaries relative to the intra-regional trade. For this reason alone, regional multipliers for employment and income will be smaller than for the entire nation. In addition, transfer payments, especially direct and indirect taxation, ensure that there are very substantial extra leakages from a regional economy that are not found in the case of nations, the effect of which is to depress the value of regional multipliers. However, estimation of the magnitude of regional multipliers is fraught with difficulty, for the reason that there are no "trade" and "financial" statistics collected for inter-regional transactions: indirect estimation is therefore necessary. Nevertheless, there is a reasonable consensus that in Britain regional multipliers are generally of the order 1·2–1·3, with Scotland probably enjoying a somewhat higher figure.[14, 45, 46]

The existence of small regional multipliers implies that much of the benefit from a given development in a particular region is reaped by the

and the development of the New Towns and Expanded Towns after the Second World War—those lucky enough to move out were generally those with skills and a history of regular employment. When hostilities ended in 1945, there was still a massive problem of slums in most of Britain's bigger cities. Apart from continuing efforts to decentralize both employment and homes, the strategy that was followed in parallel was simultaneously the clearance of slums and re-housing at high densities in tall blocks of flats. The problem was perceived essentially as a *social* matter, amenable to intervention in the housing market. The jobs were still there, although the wages were often low. In essence, therefore, the issue seemed to be how to maximize the use of the scarcest resource—land in the big cities and their vicinity. While the best use of the latter depended on the provision of good communications, the former required high-density redevelopment, for which modern building techniques seemed to hold the answer.

The perceived problem of the inner cities in the 1980s retains familiar elements—poor housing and quality of environment, high unemployment and low wages, etc. However, entirely new is the absolute loss of population and the even faster loss of employment. Although population has been moving from the central areas of big cities for much of the present century, it is only since 1951 or even more recently that there has been a net loss of jobs.[10,19] Rates of unemployment in central areas are now high, matching or exceeding unemployment rates in the assisted areas. There can be little doubt that the fundamental problem now is the lack of employment opportunities, associated with the relatively low wages of many who are in employment. In face of the rapid loss of employment and slower adjustment of the resident population, the most popular response is to argue the need to preserve existing jobs and to encourage the establishment of new firms to create additional employment. However, as Gripaios[16] concludes:

The existence of severe employment problems in inner areas like south-east London suggests that there are grounds for rethinking the present spatial employment policy of decentralisation. Given the changes in the relative profitability of an inner-city location, some dispersal of economic activity would have occurred anyway; but the particular policy adopted in the United Kingdom has increased the speed and type of response to these changes, thereby magnifying the effects on remaining inner-city residents and firms. Even so, it is doubtful whether a complete policy reversal of encouraging population and industry to move back to the inner cities is called for. The south-east London evidence suggests that industrial decline has been so extensive in the inner cities as to be irreversible, at least given the resources that could be provided by a slowly growing national economy. It is the competitiveness of the latter that must be the primary consideration for some time, and this would hardly be improved by concentrating production at uneconomic sites. The best way to help the inner cities now would be to change the emphasis of decentralisation policy from the encouragement of relatively long-distance movement to movement to the outer cities. In this way the outer cities could develop as the inner cities decline.

The major difficulty with this approach is that it would provide no solution for the very poor, since it seems unlikely that they could afford the cost of "reverse commuting" from the central areas to the expanding urban periphery. Even if such a pattern of commuting could be established, a serious problem would remain in the central areas of our cities, to adjust to the loss of both employment and population that has already occurred, and also to any further decline that may occur. There are various aspects of this adjustment process, ranging from the social problems associated with localized decline in population and economic base to the fiscal problems of our cities. At the present time, a remarkable amount of attention seems to focus on what might be called the social symptoms of the economic malaise, such as problems of ethnic relations, law and order, and inadequate housing. To the extent that consideration is given to employment in the cities, emphasis is now placed on preventing the unnecessary "death" of firms through the application of unnecessarily rigid planning "standards", on the attraction of new small firms and, for a limited number of cities, the new enterprise zones. Virtually no attention has been given to a quite fundamental economic fact concerned with the supply of and demand for the factors of production, and in particular, land.

Until the 1960s land in the major cities was a scarce resource, but it is now relatively abundant and, being abundant, ought to be relatively cheap. If the land market were perfect the abundance of central sites would result in a lowering of prices to the point at which beneficial use of some kind would take place. That this does not occur indicates the existence of serious imperfections in the land market. The essence of the problem to which the succeding paragraphs will be addressed can be summarized thus. In the nineteenth century, governments were reluctant to introduce controls over private enterprise and only did so when the

Table 6 Vacant land in four major cities[a]

	Total vacant land (ha)	Percentage of city land	No. of sites	Average size of site	Percentage of city vacant land
Birmingham	834	3·07	823	1·01	100
Glasgow	1562	7·70	1054	1·48	100
Liverpool	648	5·59	544	1·19	100
London	7727	4·89	n.a.	n.a.	100
Of which inner areas:					
Birmingham	262	7·26	512	0·51	31·4
Glasgow	418	11·93	494	0·85	26·7
Liverpool	359	10·26	426	0·85	55·5
London	1885	5·58	n.a.	n.a.	24·3

[a] Vacant land is defined as unused: this is a much wider definition than that for statutory derelict land.
Source: Burrows (1978) p.7

social cost of abstaining became insupportable. By contrast, we now seem to have reached the converse situation: only if a whole series of restraints on the urban land market is eased will public and private adjustment to the changed circumstances of our larger cities be possible.

First, some clear evidence is available that in at least a number of cases land really is in surplus supply. Burrows[2] has documented the position in four major cities (see Table 6). That these data are likely to be representative of urban areas generally is indicated by the results of a pilot scheme in which selected local authorities have been required to publish registers of vacant and under-used land. The first 32 registers record some 8000 hectares owned by public bodies (local authorities, nationalized industries, etc.), all comprising sites of at least 0·4 hectares. The Secretary of State for the Environment intends to seek powers to compel all public bodies to publish such registers (*The Guardian*, September 19, 1981). While a certain amount of land must be vacant or derelict at any one time, as part of the continuous redevelopment of the urban fabric, the greater part of the totals recorded cannot properly be attributed to this cause; many of the sites have been vacant for at least ten years. The East End of Glasgow, which is probably the worst problem area in any

British city, suffers from a vacancy rate of around 20%. Burrows estimates that about half of the vacant land is privately owned and half publicly owned. Although the recent shift of emphasis away from comprehensive redevelopment schemes may reduce the amount of vacant land, this process will be slow and meanwhile not only is there a continuing direct mis-use of land resources but there is the blight which is cast on surrounding areas.

Given the fact that much land had been vacant for many years and that Burrow's data relate to a period prior to the current major recession, it is not plausible to suggest that the high vacancy rate is a temporary phenomenon which will disappear as the national economy comes out of recession. This appears to be a long-term, structural problem which may have been exacerbated by the low level of investment but certainly has not been caused by it.

The interpretation which Burrows[2] puts on this phenomenon is curious: "The important question to pose here is not why inner city land values are so high but why the land is valued so low by potential users." This view is contrary to any reasonable interpretation of economic mechanisms, since the low valuation of potential users reflects their opportunity costs, i.e. the options available at other locations. It is the high value of inner city land to which we must turn our attention. In particular, it is the question of relaxing the land market rigidities which must be central to our concern, a point briefly referred to by Gripaios.[16] After all, the cost of servicing the capital used to acquire land, and/or the opportunity cost represented by the holding, provides an incentive to bring land into use which is manifestly inadequate.

The single most important imperfection in the market arises from deliberate planning intervention. It has become accepted practice to draw up land-use zones, designating areas as residential, industrial, commercial, etc. Indeed, the segregation of land uses is one of the cornerstones of planning as it has developed in Britain since the Second World War. There is, of course, a rational reason for this policy: to create clean and pleasant residential areas, noxious industrial and commercial activities should be undertaken elsewhere. In practice, the noxious nature of much manufacturing has been greatly ameliorated by the use of electrical power in place of coal, so although it seemed self evident in the early post-war period that "non-conforming" land uses should be eliminated, thereby providing a better living environment, this chain of causation is no longer so manifestly correct. Furthermore, there is evidence that the rigid imposition of zoning regulations has been a significant contributor to the loss of jobs, through the "death" of displaced firms. Meanwhile, vacant land commands a *potential* price related to the nature of the permitted use. Although change of use can be sanctioned by the planning authority, there is marked reluctance on the part of councils to accede to such requests, because each change implies the imperfection of the original zoning. This whole planning mechanism therefore operates to maintain artificially high prices even where the ground has been unused for decades.

The second major land market rigidity arises from the laudable activities of preservationists. Undoubtedly, the preservation of individual buildings, and even whole precincts, against destruction and replacement by modern structures must continue, but this philosophy can only be justified if viable economic activities are available and can flourish. There are circumstances where the preservation of one or more building can create a major, perhaps insuperable, barrier to useful occupation not only of the site itself but of the surrounding land as well. Possibly the clearest example of this problem is provided by the docks of London, Liverpool, Bristol and elsewhere. In limited cases, a marina can be created and new uses found for the warehouses. But there cannot be a *general* case for the preservation of all the warehouses and harbour basins; some of the buildings will have to be demolished and some basins filled. Indeed, the main road traffic hub of Bristol, Broad Quay, occupies the site of former docks. While it would be wrong to take an entirely philistine view of the monuments to past endeavours, it is equally wrong to attempt to engage in preservation without regard to the likely impact on the area around the structure being preserved. If the "revitalization" of inner cities is now high on the list of public priorities, then where this goal is in conflict with preservation, preservation almost certainly ought to take a much lower priority. In east London and the docklands of Merseyside, for example, preservation cannot be argued to be the means to regeneration in the same way that is valid for The Shambles and adjacent areas in York and similar parts of Chester, Bath or elsewhere.

Third on the list of considerations, and related to both the preceding points, is the manner in which rates are levied. Unusable buildings and vacant land are exempt from the payment of rates. For the owner of such property, there is no direct cost incurred through retaining possession, as a speculation that one day somebody may be willing to pay the "market" price for the site. As we have seen, this "market" price is inflated by the operation of land-use controls. Pricing policies for public goods and to cope with negative and positive externalities present formidable problems. In the context of rates, there is a rough and ready adjustment in the sum payable in accordance with the characteristics of the property itself and its immediately surrounding area. Favourable externalities (in the shape of public open space, well kept neighbouring properties, etc.) result in higher rateable values. Conversely, the adverse effects of dereliction and other negative externalities are reflected in lower rates. These effects are only experienced where there is a beneficial use. There is no mechanism whereby those who create positive externalities are recompensed, nor are the generators of negative externalities penalized. In many cases, the source of positive or negative externalities is diffuse and no mechanism can be envisaged to recompense or tax the sources of external effects. However, vacant land is a special case. The negative externalities are real and may affect quite a large surrounding area; the source of these effects is explicitly located in a specified area. The owners of such vacant land impose serious costs upon the local community which are very imperfectly reflected in the level of rateable values, and they do so at no direct cost to themselves. This asymmetrical relationship puts very serious obstacles in the way of maintaining a viable urban structure.

In the extreme case, it would be better if vacant land were levelled and planted as an open space of grass and trees than for it to remain as a festering pile of rubbish. More generally, it seems self-evident that any use of the land would be better than none, provided that means can be found to ensure that, where appropriate, "temporary" use did not preclude "better" long-term use of the site. Given the scale of adaptation of the urban fabric which is required, means must be found to ensure that urban land resources are used to the fullest extent possible, even if this implies unorthodox solutions.

The first necessity is to provide a powerful incentive to the owners of vacant urban land to ensure that it is brought into productive use at the earliest opportunity. The most effective way of doing this is to impose a direct penalty, in the form of a tax based on the site value of the land. As a starting point, that site value might be calculated on the basis of the use to which the land was being put immediately prior to its abandonment. As we shall detail below, it would be necessary to except certain sites from the payment of a site-value tax. However, if a site-value tax were normally payable on vacant urban land, there would be an immediate and significant cost incurred by holding land unused, and this would encourage the much better use of urban land resources to the benefit of the whole city.

A site-value tax in the particular context in which it is here being advocated would be compatible with the existing system of rates or with any other system for raising local government finance. However, about one half of all the urban vacant land is owned by local authorities. If the site-value tax on this land were treated as revenue for the local authority concerned, a paper transaction would ensure that there would be no net liability to the local authority in question. Consequently, the tax levied on vacant sites owned by local authorities would have to be payable to the national Exchequer. In this way local authorities would be faced with the same imperative as private owners. In the case of vacant land owned by public bodies such as British Rail, the site-value tax should be payable to the local authority.

Opponents of site-value taxation will object that valuation is a rough and ready matter, more of an art than a science. Without doubt this is true, but the whole of government is an art, and however rough the justice might be, the inequities that might arise under the system here proposed appear to be small in comparison to the manifest ills of our urban areas at the present time under the existing system. Furthermore, the approach here advocated avoids the bureaucratic problems involved in the various attempts to tax development value or to take development land into public ownership.

The proposal which has been made for a site-value tax on vacant urban land should be seen in the context of the scandalous waste of resources that is currently manifest, and not as part of a general advocacy of this form of taxation in preference to others. It is a pragmatic solution to a problem which, in Britain at least, has proved intractable. However, to be workable, the scheme in its final form would have to admit of exceptions, and also carries some quite fundamental implications for the concept and practice of urban planning. In the next few paragraphs, we will examine some of these issues.

Vacant land which is the subject of a planning application should be exempt from site-value taxation. The main reason for making this suggestion is that the time taken over a planning application is highly variable, and is in any case a matter outside the control of the applicant. In addition, the loss of revenue to the local authority while the application is being considered should prove a spur to expeditious

decision-making. If the application is approved, then a reasonable period
—say three years—ought to be allowed for the construction phase
during which no tax would be levied. If construction work starts almost
at the end of this period, completion may not be achieved until the sixth
year or even later. Perhaps, in such cases, the site-value tax should be
levied as a rising proportion, from one-third the assessed rate in the
fourth year to the full rate in the sixth.

Land assembly presents a different problem. For certain projects, it is
essential to acquire freehold rights from a large number of landowners
and, short of compulsory purchase, assembly may take many years.
While the land is being acquired, it may be necessary for some or all of it
to be held vacant. For projects which have been approved in principle
but for which it is premature to submit a detailed planning application,
the following provision could be made. Whether it is the local authority
or a private developer, the site-value tax should be paid into a special
fund organized nationally. If the development, or an agreed alternative,
goes ahead, the payments should be refunded, with accrued interest. If
the project falls through, the accrued sum should be passed to the local
authority except where the authority was itself the land assembler. It
might be reasonable for land assembly to be permitted for up to ten years
on this basis. Although the lump sum which has accrued up to ten years,
and the interest thereon, should remain available for refund after ten
years, the site-value tax paid thereafter would go direct to the local
authority (or Exchequer) and be forfeit. Provisions along these lines
would permit the large-scale assembly of land which is necessary for
certain projects, while imposing some real costs for failure either to push
them through or to do so in a reasonable time, costs to the developer
which would match the social costs created by blight.

Another exception is represented by temporary uses of vacant plots
pending redevelopment. Temporary car parks are a familiar sight in
many urban areas, providing welcome relief for the harassed car owner.
The payment of hourly or daily parking charges implies that a revenue is
being earned and therefore a site-value tax can reasonably be levied. A
more difficult issue arises with plots for which this is not a valid option.
On the principle that any use is better than none, and given that some
land must be held for quite long periods so that major projects can be
realized, it may be advantageous to create areas of grass and trees, even
children's play areas, on a time scale of, say, twenty years. Private
landholders might lease the land to the local authority at a peppercorn

rent for twenty years and thereby become exempt from site-value tax. Provision would have to be made for the owner to resume his title, and local authorities would be obliged not to withhold their consent for development for any reasonable project. Viewed in this context, Eversley[11] misses a fundamental point when he remarks:

> It is therefore assumed that, however much certain interests may plead for "grassing over the empty spaces" (either because they think that this is the best use for urban land or because they think that it will raise national income fastest), this is a solution expressly rejected by the Inner Areas Studies teams, by successive central and local governments, and by all planners in the field. It is a purely academic view and requires no further discussion in this book.

Temporary grassing over would not preclude future redevelopment and meanwhile would add substantially to the amenities of the area, improving the welfare of the inhabitants and also increasing the chances of attracting firms to establish plants. Furthermore, such a programme could be assisted by an extension of existing provisions for financing the reclamation of derelict land, as well as providing work ideally suited to the job creation schemes currently in existence.

The preceding paragraphs have sketched what might be termed an "end state", the fundamental purpose of which is to alter the pattern of interference in the land market so that this *locally* abundant resource may be bid down in price to the point at which beneficial uses become a viable proposition. How can we proceed to achieve this desirable goal? At present, there is no cadastral survey in Britain, so our information concerning ownership of unused and derelict land is often minimal. This particular problem obtruded as a matter of great seriousness in the case of the Lower Swansea Valley;[24] however, the problem is general throughout the country. Although it may be impossible to institute a national cadastral survey, such a survey ought to be established for all the major cities and especially those areas with much vacant/derelict land. Such a survey would make redundant the register of *public* unused land that is being compiled by local authorities. A cadastral survey could in the long run be linked with the National Land Register, to provide a continuously updated record of land ownership.

Even if attention were first to focus on vacant land, it would be some years before ownership rights could be fully established. In any case, some process would have to be envisaged whereby, in the absence of an identifiable owner, that land could be taken into public ownership. With ownership established, a site-value tax could be levied. Given the long lead times involved in property transactions and urban development generally, it would be unreasonable to impose such a tax at the full rate from the date determined. Perhaps a ten-year period ought to be envisaged, with the tax rising by annual increments from one-tenth to the full amount. On this basis, the full implementation of these proposals would take upwards of fifteen years from the time the decision to proceed had been taken, i.e. a minimum of three general elections, more probably four or five. The success of these proposals would therefore depend upon all-party assent, forming a necessary part, if not a sufficient part, of the steps necessary to maintain the major conurbations, and especially their inner areas, in an economically and socially viable condition. Such assent implies a willingness for rational debate which has been markedly absent in the context of ideologically charged issues concerned with land ownership and development.

It would be idle to pretent that interference in the land market is a sufficient condition for salvaging the inner city wreck. However, it is surely self-evident that if a factor of production, in this case land, is in excess supply, then its price must be bid down to a realistic level at which some form of use would be fully economic. If the price of land were bid down in the manner proposed, it would facilitate all forms of activity—manufacturing and commercial investment and provision of housing, hospitals, schools, swimming pools, etc. In other words, cheaper land would enable the urban economies to be substantially more economic than at present, and hence would improve the prospects for their long-term viability. This would be to the benefit of all their residents, including the poorest. Although the change here advocated is not a sufficient condition for the revitalization of our cities, that it is a necessary condition is beyond any reasonable doubt.

In this section, we have concentrated on one particular aspect of the urban problem, namely, land values. The primary reason for doing so is twofold:

1. Whatever else may be done—to create enterprise zones or build council houses—the structure of inner urban land use will have to change in a flexible manner, responsive to changing conditions.
2. The topic has been almost completely ignored in the recent welter of public comment on the problems facing our major cities.

Implicit in the argument which has been developed is the proposition that the deliberate segregation of certain land uses — especially residential and manufacturing — is a policy that makes much less sense than it formerly seemed to (however, see Chisholm[4]). Therefore, perhaps the planning profession must accept a more humble role than has been customary — a role of maintaining minimum standards of environmental quality, a mix of residential, employment and other land uses, and facility of circulation, rather than attempting to mould cities to some pre-determined pattern. This point has been eloquently made by Hughes[25] in the following remark:

> It should be made clear that the analysis of this chapter has not been primarily concerned with the wastelands in the inner areas of many large and medium-sized metropolitan areas. Indeed, perhaps the greatest future asset of these areas will be to possess larger uncommitted tracts of lands. Unfortunately, the minds of many planners and valuers are occupied with an image of these areas rebuilt to a fairly narrow range of uses.

A final comment is in order. Urban deprivation has been the subject of numerous policy initiatives from 1968 onwards. The number of these initiatives has been so great that *The Guardian* (September 7, 1981) referred to government "gimmickry" and the "law of compulsive innovation", a term coined by Anthony Downs. Certainly, the documentation provided by Lawless[29] shows just how diverse have been the various schemes, and how small the resources devoted thereto.

> Urban initiatives represent exactly the sort of commitment politicians like: minimal financial output and yet major political impact. Total resources devoted to the entire set of experiments over the last decade have in fact been minute in relation to total government expenditure. The funds allocated to all ten projects have amounted to considerably less than £200m.[29]

To the extent that there is frequent innovation and policy change, the effectiveness of any single initiative must be diminished. Indeed, it is arguable that this single reason is sufficient to explain the notable lack of success achieved to date.

CONCLUSION

Albeit briefly, enough evidence has been cited at both the regional and the urban scales to show that the economic and social problems which are evident today have long antecedents. The nature of the problems, and to some extent their location, has changed over time, at both geographical scales. Furthermore, the fundamental forces at work have altered, again at both geographical scales, and hence policy prescriptions which ought to be followed have changed. However, in both cases there has been a lag in perception, such that the remedies relevant for yesterday are apt to be applied to today. At the regional scale, attention was drawn to the inadequacy of demand-deficient explanations for high unemployment and the other symptoms associated with the assisted areas—low activity rates, low incomes, poor quality of environment, etc. Deficiencies on the supply side are probably of equal importance, especially in respect of the quality of the workforce and its willingness to accept changed industrial practices. Likewise, at the urban scale we have emphasized the supply-side problems, especially with respect to land. We have remarked the frequency with which the policy package has changed at both the regional and urban scales, and we have shown cause for thinking that regional policies have been much less successful than is commonly supposed.

With these thoughts in mind, can any general conclusions be drawn? At the outset, it is apparent that for the foreseeable future the ability to pursue social policies will be dependent upon improvements in productivity and efficiency, at least to maintain if not to improve the nation's position in competition with other industrial trading states. Reducing unemployment by creating permanent low-productivity jobs will not provide long-term relief. Efficiency must be tempered by humanity—the former must not be permitted to ride roughshod over the latter. If this premise is accepted, then the supply response to changing circumstances becomes a much more central issue than has hitherto been conceded.

Although the regional and urban symptoms of economic and social malaise are rather similar and although outwardly the cause—a lack of jobs—is the same, the reasons leading to this deficiency of employment differ between the regions and the urban areas, especially the inner urban areas. Although it is an over-simplification, the regional problem can be represented as a failure of the workforce to adapt quickly enough and thereby to create the opportunities for profitable investment in new lines of business. In the conurbations, the inadequacy of the land market has created a serious imbalance in the economy, impairing its ability to respond to the decentralization of both people and jobs. In neither case

Chapter Three

Urban Evolution in Islamic Areas

W. B. FISHER

The rise of Islam as a highly significant element in contemporary world
affairs is now an accepted major feature of the last quarter-century.
Besides the obvious contributing factors in this situation—world
dependence on petroleum as prime energy source, with Islamic countries
as principal producers, and the Israel-Palestine issue, which has now
developed world-wide ramifications—there is, further, the more
generally disturbed political situation that has become increasingly
endemic in many Islamic areas. These areas could be said to be the only
parts of the world where warfare, intermittent but recurring and
threatening at times to escalate to extremely serious levels, has now gone
on for thirty-five years. At the time of writing there are military
operations of a kind in Afghanistan, Iran-Iraq, Israel-Lebanon, Somalia,
and Morocco-Mauritania, while 1981 witnessed a pre-emptive air strike
by Israel against what it considers the threat of nuclear weapons in Iraq,
and subversion in Saharan Africa supported from Libya. Such unrest
carries considerable risk of intervention by outside powers: major and
minor, Islamic and non-Islamic. Warfare between India, Pakistan, and
Bangladesh may not be repeated, but it has caused well over a million
casualties and remains a threat, particularly as both Pakistan and India
have access to nuclear power.

The fact that this zone of disturbance forms a large part of what we can
term the geopolitical interface between the Communist and Capitalist
zones of the world adds further to its significance. American
commitment to Israel and to a less extent to Saudi Arabia and the Gulf
Emirates together with Russian attempts to gain political advantage in

THE EXPANDING CITY
ISBN 0 12 547250 1

South Yemen (Aden), Somalia, Libya, Syria and Iraq are paralleled by
the importance of many Islamic states as highly valued buyers of
sophisticated machinery—especially armaments, sales of which do much
to offset the costs of buying Middle Eastern oil. The Islamic area also
includes some of the richest states in the world in terms of GNP per head
of population in the present-day world, and also some of the very poorest,
a further possible source of instability. It is thus included, somewhat
doubtfully, in the "Third World", but might better be regarded once
again as an intermediate boundary region. Moreover because of
differential demographic growth rates the issue of Islamic populations is
becoming one of very considerable importance within Russian Central
Asia. Hitherto a minority, increases of Muslim populations at a rate
greater than that of Russian-speakers may well overturn the present
demographic balance in these areas and cannot but be a source of
considerable anxiety to Russian rulers in Moscow.

Last, as a further political and driving force, there is the growth over
the last two decades of Muslim fundamentalism. Whether this has arisen
in response to the economic and political changes mentioned above, or
whether it has been a basic contributory element is too complex to be
discussed here: nevertheless, the fact of its existence is clear and its
effects very considerable.

In brief there has occurred broadly since 1940-50 a transformation that
now compels, for extremely strong reasons, a close world interest in
Muslim affairs. The Islamic areas, which up to the Second World War
almost without exception had no more than dependent status as
partitioned, colonized or mandated to European powers under spheres of
influence, from Tashkent and Jakarta to Marrakesh and Kano are now
experiencing a very remarkable transition in economic and political
conditions. For long peripheral to world affairs, with low economic
standards, and following cultural patterns that were usually dismissed as
restrictive, out of date, ineffective and in general decline, in process of
abandonment even by the more progressive elements of its own
following, the Islamic world seemed in the early part of this century
likely to experience total political subjection and considerable cultural
decline. The Sykes-Picot Treaty of 1916 which proposed partitioning
the entire present Middle East among major European powers; the
implant of Zionists almost casually undertaken by a largely uncom-
prehending government in London; and then the decades of economic
dominance by foreign oil companies have given way to a situation in

which the world as a whole now watches anxiously not only any changes in world prices of oil as set by the Organization of Petroleum Exporting Countries (OPEC) (a majority membership of which is Islamic), but also the general economic, political and even theological trends in Islamic countries.

The result has been a much greater concern with the Islamic city as a concept. First, because there is now a more positive, confident feeling among Muslims as to the vitality and strength of Islam, which is seen by many as a real alternative form of society at the present day. The roots and origins of Islam are now increasingly analysed with the aim of charting development plans for the future. Secondly, many Islamic countries have world-wide importance as trading partners, and with their rapidly growing populations, especially urban, there is considerable interest in new town construction. Last, it is clearly the hope of many Muslims that Islamic society, obviously in our own time in certain respects now highly cohesive, locationally compact as one contiguous zone, and politically and socially resilient, could generate (as it may well have done in the past) a special urban pattern which can be identified through function and morphology as answering specifically to the current needs of Islam. Will the resurgence of Islam lead, as is now hoped, to the development of a new social order with an appropriately new and distinctive typology of urban life to sustain this?

THE ISLAMIC CITY: GENESIS AND DEVELOPMENT

Any analysis of city development in Islamic areas is subject to severe constraint. As regards the earliest phase, there was for long extremely little information: only an exiguous amount of first-hand documentation, and some of that hostile, since it was made by defeated enemies. Archaeological evidence is still limited because much has been destroyed, and building materials were often more fragile than those in northern Europe. Much also remains buried either under *tells* or more modern cities, including cemeteries, which offer especial difficulty to excavation. For later periods, too, quite often records (e.g. of civil administration) are, even when extant, neglected simply because of the lack of suitable investigators: for example the writer has seen considerable quantities of Ottoman records preserved in municipalities of south-east Turkey but being in Arabic and totally unclassified they demand inputs of research that are simply not available at the present. Only Bernard Lewis so far has undertaken for Istanbul a major study based on Ottoman evidence.[25]

Earliest work in the present century was largely but by no means entirely by French researchers in Francophone Arab areas of the south and eastern Mediterranean, with North Africa and Syria most closely investigated. In the past thirty years American, British and German workers have been active in Iran, Egypt and Turkey, and there is a growing contribution from indigenous investigators. Some Russian interest has also been shown in Turkic areas of Soviet Central Asia and adjoining areas of Iran. There is also interest of a rather different kind at the present time, mainly by practising architects anxious to develop specifically "Arab" styles from earlier models in Islamic areas of Arabia. The Indian sub-continent and Islamic areas further to the south east, however, still remain largely untouched, and the earlier Russian initiative on the Muslim cities of Soviet Asia has been subject to obvious political constraints.

Thus although there is now a fair spread of local, individual studies, often with considerable detail, little of a generalist approach can be said so far to have developed. M. E. Bonine[6] puts it perhaps rather strongly when he writes that our appreciation of Islamic cities amounts to irregular extrapolation from individual town studies "in clichés and stereotypes". Nevertheless it is apparent that important issues of a wider kind have clearly emerged and these will now be briefly discussed.

Models of the Islamic City

Over the last fifty years there have been varying suggestions regarding possible theoretical models of a traditional Muslim city. These models include the following basic elements: a citadel with related defensive perimeter walls enclosing the settlement; a large Friday mosque located close to or at the intersection of two or more street arteries; one or more bazaar areas situated close to the main mosque, with a hierarchy of trades declining towards the periphery; ablution facilities (*hammam*) also very close to the main mosque; and a pronounced segmentation into residential districts often on a confessional basis, with formerly a Jewish community usually located closest to the Citadel. Apart from some of the main traffic arteries, access to residential quarters was and remains most often intricate, winding and often extremely narrow with frequent "dead-ends". Outside the walls detached suburbs of the wealthy, of minorities, of administrative groups (native or formerly colonial), and expanses of shanty dwellings complete the pattern. Housing, except of the poorest sort, was usually of the courtyard type with a single small entrance.

We have the obvious question of how far, excluding the special element of mosques, this pattern could be said to amount to something distinctively and explicitly Muslim. The theories relating to early town growth in Europe offer considerable parallels—a strong-point of a military kind, markets, a religious centre, suburbs—one might also apply familiar sectoral theories elaborated even for the modern Western city such as those of Hoyt and others. Could, however, a network of twisting alleys, or inward looking courtyards be regarded as equally characteristic of early nineteenth-century London, Edinburgh or Vienna? Opinions differ markedly on this general point. If, looking for universalist theory, one regards town development as deriving from function—exchange, production, administration, and cultural expression—then there are common origins to most towns and cities of the world, and built form is a secondary matter. If, however, one regards urban style as closely reflecting group perception and response to the basic social and economic imperatives just listed, it is much more possible to see in the towns of Islamic areas a separately identifiable and distinctive situation.

A second important factor, deriving from the above, is the locational and environmental aspects. Hourani adverts to the dangers of applying situations characteristic of one cultural area with its characteristic patterns to another area of clearly different geographical endowment. In certain areas, cities of Graeco-Roman origin were subsumed into the Islamic polity, sometimes with minimum change. For example Christian cathedrals in Constantinople, Nicosia, Beirut, and Damascus became mosques, and similarly a number of Sassanian town foundations have continued as Islamic cities with only gradual alteration in ground plan, spread over many years. Because of their historical continuity and their greater availability of historical and site material, it has been tempting to base theories and models on conditions investigated for the limited area of Syria, Mesopotamia, and the lower Nile Valley which have hitherto been most accessible to research. It is perhaps useful to look elsewhere: Gernet[17] for instance has drawn attention to the situation in China during formative periods of Islamic development. Whilst the west had important Graeco-Roman survivals, it was also extremely closely interpenetrated by pastoral nomadic influences. In the Chinese sphere, however, there was much more of a separation, with nomadic contacts reduced if not largely excluded, and towns dominated almost entirely by influences from the surrounding agricultural countryside. The morphology of Chinese towns at the time of the expansion of Islam would thus appear to have been much more simple in pattern, modest in built form and far less detached from a rural background. All this is in sharp contrast to conditions in Islamic areas, where contact between pastoral nomads and cities was much more intimate owing to the dependence of many of the latter on trans-desert trading. Many of the earlier followers of Islam were themselves pastoral nomads, so this contact was also initially stronger, with tribal organization introduced directly into the organization of early Islamic urban development. The tribal factor therefore seems to have been particularly significant at this time of town development.

Another issue of importance is whether the early Arabs were responsible for a surge in urban growth, by the expansion of existing cities and the foundation of new ones. This has been the subject of considerable controversy. Earlier researches suggested that the undoubted increase in economic prosperity that rapidly followed the Islamic conquest resulted in an equally rapid growth in urbanization. The first reason for urban growth was given as an inferred preference for urban living as shown by the founders of Islam, with the Qur'ān cited as demonstrating strong predilection for settled rather than nomadic life, and a disdain of agriculture—which it is claimed meant that man's obligation to the divine will is best carried out in the towns. The consistent view of the Shari'a that ritual Friday prayers can only be held in a permanently inhabited settlement with at least forty responsible men present is regarded as confirmation. However, it could be argued that any large agricultural settlement could produce the necessary group of forty and that actual urban conditions are in fact not really necessary. Much of the controversy has been succinctly summarized by Cahen,[8] who regarded the ten years of residence of Muhammad in Medina with chosen companions as a unique formative period that endowed the Muslim community with its basic institutions: Medina was the model Islamic city and it "has never ceased to serve as a point of reference down the centuries". The second reason for town growth was given as the military situation, which in the earliest phases of Islamic expansion fostered the evolution of military strongpoints into settled trading and manufacturing centres. As political stability returned after conquest and economic development continued, centres such as Basra, Fustat (Cairo) and Kairouan, to name only a few, which were originally military settlements became real towns. The Russian analyst Barthold[2] also ascribed most of the towns of Turkistan to development from an original Islamic military nucleus; however, his views have been challenged by other Russian researchers.

Last, there has been a persistent tendency for new and successful rulers to establish separate capital cities as a conspicuous demonstration of a change in regime: perhaps in our own time we have seen this process operating with the designation of Ankara as the new Turkish capital. The writings of Ibn Khaldun gave this idea prominence, but earlier Muslim commentators (Yakubi and Al Mansur) write in similar vein. These general views have been sustained by later authorities who in our own time have written about the expansion of Baghdad to a city of 2 000 000 inhabitants, of Basra to over 200 000 and Kufuh to over 100 000 — all wholly new sites, as were Almeria, Fez, and Tunis.

More recently this view of rapid urbanization in early Islamic times has been strongly questioned, first by Lapidus[24] and then by Wagstaff.[36] They consider that most development occurred through expansion and replacement of populations within existing towns or by accretion of new suburbs, and that most of the new Islamic centres — usually military — either proved ephemeral or were absorbed within a short time in nearby existing settlements. Redistribution of population in existing centres rather than new development is thus held to be the chief factor in early Islamic town growth. In the present writer's view there is the great difficulty, probably insuperable, of quantifying: without actual numbers there is no way of establishing really valid general comparisons. What earlier investigators have done is to take what are in effect random samples derived from literary sources, usually based on Islamic writers (who may themselves have been by no means contemporary) with sometimes partial evidence from archaeological sources. This does not provide a clear outline of the process of town expansion, and so the idea of a rapid growth of towns due directly to a strong Islamic impulse cannot be fully sustained. Some incontrovertible instances occurred of entirely new foundations which later grew to be successful cities, and these certainly would be largely if not totally built as "Islamic" towns. Alongside these, however, would also seem to have been a greater number of other centres modified to a greater or less extent by their new Muslim regimes. How far therefore could the situation be regarded as a sufficient basis to distinguish the separate evolution of an Islamic city-type? In itself, it is perhaps insufficient, but there are further aspects that remain to be considered.

Minorities

One particular feature of the town in Islamic areas since the rise of Islam has been the presence of substantial minority groups in towns: religious, cultural and racial. These groups are to be found living in close physical juxtaposition as "ethnic quarters", nearly always as conscious elements, and the presence of such ethnic quarters in quite large numbers in most Islamic towns has often been regarded as a specific Islamic characteristic, particularly by de Planhol[11] and Lapidus.[24] De Planhol sees clustering of minority groups as something of a specific reaction to Islamic social organization: in part, the organization of rule often on a confessional basis, as exemplified in the *millet* system of the Ottomans. Nowadays advantage is often still perceived in living together: political pressures can be generated by socially conscious small groups, for example, the "incomers" of squatter Ankara, or the "tribal" housing of some Gulf States. Regrettably, too, some need for defensive clustering remains at the present day—as in Beirut or the Coptic areas of Cairo, to give only two instances. There is, of course, also the frequent forced move of populations to meet particular political crises or the edict of rulers; we have seen this in present-day Jerusalem. Moreover, economic differentials have reinforced confessional awareness over the past thirty years; here Tehran offers a remarkable example. There has been a very marked growth of wealthier, westernized suburbs up the formerly undeveloped hill slopes towards what some years ago were detached "summer station" settlements—Shemlan and Shahistan for example. These are now incorporated in one near-continuous urban development that has reached into the foothills of the Elburz mountains. Similarly, lower quality housing in Tehran has spread downhill from the city centre into what until recently were brickfields and areas of polluting manufacturing occupying a geomorphological sump.

To attempt to explain the development of ethnic quarters one must consider a wide variety of influences. In some cases, minorities were simply allotted areas by ruling authority. The minorities were often military groups in the past; more often today they are inconvenient but inescapable refugees—Armenians in Beirut in the 1920s, Palestinians in Amman and elsewhere since 1947, Bulgarian Muslims in Asia Minor, and victims of local warfare such as that between Iran and Iraq in 1980-83.

Only limited studies have been made of such minority groups, but it would seem that the situation generally is by no means the simple one of intense clustering in a particular small urban area by a migrant group drawn or forced to settle as a single community. Although this may be the initial situation, very soon there is the effect of natural demographic increase: often the immigrants have a birth rate higher than that of the local population. A process of assimilation may ensue, by which some of the minority move away, and the unwanted housing may be recolonized by the indigenous population. Sometimes this can even result in the shift or an entire minority group to a quite different locality, the original area of settlement being wholly recolonized or left abandoned. Investigation by English[14] in Kirman and by Drakakis-Smith[12] of the geçekondu areas of Turkey has elicited details of some of the factors and processes involved. One can observe more of this in the Old City of Jerusalem and adjoining areas, as both Arabs and orthodox and "modernist" Israelis are in actual process of establishing what amount to minority areas, with occasional "no-go" temporary zones set up on Holy Days.

Although much further work remains to be done, enough has occurred to establish the fact of the existence of minority groups on a relatively important scale not only in the past but also at the present time. Although the underlying causation may be very different in time and in space, it is generally clear that minority groups still form a conscious and dynamic element in the present Islamic towns. Ethnicity and social clustering still continue and still offer immense scope for investigation. Minorities may well be a characteristic element of Islamic cities, with enormous implications for future evolution that will be discussed later.

Associated with this problem is the effect of a colonialist past. Islamic areas could be held to be unique in that when they were subjected to outside colonial rule and dominance during the late nineteenth and early twentieth centuries, they already had a vigorous urban system of their own. In other parts of the world (eastern Asia for example) foreign pressure was less powerful and restricted to only a few areas: Treaty Ports or ceded territories. Elsewhere opposite conditions obtained. In Africa, North America and possibly Latin America, indigenous town development was relatively weak and unable to avoid total dominance or obliteration. Only in Islamic areas (and areas strongly penetrated by Islamic culture, such as India) could pre-existing urban networks continue to exist on more or less equal terms, with the result that during the nineteenth and twentieth centuries there was the development of parallel suburbs or quarters set up by foreign rulers alongside earlier foundations. Sometimes the occupying power added new "government" settlements, as in North Africa (Fez is a prominent example); sometimes it was a local ruler who wished by creating a totally new and distinctive settlement at a distance to modernize—as in early Safavid Isfahan, or late nineteenth century Cairo, twentieth century Sabbiya (Kuwait), and the Shahestan of Mohammad Reza Pahlavi (Tehran).

Similar kinds of expansion can be noted for cities in other parts of the world, and one cannot suggest that the existence of "ethnic quarters" with new accretions on a periphery is in any sense solely a characteristic of the Muslim towns. However, it would seem that ethnic quarters have been more numerous, more pervasive and cohesive, and more identifiable in Moslem towns, and have thus had a distinctly greater role in influencing city life—especially social patterns and forms of government. The fact that 'quarters' remain today a major and clearly identifiable phenomenon could also be regarded as tending to differentiate Islamic from other urban developments. One possible factor in the persistence of ethnicity in Muslim communities is the matter of cultural assimilation, which is regarded by many observers as low, compared with minorities in other parts of the world. In support of this statement, the same point has been made regarding assimilation of Muslim groups in present day Britain and the USA, although the validity of a transfer of ideas in this respect can be questioned.

Earlier analysts of city development, in particular Max Weber,[37] commented that, besides the basic elements of a city—fortifications, markets, and some form at least of partial autonomous administration—two other elements that characterize the city in Europe were absent in Islamic areas: partial autonomy and distinctively urban forms of association. This has led to discussion about the corporate nature or otherwise of the Islamic city, and the identity of civic groups that could be held to have contributed to this corporate activity. Controversy has arisen with, on the one hand, attempts to demonstrate the existence of Islamic medieval associations linked to religious activities—especially Sufis and Ismailis—which are then equated with the craft and trade guilds of western Europe. Some writers have even regarded early Islamic trading and apprenticeship systems, with associations that have links to saintly Muslim patrons, as direct ancestors of the medieval European guilds. Others, including Stein and Hourani,[21] with of course Weber,[37] see no links whatsoever: the European guilds eventually gained close internal organization and thus considerable authority at least in some areas as participating and sharing in the functions of local government as really effective agents: this did not occur in Islamic areas. Others again regard evidence of such craft and trade associations as deriving really from the Roman and particularly Byzantine periods; and under the Ottomans it would appear that some formal organization of the craftsmen and merchants was encouraged, not to transfer any powers of local administration but to allow regulation and control, especially of taxation, by central authorities. The strongly egalitarian philosophy of Islam, in which any privileged groups were mistrusted and the rights of individual action emphasized, prevented a full development of civic associations. Islamic law, according to some commentators, is strongly against local solidarities that could be regarded as diminishing or avoiding the common Islamic duties and obedience. As a result, Islam developed impressive corporate organization at state level but not at the urban level: local leaders tended to emerge and function only when central authority had broken down or was in eclipse. Their scope for action was limited because their authority derived from support by the city "quarters"— ethnic and sectarian—which was limited and fluctuating. Weber goes further in suggesting that this lack of local civic leadership was in part a result of nomadic tribal influence, which, as we noted, deeply penetrated urban Islamic communities and inhibited corporate organization.

Another view is that the above analysis is wholly erroneous in that it is Eurocentric, applying to Islam ideas and situations that are characteristic of a totally different physical and cultural environment. A significant number of writers have drawn attention to the fact that until very recently almost all studies of Islamic institutions and territories have been made by outsiders, and it is only now that indigenous researchers have begun to correct what has amounted to gross imbalance by ideas of their own. To argue, as many Western scholars have, that Islamic cities are somehow "deficient" because they apparently lack certain institutions characteristic of Western cities shows deficiency of another kind. There is the fact the existence of the Islamic cities themselves: one must develop appropriate and, if necessary, totally different methodology to understand them. Considerable weight can be added to this line of discussion by considering two aspects which are only now being investigated in detail: the demographic situation in Islamic cities and the extent of an "informal sector" in economic activity and housing. Further, it is necessary perhaps to re-interpret a number of other, fundamental matters. Shari'a law emphasizes the freedom of the individual, based on the family unit, which has the right to live in its own house, which is enclosed and oriented towards a courtyard not towards the street. Thus family units impinged on each other but mingled less. In many towns of the northern Mediterranean, strolling through the town is encouraged at certain times of the day, and main thoroughfares are even sometimes closed temporarily to traffic at dusk to allow this; such public contact is less common in Islamic areas. Physical constraints deriving from environmental conditions may also apply: the greater need for shade and shelter from the sun has often been invoked (e.g. by de Planhol[11]) as explaining town morphology. Another factor of less interest but no less importance could be that of water supply. Elaborate methods to ensure this led (e.g. by *jub* or *qanat*) to forms of cooperation and civic organization unknown in the West, for instance the water courts or committees which are such a prominent feature of society in arid areas. Also the presence mainly in urban centres of religious and teaching houses—mosques, schools, *zawiyas*, and their associated activities could lead to close connection of the *ulama* with a bourgeoisie—a considerable point of difference from the West, where monasteries were much more often in remoter rural areas and contacts with the town fewer.

Some of this largely refers to conditions in the past rather than the present day, for instance, water supply. Enough remains, however, to suggest that Eurocentric approaches, whether in social analysis or in the insensitive transfer of forms of architecture, are limited in their application; and we must look wider for satisfactory explanation.

We may first consider demographic trends. Analysis of "Western" situations showed that with a population movement from rural areas to the towns, industrialization was almost consistently accompanied by a marked decline in birth rates. For Islamic cities it would now seem, however, that many rural migrants move directly into service occupations, so that industrialization is far less a factor. Also, birth rates among new urban populations appear to increase, so that, unlike Western cities, natural increase provides the greater element contributing to population growth in contemporary Islamic cities. There is, too, the question of whether the present day Islamic city, as often nowadays a rapidly developing economic unit, will repeat or recapitulate the experience of the industrial cities of the west by experiencing a higher death rate due to poor living conditions. Evidence so far, though by no means conclusive, suggests that this may not be the case, for several reasons. First, industrial sector development is less important: many urban immigrants offer services on a larger scale. Secondly, industry is less extensive so the harmful effects of industrial activities are less. Thirdly, in many instances, public infrastructures (water, sanitation, health services) are not only markedly better than in rural areas, but often in absolute terms very superior indeed in a wealthy country. Hence the "western" concept, derived from nineteenth and early twentieth century experience, of a relatively healthy rural population and unhealthy urban dwellers does not necessarily hold true for Islamic populations. Against this, however, there is the fact of informal (squatter) housing, for which urban infrastructures are usually markedly deficient.

Despite considerable variations due to differing levels of national income, it is probably true that while mortality rates for most of the towns are in decline, urban birth rates still remain high and show only slight tendencies toward decline in certain countries: Egypt, Turkey, and Tunisia. Thus natural increase, already very considerable due to high natality, remains the most prominent demographic feature; and the problems arising from this are different from those of the Western city. The phenomenon of flight from the inner city with the growth of central "blight" areas is also much less a feature. Instead, informal economic activities tend to develop on a considerable scale, with high domestic occupancy of many central city areas at the present time. The gradient in density of occupancy does not rise consistently away from modern Islamic city centres, as is now the case in many "western" cities, but it could be said to be irregular, with the occurrence of densely occupied areas distributed both in the centre of the city and at the periphery—the latter often in the form of squatter areas. Alternating with these irregularly distributed high density areas are others of markedly light population densities within the same town.

THE INFORMAL SECTOR IN URBAN LIFE

One aspect of Islamic urban life is the fact of an extensive "informal sector" in economic activity. The existence of such a sector (also called traditional, unorganized, or unprotected), has been identified only within the last ten years. First used by Child[10] in 1972 for Kenya, the concept has since been applied extensively in Africa, Latin America, and South East Asia: very little investigation has so far been undertaken for the Middle East and southern Asia. It would, however, seem that the idea of an informal sector has very considerable relevance to our present examination, both as a system of analysis and as a guide to future evolution of city life. Because of the novelty of the concept and paucity of field investigation, it appears appropriate to sketch in outline the development of ideas generally on this informal sector.

Observers of Third World conditions over the last three decades became increasingly struck by a dualism in economic activity, as between a formal (modern, organized or protected) sector. McGee,[27] working mainly in south-east Asia, saw a dualism deriving from continuance of what he called a continuing peasant system alongside the new capitalist mode of production introduced from outside; Geertz,[16] working in Indonesia, expressed this as "pedlars and princes"; Sethuraman,[34] using material from the Indian sub-continent, distinguished a separate "bazaar" economy. An important contributing factor is the rapid growth of cities of the Third World: local figures of an annual urban growth of 7% are commonplace in only moderately wealthy or even underdeveloped countries, with far higher increases being found in certain cities of the wealthier oil states. Two examples will suffice. In the Sudan, recognized as one of the poorest of the Islamic group, recent International Labour Office (ILO) estimates are that urban populations are increasing at an annual rate of 6·4-7·1%. Juba, predominantly non-Moslem and in the special situation of recovering from civil war, is currently growing at an annual rate of 8%. In Pakistan, latest available estimates from the UN Demographic Office suggest growth of the urban population at an annual rate of 6·3%.[38]

The ILO has been especially concerned with the notion of an informal sector, and Table 1 incorporates criteria for definition as suggested by the ILO (1972) together with other definitions put forward by Santos (1975)[33] and Sethuraman (1975).[34] An enterprise need not meet all the criteria: a few or perhaps even one might justify recognition as an informal activity.

The general concept of formal and informal sectors has been criticized on several grounds. First, there is risk of regarding the model as a form of developed economic duality, with activity neatly categorized as in one or the other sub-systems, whereas in fact there is a fluctuating situation which preferably should be treated as a totality (Breman).[7] Analysis of

Table 1 Criteria for definition of the formal and informal sectors

Formal	Informal
Difficult entry (capital, licences, etc. necessary)	Easy entry
Bureaucratic organization	Family organized
Considerable reliance on overseas resources	Mainly indigenous resources
Corporate ownership	Family ownership
Large scale	Small scale
Capital-intensive	Labour-intensive
Extraneous technology	Adapted local technology
Price of commodities fixed	Price of commodities negotiable
Formally acquired skills (often expatriate)	Skills often acquired outside formal education system
Markets regulated	Markets unregulated and highly competitive
Fixed, regular wages	Wages may not be involved
Often government aid: provision of infrastructures, protection, legal and fiscal	Very little contact with authorities. May be harassment or evasion

Third World productive systems should not attempt a division into arbitrary sectors on the basis of definitions chosen *a priori* (Gerry).[18] Secondly, by adopting a dualistic model, there may be a tendency to regard the informal sector as a main point of entry for rural migrants into towns, i.e. a first stage and a highly temporary one in the process of urbanization. With this is the further tendency to categorize urban immigration as made up predominantly of poorly educated and poorly paid young adult males. Much of this is certainly true, but none of the assumptions is wholly valid. Here an important criticism can be made: under Third World conditions one must not regard the informal sector as chiefly a temporary and preparatory stage in the process of urbanization or as merely the first stage in a continuum. The size of the informal sector in some countries alone is an argument against this. For many it may well represent a permanent situation; here is perhaps the chief difference between Third World and Developed World conditions.

One other general important criticism has been advanced: Marxist thought regards any form of dualism as being a totally inadequate approach to analysis of relationships between small-scale economic activities and large-scale capitalist enterprise: modes of production are the essential basis for such analysis, and a dualism by sector is trivializing, distracting and therefore misleading. Further, it has been argued that pre-capitalist modes of production will never transform, as they did as a result of the Industrial Revolution in Developed World countries, and thus poverty in the Third World will not therefore be a temporary state. There are several reasons for this. First, because of the general demographic situation of high population increase, the bargaining power of the labourer will remain low. Secondly, while the increments of capital formerly remained in the hands of entrepreneurs who re-invested and expanded markets, nowadays in less developed countries a greater percentage goes to bureaucratic politicians and traders who have a more tenuous interest in mass consumption, preferring luxury consumption by an élite. Thirdly, the industrial sector in less developed countries is small, so the possibility of major stimulus from industry to the national economy is not great. This leads to the obvious deduction that only total change in the basis of economic activity can lead the Third World out of the constraints of poverty now visible from the operation of the formal and informal sectors. From the informal sector, it has consequently been suggested by Marxists, could come the frustration that generates eventual revolutionary violence.

It is also necessary to point out, as already has been done by Birks and Sinclair,[4] that in the small, wealthy oil-producing states, an informal sector can hardly be said to exist at all, because of a high level of demand for labour in the formal sector, institutional difficulties such as obtaining work permits and licences, and the dependence on high-cost imports which makes petty trading improfitable. Thus, as would be expected, the informal sector is most developed in capital-poor countries. Studies by Birks and Sinclair have shown that employment in the informal sector (in terms of actual numbers employed in towns) is greater than that of formal sector employment in the Yemen Arab Republic and the Sudan; while in Egypt 1980 estimates are of an urban informal workforce numbering 2 million, as compared with 4·1 million in the formal sector. Due to a greater volume of imports as part of the "open door" policy of the 1978–82 Five Year Plan, it would appear that the informal sector is now growing faster than the formal sector. One must therefore regard the small Gulf States as exceptional in not having an informal sector: for the rest, informal economic activity plays a significant part in most Islamic states, and can even be dominant in certain of the poorer ones.

INFORMAL HOUSING

Associated with, or possibly derived from, the general notion of an informal sector in economic activity is a somewhat similar situation in housing, with the development of "unconventional" housing patterns alongside more normal conventional dwellings. With the high rate of migration to towns and a high rate of natural increase for urban dwellers, there are acute problems of urban housing in most Islamic states. The problem is not just one of indigence. Although the development of shanty-towns is a well-known phenomenon, it is necessary to make a distinction between habitation of totally inferior quality, using rudimentary materials (the *bidonvilles* or *sarifas*) and housing which may be of intrinsically sound construction but which lacks legal title and therefore may not have the necessary infrastructures—roads, drainage, energy supplies. Here the influence of Islamic legal systems is felt, and the question of title to land and tenure and its use can be viewed very differently from western practices. A new factor is the development of temporary migration abroad on a fairly large scale, often leading to the repatriation of funds that (given prevalent world inflation) are very frequently channelled into house building. Turkish workers in West Germany, Yemenis in the Gulf States, Egyptians and Palestinians in many Arab countries, and Pakistanis elsewhere generate a flow of funds that, for some countries, is now very considerable. The investigation by Drakakis-Smith[12] in Ankara showed how extensive squatter (geçekondu) housing has become—almost two-thirds of the total domestic level in Ankara—and the houses built are often of good construction. It is the lack of infrastructures, congested or difficult sites, and the "unplanned" agglomerations that develop, which give rise to problems, rather than actual quality of buildings. Newly acquired skills through foreign employment, together with some communal and family help can produce a satisfactory building, and difficulties over provision of some infrastructures can be overcome through joint communal political action, particularly during a period of uncertain or "hung" government, such as that of Turkey up to 1980. However, some other difficulties due to site limitations cannot be overcome even if a squatter housing group becomes legalized. Illicit building can also reduce pressure on other, property in the city, usually slums, and Keleş[23] has shown how, in some parts of Ankara mobility between habitations has been facilitated with some easing of rent charges through geçekondu building. Detailed investigation of a similar kind has not yet been carried out in other areas, but parallel situations could well exist, certainly in Turkey and possibly in Egypt and the cities of Pakistan.

FUTURE EVOLUTION

We have noted the generally high rate of increase in urban populations of the Islamic world, particularly south-west Asia, north Africa and Soviet Central Asia. There are, however, considerable differences as between countries, and due to their very high in-migration and superior public health services, the oil-producing states show especially high rates of urban growth. As regards overall numbers, estimates by United Nations and the World Bank now suggest that the population of the north African area, 110 million in 1980, could reach 174 million (low variant) or 192 million (high variant) by the year 2000. For south-west Asia the corresponding figures are 98 million (1980), 158 million (low variant), 170 million (high variant). For the rest of Asia (Afghanistan, Iran, Pakistan, Bangladesh, Indonesia, Malaysia and Singapore together), a population of 372 million (1980), and a median figure of 635·5 million by the end of the century. In Soviet Central Asia the Islamic population by the year 2000 is reckoned to approach 65 to 75 million: approximately one-quarter of the total for the whole Soviet Union. The Arab countries, Turkey, and possibly Iran and Indonesia have very young populations as compared with world averages and even with most Third World countries: a median age of 18 years (north Africa) and 17, (south-west Asia) is expected to become respectively 20 and 19; for all less developed countries together the corresponding figures are 19 (1975) and 23 (2000). Urbanization in Muslim areas (except for the states of sub-Saharan Africa) is thus above world average and particularly so within the oil producing states. Urbanized populations estimated by U.N. researchers in 1975 at 40% of the total population of north Africa, 24% of sub-Saharan Africa, 51% in south-west Asia and 22% for Muslim countries further east, are projected to reach by 2000 58% in most areas and 68-70% in others where population is particularly mobile. Already the level of urbanization in south-west Asia is closer to that in more developed countries rather than to that of the less developed ones.

As regards general future trends, it may be instructive to make limited comparisons with other important patterns of urbanization recognized as distinctive, so it is now proposed to consider very briefly two of these: the African town, and the Socialist city.

Mabogunje[26] has drawn attention to the fact that many modern African towns represent wholly modern implants developed at least for much of their formative period under Colonial rule. The indigenous population had only at best highly restricted access to means of acquisition of productive skills, whether for processing products of the new economic order—palm oil, coffee, sisal, or minerals—or also in developing organizational skills for handling and marketing foreign imports, usually consumer goods or sophisticated machinery. The town as developed in colonial times tended to be a place where Africans held not very meaningful jobs, and the wages they earned were spent only too easily on imports: consumerism largely unrelated to local production. Similarly, urban life and education, being to a considerable extent foreign led, conferred literary and numerate skills often of little relevance to indigenous cultures. At the same time, townspeople were given the opportunity to escape from and abandon cultural restraints and indigenous *mores* derived from rural life as practised by the majority in their own country. Last, with the ending of colonial rule and its restriction on consumption and job opportunities, there has in recent years been a rush towards satisfying pent-up feelings of deprivation by conspicuous consumption and by even further relaxation of social constraint.

This analysis clearly has certain aspects closely relevant to the Islamic cities of north Africa and southern Asia, but it is suggested by the present writer that because of two special factors not present in Mabougunje's description of tropical Africa there has been a significantly different response. The two factors are the strength, pervasiveness and cohesion of Islam as a total social system and the fact that the Muslim city was a vigorous, strongly functioning system with long traditions and roots and when confronted and encroached upon by Colonial and Imperialist expansion it was able to resist Western economic and social pressures to far more effect and with much greater success. How far one may see the contemporary revival of Muslim fundamentalism as a major and direct response to the impact of Western systems upon Muslim urban life is of much relevance. Jansen[22] sees the area in which Islam has been most able to resist Western challenges as city-based education, particularly in north Africa, through changing and controlling national school systems.

Attempts at westernization, such as those by Kemal Ataturk, by the founder of Aligarh Muslim Anglo-Oriental College, and by the Muhammadiya schools of Indonesia have largely failed. Even Rodinson,[31] although convinced that "the Muslim religion seems poorly fitted to play the role of bringing about socialist economic construction", nevertheless believed that revival of Islam is the greatest single achievement brought about by "the process of putting Islam back into the educational system of Muslim countries where it was not before has been going on during the past 75 years, while in the Christian West the last remnants of religion had been pushed out of education; proof of bold assertiveness" by Islam. All this has taken place almost entirely in an urban environment, with leadership drawn from the larger mosques and madrassehs. It is in the towns, where contact is closest, that the resurgence of fundamentalist Islam has been most marked and the effects of this revival have been most apparent, particularly in the political sphere. The concept of a Holy City of Islam, thirty years ago usually dismissed by outside observers as quaint and archaic and of rapidly declining influence, has latterly taken on extreme significance as a valid expression of political power.

The relationship of ideology to urban form has recently also been investigated in Communist areas: is there an identifiable and distinctive Socialist city? Recapitulating in Russia as it were the experience of Islam but in the present century, there has been adaptation of pre-existing cities to socialized patterns followed by construction of entirely new centres explicitly on socialist models. A rationally planned and highly ordered spatial arrangement was aimed for, with emphasis on the micro-district; a residential neighbourhood linked to productive units, mainly industrial, with trading, particularly in consumer goods, on a very much smaller scale than is usual in the western or in south Asian towns.

City growth has been carefully regulated for some time in the centrally planned states by the internal passport and permit system, with the basic aims of controlling the growth of large cities and improving the status of smaller ones, a planning policy described by French and Hamilton[15] as not entirely successful. Because of a very even spread of industry, with each industrial zone linked to smaller clusters of neighbourhood units, the outstanding feature of the Socialist city is its uniformity. Architectural styles recur, varied in older cities by survivals from the historic past, and generally by new cultural parks, exhibition areas and gathering places for parades.

The segregation by sectors, prominent in Western and Islamic cities, is almost entirely absent; instead, variation by apartment blocks, sometimes built as "cooperatives" by more affluent groups. With the widespread uniformity of building styles, differentiation is more visible on the basis of the period of building. Within this uniformity are slight variations derived from regional cultures and traditions, some of which are relics of the past and others deliberately introduced as following these cultures.

To what extent do these differences justify recognition as specifically socialist? In their spatial arrangement and built forms perhaps only to a limited degree but as the matrix of a particular social consciousness of way of life possibly much more. The two aspects together, reinforcing each other, certainly amount in the view of Giese to the creation of distinctive and separate urban styles with recognizable aims.

However, there is another evolutionary process which transcends both those so far discussed: the tendency of capitalist and socialist styles to converge in built form, spatial arrangement, and function, particularly as many large cities throughout the world are now passing into a post-industrial phase with service activities predominant.

Specialized modes of transport, particularly by air, growth of traffic, and the revolutionary effect, pointed out by Jean Gottman,[19] of electronic forms of communication affect all cities to an increasing extent, producing the same attempts to find solutions to what are largely similar problems. The desire for rapid modernization, together with availability of most sophisticated plant and technology designed and produced from only a few manufacturing sources, has led to wholesale export of standardized approaches, especially with the growth in demand for "turnkey" construction. The dominance in many parts of the world of multinational enterprises further strengthens this tendency. The effect is perhaps seen at its strongest—and worst in the view of some—in the international hotels which present an almost uniform environment with a few trivial touches of local colour to provide in an otherwise largely undifferentiated living style some meaningful identification with or piquant contrast to the country they happen to be in. Although the pattern of incidence and speed of attainment may vary, a general rise in living standards, an increase in car ownership, and increased social stratification prominent in the Western countries are now also becoming characteristics of Islamic and even socialist societies. Moreover, faced with the problems of city dereliction and deterioration of the environment, the West is increasingly abandoning individualist enterprise, with its uncertain and uncontrolled effects, in favour of restriction through planning, whether by central governmental action or by public pressures directed to preservation of the environment. As Lenin remarked, industry is neutral and can lend itself either to centrally planned economies or to capitalist enterprise. More often, as now seen in many parts of the world, both coexist in a mixed economy. The modern city may thus have a single fundamental basis which ultimately will generate convergent solutions to its problems. Already the 6·5% annual growth in Russian urban population during the period 1926-39 has given way, as in the West, to absolute decline in some cities since 1970. Will the Third World and in particular the Islamic areas experience ultimately the same trend? There are, as we have noted, only a few and not yet wholly convincing patterns of a potentially similar kind in Islamic areas, providing possible further evidence for convergence in the demographic aspect. However, this is so far only a small divergent aspect of the wider and different demographic pattern characteristic of Islamic regions.

Will the inevitable final result for all cities that have sufficient wealth be a broad similarity of form, structure and architectural types that is now so apparent in Western countries, with constraints partially exercised only by effects of local terrain and availability of finance? For Islamic areas there are especially pressing issues. Sudden availability of modern resources, material and intellectual, has fostered a spirit of iconoclasm which has resulted in the destruction of parts of Muslim cities on a considerable scale and in the opinion of some has produced a vacuum in the contemporary search for solutions to design, construction and environment problems. City walls and their gates have disappeared; monuments have been destroyed and allowed to decay; whole quarters razed to provide wide avenues for access by automobiles and the military. San'aa and Esfahan offer two dramatic examples of what can happen. The modern fashion of building in glass—which, many would argue, is especially badly adapted to the Middle Eastern environment in concept and heavily dependent on air conditioning and thus abundant cheap energy—has rapidly spread; and high rise apartment living, now increasingly rejected in the West for all but the wealthy, may in time as the older courtyard house types are replaced, produce the same social problems now encountered in the West. Where opportunity offers and there is the will on the part of local or national administrators, some efforts are being made, generally on small scale, to counter or remedy this slide towards universal convergence in built form. Conservation of the remaining urban historic areas is now practised by some municipalities with major efforts at restoration and rehabilitation using local architectural styles and building material. In Jeddah some 600 buildings and building groups in the centre of the city have recently been proposed for conservation and close planning control, at a projected cost of US $400 000 000, exclusive of disturbance costs and compensation. This approach, if applied more widely but at less cost and with appropriate regional variation, could produce a truly Islamic style for modern cities. However, some may regard the proposals as unduly sophisticated and cosmetic palliatives—twee ornamentation devised by non-Muslim outsiders without real appreciation or feeling for Islam, and within the financial scope only of richer oil states. The proponents of the Jeddah scheme ruefully admit that the proposals have "yet to win the hearts and minds of the inhabitants", and an alternative scheme is now under partial implementation.

One other important trend can be observed in the large modern city: detachment from its earlier role as regional centre, with development of what may be termed network relations with other cities of similar size. This is especially true of the Middle East, where transactions involving numerous other cities of the world—through commerce, politics or pilgrimage—have grown on a considerable scale. Elsewhere in the Islamic world the trend is less pronounced. Cities are breaking out, so to speak, of their earlier locational framework and at least partly replacing functions based on regional centrality by new linkages, chiefly on a basis of service provision and trading rather than on production, with cities of similar size and function located at considerable distances. The new cities of the Gulf, with their polyglot populations and in many respects increasingly detached from a regional hinterland, are extreme examples, but a similar development of international linkages can be observed for many other cities of the Islamic world. This is clearly a further factor in the general trend described earlier as convergence.

Of a contrary nature, however, is the fact that the extensive programmes of building and town expansion (not always sustained by large oil revenues) have generated attempts so far on a small scale to reduce unit costs by developing cheaper materials and alternative infrastructures. In recent years a number of conferences and special studies have elicited specific answers: reduction in demand for water by recycling; use of brackish or marine sources and "dry" treatment of effluent; use of local materials as substitutes for timber; and new arrangements of building. From all this have begun to develop systematic attempts to quantify the inputs of materials and energy appropriate to the environmental conditions. Interesting results are emerging which could suggest that a novel, though limited, technology of construction might be developing specifically in Islamic areas, where the problems of urban growth are urgent but also partially sustained by availability of funding.

Yet another view is that analysis of the city based on morphology, spatial analysis, and built form is bound to be inconclusive because it fails to take account of psychology, culture and tradition. A conference on European town planning recently held (1981) in Holland came to the conclusion that changes in the built environment, urban management, and the social and physical phenomena involved are now so complex and interdependent that no single academic discipline is capable of analysing and elucidating them, let alone producing answers to the issues involved. At the time of writing one is aware of the desperate and inconclusive attempts to grapple with the fundamental problems of English cities. The importance of this non-material aspect of city life is stressed by Serjeant, who remarked that to understand the Islamic city one needs to have lived in a Muslim town during Ramadan. Jean Gottman[19] makes a valuable point in reminding us that cultural variations are not simply ephemeral and volatile, but some of the basic pillars of urban stability. Values, tastes and perception of particular urban populations change only slowly and at highly irregular rates, almost always slower than the ideas of those involved in city government and reconstruction, who are thus apt to ignore or underestimate the outlook of the average citizen.

If an answer is desired to the question of whether there is an Islamic city, the reply must be a partial one. In many respects, particularly in the economic aspects of city life and built form, it would seem that universal, international styles are developing and often predominate, with only limited attempts in patterns of building—types of architectural design and details like fenestration, with local use of materials—to import some sort of Islamic appearance. But it would be wrong to consider this as the totality. Alongside outward built modernity is an *élan vital* amongst the population released by the political and economic changes of the past half century.

Logic and reasoning suggest that those towns of larger size and expanded activity will, independently of their geographical location, develop strong interconnections with similar cities throughout the world, and thus any important Islamic basis will decline to negligible proportions.

Only the smaller urban centres, those retaining predominantly local and regional connections, can expect to retain a strong and distinctively Islamic quality in their life. Given this, it would seem that for the smaller towns and cities at least, an Islamic ethos, mainly of attitude and way of life rather than in built form, will continue for an indefinite time.

BIBLIOGRAPHY

1. Abu Lughod, J. (1972). Problems and policy implications of Middle Eastern urbanisation. *In* "Studies on Development Problems in Selected Countries." New York.
2. Barthold, W. (1963). "Istoriya Kultur'noi Zhizni Turkestana." Moscow.
3. Baer, G. (1964). "Egyptian Builds." Jerusalem.
4. Birks, J. S. and Sinclair, C. A. (1980). "Arab Manpower." London.
5. Blake, G. H. and Lawless, R. I. (1980). "The Changing Middle Eastern City." London.
6. Bonine, M. E. (1979). The morphogenesis of Iranian Cities. *Ann. Assoc. Amer. Geographers* **69**.
7. Breman, J. (1976). A Dualistic Labour System? *Econ. and Pol. Weekly*, Vol. 11 No. 48.
8. Cahen, C. (1970). Y a-t-il eu des corporations professionnelles dans le monde musulman? *In* Hourani and Stern (1970).
9. Cambridge History of Islam Vols. I, II, Cambridge 1970.
10. Child, F. C. (1973). "An Empirical Study of Small Scale Rural Industry in Kenya." Nairobi.
11. de Planhol, X. (1975–76). "Kulturgeographische Grundlegen der Islamischen Geschichte." Zurich-Munich.
12. Drakakis-Smith, D. W. and Fisher, W. B. (1976). "Housing Problems in Ankara." Durham.
13. Dwyer, D. J. (ed.) (1972). "The City as a Centre of Change in Asia, Hong Kong."
14. English, P. W. (1966). "City and Village in Iran." Madison, Wisconsin.
15. French, R. A. and Hamilton, F. E. Ian (1979). "The Socialist City." Chichester.
16. Geertz, C. (1963). "Pedlars and Princes." Chicago.
17. Gernet, J. (1970). Note sur les villes chinoises. *In* Hourani and Stern (1970).
18. Gerry, C. (1974). "Petty Procedures and the Urban Economy." Stern, Geneva.
19. Gottmann, J. (1978). Urbanisation and employment. *Town Planning Rev.* **49**, No. 3.

20. Herbert, D. T. and Johnston, R. J. (1977). "Geography and the Urban Built Form." Oxford.
21. Hourani, A. H. and Stern, S. M. (ed.) (1970). "The Islamic City." Oxford.
22. Jansen, G. H. (1979). "Militant Islam." London.
23. Keleş, R. (1966). Urbanisation and balanced regional development in Turkey. *Ekistics* **21** (129).
24. Lapidus, I. M. (1967). "Muslim Cities in the Later Middle Ages." Harvard.
25. Lewis, B. (1961). "The Emergence of Modern Turkey." Oxford.
26. Mabogunje, A. L. (1977). Urbanization problems in Africa. *In* S. El-Shakhs and R. Ubodho. *"Urbanization, National Development and Regional Planning in Africa."* New York.
27. McGee, T. G. (1971). "The Urbanization Process in the Third World." London.
28. Mills, L. R. (1977). "Population and Manpower in the Southern Sudan." ILO, Juba.
29. Pirenne, H. (1958). "Economic and Social History of Mediaeval Europe." London.
30. Rapoport, A. (1978). "Human Aspects of Environment." Chichester.
31. Rodinson, M. (1974). "Islam and Capitalism." London.
32. Said, E. W. (1978). "Orientalism." New York.
33. Santos, M. (1975). "L'Espace Partagé: les Deux Circuits de l'Economie Urbaine. Paris."
34. Sethuraman, S. V. (1976). The Urban Informal Sector. *Int. Labour Rev.* **114** (1).
35. Serjeant, R . B. (ed.) (1980). "The Islamic City." Paris.
36. Wagstaff, J. M. (1980). The Origin and Evolution of Towns, *In* Blake and Lawless. (1980).
37. Weber, M. (1958). The City (tr. W. D. Martindale and G. Neuworth). Glencoe, Illinois.
38. Population Division United Nations (1980). ECWA Bulletin 18 June, 1980, Beirut.
39. United Nations Conferences on Human Settlements (1978). (1) Baghdad, (2) Tripoli, Libya.

Chapter Four

The Geographical Impact of Technological Change

J. B. GODDARD

INTRODUCTION

The Micro-Electronics Revolution

Jean Gottmann has drawn attention on a number of occasions to the impact of technological change on cities. In particular, he highlighted the historic role of the telephone in permitting the geographical separation of managerial and production activities within industry, thus enabling the headquarters of companies to congregate in large cities where their senior management could take advantage of face-to-face contact for higher-level communications, while using the telephone to monitor production at a large number of factories. He also suggested that the telephone was a key innovation that permitted the development of skyscrapers because it made possible a larger amount of routine internal communication within the office building.[9]

The aim of this chapter is to explore the impact on the spatial organization of society of a technical revolution which has developed out of the telephone industry and is having wide-ranging implications outside that industry. This innovation is micro-electronics technology which has evolved out of the semiconductor, first developed in the laboratories of the Bell Telephone Corporation in the United States.[2] The discussion will not be confined to micro-electronics but will be more wide-ranging, because this technological revolution has re-awakened the

interest of the public, politicians and academics to the role of technological change in national development generally.

Micro-electronics technology is, however, a useful starting point
simply because of its all-pervasive influence, resulting in the diffusion of
the power of the computer into a wide range of existing products (such as
ignition control systems in vehicles) and creating totally new products
(such as video games). Such changes can undermine the market for
existing products which fail to exploit the new technology, resulting in
inevitable job losses. Similar developments can be observed in the service
sector where totally new services, such as Videotext, are likely to partly
displace conventional services, such as across-the-counter purchasing and
booking.

However, in addition to the direct impact on products and services,
micro-electronics technology will affect the *way* in which products are
produced or services provided. In manufacturing, developments such as
computerized numerically controlled machine tools and robots are
facilitating a further spurt of automation. In the service sector, word
processing is considerably enhancing the productivity of office activity,
an area in the past where the growth of output has more or less of
necessity been matched by a growth of employment and office buildings
to accommodate low-level clerical workers. While new process
technologies may break down the relationship, leading to short-term job
losses, in the long term higher unit labour costs in traded services on the
part of enterprises may lead to a loss of competitiveness and even greater
job shedding.

The fact that the applications of micro-electronics technology has a
potential to act as both a product and a process innovation has important
implications for employment. It means that the new technology will
affect both the industries in which individuals work and the jobs they do.
In other words, there will be positive and negative effects along the rows
and columns of the conventional industry by occupation cross-classifica-
tion of employment. Process innovations such as word processing will
affect virtually all industries simply because of the all-pervasive nature of
the office function. Other occupations have a more limited spread across
industries. Technological changes which displace a whole industry will
obviously affect all occupations, while other changes may result in a shift
in skill requirements, for example from mechanical to electronic skills as
has occurred already in such industries as the manufacture of cash
registers and telephone exchanges.

This perspective does, however, overlook a third dimension of the micro-electronics revolution, already alluded to in the discussion of the telephone, namely the role of this technology as a managerial innovation. Micro-electronics is bringing about a convergence of two technologies, telecommunications and computing; as well as affecting the information-processing function carried out within offices, it is also having a profound impact on the exchange of information within and between organizations. Improvements in communication are likely to have important implications for the structure of organizations. Just as the telephone made possible the growth of national corporations, recent advances in telecommunications on a global scale are facilitating the growth of multi-national enterprises and the integration of the global economy. Indeed, the communication needs of large corporations is one of the key forces shaping development in the international communications network, including the de-regulation of services once the monopoly of PTTs.

The Place-Specific Impact of Technological Change

Although all of these developments have been widely discussed in the debate about micro-electronics, what has been generally ignored is that they will occur in a place-specific context. New products will be manufactured in particular locations and new skills demanded there. Areas whose industries' markets are undermined by these developments will experience job displacement. This adjustment process will take place at a fairly local scale, within city regions, simply because of the relative immobility of labour. Moreover, the characteristics of cities, particularly their relative location within the national and international urban system, will affect the nature of the adjustment process.[7]

This point can be elaborated by taking the argument about technical change down from the national level, through industries and enterprise to individual establishments or workplaces. The contribution of technical advance to national economic development was much researched in the 1960s, and Denison suggested that over the first fifty years of this century more than three-quarters of the growth of the US economy as a whole was due to technological change.[4] It is also clear that the same rate of technological change has not been experienced in all countries. Indeed, some governments, notably in Japan and France, have adopted a national offensive strategy towards industrial innovation in key sectors like micro-electronics and the related information industries in order to challenge US supremacy in this area. Globally, therefore, one may talk of some countries that are technological leaders and others that are laggards.

Within industry evidence from a number of sources reveals that technological change does not take place at an equal rate within all sectors.[5] For example, using information provided by industry experts on significant new products produced in British manufacturing industry compiled by the Science Policy Research Unit at the University of Sussex, and data from the annual competition for the Queen's Award to Industry for Innovation, Oakey, Thwaites and Nash have ranked the sectors of British manufacturing industry according to their degree of innovativeness in absolute terms, and relative to their size (Table 1).[14] Rees has classified US industry into high and low technology using National Science Board data on innovations per net sales.[13]

Although interesting, such rankings do not highlight the point that innovations occur in enterprises. There is an extensive literature which suggests that the ability to produce and adopt new technologies varies

Table 1 Significant innovations in British manufacturing industry by sector 1965-76 (GB = 100)

1	Instrument engineering	480
2	Mechanical engineering	218
3	Chemicals	200
4	Electrical engineering	169
5	Shipbuilding	120
6	Bricks, glass, cement	105
7	Other manufacturing	86
8	Vehicles	86
9	Timber and furniture	52
10	Textiles	45
11	Metal manufacture	45
12	Paper and printing	28
13	Metal goods	19
14	Food, drink, tobacco	14
15	Clothing	12

Sources: Science Policy Research Unit, University of Sussex; Queen's Award to Industry Scheme; Oakey *et al.* (1979).

between enterprises.[11] Factors associated with successful innovation include large size, the employment of professional, technical and market research staff, contact with the wider research community, and access to the use of the necessary factors of production, particularly labour and capital.

Finally, and most important in terms of a consideration of the geographical impact of technical change, new products, processes and services are introduced by enterprises into particular establishments or workplaces. These establishments may be single-site enterprises or part of a large group operating over a range of locations. In the case of the single-site enterprise, the characteristics of the local industrial and commercial milieu may be very important in influencing its ability to participate in technical change—for example in terms of the availability of specialist information, sub-contractors, components, and service suppliers. Establishments which are part of a larger group may be able to substitute the intra-corporate environment for on-site facilities or, alternatively, off-site facilities in the local area—for example, through making use of centralized research and development laboratories. Nevertheless, even in this case, where these facilities are located may in turn influence the ability of the enterprise to tap into sources of information, finance and skills, and also the ease with which such information can be transferred to the establishment in question. Finally, it could be suggested that since innovations are actually introduced into specific workplaces, the push for technical change may come from the bottom upwards in organizations as well as from the top downwards. The characteristics of the local industrial and commercial environment may therefore have some importance in the case of multi-site as well as single-site enterprises.

The utilization of developments in telecommunications technology as a managerial innovation, through its influence on the ability of the enterprise and the establishment to tap into an international technological environment, could have a very important spatial impact on innovative activity in different areas. Single-site enterprises may be able to overcome the disadvantages of peripheral locations or a poor local industrial and commercial milieu. Telecommunications may also influence the spatial structure of multi-site organizations, as defined in terms of the location of information processing and exchange functions. In theory, a strategy of administrative decentralization could be translated into a spatial dispersion of functions such as accounting, research and development and marketing.

However, the experience of the spread of the conventional telephone which was associated with a spurt in the concentration of ownership of national enterprises in Europe and North America and a not unrelated concentration of head office functions within capital cities does not augur too well for the future. Improved telecommunications can further enhance remote control of production and service establishments. Branch factories may need an even more limited range of office functions, such as accountants and solicitors, because all these functions can be more readily provided from a remote headquarters. Similarly, insurance branch offices may obtain quotations from a computer terminal without recourse to the judgements of a local manager. At the same time the articulating role of the city near to a factory or office, be it a provincial centre within a country or even a national capital, which is not one of the control centres of the international financial community, may be superseded. Aggregating these effects across a number of organizations may produce significant shifts in the occupational structure of employment in particular areas, suffering from the removal of information-exchanging job functions.

Technological Change and Local Economic Development

To sum up the argument so far, it seems reasonable to suggest that because technical advance can vary between nations, industries, enterprises and establishments, it also can vary between cities, simply because of differences in industrial structure and the mix of enterprise type located within the area. Moreover, if we consider any one city in its totality, it may be that because of its history of industrialization which in turn has influenced the skill structure of the labour force and the local institutional environment, there may be considerable local constraints influencing the rate of technological change. One might suggest, for example, that many of the older industrial areas of Europe and North America which rose to pre-eminence industrially on the basis of mechanical and electromechanical technologies, now have an inappropriate skill base to match the challenge of the micro-electronics revolution. Institutional structures which were an important external economy to the older industries are now fossilized and rigid and act as a barrier to change rather than being supportive of it. In Britain such areas suffer a problem of national peripherality, while in other countries areas such as the Ruhr in West Germany have a core location which does not seem to compensate entirely for the disadvantage of history. In contrast, there are other areas such as the Thames Valley in south-east England, and "Silicon Valley" in California, where a number of factors have combined to create a favourable environment for industrial innovation and self-sustained economic growth.

The use of the phrase "self-sustained growth" leads to the question of policies for local economic development. In the past governments have attempted to tackle the problems of lagging areas by the attraction of mobile investment from more prosperous regions inside the country or from overseas. At the present time the amount of mobile investment available is declining, and the competition and therefore the cost of attracting that investment are increasing. Moreover, theories of the product life-cycle would suggest that such investment may not necessarily embody the latest technology but be seeking out cheap labour or government subsidies in order to produce goods nearing the end of their commercial life at the lowest possible unit costs. Such investment is particularly vulnerable to the introduction of new products elsewhere or the discovery of even lower labour cost areas which can be exploited by further standardization of production.

In the light of these circumstances there is a strong case to be made, at the local scale, for a policy of fostering innovation in indigenous enterprises. The case for such a policy can also be argued from a national point of view, regardless of any question of local objectives. If it can be demonstrated that the ability of an establishment to participate in technical change is in part spatially determined, then it seems imperative to target national policies at the local level, rather than relying upon the normal filtering of information down the urban and corporate hierarchy. Policy makers concerned with industrial innovation must learn from their counterparts working in agriculture where the need to stimulate change through advice delivered to the farm gate is widely acknowledged.

Although the preceding argument may seem obvious, policy makers in many countries have until recently remained sceptical about the spatial dimension to technological change. The remainder of this chapter will present some evidence which may convince sceptics, at least in Britain. Consideration is first given to evidence which a priori would suggest that there might be local variations in innovative activity; evidence is then presented which confirms the existence of such variations expressed in terms of the introduction of new products and processes into manufacturing industry. The chapter concludes with some research results on the potential contribution of developments in telecommunications technology as a managerial innovation to ameliorating spatial differences in rates of technological change.

INPUTS TO THE INNOVATION PROCESS

Research and Development

The contribution of formalized research and development (R and D) to technological change within the enterprise is widely acknowledged in the economics literature. However, the fact that this effort is not evenly distributed geographically is perhaps less well known. Aggregated data on the distribution of R and D employment in Britain indicates a concentration of jobs in the south-east core region.[3] This concentration remains even after allowing for industrial structure, that is, the tendency for certain industries which are R and D intensive to be localized in particular areas. A recent survey of approximately 800 (60%) establishments within three particularly innovative industries—scientific instruments, metalworking machine tools, and electronic components—in Britain has suggested that there are organizational explanations for this tendency, with multi-site companies tending to concentrate their R and D activity in core regions of the country, and single-site enterprises devoting less resources to R and D in peripheral regions than their counterparts elsewhere.[16] For example, Table 2 reveals that within these industries the mean size of on-site R and D employment in establishments which are part of a larger company group and are located in the

Table 2 Research and development employment by establishment status and area

	Northern Region		North west		South east	
	Single	Group	Single	Group	Single	Group
Minimum	1	1	1	1	1	1
Maximum	9	60	16	120	9	300
Mean	3·1	13·7	3·1	20·8	3·3	34·1
No. of establishments	15	25	17	34	22	32

Source: Thwaites *et al.* (1981)

Table 3 On-site research and development by area and ownership status of establishment

Region	Percentage of establishment without on-site R and D facilities	
	Single-site companies	Group establishments
South-east	10·4	11·9
Non-assisted area outside south-east	11·9	23·9
Intermediate areas	16·3	9·6
Development areas	30·2	15·9
Great Britain	13·9	15·2

Source: Thwaites *et al.* (1981)

north of England is 13·7 workers, compared with 34·1 in the south-east, while the maximum numbers range from 60 to 300. In contrast Table 3 reveals that 30% of single-site establishments in the peripheral regions as a whole have no on-site R and D facility at all, compared with only 10% of similar establishments in the south-east core region.

Other Managerial Functions

Successful innovation involves linking research and development activity with the needs of the market place; it may therefore be associated with high levels of activity across a broad range of managerial functions. A survey of a representative sample of 96 manufacturing establishments in the northern region of England, however, has revealed that locally owned companies on average have a smaller proportion of their total employment devoted to non-production activities (28·0%) than do subsidiaries or branches of larger company groups (37·0% and 36·0%).[12] Not surprisingly, white-collar employment in branch establishments is heavily concentrated in production management. Moreover, another study undertaken of all the manufacturing establishments of the largest 100 UK companies has revealed that branches in the north have a lower proportion of white-collar workers than similar status establishments elsewhere.[3]

Specialist Information

A lack of research and development facilities and other management functions on-site may be compensated for by contact with sources external to the establishment, either within the enterprise or outside it. The three industries survey carried out by Thwaites, Oakey and Nash revealed that establishments that are part of a large group and which are located in a peripheral area in Britain are most likely to have another company site as their primary source of technical information; similar establishments located in the core region are more likely to use an extra-company source of information.[16] In other words, core region establishments of large enterprises are more clearly linked to the broader information environment, while those in the periphery rely more on the intra-corporate transfer of informaton.

These conclusions are reinforced by surveys carried out in the North of England on a wide range of indicators of extra-establishment linkages, in addition to R and D contacts.[12] In terms of business services, independent firms purchase 72% of their needs from within the region, compared with only 27% for non locally owned firms. In terms of business contacts as a whole, dependence on the local environment is a feature of small independent firms using jobbing technology, while large branch establishments using mass production technology are less locally orientated. Finally, research undertaken on business travellers leaving the northern region has shown that the less travel-intensive sectors are characterized by a predominance of top management from small independent enterprises, while the more travel-intensive sectors are characterized by individuals working in technical occupations in large branch establishments.[6]

From these various studies the northern region of England may be characterized as one where the indigenous sector of industry is dependent upon the less information-rich local environment, while the non-indigenous sector is locked into an intra-corporate system of information transfer. In contrast, we can say that both independent firms and branches in the south east core region have more commitment to in-house research and development effort, and more ready access to extra-corporate information sources.

THE REGIONAL DIMENSION TO INNOVATIVE ACTIVITY WITHIN MANUFACTURING INDUSTRY

The Location of the First Commercial
Manufacture of Significant New Products

Are the contrasts in the inputs to the innovation process that have been described in any way correlated with the output, measured in terms of the introduction of new products to manufacturing establishments? This question was first addressed in a study of the location of the first commercial manufacture of 287 expert-adjudicated significant new products introduced in Britain between 1965 and 1976.[14]

These may be classified as being at the earliest stage in their product life cycle and form the basis of the inter-sectoral rankings given in Table 1. Table 4 reveals that the inter-regional variations in rates of innovation are almost as pronounced as the inter-sectoral differences. Furthermore, the regional contrasts remain even after standardizing for regional variations in industrial structure. The only aggregate factor which accounts in a statistical sense for the good performance of the core regions is the distribution of non-production employment within manufacturing industry.

In a sub-sample of 44 of the new products which were developed on one site within a company and put into production at another very little inter-regional transfer of new products is observed (Table 5). In other words, local innovative activity tends to produce local results. Attempts through industrial dispersal policies to stimulate the transfer of technology to peripheral regions, by controls on industrial development in the core, may therefore only frustrate the national innovative effort and not benefit peripheral areas.

In the study described above innovation was strictly defined as products that were new to the country as a whole. However, many technical changes that are significant from the point of view of the enterprise or establishment are of a marginal or incremental nature. In a

Table 4 Significant innovations by region per thousand manufacturing employees 1965-76 (GB = 100)

1	East Anglia	154
2	South-West	136
3	South-East	130
4	North	117
5	East Midlands	84
6	Yorkshire	84
7	West Midlands	82
8	North-West	80
9	Scotland	76
10	Wales	48

Sources: As for Table 1

Table 5   Inter-regional transfer of company developed new products

		Destination		
Origin	Development area	South-east	Other	Total
Development areas	2	0	0	2
South-east	2	15	8	25
Other regions	3	0	14	17
Total	7	15	22	44

Source: Oakey *et al.* (1979)

further study of technical change in the three high-technology sectors already referred to, Thwaites, Oakey and Nash have defined innovation as new products and processes introduced to the establishment.[16] Managers were asked to identify the most economically significant new product and new process introduced into their establishments between 1973 and 1977. In addition the most technologically advanced product and process currently manufactured or used in the establishment was identified. The products and processes were then independently classified along a five point scale of technical and economic significance by industry experts.

The Introduction of New Products and Production Processes into Manufacturing Establishments

A key finding of the above study was that there was surprisingly little regional variation in the rate of adoption of process innovation. This is because most process innovations take the form of bought-in machinery about which information is generally available from manufacturers' catalogues and the trade press. Little on-site R and D effort is required in adopting new process machinery, hence there is only a weak relationship between the presence or absence of an R and D facility in a factory and the incidence of process innovation as a whole. However, if only process innovations developed on-site are considered, then a strong positive relationship with R and D effort emerges.

The role of group establishments in relation to process innovation is particularly interesting. Such establishments are not surprisingly more likely to rely on intra-corporate transfer of process technology, and in the case of those group establishments located in peripheral regions, the technical quality of such transfers is likely to be on average lower than group transfers as a whole. Moreover, group establishments *without* control over business functions, such as marketing, purchasing and R and D, are more likely to introduce process innovations than those with *more* autonomy. Such establishment are also more likely to be involved in mass production than small batch production or jobbing work. In terms of capital investment peripheral region group establishments spend a higher proportion of their total investment, and have a higher expenditure per capita, on process innovations than similar plants elsewhere.

It should be recalled that the peripheral regions of Britain benefit from considerable government capital investment subsidies, and it is apparent from the above results that these subsidies are being heavily utilized by large multi-site enterprises to foster process innovation, that is, the manufacture of existing products at lower unit costs. There is considerable doubt whether this form of innovation lays the basis for self-sustained regional economic growth.[15]

Regional variations in product innovation are more pronounced, particularly in the case of independent companies. Thus 45% of such establishments in peripheral regions had not introduced a new product in the five-year period under study compared with only 15% in the south-east core region. The corresponding figure for establishments that are part of a larger concern are 14% and 9% (Table 6). These contrasts may be related to the inter-regional variation in R and D effort already noted. Because of its confidential nature new product development is closely related to on-site R and D. Thus 44% of establishments without an on-site R and D facility had not introduced a new product, compared with only 11% of those with such a facility (Table 7). In the case of independent companies with no R and D facility on-site as many as 64% had not introduced a new product. Moreover, if the quality of the new products introduced into independent firms as a result of on-site R and D is considered (as opposed to those obtained through licensing) it is apparent that 69% introduced into the periphery are classified as low technology, compared with only 40% in the south-east core region.

Clearly, there are important corporate effects on the likelihood of on-site R and D effort and product innovation which need to be distinguished from those variations associated with location. The critical question is whether locational contrasts remain after these corporate

Table 6 The introduction of new and improved products by establishment status and region 1973–77

	Percentage of all establishments in region	
	Single site	Multi-site
South-east	85·3	91·2
Non-assisted areas outside south-east	74·2	88·0
Intermediate areas	75·8	87·4
Development areas	54·8	86·8
Great Britain total	77·9	89·0

Source: Thwaites, Oakey & Nash 1981.

Table 7 On-site research and development and product innovation

Type of company	Product (%)	Innovation (%)
	Yes	No
Single-site with on-site R and D	87·1	12·9
Single-site without on-site R and D	36·0	64·0
Multi-site with on-site R and D	91·3	8·7
Multi-site without on-site R and D	66·6	33·4

effects have been accounted for. An attempt has been made to do this by the use of logit analysis which seeks to account for the probability of product innovation in an establishment in terms of a number of categorical explanatory variables.[1] In this analysis an attempt is made to predict the probability of the incidence of a product innovation in an establishment in terms of the size of its R and D effort, ownership status, enterprise size, sector and location.

This analysis reveals that R and D effort is the single most important influence on the likelihood of product innovation, followed by sector and corporate status of the establishment. Nevertheless, location is an important and statistically significant influence. More specifically, the table of predicted probabilities from the model (Table 8) reveals that single-site-enterprises with fewer than 5 R and D workers in the radio and electronics components sector in development areas have only a 0·47 probability of recording a product innovation compared with a 0·71

Table 8 Predicted possibilities of product innovation

No. of R and D workers	No. of sites	Metal-working machine tools				Scientific instruments				Radio and electronic components			
		South-east	Other	Inter-mediate area	Develop-ment area	South-east	Other	Inter-mediate area	Develop-ment area	South-east	Other	Inter-mediate area	Develop-ment area
<5	1	0·77	0·68	0·68	0·55	0·86	0·79	0·79	0·69	0·71	0·60	0·60	0·47
<5	2–10	0·80	0·72	0·72	0·59	0·88	0·82	0·82	0·72	0·74	0·64	0·64	0·51
<5	>10	0·94	0·91	0·91	0·85	0·97	0·95	—[a]	0·91	0·92	0·88	0·88	0·81
≥5	1	0·94	0·90	0·90	0·84	0·96	0·94	0·94	0·91	0·91	0·87	0·87	—
≥5	2–10	0·95	0·92	0·92	0·86	0·97	0·95	0·95	0·92	0·93	0·89	0·89	0·82
≥5	>10	0·99	0·98	0·98	0·96	0·99	0·99	0·99	0·98	0·98	0·97	0·97	0·95

[a] Denotes data not available

Table 9 Grouping of establishments in relation to their organizational
characteristics and innovative activity

Group 1
Small single-site enterprises in development areas (13·0% of cases)

    Product innovation: 16·2% of group
    Process innovation : 41·9% of group

Group 2
Small single-site enterprises in the south-east (19·0% of cases)

    Product innovation: 100·0% of cases
    Process innovation :   54·9% of cases

Group 3
Small branch establishments with low autonomy and located in development
areas (17·7% of cases)

    Product innovation: 79·7% of cases
    Process innovation : 60·1% of cases

Group 4
Small headquarters establishments of small company groups in intermediate
areas (10·3% of cases)

    Product innovation: 88·0% of cases
    Process innovation : 69·9% of cases

Group 5
Large branch plants of large company groups located in development areas
(10·6% of cases)

    Product innovation: 98·8% of cases
    Process innovation : 89·8% of cases

Source: Thwaites *et al.* (1981)

probability for similar establishments in the south-east. Similar contrasts
occur for single-site establishments in all of the other sectors. However, if
the number of R and D workers is increased in single-site companies, the
disadvantage of the peripheral region is almost eliminated. So more R
and D effort would appear to compensate for the disadvantages of
peripheral locations. In the case of multi-site enterprises the lowest
likelihood of innovation occurs within the establishments of small
enterprises (those with fewer than 10 sites) located in development areas.
Again this disadvantage is reduced by increasing the number of R and D
workers on site, with the highest probability of innovation occurring in

the development areas in establishments of multi-site companies which have R and D facilities on the premises.

In this analysis the variable location has no direct meaning. What is indirectly suggested is that different types of establishment characterize different localities. This can be made apparent by a cluster analysis of a wide range of features of the establishment, with each cluster being contrasted in terms of its representation of innovative establishments in each group. Such an analysis suggests that small independent enterprises are not all technological laggards (Table 9). A clear group of individual establishments in which all have introduced a new product can be identified. The bulk of these are, however, located in the south-east. In contrast, only 16% of another cluster of small firms in peripheral regions had introduced a new product. Within the multi-site group those establishments with headquarters in the intermediate regions and low autonomy branches of small company groups in the periphery had the poorest innovative record. (Significantly the highest representation of process innovations could be found in the branches of large companies located in peripheral regions.)

One shortcoming of both the logit and cluster analysis is the measurement of innovation simply in terms of new products and processes with no consideration as to their technical quality or economic impact on the establishment. However, by comparing the characteristics of the innovation (such as its product group) and its relationship to the main product line, it is possible to determine whether an innovation is associated with product diversification. Moreover, by using information in the Census of Production it is possible to ascertain whether this diversification is taking the establishment into high or low growth market areas. Together with the experts' rating of the new products and processes it is possible to derive a variety of measures of the quality of an innovation. Fifteen such measures have been input into a cluster analysis with a view to identifying technologically leading and technologically lagging groups of establishments.

Six clusters provide the most parsimonious classification. One group, containing 23·4% of the establishments, can be identified as containing the technological laggards, while two groups, with 17·2% and 11·9% of establishments, contain the technological leaders. The main distinction between the two leading clusters is that the smaller group shows a greater propensity towards process innovation. The critical question is whether there is any tendency for technologically leading or lagging establishments

Table 10 Grouping of establishments by quality of innovation and location of company headquarters[a]

Headquarters location	High technology product	High technology process	Low technology product/process
South-east	1·14	1·12	0·89
Non-assisted areas outside south-east	0·73	0·78	1·26
Intermediate areas	0·69	0·63	1·47
Development areas	0·15	0·88	1·35
Overseas (excluding US)	1·45	1·05	0·80
United States	1·42	1·19	0·55

[a]Figures refer to the proportion of establishments in each group in each region divided by proportion in each region in the whole sample
Source: Thwaites et al. (1981)

to be located in particular regions. Table 10 confirms the south-east as having the highest concentration of leading edge establishments and the intermediate areas of laggard establishments. The development areas perform much better than expected. However, if headquarters location is considered rather than the location of the establishment itself, the performance of the development areas is depressed dramatically. Thus it would seem that non locally owned establishments boost the level of technology within development areas, while overseas owned establishments appear to embody the most advanced technology of all.

MANAGERIAL INNOVATION

The analyses presented in this chapter suggest that the greatest barrier to innovation are faced by small independent firms in peripheral regions. Such enterprises are particularly constrained by problems of access to specialist information related to the innovation process. The chapter will conclude by considering the way developments in telecommunication technology as a managerial innovation might assist such enterprises. Unfortunately the conclusions about to be presented are not very encouraging.

A study of the availability and the use of these technologies by approximately 300 managers in 98 manufacturing establishments in the

Northern Region of England has revealed small independent firms involved in jobbing production are less likely to take advantage of telecommunications technology than their counterparts in large branch establishments involved in mass production.[10] In addition an assessment of the potential for substituting telecommunications for the face-to-face meetings held by approximately 6000 business travellers between the north of England and the south-east suggested the greatest substitution potential was to be found in the case of meetings held by representatives from multi-site companies compared with independent companies, within the manufacturing sector compared with the service sector, and taking place in the Northern Region compared with the South East. Communications by branches frequently involve research staff on matters internal to the organization, and for these communications the company has the facility of installing compatible equipment throughout the organization. In contrast communications generated by independent firms frequently involve senior staff in negotiations with customers and suppliers who may not have compatible facilities. Thus developments in telecommunications may permit further remote control of production in peripheral regions and not greatly assist independent firms.

CONCLUSION

A number of important themes have not been developed in this chapter. Athough a clear geographical dimension to contemporary technological change in Britain has been identified, the causes of these differences have not been really explained. In part they are due to the characteristics of firms in different areas. It is uncertain how far particular types of firms tend to predominate in certain areas and thereby endow their locality with a character which either stimulates or retards technological change. Nevertheless there is some evidence that environmental factors like the quality of shopfloor and managerial labour does vary between areas, as does the availability of finance and access to specialist information. However, the geographical range (e.g. local labour market to a major region like the south-east of England) over which variations in these factors occur needs further investigation.

Little direct evidence has been provided about the geographical impact of technological change, particularly on employment. However, here it is extremely difficult to disentangle the effects of technical change *per se* from other influences on the competitive position of firms. Nevertheless, an important point made in the introduction to this chapter must be reiterated: failure to introduce new products and processes will ultimately lead to a loss of competitiveness and thereby jobs. Regions in which firms do not advance technologically are liable to decline, come what may. Policies designed to stimulate technological change must therefore form an integral part of any regional development strategy.

Very little has been said about the impact of technological change on the quaternary sector. The main emphasis has been placed on the secondary sector and related producer services, either within or outside manufacturing companies. This chapter has been written in Newcastle upon Tyne, in a lagging region of Britain whose prosperity has been built upon a competitive manufacturing sector, and from this perspective it is difficult to see a role for an autonomous quaternary sector unrelated to the manufacturing base. Only a limited number of regions in any nation —usually that containing the capital city—possess the possibility of sustaining an export-based quaternary sector. In other cities it seems that the increasing concentration of control of manufacturing industry outside the region has been associated with a collapse of Jean Gottmann' "interwoven network of quaternary activities"[9] such as banks, stock exchanges, and professional and trade associations. As the industries in the hinterlands of these provincial cities which such functions serve have declined or have become increasingly national and international rather than purely regional in character, so the *real* quaternary sector has retreated. Office jobs have expanded but in population-serving functions related to Local Government and in routine parts of dispersed Central Government. And it is just these routine jobs that are vulnerable for displacement by new office technologies.

There is one final theme that has only been alluded to in the Chapter— the international dimension to technological change. The emphasis has been on the local scale and the fact that new technologies are physical realities that are introduced into particular workplaces in specific geographical settings. Clearly, these local changes must be seen in the context of international movements of disembodied capital, a phenomenon much studied by economists and now also by geographers. In such analyses technology is a very abstract concept or is merely a residual factor remaining after taking account of all other influences on patterns of corporate or national development. The analyses presented in this chapter have clearly indicated that in spite of the apparent ease communication in a small country like Britain there are strong local contrasts in technological capacity. These contrasts are likely to be even more marked at the international scale and to be both a cause and a consequence of different levels of development in the global economic system.

ACKNOWLEDGEMENTS

This paper draws heavily on research undertaken in the Centre for Urban and Regional Development Studies in the University of Newcastle upon Tyne, and I am particularly indebted to Alfred Thwaites who has led the Centre's research on technological change in a regional context. Numerous findings from a research project on *Industrial Innovation and Regional Economic Development*, sponsored by the Department of the Environment and undertaken by Alfred Thwaites, Raymond Oakey and Peter Nash are quoted in the paper and their contribution is gratefully acknowledged. A further study of *Telecommunications, Industrial Organisation and Regional Development*, also sponsored by the Department of the Environment in the Centre and undertaken by Vicky James, Neill Marshall and Nigel Waters is another major source that is gratefully acknowledged.

REFERENCES

1. Alderman, N., Goddard, J. B. and Nash, P. A. (1981). "The Application of Logit Analysis to Industrial Survey Data." Discussion Paper Number 42 Centre for Urban and Regional Development Studies, University of Newcastle upon Tyne.
2. Braun, E. and MacDonald, S. (1978). "Revolution in Miniature: The History and Impact of Semiconductor Electronics." Cambridge University Press, Cambridge.
3. Crum, R. E. and Gudgin, G. (1978). "Non-Production Activities in UK Manufacturing Industry" Regional Policy Series Number 3. Commission of the European Communities, Brussels.
4. Denison E. F. (1967). "Why Growth Rates Differ." The Brookings Institute, Washington.
5. Freeman, C. (1974). "The Economics of Industrial Innovation." Penguin, Harmondsworth.

6. Goddard, J. B. (1979). "Office Development and Urban and Regional Development in Britain" *In* P. Daniels (ed.) "Spatial Patterns of Office Growth and Location." John Wiley, Chichester.

7. Goddard, J. B. (1980). Technological forecasting in a spatial context *Futures* **12**, 2, 91-105.

8. Gottmann, J. (1966). Why the skyscraper? *Geographical Review* **15**, 190-212.

9. Gottmann, J. (1970). Urban centrality and the interweaving of quaternary activities. *Ekistics* **29**, 322-331.

10. James, V. Z., Marshall, J. N. and Waters, N. (1979). "Telecommunications and Office Location" Final Report to the Department of the Environment. Centre for Urban and Regional Development Studies, University of Newcastle upon Tyne.

11. Le Heron, J. (1973). Best practice technology, technical leadership and regional economic development" *Environment and Planning* **5**, 735-749.

12. Marshall, J. N. (1979). Ownership, organisation and industrial linkage a case study of the Northern Region of England. *Regional Studies* **13**, 531-557.

13. Rees, J. (1979). Technological Change and Regional Shifts in American Manufacturing. *Professional Geographer* **31**, 45-54.

14. Oakey, R. P., Thwaites, A. T. and Nash, P. A. (1980). The regional distribution of innovative manufacturing establishments in Britain *Regional Studies* **14**, 235-254.

15. Thwaites, A. T. (1978). Technological change, mobile plants and regional development. *Regional Studies* **12**, 445-462.

16. Thwaites, A. T., Oakey, R. P. and Nash, P. A. (1981). "Industrial Innovation and Regional Development" Final Report to the Department of the Environment. Centre for Urban and Regional Development Studies, University of Newcastle upon Tyne.

Chapter Five

Decentralization without End?
A Re-evaluation

PETER HALL

"Men come together in cities in order to live; they remain together in order to live the good life." Thus Aristotle.[1] Then and for a long time after, that dictum may have been true. Now, however, it seems that it is true only in part. In one part of the world—true, the bigger and by far the more rapidly growing part—men and women come into cities in order to live, but, whatever their hopes and aspirations, it appears that all too few of them remain to live the good life. While in the other part of the world—the smaller but overwhelmingly the richer part—they are flooding out of the cities both to live and to enjoy what, by their definition and according to their lights, is the good life. Cities, in other words, can no longer be equated with urbanity.

The purpose of this chapter is to chronicle these processes and to attempt (at least in part) to explain them. Particularly, this chapter seeks to develop a general theory of urban evolution that encompasses different cities at different stages of socio-economic evolution at different periods in recent history. It asks what forces are attracting people and jobs into or away from cities, or into different kinds of location within urban areas. It does this with the aim of answering a general question: whether there is a general tendency for cities progressively to move from centralization to decentralization and from growth to decline.

THE EXPANDING CITY
ISBN 0 12 547250 1

THE AMERICAN MODEL: STATISTICAL TRENDS

The processes of decentralization are longest and best documented in tl United States, where a veritable flood of literature has quantified tl trends and has attempted some explanation of the contributo causes.[4,5,6,18,21,22] The broad conclusions emerging from this literature ca be easily summarized.

First, there appear to be negative returns to urban scale: larger urbi areas are either increasing much more slowly than smaller ones actually declining. Secondly, urban areas are decentralizing: central citi are either increasing much more slowly than suburbs in the san metropolitan areas or actually declining. Thirdly, more recently they a decentralizing in an even more radical way: metropolitan areas as a who are increasing less rapidly than nonmetropolitan areas, and there is n migration out of metropolitan into nonmetropolitan areas. And fourthl over these is laid a powerful inter-regional shift: urban areas in the nor and east are increasing much less rapidly than those in the south ai west, and many of the former group are actually in decline.

Viewed more closely and with the aid of the most recent data, some these trends appear to be confirmed; however, one must be doubted. It true that population is progressively shifting from city cores to suburbi rings, but it is not true that nonmetropolitan areas are gaining at tl expense of metropolitan areas. This interpretation arose from lookii merely at a fixed number of metropolitan areas. Between 1970 and 197 however, some 41 new Standard Metropolitan Statistical Areas (SMSA were added on the basis that they satisfied the criteria for metropolitt area defintiion. When these are included, it is found that from 1970 1978 metropolitan areas grew by 14·4%, while nonmetropolitan are actually declined by 8·0%: double the rate of decline during the 196 (Table 1).

Table 2 presents data on an alternative basis: the 243 SMSAs defined at the 1970 Census. On this basis, during the 1970s nor metropolitan areas grew nearly twice as fast as metropolitan area 1·2% per annum against 0·7%. The difference between Table 1 ai Table 2 strongly suggests that the rapid growth in the period w concentrated in those areas which achieved SMSA status during tl decade. In fact, of the net metropolitan increase of 20·1 million Table 1, nearly half—9·0 million—came from the 41 new SMSA

Table 1 United States: metropolitan and non metropolitan population (in 000s) 1940-1978

	1940	1950	1960	1970	1978
No. of SMSAs	168	168	209	243	284
Metropolitan	69 535	84 854	112 885	139 419	159 514
Percentage change		+22·0	+33·6	+23·5	+14·4
Non-metropolitan	62 135	66 742	66 438	63 793	58 750
Percentage change		7·4	−0·5	−4·0	−8·0

Source: *Statistical Abstract of the United States 1980*, based on *Censuses 1940-1970* and *Current Population Reports 1978*.

Table 2 United States: Metropolitan cores and rings and non metropolitan areas: population (in 000s) 1960, 1970, 1979 (for 243 SMSAs as defined in 1970)

	Total resident population			Non-Institutional population	
	1950	1969	1970	1970	1979
SMSAs	94·6	119·6	139·4	137·1	145·4
Percentage change		+2·3	+1·5		+0·7
Central cities	53·7	59·9	63·8	62·9	60·6
Percentage change		+1·1	+0·6		−0·4
Suburbs	40·9	59·6	75·6	74·2	84·8
Percentage change		+3·8	+2·4		+1·5
Nonmetropolitan	56·7	59·7	63·8	62·8	69·9
Percentage change		+0·5	+0·7		+1·1

Source: *Statistical Abstract of the United States 1980*, based on *Census 1950, 1960* and *1970* and *Current Population Reports*.

Conversely, this 9·0 million was nearly double the nonmetropolitan loss of 5·0 million. Figure 1 shows that the new SMSAs were located disproportionately outside the traditional manufacturing belt of the North-East and Midwest. Twenty-one of them are unambiguously in the southern and western "Sunbelt". Of those that are found in the north and east, most seem to represent further suburban outgrowth from New York and Chicago.

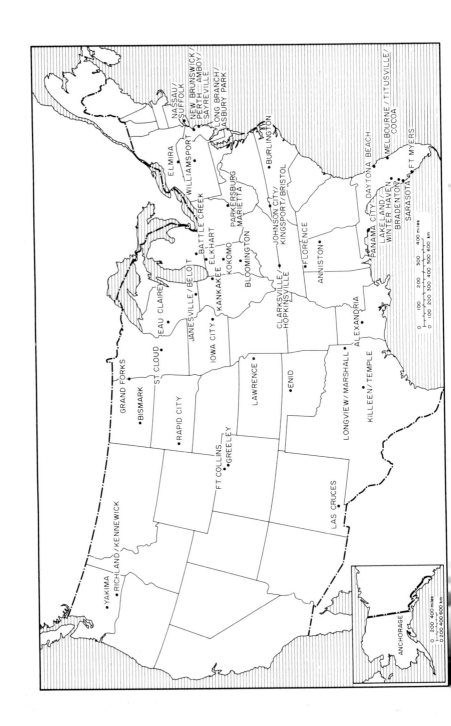

NASSAU/
SUFFOLK

NEW BRUNSWICK/
PERTH AMBOY/
SAYREVILLE

LONG BRANCH/
ASBURY PARK

ELMIRA

WILLIAMSPORT

BURLINGTON

MELBOURNE/TITUSVILLE/
COCOA

PARKERSBURG
MARIETTA

JOHNSON CITY/
KINGSPORT/BRISTOL

DAYTONA BEACH

PANAMA CITY

LAKELAND/
WINTER HAVEN

FT MYERS

SARASOTA

BRADENTON

BATTLE CREEK

ELKHART

KOKOMO

FLORENCE

ANNISTON

400 miles

400 km

300

200

500 600

100

100 200 300 400

0

0

BLOOMINGTON

CLARKSVILLE/
HOPKINSVILLE

JANESVILLE/BELOIT

KANKAKEE

EAU CLAIRE

ALEXANDRIA

IOWA CITY

LAWRENCE

ENID

GRAND FORKS

ST CLOUD

LONGVIEW/MARSHALL

BISMARK

RAPID CITY

KILLEEN/TEMPLE

FT COLLINS

GREELEY

LAS CRUCES

RICHLAND/KENNEWICK

YAKIMA

ANCHORAGE

0 200 400 miles

0 200 400 600 km

Table 3 United States: 32 largest SMSAs: population
1960, 1970, 1980

| | Percentage population change | | Population (000s) |
	1960-70	1970-80	1980
SMSAs	18·2	6·7	100 173
Central cities	4·1	− 4·9	38 350
Suburbs	31·7	18·5	61 823

Source: United States Bureau of the Census, *1980 Census Report*,
2548-(9) (March 1981).

On the other hand, the long-observed movement from cities to suburbs continued in the 1970s. Table 2 also shows that by the 1970s, central cities were showing a marginal net loss of population against a 1·5% gain for the suburban rings. For the 32 largest metropolitan areas, Table 3 shows the same trend for the entire intercensal decade 1970-80. Table 3 also shows that overall the largest SMSAs showed a striking reduction in their rate of population gain after 1970. In addition to New York, which lost nearly 1 million during the 1970s, eight other SMSAs lost population. The highest rates of loss, in order, were Buffalo, Pittsburgh, Cleveland and New York. Most other metropolitan areas in the North-East and Midwest were stagnant. However, ten metropolitan areas, all in the South or West, grew at least twice as fast as the average growth of the entire US population (10·9%). In order, these were Phoenix (55·6%), Tampa-St Petersburg (42·4%), Houston (42·3%), San Diego (37·0%), Miami-Fort Lauderdale (36·6%), Denver (30·3%), Atlanta (26·0%), Sacramento (25·8%), Dallas-Fort Worth (24·7%) and Portland, Oregon (22·8%).[20]

These overall trends, however, conceal a significant distinction: the largest areas of all (with 2·5 million or more people in 1980) grew by only 4·5% during the decade, or less than half the national increase of 10·9%, while the areas in the 1-2·5 million group grew by 11·9%, faster than the national average. During the previous decade, the growth rates of these two groups had been almost the same: 18·2 and 18·4% respectively. In other words, there has been a striking reduction in the growth rate of the very largest areas, while the next size group has only slowed down in line with national trends.[20]

The slowing down in the growth of the bigger SMSAs as a group can be explained very largely by the declines in their central cities. These losses have occurred not merely in the declining SMSAs of the North-East and Mid West, but also in some of the burgeoning metropolitan areas of the South and West: Atlanta, New Orleans, Seattle, and Denver. Where central cities were still growing—as in the cases of Phoenix, Houston, San Diego and San Antonio—it was notable that they had recently annexed territory because of state laws that allowed them to do so relatively easily. In general terms, then, central cities almost everywhere tended to be declining or at least stagnating; the difference is that in the South and West the vigorous growth of the suburbs more than compensated, but in the North-East it did not and in the North Central (Midwest) division it barely did.

Thus the most recent figures appear to confirm at least three trends: a continuing regional shift, a continuing city-to-suburb shift, and a continuing trend for larger metropolitan areas to grow more slowly than smaller ones (or even to decline). Table 4, which uses slightly earlier data for the whole array of SMSAs, powerfully confirms this last trend. Whereas in the 1960s the second largest size group (1–3 million) recorded the highest rate of growth, by the 1970–78 period there was a systematic array, with the largest size group (more than 3 million) recording an actual loss and the smallest (less than 100 000) recording the biggest gain. American urban areas, it seemed, were massively exhibiting what the economists call negative returns to scale.

Thus three of the trends are confirmed by the most recent available data. The fourth is not—or rather, it is replaced by an alternative formulation: there has been a rapid growth of population in newly designated SMSAs, which in earlier analyses were correctly described as nonmetropolitan but were in fact on the verge of qualifying as metropolitan areas. The 1980 census data will undoubtedly result in the designation of yet further SMSAs, so it is certain that Table 1 underestimates the extent of this phenomenon during the 1970s.

To some degree, all four trends run in the same direction and reinforce each other. Much, though by no means all, of the movement into the South and West is a movement into smaller SMSAs, a number of them newly designated during the 1970s. The city-to-suburb movement, though evident everywhere (save in a few Sunbelt SMSAs with generously bounded central cities) is producing stagnation and decline in Frostbelt SMSAs because of weak suburban growth, in turn reflecting an

Table 4 United States: SMSAs, by size group: population change, 1960-70, 1970-78

Size class	Percentage population change	
	1960-70 (243 SMSAs)	1970-78 (268 SMSAs)
All SMSAs	16·6	6·2
3 000 000 or more	11·9	− 1·6
1 000 000-3 000 000	21·4	8·0
500 000-1 000 000	18·0	7·6
250 000-500 000	16·3	10·5
100 000-250 000	14·5	11·6
Less than 100 000	12·3	13·2

Source: *Statistical Abstract of the United States 1980*, based on *Census of Population 1970* and *Current Population Reports*.

unfavourable net migration balance for the metropolitan area as a whole. The stagnation of these areas partly reflects the fact that many of them are big. Thus the archetype of the static or declining SMSA is the big North-Eastern or Midwestern area that reached its economic peak sometime in the first half of the twentieth century and now suffers serious problems of erosion of its central city's economic base. The archetype of the growing SMSA is the smaller, newly designated metropolitan area of the Sunbelt. True, there are many qualifications and exceptions to these archetypes. Much of the growth of the Sunbelt still comes from its larger SMSAs, which added over 7·6 million to their populations during the 1970s. But against that, the rest of the Sunbelt — the smaller SMSAs and the Nonmetropolitan Areas — grew by no less than 10·5 million. In the Frostbelt, in contrast, the larger SMSAs lost 1·3 million and the remaining areas gained only 3·3 million (Table 5).

THE AMERICAN MODEL: SOME EXPLANATIONS

The American literature has exhaustively examined the main causative forces behind these trends. Although fierce controversies rage among the schools of urbanism, especially between the Marxist or Political

Table 5 United States: population change by region and metropolitan status, 1960-70, 1970-80

Region, status, size class	Population change (000s)		Percentage population change	
	1960-70	1970-80	1960-70	1970-80
UNITED STATES	23 991	22 177	13·4	10·9
SMSAs over 1 000 000	14 480	6331	18·2	6·7
Over 2 500 000	10 030	2912	18·2	4·5
1-2 500 000	4451	3419	18·4	11·9
Other areas	9511	15 846	9·5	14·5
NORTH-EAST	4383	− 59	9·8	− 0·1
SMSAs over 1 000 000	2484	− 1419	9·4	− 4·8
Over 2 500 000	2484	− 1171	10·7	− 4·5
1-2 500 000	36	− 248	1·0	− 6·6
Other areas	1860	1361	10·5	7·0
NORTH CENTRAL	4971	2078	9·6	3·7
SMSAs over 1 000 000	3046	118	13·3	0·5
Over 2 500 000	1628	− 145	11·9	− 0·9
1-2 500 000	1417	262	15·2	2·4
Other areas	1926	1960	6·7	6·4
SOUTH	7852	12 000	14·3	19·1
SMSAs over 1 000 000	4040	3654	31·8	21·8
Over 2 500 000	2754	2350	39·2	24·0
1-2 500 000	1286	1304	22·7	18·8
Other areas	3813	8346	9·0	18·1
WEST	6785	8157	24·2	23·4
SMSAs over 1	4872	3976	29·1	18·4
Over 2 500 000	3163	1877	28·1	13·0
1-2 500 000	1709	2101	31·0	29·1
Other areas	1913	4178	16·9	31·6

Source: United States Bureau of the Census, 1980 Census Report: 2548-(9) (March 1981).

Economy school and the rest, general agreement exists as to the main forces of change.

The most important forces are economic. Perhaps to a greater extent than any other nation, the United States is now "post-industrial".[3] More than 65% of all workers are now in the so-called tertiary sector. The manufacturing base, though immensely productive, needs fewer and fewer workers to maintain a given volume of output. At the same time, profound shifts have occurred and are occurring in the location of manufacturing activity. Basic industries like textiles, apparel, steel and automobiles, which are traditionally located in the manufacturing belt of the North-East and Midwest, are experiencing increased competition from overseas, especially from Japan and the so-called Newly Industrializing Countries (such as Mexico, Brazil, Korea, Taiwan and Hong Kong), and many are facing recession and are cutting their workforces. Newer industries, such as aerospace and electronics, tend for various reasons to be concentrated outside the manufacturing belt, especially in such Sunbelt states as Florida, Texas, Arizona and California.

These reasons include strategic considerations during and after World War Two, the spinoff factor from fundamental research in Sunbelt universities (Silicon Valley, the micro-electronics area of California, is next to Stanford University), and the need to attract scarce and highly skilled labour—especially in engineering—by offering a location in an environmentally attractive area.[2] However, the term "Sunbelt" is misleading if it suggests that environmental factors are the only significant ones. Rather, the Sunbelt now constitutes the new industrial belt of America, resulting from a separate and subsequent wave of industrial innovations. Just as the manufacturing locus developed first (in the textile era) in New England, moved (in the age of iron and steel) to the Appalachians and Great Lakes, and then (in the automobile period) to Michigan, so in the most recent wave it has moved to where the innovations have been made.[11]

Increasingly, however, it is the location of the service industries that provide the key to the changing geography of the United States. Many, of course, are residentiary, in that the location of the workers is tied to the location of the customers: thus local shopping, local schools, local construction and real estate, local entertainment. In so far as the newer industrial areas generate high incomes, so by a multiplier effect do they generate many such local service jobs. But a significant part of the growth of service industry is not residentiary in this strict sense. This part embraces: the headquarters of multi-locational corporations, including both manufacturing and service companies, in particular the so-called FIRE (finance insurance and real estate) groups; recreation and entertainment of all kinds away from the immediate home area; provision for the retired population, now a very large industry in its own right; higher education and research; and nonprofit corporations.

Even at first glance, the locational patterns of these different activities are clearly very varied. But certain key points can be made. First, there appears to be a tendency for the United States economy to become increasingly regionalized, in the sense that an increasing part of commercial and financial activities, plus the associated transportation and lodging services, become concentrated in a relatively small number of major commercial centres located next to major "hub" airports. This is related to shifts in the pattern of corporate organization and control in the contemporary United States.[8,17] Such centres as Los Angeles, Phoenix, Houston, Denver, Dallas and Miami have clearly been major beneficiaries of this process. So have older centres like Boston and Chicago, but because their tributary areas are either growing slowly or are actually declining, they do not exhibit the same dynamism as the newer cities. Secondly, major recreation areas seem to display an inbuilt momentum as they attract additional activities such as retirement, entertainment, luxury shopping, transportation, construction and real estate. This explains the continued growth of some major metropolitan areas (Los Angeles, San Francisco, Denver, Miami) as well as the emergence of many smaller ones. Thirdly, government expenditure is still a crucial factor for many areas, either through defence or through civil research in universities or specialized laboratories. San Diego, San Francisco, Denver, Houston and Melbourne-Titusville-Cocoa are among the major beneficiaries here. Fourthly, only the first of these processes tends to aid the bigger metropolitan areas. Some, such as recreation and retirement, tend to benefit smaller places. Others, such as research and government spending, seem to have gone to a great variety of places large and small but predominantly in the Sunbelt.[13]

This second set of forces has been social and cultural. People have continued to express a preference, *en masse*, for living in suburbs rather than in central cities. The exceptions have been those few cities (Houston, Phoenix) where the cities have themselves been able to incorporate the suburbs. For this suburban trend there remain a number of powerful reasons. First, many of the new jobs are being created in the suburbs rather than in the inner city areas. Almost the only new jobs being created on any scale in many cities are the office and related jobs in central business districts, and these barely compensate for the big associated decreases in manufacturing and related employment. Secondly, the more attractive new housing is overwhelmingly created at or near the suburban-rural fringe, while the outworn housing is concentrated in the inner city. Thirdly, the associated shopping, schools and other services in the suburbs are perceived as superior to those in the central city. Fourthly, fear of crime may continue to be a deterrent to life in the city.

All these factors were already observable in the 1960s, when they were associated with a strong tendency for whites to leave the cities as blacks came in from the rural South. Now in many SMSAs a new wave of immigrants is arriving in the cities—a wave as large, during the late 1970s and early 1980s, as has ever been observed in the history of American immigration. It is composed of Mexicans and other Spanish-speaking people from Central and South American, Chinese from Taiwan, Hong Kong and other parts of South-East Asia, Filipinos, and many other non-European groups. Most of this immigration is apparently going into central cities. The full evidence will not be available until publication of the details of the 1980 Census, and even then will not be easy to interpret because of changes in ethnic classifications since 1970. The fact that the cities have nevertheless declined is powerful witness to the fact that the outflow of longer-established whites is continuing and that indeed it may be joined by a flow of blacks from the cities into some suburbs.

Some observers have noticed a possible counter-movement to this trend in the form of "gentrification" of selected inner city areas by returning white, middle-class, relatively high-income people. Generally young and either single or at any rate childless, they seem to be rejecting the suburban milieu in which they grew up, in search of what they see as the more cosmopolitan virtues of the city. The process is invariably accompanied by an upgrading of local shops and other services, with a growth of boutiques, speciality stores, restaurants and bars, specialized cinemas and the like. Originally limited to a handful of major cities like New York, Washington and San Francisco, gentrification now seems to be affecting a very wide range of American cities. But two comments are in order. First, the process is still very partial and very local: even in a city such as New York, it leads to middle-class enclaves close to badly decayed slums. Secondly, because the middle-class incomers live at lower densities than the displaced blue-collar renters, the effect paradoxically is usually to increase the rate of population outflow from the city. This process, first noted for London in the 1960s, is certainly a factor in the continued decline of American central cities in the 1970s. How far quantitative decline is compensated by qualitative improvement in quality of life, of course, is a matter of judgement.

THE EUROPEAN EXPERIENCE

In the other great concentrations of urban life within the advanced industrial world, the processes do not seem to have gone so fast and a far, at least on the basis of data up to the mid-1970s. This is the most important conclusion to emerge from a study of over 500 urban areas in Europe[10,12] and a parallel study of over 100 similarly defined areas in Japan.[9]

The European study shows that the great majority of Europeans lived in metropolitan areas (as they were defined for the purpose) and that the proportion actually increased during the period under study, 1950–1975 (Table 6). The remaining, nonmetropolitan areas actually contained slightly fewer people at the end of the period than at the start. However, in a striking parallel with the American experience reported above, there was a pronounced shift toward decentralization within metropolitan areas, from cores to rings. This became evident only after 1960: overall in the countries studied, the metropolitan rings had a decreasing share of total population in the 1950s but an increasing share in the 1960s, when their aggregate population growth exceeded that in the cores (Table 7). After 1970, admittedly on the basis of incomplete data that exclude five of the countries, the process of decentralization accelerated: the urban cores, which had had two-thirds of total growth in the 1950s but less than half in the 1960s, had a negligible share in the first half of the 1970s. In contrast, the rings had one-third of the growth in the 1950s, more than half in the 1960s, and the whole of the net growth in the first half of the 1970s. Even in this last period, however, people were still leaving nonmetropolitan areas for metropolitan ones.

For employment, the evidence is more limited. The available evidence suggests that a very high proportion of all jobs were concentrated in the metropolitan areas and that within these the proportion of employment within the cores increased during the 1950s but decreased marginally during the 1960s, indicating that jobs as well as people were beginning to decentralize outwards. However, the group of countries that reported employment data were in general the most highly industrialized and urbanized ones where such a process might have been expected to start earliest, so this may not be a representative picture.

These overall trends are to some extent misleading because they conceal very large differences as between one European country and another. Britain led the way toward deconcentration: there, partly in the 1950s and almost universally in the 1960s, urban cores were growing more slowly than rings or were actually declining; this process accelerated after 1970, with massive losses in the cores and gains in the rings. The process started earliest and was most marked in the larger metropolitan areas around the leading cities—to such an extent that even by the 1960s they were losing population overall, a process that accelerated in the early 1970s. Belgium and the Netherlands were the two countries on the European mainland where the same process was observed, partly in the 1950s and more widely in the 1960s and early 1970s. With an important group of countries, the Scandinavian nations, Germany, and Switzerland, the process came later, in the 1960s; it almost certainly continued in the 1970s, although data for Germany and Switzerland are lacking. In Southern Europe—Spain, Portugal, Italy—the process only really made itself felt in the early 1970s. In France, and still more strikingly in the Eastern European nations of Hungary and Poland, it was not generally evident even by the mid-1970s. Although there are considerable differences, one element is almost universal: the nonmetropolitan areas show very little dynamism. Only France after 1970 appears as an exception, and even there, the non-metropolitan areas were taking no more than 15% of total growth.

These differences are associated with others. In Britain, for instance, the growth of the largest urban areas shows a progressive retardation; by the 1970s they were actually declining. The process is much less evident elsewhere in Europe, and in some countries—notably Germany, Italy, Spain and Eastern Europe—the largest metropolitan areas continued to grow very rapidly throughout the period under study. Further, in some of these areas, the bulk of the growth over much of the period was actually occurring in the central cities. It is notable that these fast-growing major metropolitan areas are highly concentrated within those

Table 6 Europe and regional groups: metropolitan and non-metropolitan population (in 000s) 1950–1975

	1950[a] Total	1950[a] Per-centage	1960[a] Total	1960[a] Per-centage	1970[a] Total	1970[a] Per-centage	1960[b] Total	1960[b] Per-centage	1970[b] Total	1970[b] Per-centage	1975[b] Total	1975[b] Per-centage
ATLANTIC EUROPE												
Core	27 322	51·25	27 833	50·01	27 160	46·29	26 665	51·87	25 992	47·99	25 364	46·58
Ring	22 575	42·34	24 550	44·12	28 178	48·02	23 012	44·77	26 354	48·65	27 305	50·15
Non-Met	3419	6·41	3267	5·87	3340	5·69	1728	3·36	1822	3·36	1781	3·27
TOTAL	53 316	100·00	55 650	100·00	58 678	100·00	51 405	100·00	54 168	100·00	54 450	100·00
NORTHERN EUROPE												
Core	4959	33·94	5554	35·54	5960	35·23	5554	35·54	5950	35·23	5683	32·90
Ring	6274	42·94	6589	42·16	7403	43·83	6589	42·16	7403	43·83	8007	46·35
Non-Met	3378	23·12	3485	22·30	3536	20·93	3485	22·30	3536	20·93	3585	20·75
TOTAL	14 612	100·00	15 628	100·00	16 889	100·00	15 628	100·00	16 889	100·00	17 275	100·00
WESTERN EUROPE												
Core	22 744	37·84	26 725	40·29	30 717	41·60	26 653	40·37	30 641	41·69	31 169	40·93
Ring	27 674	46·05	29 711	44·79	32 760	44·36	29 468	44·63	32 496	44·21	34 308	45·05
Non-Met	9683	16·11	9900	14·92	10 368	14·04	9900	15·00	10 368	14·10	10 673	14·02
TOTAL	60 101	100·00	66 336	100·00	73 845	100·00	66 021	100·00	73 505	100·00	76 150	100·00
SOUTHERN EUROPE												
Core	22 801	27·94	27 821	31·82	33 346	35·37	26 389	33·32	31 896	36·81	32 974	37·05
Ring	37 747	46·26	38 696	44·25	41 425	43·93	34 282	43·29	37 115	42·84	39 473	44·36
Non-Met	21 045	25·79	20 927	23·93	19 515	20·69	18 522	23·39	17 619	20·33	16 543	18·59
TOTAL	81 593	100·00	87 444	100·00	94 286	100·00	79 193	100·00	86 630	100·00	88 990	100·00

CENTRAL EUROPE												
Core	19 256	31·66	22 719	34·35	23 632	32·60	18 404	34·51	19 186	32·86	NA	NA
Ring	41 240	67·80	43 066	65·11	48 453	66·84	34 919	65·49	39 194	67·14	NA	NA
Non-Met	329	0·54	360	0·54	408	0·56	0	0	0	0	0	NA
TOTAL	60 825	100·00	66 144	100·00	72 493	100·00	53 322	100·00	58 380	100·00	59 802	100·00
EASTERN EUROPE												
Core	NA	NA	NA	NA	NA	NA	11 961	30·39	13 935	32·61	15 148	34·07
Ring	NA	NA	NA	NA	NA	NA	27 396	69·61	28 796	67·39	29 312	65·93
Non-Met	NA	NA	NA	NA	NA	NA	—	—	—	—	—	—
TOTAL	NA	NA	NA	NA	NA	NA	39 357	100·00	42 731	100·00	44 459	100·00
EUROPE												
Core	97 082	35·89	110 652	38·00	120 805	38·20	97 222	38·64	108 414	39·57	NA	NA
Ring	135 510	50·11	142 612	48·97	158 219	50·04	120 747	47·99	132 164	48·25	NA	NA
Non-Met	37 854	13·99	37 939	13·03	37 167	11·75	33 635	13·36	33 345	12·17	32 582	11·58
TOTAL	270 446	100·00	291 203	100·00	316 919	100·00	251 505	100·00	273 923	100·00	281 324	100·00

[a]All countries.

[b]UK, Sweden, Norway, Denmark, France, Belgium (excluding Luxembourg), The Netherlands, Spain, Italy, Hungary, and Poland only.

NA: separate core and region figures not available for Germany.

Source: Hall and Hay (1980) plus new data on Eastern Europe.

Table 7 Europe and regional groups: metropolitan and non-metropolitan population change, 1950–1975

	1950–1960[a]			1960–1970[a]			1960–1970[b]			1970–1975[b]		
	Absolute change (000s)	Per-centage change	Per-centage of total	Absolute change (000s)	Per-centage change	Per-centage of total	Absolute change (000s)	Per-centage change	Per-centage of total	Absolute change (000s)	Per-centage change	Per-centage of total
ATLANTIC EUROPE												
Core	511	1·87	21·92	−673	−2·42	−22·23	−673	−2·52	−24·36	−628	−2·42	−222·74
Ring	1975	8·75	84·63	3628	14·78	119·82	3342	14·52	120·96	951	3·61	337·20
Non-Met	−153	−4·47	−6·54	73	2·25	2·41	94	5·44	3·40	−41	−2·24	−14·46
TOTAL	2334	4·38	100·00	3028	5·44	100·00	2763	5·37	100·00	282	0·52	100·00
NORTHERN EUROPE												
Core	594	11·99	58·49	396	7·14	31·45	396	7·14	31·45	−267	−4·49	−69·17
Ring	315	5·02	30·98	814	12·35	64·54	814	12·35	64·54	604	8·16	156·48
Non-Met	107	31·70	31·70	51	1·45	4·01	51	1·45	4·01	49	1·39	12·69
TOTAL	1016	6·95	100·00	1261	8·07	100·00	1261	8·07	100·00	386	2·29	100·00
WESTERN EUROPE												
Core	3981	17·50	63·85	3992	14·94	53·16	3988	14·96	53·29	528	1·72	19·96
Ring	2037	7·36	32·67	3049	10·26	40·60	3028	10·28	40·46	1812	5·58	68·51
Non-Met	217	2·24	3·48	468	4·73	6·23	468	4·73	6·25	305	2·94	11·93
TOTAL	6235	10·38	100·00	7509	11·32	100·00	7484	11·34	100·00	2645	3·60	100·00
SOUTHERN EUROPE												
Core	5020	22·02	85·80	5525	19·86	80·75	5507	20·57	74·05	1078	3·38	45·68
Ring	949	2·51	16·22	2729	7·05	39·89	2833	6·58	38·09	2358	6·35	99·92
Non-Met	−118	−0·56	−2·02	−1413	−7·25	−20·65	−903	−4·88	−12·16	−1076	−6·11	−45·56
TOTAL	5851	7·17	100·00	6341	7·82	100·00	7437	9·39	100·00	2360	2·72	100·00

CENTRAL EUROPE												
Core	3463	17·98	65·11	914	4·02	14·39	782	4·25	15·46	NA	NA	NA
Ring	1825	4·43	34·32	5387	12·51	84·85	4276	12·25	84·54	NA	NA	NA
Non-Met	31	9·28	0·57	48	13·38	0·76	0	0	0	0	0	0
TOTAL	5319	8·74	100·00	6349	9·60	100·00	5058	9·49	100·00	NA	NA	100·00
EASTERN EUROPE												
Core	NA	NA	NA	NA	NA	NA	1974	16·50	58·50	1212	8·70	70·15
Ring	NA	NA	NA	NA	NA	NA	1400	5·11	41·50	516	1·79	29·84
Non-Met	NA	NA	NA	NA	NA	NA	—	—	—	—	—	—
TOTAL	NA	NA	NA	NA	NA	NA	3374	8·57	100·00	1728	4·04	100·00
EUROPE												
Core	13 570	13·98	65·38	10 153	9·18	40·63	11 192	11·51	50·15	1212	8·70	70·15
Ring	7102	5·24	34·21	15 607	10·94	62·46	11 417	9·46	51·16	516	1·79	29·84
Non-Met	85	0·22	0·41	−772	−2·32	−3·09	−290	−0·00	−1·30	−763	−2·29	−10·30
TOTAL	20 757	7·68	100·00	24 988	8·58	100·00	22 318	8·87	100·00	7401	2·70	100·00

[a]All countries, except Hungary and Poland.

[b]UK, Sweden, Norway, Denmark, France, Belgium (excluding Luxembourg), The Netherlands, Spain, Italy, Germany, Hungary, and Poland only.

NA: separate core and region figures not available for Germany.

Source: Hall and Hay (1980) plus new data on Eastern Europe.

parts of Europe that were marked by generally high economic and demographic growth during the period. These include not merely the European "Sunbelt" of Spain and Portugal but also (again in contrast to the American experience) the European industrial heartland or "Golden Triangle", the corners of which are conventionally taken to be Birmingham, Dortmund, and Milan. This suggests that, as in the United States, large metropolitan areas may grow if they are located in regions favourable for growth. Further—and this is fairly common in Europe, much rarer in America—as long as the central city areas are broadly bounded they may not experience notable core-to-ring deconcentration.

The precise mechanisms underlying growth in Europe are very different from the United States. In the United States they involve the growth of the post-industrial economy. In Europe, at least until 1975 they have been the development of an industrial economy coupled with the rationalization of peasant agriculture, which has taken millions of workers off the land and into urban industry. The nations that experienced the most rapid urban growth, including even the biggest metropolitan areas, have been rapidly industrializing nations such as Germany in the 1950s, France and Italy throughout the period, Spain and Eastern Europe after 1960. Conversely the United Kingdom, the nation farthest along the path to the post-industrial economy, exhibits trends similar to those of the United States: decline of the largest metropolitan areas, general inner city decline, a rapid rate of sub-urbanization and a general tendency for growth to take place at lower levels of the urban hierarchy.

The evident reason for these differences was that until 1975, much of Europe was at a rather earlier stage of urban evolution than either the United States or the United Kingdom, the European country most clearly following the American trends. Between 1950 and 1972, the numbers employed in primary industries in the extended European Economic Community declined from 17·0 million to 9·7 million, or from 17·1% of the total workforce to 9·4%.[16] Naturally all the ex-farmworkers went into manufacturing or service jobs in the urban areas. In many regions, the local urban economies could not expand rapidly enough to cope, and the displaced farmworkers had to join longer-distance migration flows to the larger metropolitan areas.[7,15] Such areas included Corsica, Sardinia, much of southern Italy, Scotland, Ireland, the Massif Central of France and the so-called *Zonenrandgebiet* (Border Area) on the eastern margin of the Federal Republic of Germany. From some of these migrants left not merely their own region but their own country, to join the more than 6 million migrant workers counted within the EEC by the early 1970s.

The evidence for Japan closely parallels that for Europe. Glickman's work[9] shows that since World War Two the Japanese population has been highly concentrated into a limited number of metropolitan areas. Further, between 1950 and 1970 the largest centres, especially in the Tokyo and Osaka regions, grew faster than average. Within the metropolitan areas, the 1950s were a period when population was still concentrating in central cores, but during the 1960s the rings began to grow more rapidly than the cores. After 1970, although the bigger metropolitan areas continued to grow faster than the smaller ones, their rate of growth slowed down, the rate of decentralization from city to suburb tended to increase, and the central cities of Tokyo and Osaka actually lost people while cities close by gained rapidly. However, this was mainly true of the larger areas; smaller metropolitan areas, with fewer than 800 000 people, continued to exhibit faster growth in central cities than in suburban rings. Overall, Glickman found that in the slowing-down of increase in the largest centres in the 1970s, the absolute losses from the larger central cities, and the growth of medium-sized cities near to major cities and even of medium-sized cities in rural areas Japan was coming to resemble western, particularly American, models. But in other respects, particularly in the strong continuing tendency to centralize in the smaller and medium-sized places, it was still perhaps at an earlier stage of evolution.

THE INDUSTRIALIZED NATIONS: TOWARD A GENERAL MODEL

From these observations of the major industrialized and urbanized regions of the world, we can begin to construct a tentative, descriptive model of urban evolution. It appears that most cities, in most countries, fit reasonably well into this model. It is based on the notion of a continuum of industrialization and urbanization on which different nations and city systems appear at different stages of evolution.

In the first stage, corresponding to primary industrialization and agricultural rationalization, people begin to leave the land for jobs in the cities. In many agrarian regions, the local cities cannot absorb the

Table 8 Europe and regional groups: population shifts, 1950–1975

							Type of shift[a]						
	LC		AC		RC		RD		AD		LD	
	No. of regions	Per-centage	No. of regions	Per-centage	No. of regions	Per-centage	No. of regions	Per-centage	No. of regions	Per-centage	No. of regions	Per-centage
EUROPE												
1950-60[a]	74	13·73	118	21·89	215	39·89	93	17·25	21	3·90	18	3·34
1960-70[a]	35	6·49	61	11·32	196	36·36	158	39·31	74	13·73	15	2·78
1960-70[b]	33	6·38	61	15·67	215	41·59	123	23·79	51	9·86	14	2·71
1970-75[b]	30	5·80	46	8·90	141	27·27	144	27·85	112	21·66	44	8·51
ATLANTIC EUROPE												
1950-60	10	6·99	8	5·59	56	39·16	39	27·27	15	10·49	15	10·49
1960-70	4	2·80	2	1·40	31	21·68	58	40·56	36	25·17	12	8·39
1960-70[c]	4	2·90	1	0·72	30	21·74	57	41·30	34	24·64	12	8·70
1970-75[c]	3	2·71	1	0·72	37	23·19	54	39·13	25	18·12	23	16·67
NORTHERN EUROPE												
1950-60	3	6·82	15	34·09	19	43·18	6	13·64	1	2·27	0	0·00
1960-70	3	6·82	4	9·09	28	63·64	6	13·64	3	6·82	0	0·00
1970-75	2	4·55	0	0·00	3	6·82	16	36·36	19	43·18	4	9·09
WESTERN EUROPE												
1950-60	5	4·17	47	39·17	41	34·17	22	18·33	4	3·33	1	0·83
1960-70	3	2·50	21	17·50	59	49·17	25	20·83	10	8·33	2	1·67
1960-70[d]	3	2·52	21	17·65	59	49·58	24	20·17	10	8·40	2	1·68
1970-75[c]	11	9·24	9	7·56	40	33·68	25	21·85	30	25·21	3	2·52

	LC		AC		RC		RD		AD		LD	
SOUTHERN EUROPE												
1950-60	30	23·08	35	26·92	55	42·31	10	7·69	0	0·00	0	0·00
1960-70	24	18·46	32	24·62	53	40·77	19	14·62	2	1·54	0	0·00
1960-70[e]	22	17·60	32	25·60	51	40·80	19	15·20	1	0·80	0	0·00
1970-75[d]	14	11·20	9	7·20	26	20·80	40	32·00	26	20·80	10	8·00
CENTRAL EUROPE												
1950-60	26	25·49	13	12·75	44	43·14	16	15·67	1	0·98	2	1·96
1960-70	1	0·98	2	1·96	25	24·51	50	49·02	23	22·55	1	0·98
1960-70[f]	1	3·85	2	7·69	6	23·08	14	53·85	3	11·54	0	0·00
1970-75[f]	0	0·00	1	3·85	6	23·08	4	14·38	11	47·31	4	15·38
EASTERN EUROPE												
1960-70	—	—	71	32·30	41	63·07	3	4·62	—	—	—	—
1970-75	—	—	26		34	52·31	4	6·15	1	1·54	—	—

[a] Excluding Hungary and Poland.
[b] Excluding Ireland, Luxembourg, Portugal, Germany (most areas), Switzerland and Austria.
[c] Excluding Ireland.
[d] Excluding Luxembourg.
[e] Excluding Portugal.
[f] Excluding Germany (most areas), Switzerland, and Austria.
[g] LC—Centralization during region decline in population.
AC—Absolute centralization.
RC—Relative centralization.
RD—Relative decentralization.
AD—Absolute decentralization.
LD—Decentralization during region decline in population.
Source: Hall and Hay (1980) plus new data on Eastern Europe.

migrant flows, which then go on in longer-distance migration flows to the larger centres (normally national or provincial capitals). This leads to a "primate" pattern of urban size, in which one city (or a very few cities) grows more rapidly than the rest and thereby dominate the hierarchy. At this stage, the migrants tend to go straight into the central cities because there work opportunities (and also knowledge of work opportunities) are concentrated. In terms of intra-urban change, therefore, this period is dominated by metropolitan areas experiencing the phenomenon of centralization during loss. In the regions of outflow, the city will be growing but it cannot make up for the loss in the ring (still not sub-urbanized and hence completely rural) around it. Thus the whole metropolitan area will be losing people. Only a few larger centres will provide an exception to this rule.

These few centres have already reached the second stage, which can be termed absolute centralization. Here the city grows, the surrounding ring loses, but overall the system grows because the central city growth is greater. In time, the rural outflow from the peripheral regions begins to exhaust itself, while the cities in these regions begin to develop as local manufacturing and service centres, thus providing more employment opportunities and intercepting more of their local rural migrants. At the conclusion of this stage, therefore, the domination of the system by the primate city or cities is beginning to weaken, while within most systems centralization during loss is replaced by absolute centralization.

In the third stage the rural loss is more or less stemmed and suburban out-movement begins. This process tends to begin earliest in the larger metropolitan areas which have experienced such rapid growth in stages one and two. However, as the central city is still adding population, indeed more rapidly than are the suburbs, we can call this the phase of relative centralization.

The fourth stage reverses this process. Suburban out-migration continues apace, until the rate of growth of the suburban ring exceeds that of the central city. We now have the mirror image of the third stage: relative decentralization.

The fifth stage takes the process one stage further. Starting with the largest and most congested cities, the central city actually starts to lose poeple through a combination of urban redevelopment, slum clearance, displacement of residences by commercial uses, and a general tendency to lower densities of occupation. This then is a phase of absolute decen-tralization. During this phase, it is often observed that the growth of the largest metropolitan areas has begun to slow down in relation to places lower down the hierarchy. Thus the principle of primacy begins powerfully to be eroded.

The sixth and final stage completes the process. The slow growth of the large metropolitan areas has now turned into actual decline. Although their suburban rings are usually still gaining people, this process is insufficient to counterbalance the decline of their central cities. Accordingly this stage is termed decentralization during loss. This is never a general condition; even in advanced industrial (or post-industrial) countries like the United States and the United Kingdom, it represents the state only of a few very large metropolitan areas. But, speculatively, it might be an end to which other places will eventually tend. If this progressively affected lower levels of the urban hierarchy, it would of course tend to steady erosion of the primacy principle. The work on European urban systems indeed showed that countries like the United Kingdom and Belgium tended most closely to have urban systems that corresponded to the so-called rank-size rule; in other words, they had virtually no trace of primacy. However, it also suggested that primacy might represent at least in part the special historic legacy of each country. Within Europe, for instance, France and Austria still had highly primate urban systems by the 1970s.

With this proviso, it can be suggested that different nations are indeed at different positions on this continuum. Table 8 shows that Eastern and Southern Europe are still in Stages 1 and 2 (though the latter may well be moving into Stages 3 and 4). Much of Europe has recently passed from Stage 3 to Stage 4, with some areas in Stage 5. Japan may also be reaching this stage of transition. Relatively few countries have reached a general Stage 5 position, and even the United Kingdom and the United States — the countries apparently most advanced on the continuum — still show only a partial transition to Stage 5. Stage 6, up to 1975, is restricted to a few very large metropolitan areas in these two countries; and perhaps in a few others after that date, but data so far are lacking.

THE DEVELOPING WORLD

The usefulness of this model can be gauged by testing it on the other half of the world. As everyone now knows, this world is characterized by a dizzying rate of urban growth. The process echoes that in the countries

Table 9 Populations of 25 largest urban agglomerations in the developing countries, 1950, 1980 and 2000

City[a]	Population in 000s			Percentage change 1980-2000
	1950	1980	2000	
Mexico City	2967	15 032	31 025	106·4
São Paulo	2483	13 541	25 796	90·5
Shanghai	5781	13 410	22 677	69·1
Beijing	2163	10 736	19 931	85·6
Rio de Janeiro	2937	10 653	18 961	78·0
Bombay	2901	8343	17 056	104·4
Calcutta	4446	8822	16 678	89·1
Jakarta	1725	7263	16 591	128·4
Seoul	1113	8490	14 246	67·8
Cairo/Giza/Imbaba	2466	7464	13 058	74·9
Madras	1397	5406	12 882	138·3
Manila	1598	5664	12 313	117·4
Buenos Aires	5251	10 084	12 104	20·0
Bangkok/Thonburi	1414	4870	11 936	145·1
Karachi	1127	5005	11 774	135·2
Delhi	1390	5414	11 683	115·8
Bogota	633	5493	11 663	112·3
Teheran	1126	5447	11 320	107·8
Istanbul	969	5162	11 221	117·4
Baghdad	579	5138	11 125	116·5
Dacca	325	2841	9725	242·3
Lagos	300	2900	9400	224·1
Lima	1091	4682	8930	90·7
Kinshasa	199	3089	8411	172·3
Tienjin	2392	4810	7775	61·6

[a]By size order as projected 2000.

Source: United Nations, Department of International Economic and Social Affairs, *Patterns of Urban and Rural Population Growth*. (*Population Studies*, 68) (ST/ESA/SERA/ 68) (United Nations, New York, 1980). Richardson, H. W., The Future Metropolitan Region. In: *Proceedings of the First International Congress of Planning for Major Cities*. Mexico City (1982, forthcoming).

of the developed world when they experienced their own industrial revolutions, but in scale it appears to go far beyond it. Table 9, based on United Nations compilations and projections, gives a useful overview of it.

Table 9 shows an unprecedented rate of growth in the recent past: many of the 25 metropolitan areas increased their populations fivefold during the 30-year period 1950-1980, and a few even managed to grow tenfold. In general, the projected rate of growth for 1980-2000 is slower; it could hardly be otherwise. Nevertheless, many areas will double in population and a few will triple. Because the base is by now so large, the absolute increases are very large and will, if realized, create urban areas by the year 2000 that are quite without parallel in history. Three cities will have exceeded 20 million, eight will be over 15 million, and 45 will have more than 5 million. Further, out of the 30 biggest urban agglomerations in the world by the year 2000, no fewer than 21 will be in the Third World.

This rapid growth of the biggest cities almost certainly will mean that many developing countries will retain a somewhat primate urban

Table 10   Size and growth of 12 biggest cities, Mexico, 1970-80

City by size order	Population 1980	Percentage growth 1970-1980
Mexico City[a]	9 500 000	35·7
Guadalajara	2 369 420	62·8
Monterrey	1 930 891	59·1
Puebla	861 029	114·4
Torreon	774 568	76·6
Leon	599 983	64·4
Ciudad Juarez	564 082	38·5
San Luis Potosi	499 300	68·1
Chihuahua	367 088	42·8
Mexicali	319 369	21·2
Cuernavaca	311 872	132·5
Jalapa	311 090	154·2

[a]Federal District. The actual urban area was far larger, with a total population of about 15 000 000.
Source: Census of Mexico, 1980.

hierarchy dominated by one (or a few) giant urban areas. Admittedly, Table 9 does not show the other significant fact that in these same countries, smaller cities are also growing rapidly, in some cases more rapidly than the giants. However in many of these countries these second- and third-order cities are very much smaller than the first-rank ones, so the rule first enunciated by Taafe, Morrill and Gould in 1963[19] still stands: countries in early stages of rapid development tend toward a primate system of urban population distribution, which is only modified at later stages in the development process. Table 10, which presents figures for size and growth of leading Mexican cities, demonstrates the point that although second- and third-order cities have grown faster than Mexico City, they have a considerable way to catch up. In fact, since 1940 Mexico City has retained almost the same position in the urban hierarchy in relation to the next largest cities.[19] Notoriously, these cities find it almost impossible to cope with such a flood of humanity; even highly organized cities in the developed world, with immeasurably greater resources, would find the task almost beyond them. In the developing world, with extremely scarce money and manpower, they can do almost nothing; the city develops in conditions of extreme *laissez-faire* only lightly mediated by any form of planning and control. The result is a very distinctive pattern of activities and land uses, common to most such rapidly developing cities. It has three main features:

(1) *Housing*. Many of the new arrivals, typically over 50%, cannot afford any form of shelter in the conventional tenure systems (purchase, private renting or public conventional housing) and erect makeshift shacks on a self-help basis. Because they cannot afford to buy the land, this process can take place only in locations where squatting is countenanced, that is, far from the city centre. Often, such areas are outside the city limits where planning and building controls are more strictly enforced; the extraordinary case of Nezahualcoyotl, a spontaneous settlement in Mexico that now houses probably 2 million people, arose because the site was just outside the boundaries of the Mexico City *Distrito Federal*. The houses are often unserviced or extract utility services illegally; water supplies are limited and may be polluted; drainage is absent, further adding to the problems of the water supply; electricity is often lacking or very limited; roads are unsurfaced and may be difficult to traverse in bad weather. The characteristic pattern of growing third world cities is therefore generally contrary to that in the United States or much of Europe, with the rich living near the centre and the poor living at the distant periphery.

(2) *Employment.* The new arrivals commonly have no marketable skills in urban employment and arrive in a labour market that is often already saturated, so they must make do with a variety of extremely irregular and low-paying jobs in the so-called informal economy. (More than half the workforce of Mexico City, for instance, lacks permanent employment.[14] Both these, and more regular employment, are often located far from where the new arrivals can make their homes: they tend to be either in the central business district or in industrial areas that may be on the other side of the city altogether. Consequently, a third problem arises.

(3) *Transportation.* With housing at the distant periphery and jobs at the centre, there is obviously a major commuting problem. It is compounded by the fact that, compared with the great cities of the developed world, these cities started underground railway construction very late and either have skeletal networks or none at all. Mexico City, for instance, has only 47 kilometres of underground railway (as of 1980) for its 9·5 million people. So commonly, public transport is poor and irregular. It takes the form either of buses or of para-transit vehicles (jitneys, shared taxis) using a street network that for a variety of reasons — lack of street space (as in Bangkok), high car-ownership associated with very low fuel prices (Mexico City), poor traffic management and control (almost everywhere) — is severely congested. As well as being long, journeys are often very slow. They eat into the time budget of the low-income worker, giving him less time with his family that might have been spent on improving the condition of his housing. (In Mexico City, for instance, many workers spend five or six hours a day on travel to and from work.[14]) So the elements interact in a vicious circle.

The central point is that the crisis of the giant Third World city leads to an odd and distinctive pattern of decentralization. The new arrivals, who are poor, constantly tend to find homes very far from the centre — farther indeed than they would if they were buying or renting legally. The jobs they perform tend to be in the centre, leading to an exaggerated form of long-distance commuting. If they find factory jobs outside the centre, these are likely to be peripheral in some other sector of the urban area, again leading to very long commuter journeys. In time, probably, employment too will tend to decentralize, but that would presuppose stable employment for all or most of the population, which is unlikely in the foreseeable future.

Although systematic analysis has not so far been made and would be difficult because of data problems, the result of these patterns is that almost certainly many cities of the developing world have reached the stage of relative decentralization of population; the main weight of population growth is found outside the limits of the legally defined central city. Employment, on the other hand, is almost certainly still centralizing in these cities. Long and arduous commuter journeys are the result.

A DECENTRALIZING WORLD?

Thus in very different ways, the cities of both the First (western) and the Third World are deconcentrating. Only in the Second (socialist) World does it appear that the central city is truly maintaining its position. The basic mechanisms, however, are very different. At one extreme, the United States and United Kingdom present the picture of advanced deconcentration associated with the transition to a post-industrial or service economy. Such countries demonstrate strong growth of medium-sized and smaller cities and a general tendency to stagnation or decline of the older, larger urban systems. At another extreme, the most rapidly urbanizing countries of the Third World are those in course of rapid industrialization. In this regard they are probably no more than two or three decades behind European countries such as Spain and Italy. Wherever this process occurs, it seems to lead to rapid growth of the leading cities and thus to an accentuated primate distribution of urban population.

The odd feature about the urbanization of the Third World is the process of instant deconcentration occasioned by the phenomenon of mass squatting. In this regard, the developed world offers few parallels. Paris had shanty towns in the suburbs in the 1930s, but these appear to have been settled mainly by migrants from the congested inner city.[2] Generally, new arrivals in the city have tended to seek accommodation in the congested inner city where they found work opportunities, work information, and the culture of fellow-migrants. It is too early to say how, in the course of the coming decades, this inside-out pattern of urbanization might evolve. Just conceivably, if prestige continues to lie with the central city address, we might witness an inward movement as the new arrivals become more affluent: a strange reversal of the traditional process of western urbanization. If it did, however, it would probably be accompanied by the same puzzling phenomenon that attends the process of gentrification in British and American cities: net population loss.

Apart from such changes resulting from social or cultural aspiration, little seems likely to disturb the tendency for the world's urban areas progressively to expand. It now appears clear for instance that rising energy costs can be met through a series of adaptations (particularly the use of smaller, fuel-efficient cars) without fundamental changes in the car-oriented, suburban way of life. At the same time, rising fuel costs plus rising labour costs have meant hard times for the public transportation systems on which the larger, older, higher-density cities so critically depend. Rising crime rates and other forms of social malaise continue to tarnish the image of the city as a good place to live; in the United States, this reputation has extended from cities like New York to places like San Francisco and Los Angeles, which not long ago felt themselves relatively immune.

These trends are likely to continue. The prospect is for new generations of even more fuel-efficient cars by the mid-1980s and even of very small, hyper-economical cars which the Japanese are testing in their own home market. Public transport, starved of both capital investment subsidy and operating subsidy by governmental cuts in many countries, may well go into greater and greater deficit and become increasingly unattractive to its customers. This in turn could lead to mass movement of central office and other commercial functions from the central business districts of the larger cities. Finally, the forthcoming explosion of information technology during the 1980s, in the form of mini- and microprocessors, satellite transmission of electronic data, word-processing and remote processing of data, promises to erode the traditional advantages of the CBD as places for face-to-face contact.

Cities will never be entirely depopulated, of course. They will always remain highly attractive places for some. Single people, young people, either unmarried or without children, students, people who value social interaction or the proximity of cultural monuments, people whose work and social life interact, people who want or need to be near the heart of social and cultural and political interaction will all continue to seek their niches near the heart of the city. And many of them will be willing and able to pay the price (paradoxically it seems that at the same time as cities depopulate so their land and property values are at their highest). However, for the rest, it seems that the future lies in the suburbs to an increasing extent in the smaller cities that combine low costs of producing goods and services with an agreeable way of life.

REFERENCES

1. Aristotle, quoted in Mumford, L. (1938). "The Culture of Cities" 492. Harcourt, Brace, New York.
2. Bastie, J. (1964). "La Croissance de la Banlieue Parisienne." P.U.F., Paris. 229-323.
3. Bell, D. (1973). "The Coming of Post-Industrial Society: A Venture in Social Forecasting." Basic Books, New York.
4. Berry, B. J. L. (1970). The geography of the United States in the year 2000. *Transactions of the Institute of British Geographers* **51**, 21-53.
5. Berry, B. J. L. (1976). The counter-urbanization process: urban America since 1970. *In* Berry, B. J. L. (ed.). "Urbanization and Counter-Urbanization." (Sage Urban Affairs Annual Reviews, 11). Sage, Beverly Hills and London.
6. Berry, B. J. L. (1980). Inner city futures: an American dilemma revisited. *Transactions of the Institute of British Geographers NS* **5**, 1-28.
7. Clout, H. (1976). "The Regional Problem in Western Europe." Cambridge University Press, Cambridge, 5.
8. Cohen, R. B. (1981). "The new international division of labor, multinational corporations and the urban hierarchy. *In* Dear, M. and Scott, A. J. (ed.). "Urbanization and Urban Planning in Capitalist Society." Methuen, London.
9. Glickman, J. (1978). "The Growth and Management of the Japanese Urban System." Academic Press, New York and London.
10. Hall, P. (1981). Urban change in Europe. *In* Pred, A. "Geographical Essays for Torsten Hägerstrand." Gleerup, Lund.
11. Hall, P. (1982). Keys to regional growth. *Transactions/SOCIETY*, **9/5**, 48-52.
12. Hall, P. and Hay, D. (1980). "Growth Centres in the European Urban System." Heinemann Education, London.
13. Malecki, E. J. (1980). Science and technology in the American urban system. *In* Brunn, S. D. and Wheeler, J. O. (ed.). "The American Metropolitan System: Past and Future." Arnold, London.
14. May, C. D. (1981). Mexico City: omens of Apocalypse. *GEO*, **3/5**, 21-36.
15. Merlin, P. (1971). L'Exode rural *Cahiers de l'Institut National d'Etudes Demographiques*, **59**, 1-228.
16. Salt, J. and Clout, H. (1976). "Migration in Post-War Europe." Oxford University Press, Oxford, 34-5.
17. Stephens, J. D., Holly, B. P. (1980). The changing patterns of industrial corporate control in the United States. *In* Brunn, S. D. and Wheeler, J. O. (ed.). "The American Metropolitan System: Past and Future." Arnold, London.

18. Sternlieb, G. and Hughes, J. (1975). "Post-Industrial America: Metropolitan Decline and Inter-Regional Job Shifts." Rutgers University, Brunswick, N.J.
19. Taafe, E. J., Morrill, R. J., Gould, P. R. (1963). Transport expansion in underdeveloped countries: a comparative analysis. *Geographical Review* **53**, 503-29.
20. United States Bureau of the Census (1980). "Census Report: 2548-(9)", 2. Washington D.C.: Bureau of the Census (mimeo).
21. Vining, D. R. and Strauss, A. (1977). A demonstration that the current deconcentration of population in the United States is a clean break with the Past. *Environment and Planning, A,* **9**, 751-8.
22. Vining, D. R. and Kontuly, T. (1977). Increasing returns to city size in the face of an impending decline in the size of large cities: which is the bogus face? *Environment and Planning, A,* **9**, 59-62.
23. Violich, F. (1981). Mexico City and Mexico: two cultural worlds in perspective. *Third World Planning Review,* **3**, 361-386.

Chapter Six

National Cultures and Academic Geography in an Urbanizing Age

DAVID HOOSON

THE NATIONAL ROOTEDNESS OF GEOGRAPHY

One paradox of geography as an organized subject of study is that although its whole history, aura and etymology emphasize its global viewpoint, its actual evolution has partaken heavily of the particular national, cultural and environmental traditions and outlooks in which its leading scholars were nurtured. In practice, of course, there is an inevitability—even a legitimacy—about this state of affairs, which implicitly recognizes the relativity even of "world-views" to the particular vantage-point of the viewers.

As a modern academic discipline, geography crystallized in the quarter-century or so before the First World War in the leading countries of Europe and their American and Russian offshoots. Competitive nationalism, imperialism and free trade were developing apace alongside such basic processes as urbanization and universal education, which in turn facilitated the mobilization and dissemination of national cultures and the "state-idea". Therefore the leading scholars of the day, however independent-minded and committed to a global and "objective" geography, were inevitably guided to greater or lesser degree by the general climate of opinion and preoccupations of their home-country, its recurrent crises and urgent priorities, imperial rivalries and principles of educational reform, for example, as well as ingrained perceptions of its own national and natural environments. Thus it is not surprising to find

THE EXPANDING CITY
ISBN 0 12 547250 1

that, particularly in these formative decades before the First World War, recognizably distinct *genres* of thinking and writing, approaches, methods and emphases developed in each of the geographically significant countries, although it is debatable whether they can, or should, be dignified by the term National Schools. In other words, a marked national *rootedness* developed in geographical scholarship, and the firmness, vigour and depth of these roots seem to have had a strong influence on the strength with which the image and role of geography has "taken" in its subsequent history in the various countries concerned. For instance the somewhat hazy and insecure image of geography in America today may derive from the fact that the two dominant concepts developed before the First World War—"cycle" geomorphology and a sometimes crude form of environmental determinism—were later disowned by most of the profession there. In contrast, the prevailing theoretical framework and even practical preoccupations of the pre-Soviet Russian School proved resilient enough to survive the severe stresses of the Stalin era and to provide a vital spirit of continuity and inspiring tradition for contemporary Soviet geographers. As one contemplates the very different ways in which the basic thought-structure of geography evolved in the early stages in different countries, many questions of a comparative nature come to mind. For instance, why did the Russian geographers, in a social climate where fatalism was endemic and where some prominent historians were attracted by environmental determinism, avoid the latter position and focus instead on man's impact on nature; while on the other hand in America with similar natural environments and frontier history, the dominating philosophical stance markedly diverged? Why did a closely knit coherent school of thought develop in France but not in Britain at the same time, and how much can this be attributed to divergent traditions of educational and political philosophy and world-wide situation and how much to the dominance of mind, temperament and "charisma" of some leading scholars?

TRANSCENDING NATIONAL CULTURES

As always a few individuals stand out, and I wish at this point to pay tribute to Professor Jean Gottmann, who is truly exceptional not only in the range and impact of his scholarship but in the way he has absorbed, transcended and eventually become prominent in several national geographical traditions and *milieux*. I cannot think of any other geographer in history who has pulled off anything like the "hat-trick" of chairs at the Sorbonne, Princeton's Institute for Advanced Study and then Oxford, acquiring a remarkably subtle understanding of the respective national cultures. Several of us like to pay lip-service to the concept of "citizen of the world" as most appropriate to the shrunken and interdependent "space-ship earth" of our day, but Gottmann comes closer than any other geographer to embodying this ideal, while remaining, in many essential respects, profoundly French—reflecting the cultural hearth of his formative years.

It would be superfluous, in a volume specifically dedicated to him, to expatiate further on Gottmann's achievements and career. I wish, however, to make two points. First, I regard him as squarely in the French tradition of regional, human and political geography, following particularly his teachers Siegfried and Demangeon, and that his more recent (post-Megalopolis) success as a student of cities is quite naturally infused and informed with this humanist tradition. Secondly, the four national traditions I intend to compare in this paper—Britain, France, Russia and the United States—have all been home to him at various phases of his life and have contributed to his international outlook.

Divining Personal Histories

The basic problem in attempting to divine and interpret the impact of national culture and circumstances on the questions and emphases in his geographical work chosen by an individual scholar in the past is, of course, as elusive and subject to inference and speculation as any of the myriad decisions that move intellectual history. One needs to put oneself in the individual's shoes with respect to his situation, in relation to the thought, needs and opportunities of his time and place. It also helps to try to imagine his formative experiences, both local and global, and the attitudes and assumptions presumably underlying them. If he moves to another place, let alone another culture and part of the world altogether, he will be inescapably tarred with the brush of his earlier situation, preconceptions and place in the world. Presumably, as a geographer above all, he will have a professional as well as a personal interest in transplanting himself reasonably successfully and adapting himself to the viewpoints and necessities of another region, culture or scale. Effective comparative analysis and the development of a many-sided world-view, both desirable staples of geographical studies, should be helped by such transplanting, because we can never jettison entirely (even if we wanted to) the ingrained assumptions and mind-sets deriving from our earlier experiences. Just as it is easier to learn further foreign languages once one has been mastered, so the effort of imaginatively empathizing with other world-views, not experienced at first hand, becomes progressively easier to the extent that we have experienced more than one base of living and working.

On this score Jean Gottmann should be a good guide and source of wisdom, and I hope that soon he will give us an autobiographical account of the insights of his geographical Pilgrim's Progress. Only through a series of reflective personal testimonies of this sort can a truly clear light be thrown on the question at issue here and the individual reactions be placed in significant groupings such as cultures and national or local "schools". Since the process of analysing in some depth one person's experience is a prerequisite to any plausible projection on a broader canvas, and since one is presumably only a relatively unchallenged authority on oneself, I propose now, with, I hope, appropriate measures of diffidence and curiosity, to describe my own odyssey in those terms.

The Geography of One Geographer

I believe I was lucky, though I did not feel so at the time, to be brought up on a farm in the Vale of Clwyd, North Wales, when Britain in general was already overwhelmingly urban. The beautiful encircling hills bounded my world in a way which was at once reassuring and claustro-phobic, and the working farm served as a microcosm of the interplay of physical, social and economic factors in the context of world-wide depression. Since my father ran the farm on "organic", "re-cycling" lines long before the current fashions emerged, I became conscious early of the profound inter-connectedness of the elements of the natural world with each other and with people and also the pervasive human role in modifying their world, creating new environments for future generations to contend with and be nurtured by. Although in some ways the valley seemed to me a backwater, consciousness of the wider world flooded in in the form of the low prices for the produce of the farm, queues at the Labour Exchange in the nearest town, and the gathering storms in various parts of the world. Increasingly my reading crowded out work on the farm as I learnt about the various ways in which nations were attempting to cope with their own environments and development in the context of their national traditions and political systems—the New Deal and the Dust Bowl in Roosevelt's United States, the "transformation of nature" and Five Year Plans in Stalin's Soviet Union, and the clamour for *Lebensraum* in Hitler's Germany, to mention only the more dramatic of the day. But these were all "foreign"—the global context in which we children were made to feel cosily at home was that of the British Empire, then still entirely intact and occupying (usually in red) an imposing proportion of the world on our (Mercator) school wall-maps. It did seem to be a world in itself, on which "the sun never set", with our tiny island improbably acting as a metropolitan fulcrum, balancing and ruling an astonishing collection of populous, raw-material-producing, "native" tropical colonies as well as the "white" Dominions in which predominantly British settlers were still feeling out their "pioneer fringes".

Following this early cultural conditioning, my entire teenage years were spent in a state of world war which, if nothing else good can be said about it, did round out my geographical education. The crucial significance of distance, harsh environments, population concentrations, and the fragility of national power came home to me dramatically through following the campaigns, which at the end even propelled me physically for the first time outside the confines of my island, to spend two years among the still colonial civilizations of South and South-East Asia. This sudden pitchforking into the strange and intense physical world of the tropics on the one hand, and the ancient, "teeming", poverty-stricken cultures on the other—all so starkly different from Britain and British life but somehow tied to it—made an indelible impression on me.

On returning to Britain and to Oxford University and the London School of Economics, universities with continuing imperial connections, albeit from distinctive viewpoints, but also to the ferment of social change, I experienced an exhilarating yet perplexing transition period with the shape of the new world emerging but not yet clearly crystallized. Oddly enough, I was being seriously drawn, even in the year of Indian independence, to join the Colonial Service, while at the same time being strongly influenced by Marxism in the aftermath of the war. Despite my travels and studies of the world, the telescope for my world-view was planted firmly in Britain and its special concerns, and I settled down to teach there and do research on a British topic.

However a major turning-point in altering my geographical perspective and orientation came in 1956 when, at the age of thirty, I accepted an offer to move to the United States to develop a speciality in the geography of the Soviet Union. This year also happened to be a fateful turning point in world affairs which, no doubt, encouraged my personal transition to a new perspective. The "year of Suez", it signalled, once and for all, the demise of the old British Empire. Further, the Hungarian uprising notwithstanding, it marked, for the Soviet Union, not only the clear accession to "super-power" status after the devastating war, but also, with Khrushchev's "secret speech" denouncing Stalin, a new, more hopeful and even heady, era of reform. There could therefore hardly have been a more propitious year for plunging wholeheartedly into Soviet studies and my well-remembered vicarious "experience" of that country from the war years was quickly reactivated and deepened, with travel and language study. Being based in Washington D.C. in the late 1950s, at the nerve-centre of the "other" super-power, was an additional bonus and catalyst for changing the scale and angle of vision of my studies, enabling me to adopt a meaningful comparative perspective, which I had always regarded as an essential component of geographical analysis, and which in these frenetic "Sputnik" years was given full play. Quite apart from the balance of power question, the few years around 1960 saw the most fruitful "competitive coexistence" in the history of the USA and the USSR, and it also happened to coincide with as far-reaching theoretical and methodological disputations as we have seen in the geographical professions of both countries. Unfortunately it was a short-lived Golden Age—by the mid 1960s, with the ousting of Khrushchev, the death of John F. Kennedy, the onset of the Sino-Soviet split and the Vietnam War, the atmosphere became less exciting and more restrictive for Soviet and comparative studies, with less information and less fruitful contacts. For those few years, however, the locale of Washington was heaven-sent, enabling me to move to a new scale and a new set of significant problems at a propitious time. The studies launched from this vantage-point eventually enabled me to move to the Pacific coast, where I have lived for the past two decades and where I feel more comfortable from environmental and intellectual points of view. I have always felt that the western side of the continents, at temperate latitudes, are the most congenial for living and working and, in particular, the combination in the San Francisco Bay Area of the gentlest climate and one of the most beautiful landscapes I have ever encountered with a stimulating cultural and intellectual environment is hard to beat as a favourable place in which to settle and practise geography.

In addition to this personal "amenity" factor, coming to live on the shores of the Pacific has also inevitably shifted the focus of my personal world-view as well. With the largest concentration of East Asians outside Asia and the harbours full of ships plying to and from Asia, the frame of reference of a Pacific Basin world has become quite a rational one for me. The phenomenal resurgence of Japan, the re-awakening and re-orientation of China, the emergence of Australia and "Pacific Siberia" as vital sources of industrial raw materials, as well as the Vietnam War and the continuing westerly movement of the American population have combined to make unrecognizable the picture of the Pacific as a remote and dependent backwater portrayed in my youth. Thus my outlook, identification and world-view as a geographer have changed radically since my upbringing in Britain, although I will always be inescapably tarred with the brush of my formative national culture and preconceptions.

FOUR DISTINCTIVE TRADITIONS

I have tried to illustrate from my own experience the interplay between the contingencies and circumstances of place and time in which a geographer finds himself at various stages of his life and the nature, direction and perspective of his scholarly work. Along the way I have inevitably become acquainted and to a degree imbued with the ingrained ways of thought, cultural assumptions and historical background of the Americans, which is both superficially easy and subtly difficult for one reared in the British tradition to do. Further, although I have not lived in Russia I have travelled there frequently and made it my business over the past quarter-century to try to get under the skin of its traditions and ways of thought (both Russian and Soviet), in particular of course those of the geographers, and interpret them as best I could to my English-speaking colleagues. Finally, though I can claim no special expertise in it, I have long felt a special affinity with French traditions and styles in geography.

These four national cultures have thus permeated my consciousness to greater or less degree and caused me to ponder their differences in relation to the achievements and failures in respect of my chosen field of study. Therefore, having indulged in an autobiographical digression, I shall now proceed from the scale of this personal narrative to speculate on the nature of the geography which emerged in each of these four countries in the formative urbanizing decades before the First World War. Obviously Russia and America had a lot in common in their frontier history, youth, large size and similar natural regions, in spite of the great difference of cultural and political traditions. Similarly France and Britain, both small mature nation-states long at the heart of world empires and at the centre of Western civilization, nevertheless have recognized, possibly over-caricatured, differences of style, philosophy, taste and social proclivities as well as degree of urbanization, which may go some way to explain the fact that no closely knit recognizable "school" of geography emerged in Britain to compare to that of France. Similar comparisons and contrasts may occur as between France and America or Russia, or with Germany (well-known but not considered here in any detail) as the exploration proceeds.

Britain and Russia, on the face of it, seem to be archetypal polar opposites—the epitome of insularity and continentality respectively, of sea-power and land-power, urban and rural, democracy and autocracy, of the "tight little island" and the endless steppes and wild "frontiers" and so on. I will begin with a discussion of the Russian case because it is the one of the four national schools under review on which I have done the most substantial amount of original research (e.g. Hooson, 1968) and also because it has, until recently, barely been recognized in the rest of the world, in spite of its distinguished and distinctive history. Moreover its progress and emphases do seem, as closely as any of them, to have been sensitive and responsive to the recurring developments and needs of the country and its people.

The Russian Tradition

Building on a vital tradition of geography in the service of the state, its expansion and development, which goes back prominently to Peter the Great, the subject may be said to have experienced its Golden Age between about 1870 and the First World War. In the volume, variety and originality of work done, it can stand comparison with that of any other country of that period. Moreover its progress and directions do seem, at least as closely as in any other country, to have been responsive to the distinctive developments and needs of the people and their regions.

In the middle of the nineteenth century agrarian feudalism still reigned in Russia and the cities counted for relatively little in the life of the Russian people. Only one in ten of them lived in towns of any sort, and there were still only two cities of over 100 000 inhabitants in the whole country (excluding Poland). By 1913, however, the two had become 25 (or over 30 if Siberia, Caucasia and Turkistan were included), while Moscow and St Petersburg had each reached about two million. They had come to reflect the new locus of power and innovation, the spread of the railway, and the rapid building of industrial foundations.[14] They were full of peasants at one remove, although a skilled proletariat was also gradually becoming divorced from the villages. As elsewhere, the cities were the centres of change — both peaceful and violent — but it should be stressed that even up to the late 1920s, fully four-fifths of the total population was still rural. The urban population did not begin to outnumber the rural in the Soviet Union until about 1960, a full century after this occurred in Britain, so although the new cities were assuming an influence out of all proportion to their numbers, the "agrarian question" remained of paramount importance.

Apart from the unprecedented economic growth, railway building and imperial expansion which was getting under way in the mid nineteenth century, a great national intellectual awakening was taking place. It was greatly influenced by European philosophers, especially Hegel, and by European revolutionary and reform movements and led eventually to the emancipation of the serfs in 1861, to intense reforming zeal for promoting the betterment of the peasants and, to this end, a plethora of schemes for improving the organization of the national and regional economy. People from many different interests and political persuasions came together in an unprecedented surge of patriotic resolve.

In this connection, the Imperial Russian Geographical Society, which was founded in 1845, quickly became recognized as one of the most successful and popular — in the best sense — of the country's learned societies and seemed to strike many chords in tune with current national aspirations, needs and ways of thought. It strengthened the rationalist forces in the Russian intellectual tradition by vigorously disseminating knowledge about nature and man through the Empire, with regional branches rapidly set up in such places as Siberia and Caucasia. There existed a remarkably propitious and fruitful combination of patriotism and philanthropy, which had deep roots among Russian intellectuals. In the context of the Geographical Society, this meant a marriage — uneasy sometimes, owing to political divisions — between the drive for exploration and the appraisal of resources, often within an imperialist framework, on the one hand, and the striving for liberal reform in the social and economic condition of the peasants through surveys and plans, on the other.

Peter Petrovich Semënov, having entered the ferment of St Petersburg life after a quiet privileged rural upbringing during which he had become painfully aware of the conditions of the serfs on his father's estate in Central Russia, joined the Geographical Society at the age of 22, having pledged himself to "devote [himself] completely to scientific work and . . . to search for some sort of civic activity connected with science". Shortly afterwards he went to Berlin where he met Humboldt and was particularly inspired by the ageing Carl Ritter, at whose feet he sat for a year, and on his return to Russia he set out to translate Ritter's books on Asia and also to plan an expedition to the then hardly known Tien Shan ranges in Central Asia. At the same time he was also a member of the "Committee for the Emancipation of the Peasants from the Bonds of Serfdom". The Geographical Society, in its first few years, was dominated by a rather conservative group, frequently military officers of German extraction, and in the nationalist upsurge of the late 1850s there was an increasing move to bring more thoroughgoing culturally Russian persons into positions of power. Semënov was made secretary of the Physical Geography section at this time, marking the beginning of a half-century's reign as the chief guiding hand of the Geographical Society.

The timing of his assumption of this dominant role was crucial, as was his own temperament, education and breadth of interest. His over-whelming desire to devote his life to "some civic activity connected with science", was combined with the early geographical inspiration he had received from Carl Ritter and the heady spirit of reform which was in the air when he returned from Germany. It was indeed a propitious time for the launching of expeditions with the stepping up of Russia's imperialist expansion, and all this conspired to put the young Semënov in the right place at the right time. He thenceforth had a profound impact on the fortunes and directions of geography in Russia, lending it coherence and unity both in his own work and through his institutional guidance.[13] He became as "compleat" a geographer as any of his European contemporaries and may be said to be *the* figure linking the subject's early history in Russia with the remarkable flowering of activity of the last few decades of Tsardom.

However, in the unpredictable swings between repression and reform that characterized the Russian autocratic political climate it is hard to exaggerate the critical importance of Semënov's temperament, which, while high-minded and dedicated, nevertheless allowed for the necessity of compromise to achieve the tasks he had set himself to do without going out of his way to alienate the Tsarist authorities to the point where he would have been prevented from carrying them through. His circle was very broad, ranging from liberal "dissident" writers like Dostoevsky and Danilevskii to conservative military imperialists who were nevertheless patriotic and high-principled according to their lights. Semënov's skills as a mediator between such people of very different convictions were legion and contributed in large measure to creating and preserving a geographical community, cohering largely around the Geographical Society, which was hospitable to diverse interests and temperaments and reached out to a broad and enthusiastic section of the lay community. He was thus enabled to stay in Russia and devote himself effectively to promoting and executing far-reaching projects concerning population, landownership and regionalization, in addition to exploration, which did much to improve the general understanding of some of the most fundamental structures of the national and regional economy, society and environment, providing a better framework for planning and eventually for improving the lot of the people. Oddly enough, Semënov's long-term work in this direction was commented upon favourably by Lenin and even Marx himself, at the same time as he was being honoured by the Tsar with the addition of the suffix Tian-Shansky to his name (rather like the place-names assumed by the British peerage) in recognition of his path-breaking expeditions to the Tien Shan mountains in Central Asia.

By way of contrast stands the destiny of his friend and fellow-geographer Prince Peter Kropotkin, 15 years younger, who had also at an early age carried out strikingly original exploration and scientific work in Siberia and was also offered the secretaryship of the Geographical Society in 1871. Although he was initially delighted to receive this invitation, loved geography and was in his element when doing research in it, he felt he had to decine, with great regret, saying many years later "But what right had I to these higher joys [his scientific research] when all round me was nothing but misery and struggle for a mouldy bit of bread".[6] He had been deeply hurt by the suffering he saw in Russia, initially at the hands of his father, who was cruel and arrogant to his serfs, and the vision of the crass contrast between abject misery and great wealth had eaten into his sensitive soul. So, on painfully renouncing a comfortable and promising job, in which he could have done a great deal for his subject, his country and his people if he had gone into it with the temperament of a Semënov, he plunged into revolutionary activities, courting almost inevitable imprisonment, from which he was lucky to escape to England in 1876. Here he spent the next forty years of his life, his main energies being spent in spreading his personal anarchist faith as well as writing prolifically on a wide variety of interesting and significant topics, such as his original counterpoise to Darwinism, *Mutual Aid*[7] which stressed the lessons of cooperation, rather than competition, in the natural world. He did maintain his interests and activities in geography, becoming widely and affectionately known even in such a typically Establishment institution as the Royal Geographical Society. This work was mainly concerned with interpreting developments in Russia, but he also wrote on his ideas about geography as an academic discipline and what it ought to be[5] and was keenly interested in its emerging place in the British universities. Like most Russian political exiles, however, he deeply wished to return home and had to be dissuaded several times from doing so. He finally did, in 1917, but died a disappointed man four years later. His absence from Russia coincided with an extraordinary flowering of geographical activity there (as it did in Britain), but in a fundamental way his "disembodiment" in a national cultural sense meant that geography as a subject lost a leader of genius. Given his temperament, his traumatic early experiences, and the political climate in Russia, this now seems inevitable, and geography's loss was no doubt more than compensated for by his widespread political influence. But however fruitless speculation about the "What ifs?" of history may be, it is hard not to be wistful and curious about the effect on the character and development of Russian geography (or British for that matter) if Kropotkin had been in a position of institutional leadership, combined with peace of mind and freedom to develop his ideas in a congenial cultural and political context.

The very different temperaments of Semënov and Kropotkin, deriving from their own personal experiences and circumstances within the fermenting, and yet periodically repressive atmosphere of Russia in the third quarter of the nineteenth century, illustrate the tenuous contingency of the course of geographical thought.

The British Tradition

The *milieu* into which Kropotkin was transported in 1876 could hardly have been more different from that of his Russian homeland. Britain had already been predominantly urban for a quarter-century and by the First World War was to reach its climax of about four-fifths urban. Russia, at this time and later, was still four-fifths rural. Further, perhaps even transcending the stark urban–rural population contrast, was that of their place in the world and the outlook stemming from it. Britain, the small island at the heart of a world-wide Empire, made up of a great variety of cultures, heavily dependent on international trade, and a world financial centre, might be expected to reflect those concerns in the orientation and spirit of its intellectual endeavours. This should presumably have applied in particular to the emerging social and natural sciences, including geography, which were beginning to crystallize and make inroads on the traditional classical education in the latter half of the nineteenth century. The vague public consciousness of the breadth and significance of the Empire, as expressed in periodic Victorian celebrations of it, was increasingly given more direct significance for ordinary citizens by the waves of emigration to the "new lands", with the network of personal communications and broadening geographical perspective resulting from it. The influence of novel and pervading general theories, from Adam Smith to Darwin, coupled with a succession of brilliant scientific sea expeditions, going back to Cook, infused the atmosphere immediately preceding the formal establishment of geography as a university subject in Britain, following the Keltie report of 1885. The Royal Geographical Society, which had hitherto heavily concentrated its energies on the promotion of exploration, began to play an effective role in the promotion of geographical education, by initially helping to finance the appointment of trained geographers at Oxford and Cambridge.

The first such person to be appointed, the 25-year-old Halford Mackinder, to Oxford in 1887, was surely a classic case of "the right man in the right place at the right time". He was equipped with just the right mixture of breadth of academic training, high visibility and articulate brilliance, having just delivered at the Royal Geographical Society a strikingly well-argued thesis of what geography ought to be[8] following a series of very successful extramural lectures given around the country. His background in both natural science and history lent authority to his plea for a synthesis of the physical and human aspects of the subject, largely through the medium of regional studies, which turned out to sound surprisingly revolutionary in Britain at the time. The Keltie report had revealed Britain to be lagging seriously behind Germany in geographical education, and since Germany was increasingly felt to be a threat and a competition in many fields to the hitherto assured confidence and superiority of the British Empire, the potential impact was rather like the electrifying effect of the striking Soviet scientific prowess on American educational reform in the 1950s. Mackinder had the additional advantage of possessing "sound" Imperialist convictions and was therefore more to be trusted with guiding the infant steps of university geography in Britain than, for instance a Kropotkin or a Geddes. In the event, Mackinder, like those two, was deflected into other, primarily political, activities and did not have the sustained, follow-up role in the building and guiding of geography in the British universities which he undoubtedly would have had if he had been more single-minded about developing the adopted academic subject which he had launched with such *éclat* in 1887. But his genius lay in his powers of suggestion and innovation and in an almost Churchillian choice of words and ringing tones. His political-geographical vision and world-view struck a chord very much in tune with his times and with the imperial thought-structure and carried his message across the world in a dramatic way as the new century unfolded. His dramatic sense of timing was uncannily exemplified when he first expounded his famous Heartland theory[10] at the very high-water-mark of four centuries of continuous expansion by the Russian Empire—just months before its traumatic defeat at the hands of Japan.

Although very different from Mackinder in politics and temperament, Patrick Geddes had a similar effect on young geographers, inspiring them with his fertile and exciting ideas and schemes which he was usually content to leave to others to develop and test out in detail. They were also at one in their emphatic recognition of the fundamental importance of a regional, synthetic approach to problem solving and to geographical understanding. This was probably what, above all, made Geddes a true geographer, although he was originally an evolutionary biologist and was later to be characterized more as a sociologist and town planner. Thus although never a "professional" geographer, he was the formative stimulating influence on such notable geographers as Fleure, Herbertson and Fawcett, all of whom played key roles in guiding academic geography in Britain.

Geddes was, remarkably, the only "geographer" who came to focus major attention on cities in this period when the "urban fact" had become so overwhelming in Britain. Why urban geography as such should have been so undeveloped under such circumstances is still hard to understand. Perhaps the fact that Geddes' models for geographical method were taken from France—notably LePlay and Reclus—within a basically rural and regional, rather than primarily urban, tradition, explains why the regional framework was so fundamental to his work on cities,[3] and why he failed to fashion what Robson has termed "a robust urban sociology".[12] Incidentally, Mackinder's vivid description of the human dynamics of Metropolitan London[9] is very Geddesian in spirit and tone. Although other scholars developed some rather typically British strands of the time, such as Chisholm and his "commercial geography",[2] it seems that Mackinder and Geddes provided the most powerful sparks for the development of British academic geography at the beginning of this century and both were keenly attuned to the context and the needs of their times and their country. It is a kind of tribute to the openness and tolerance of British society of the time that two men so different politically and temperamentally should have made the subtle but great impact that they did. A. J. Herbertson, a devoted but measured disciple and assistant of Geddes, who later became Mackinder's right-hand man and successor at Oxford, may be said to be a link figure between them, lacking their charisma but full of intellectual integrity and devoted to the regional approach and to the promotion of geographical teaching. Together with H. J. Fleure, another disciple of Geddes and admirer of Mackinder, he launched and nurtured the Geographical Association to spread the gospel among the school teachers of the country. Although Herbertson died prematurely in 1915 and neither Mackinder nor Geddes was playing a very active part in geography by that time, the torch of a humane British geography was fully kindled and ready to be duly institutionalized after the First World War. In many ways the highly successful Summer Schools held in Edinburgh and in Oxford just before the First World War, which brought in notable and unconventional scholars from Europe and America as well as aspiring geographers from other fields, must be regarded as important catalysts in the crystallization and inspiration of the next generation when the subject was able to "take off". In them exploration, and excitement, had full play.

The American Tradition

The burgeoning United States of America in the second half of the nineteenth century was dominated by the vision and the reality of "the frontier", the population movements—ever westward—and ideas of continental destiny. Expansive, naive optimism, taken to be typical of "the American spirit" and belief in limitless opportunities and freedoms alternated at times with pessimistic images of "wilderness" or the "American desert". In the surge of new-found nationalism following the Civil War, the passing of the Homestead Act, and the threading of the railways across the continent, both the ideas and the reality continued to be fluid and the geography of the Western half of the continent, by painful trial and error, was being discovered and frequently misunderstood at the same time as it was being used and abused. In spite of the rapid growth of cities in the east, the country as a whole was overwhelmingly rural, to the extent of some two-thirds even at the end of the century. The phenomenon of the American "frontier" itself, which was considered to have come to a close by the 1890s, was being identified as a key catalyst of the apparently perennial rebirth, vigour and enterprise of American society and the American character.[16]

In this basically optimistic—at times even euphoric and arrogant—view in which Man was seen to be "conquering", altering and taming Nature, and where the dominant theme of the country's history had been that of the colonization of a supposedly rich and open land, an academic geography primarily focused upon man's impact on nature, rather than the reverse, might have been expected to develop. But when it did emerge, with an institutional and professional identity at the end of the century, the dominant concerns were with the evolution of landforms *per se* and on the environmental "influences" on human phenomena, while both themes were plagued with simplistic and dogmatic assertions, generalizations and thought-structures, beguiling and even fascinating though they often proved to be to their readers. The interesting questions are why the subject took root in this way, to a greater extent than it did in any other country, why it was so popular and persistent, and what there might have been in the particular historical and environmental context of nineteenth century American life and thought which precipitated such distinctive geographical preoccupations.

It may indicate a capricious, subliminal reaction to the aggressive optimism and assumptions of omnipotence over nature. The sobering shocks and forebodings of Great (American) Deserts and other intractable impediments may have contributed to the prevalence and force of this philosophy. Certainly the massive physical barriers to close settlement of the West, and the gradual public perception of their reality, created a receptive climate for environmentalist beliefs. Added to this is the fact that the key figures who were to guide the infant steps of academic geography in America were geologists, notably W. M. Davis and R. D. Salisbury. Their overwhelming interests being in the landforms themselves, it might be said that they had an understandable vested interest in asserting that the intellectual study of environmental influence, conceived as cause and effect, naturally according a proper primacy to geomorphology, was the obvious way to proceed in dealing with the human phenomena of geography, in which in any case they had little interest and did no research on personally. It also seemed easy to invoke Darwin, as Davis freely did in respect of both his geomorphological cycle and his environmentalist views, although it should be noted that geological forerunners such as Powell[11] and Shaler[15] had eschewed any literal extension of Darwinism to human behaviour, in which they (especially Powell) became more and more interested. But the spirit and practice of academic geography before the First World War was in fact dominated by a misplaced and dogmatic evolution and environmentalism, however beguiling, exemplified by Semple and Huntington as well as Davis. Since these ways of thought were subsequently disowned by the profession, with a consequent lack of that corporate intellectual continuity enjoyed by other countries (including Russia, in spite of the complete political overturning) they may well account in part for the confused public image and institutional vulnerability under which the American profession and discipline still labours. The original fact that American institutionalized academic geography was born of geological parentage was crucial to its early life, in particularly marked contrast to the situation in France, where it largely grew out of history.

The French Tradition

I do not propose, partly because of lack of space but more importantly because of lack of expertise in comparison with many other geographers —not least Jean Gottmann—to do more than accord France a brief comparative mention in the context of this paper. Although France, like the USA, was heavily rural during most of the period under review and only crossed the line to majority-urban in the 1920s, the whole context, *milieu* and *genres de vie* could not have been more fundamentally different. Instead of a mobile, heterogeneous and basically rootless society pressing against the seemingly endless frontiers, coming upon adventitious wealth as well as great physical impediments, France presented an apparently exquisitely harmonious climax of distinctive *pays*, "medals stamped in the image of a people", of closely knit cultural and geographical kinship over centuries. But the peace and harmony had been rocked by the national defeat by the Germans in 1870 and the educational system was challenged into fundamental reforms, as to some extent Russia and Britain also were, and like America when challenged by Russia in the 1950s. Like Britain, France took pride and refuge in its colonial empire, which imparted a world-wide dimension to its geographical and philosophical canvas. Although it was very much less urbanized than Britain—when the latter began to count the majority of its population as urban around 1860 the French were still well over two-thirds rural and they were still predominantly rural when Vidal de la Blache died in 1918—paradoxically this was a period of steady and significant growth for the major cities of France. Compared with Russia, however, which was still nearly four-fifths peasant when France crossed the line over into majority-urban in the late 1920s, the contrast in social fabric was still stark, even though Russia had also, as we have seen, experienced hitherto unprecedented city growth over the previous half-century.

The atmosphere of French geography in the formative decades before the First World War was undoubtedly more humanistic, more historical, and more philosophically cohesive as a School than that of any other nation at the time. It was probably also less environmentally deterministic than any, characterized by a particular French idealism, spiritualism and eclecticism leading to the formulation of the well-known but often misunderstood Possibilist philosophy. Vidal de la Blache, the acknowledged leader of the academic School of the period, was clearly suffused with a historical sense not only by his training in history but by his Mediterranean upbringing and travels, including several years of teaching in Greece in the 1860s, followed by his teaching in Lorraine, beginning in 1872 in the aftermath of the Germany victory which affected that region, and also Vidal himself, so painfully. His great forerunner, Elisée Reclus, who had studied with Ritter in Berlin in the pre-Darwinian 1850s was affected by some of the same events as Vidal, but reacted to them much more radically, especially to the Paris Commune following the collapse of France in 1871, so much so that he was banished from France for most of his working life and had therefore no direct influence on development in French "academic" geography.

His geography, like that of his friend Kropotkin, became thoroughly suffused and interwoven with his anarchistic philosophy, and his deep human sympathy and compassion for the peoples of all countries shine through his prolific works, effectively preventing any hint of environmental determinism or social Darwinism. Thus basic temperamental tendencies, easily transmuted into political action and doctrine, are seen to take their place alongside the chronological and spatial context of their "life-paths", accidents, and practical opportunities, in forming the character of geography as it had crystallized in France before the First World War. Although both of these men were intellectually nurtured in a country which was still profoundly rural—even parochial—and with deep and stable historical roots, they both retained a remarkable sympathy for and understanding of the very different circumstances and *genres de vie* of peoples around the world. In fact, however different these two great men were in political expression, institutional affiliations and in their general "constituency", they had in common a marvellously humane, literary and scientific ability to portray the world as a whole, moving effortlessly from the local to the global scale. That Vidal de la Blache, in his last work, *La France de l'Est*[1] was groping towards a firmer and more systematic integration of "the urban fact" in the regional and human geographical tradition which he had built up, is well known. The framework could accommodate it logically and easily, but the deeply rural cast of France, and most of the world in which Vidal lived, inevitably set the tone. The full transforming surge of modern urbanism has only really come to France since the Second World War, and it has fallen to scholars like Gottmann and Pinchemel to come fully to grips with it, still broadly within the tradition of the "French School".

PERSONALITY, CONTEXT AND CONTINGENCY

It is in the very nature of these discussions that they do not conduce to the formulation of novel or comprehensive theories or even particularly startling conclusions. What emerges above all is the necessity, in the history of geographical thought, of focusing on the interplay between the personality of the leading individuals and the ensemble of the total historical context of their times. Particularly crucial is the nature of the interplay at the very moment when the key opportunities appeared, with

all the contingencies and unforeseen developments involved. The main
problem is for anyone else adequately to enter imaginatively into the
predicament, state of mind and basic early influences and world-view of
the person being examined. Although the pitfalls attending even this are
obvious, the evidence provided by a careful *autobiographical* account of
the person's own impressions of how, when, where and why he evolved
as a geographer the way he did is the indispensable and irreducible raw
material for deciphering the true history of geographical thought. In fact
perhaps the chief concrete recommendation I wish to make, arising from
this paper, is that each geographer should make an effort to set down his
thoughts on his own history (and geography) at some late, but not too
late, point in his career.

It is difficult to discount the importance of the national-cultural
context in which an individual scholar has his being and has been
nurtured, including its inevitably distinctive view of the world.
Mackinder, Semënov, Vidal de la Blache and Powell seem in so many
ways quintessentially *of* their respective national nineteenth century
cultures—British, Russian, French and American—and it is hard to
think of any of them successfully transplanted to another. Of course it
could have been done—Mackinder was reportedly offered a job at
Chicago, but it would have involved a radical reorientation on both sides.
It is fascinating to speculate about how differently American geography
might have turned out if Mackinder, rather than Salisbury, had been the
guiding hand of the infant Chicago department of geography, or if Franz
Boas—who was after all originally a geographer, had been "called" to
Harvard instead of W. M. Davis and had been thrust into a position of
leadership in American geography, rather than anthropology. Or,
alternatively, if Reclus or Kropotkin had been allowed, or had felt able,
to remain in their own nations and were given the power to influence the
nature of the crystallization of academic geography and guide it
institutionally.

It is not difficult to discern the effect of such things as the Empire on
British geography, the rural cast and regional stability on French
geography, the broad bioclimatic zones of life and the peasant lot on
Russian geography, and the Western "Deserts" and "Frontiers" on
American. What is difficult to comprehend is the relative absence of a
proper professional study of the phenomenon of urbanization from a
geographical point of view before the First World War. Although Britain
was the only one of the four countries reviewed here which was

predominantly urban throughout the period, it was an urbanizing age for the others, with expanding cities developing as centres of innovation and change, with a significance out of all proportion to their numbers. The idiosyncratic work of Geddes, who was never a "professional", though in many ways a "born", geographer represented the only serious geographical attempt to study cities in Britain. He was influenced heavily by regional and ecological methods developed in rural France, notably by LePlay, and his most influential geographical disciples in Britain — Herbertson and Fleure — were known for their regional and ecological approaches, rather than urban as such. But perhaps, after all, it is time, following the somewhat disembodied nature of much urban geography in recent years, to reassert the essential regional, ecological and political contexts within which our cities grow, disperse and decay. Jean Gottmann, squarely within the French regional tradition and its spirit in tune with the times, has shown us the way.

REFERENCES

1. Blache, V. de la (1917). "La France de l'Est." Paris.
2. Chisholm, C. G. (1899). "Handbook of Commercial Geography." London.
3. Geddes, P. (1915). "Cities in Evolution." London.
4. Hooson, D. (1968). The development of geography in Pre-Soviet Russia. *Annals A.A.G.* **58**, 250-272.
5. Kropotkin, P. (1885). What geography ought to be. *The Nineteenth Century* **18**, 940-56.
6. Kropotkin, P. (1899). "Memoirs of a Revolutionist." New York.
7. Kropotkin, P. (1902). "Mutual Aid: a factor in evolution."
8. Mackinder, H. J. (1887). The scope and methods of geography. *Proceedings, Royal Geographical Society* **9**, 141-60.
9. Mackinder, H. J. (1902). "Britain and the British Seas." London.
10. Mackinder, H. J. (1904). The geographical pivot of history." *Geographical Journal* **23**, 421-4.
11. Powell, J. W. (1882). Darwin's contribution to philosophy. *Proceedings, Biological Society of Washington* **1**, 60-70.
12. Robson, B. T. *In* Stoddart, D. R. (ed.) (1981). "Geography, Ideology and Social Concern." Blackwell, Oxford.
13. Semënov Tian-Shanskii, P. P. (ed.) (1896). "Istoria poluvekovoi deiatelnosti Imperatorskago Russkago Geograficheskago Obshchestva 1845-1895." St Petersburg.

14. Semënov Tian-Shanskii, V. P. (1910). "Gorod i Derevnya v Yevropeiskoi Rossii." St Petersburg.
15. Shaler, N. S. (1891). "Nature and Man in America." New York.
16. Turner, F. J. (1920). "The Frontier in American History." New York.

Chapter Seven

Urbanization and Population Change in Nineteenth-Century England

RICHARD LAWTON

In the great surge of interdisciplinary interest in historic population studies over the past twenty years, geographers have been mainly concerned with spatial analysis of change, especially through migration. Their work has been primarily descriptive in character, although Brian Robson's study of urbanization suggests the potentialities of a more analytical approach.[1] Regional accounts are few and mainly exploratory, while detailed studies of the underlying processes are relatively few and recent in origin. Yet the study of British nineteenth-century population is both of intrinsic historical value and also of contemporary interest to social scientists with a concern for the developing societies which are at present undergoing similar demographic, economic and social transitions to those experienced in Britain in the eighteenth and nineteenth centuries.

This chapter concentrates primarily on the effects of urbanization on the distribution and dynamics of population in nineteenth-century England, although the relationships between population change and some of the processes involved in the growth of a new mainly urbanized society are also discussed.

GENERAL POPULATION TRENDS

Following a period of little growth in the early eighteenth century, population growth accelerated to an estimated 0·66% per annum between

1740 and 1780 leading, in the 1780s to 1820s, to a phase of hitherto unprecedented population growth averaging 1·48% per annum in England and Wales.[2] Relatively high rates of growth were maintained until the end of the nineteenth century, although they slackened somewhat after 1851, and right up to the First World War increments were progressively greater averaging 338 000 per annum in England and Wales between 1871 and 1911. Cumulatively, the population of England increased fourfold from around 9 millions in 1801 to 36·1 million in 1911: this was indeed a demographic revolution.

There was a substantial reduction in general mortality from 32/1000 in the early eighteenth century to 22/1000 in the early nineteenth. An earlier, and perhaps higher, incidence of marriage from the late eighteenth century, especially in proto-industrial areas, saw crude birth rates increase to 40–41/1000 by the early nineteenth century compared with 35–36/1000 in the mid eighteenth and mid nineteenth centuries.[3]

From the 1830s, national rates of population increase slackened. Unhealthy conditions in urban and industrial areas prevented general improvements in mortality rates, which remained around 33/1000 until the early 1880s. Only with improved housing, sanitation and public health, and better scientific and medical knowledge, especially of infectious diseases such as cholera and typhoid, did the towns become safer places—especially for the working classes—a fact reflected in the rapid improvements in infant mortality after the turn of the century.[4]

A decline in the birthrate from the late 1870s initiated the third phase of the British demographic transition, with the results of birth control progressively reflected in the restriction in the size of middle-class families evident from the 1880s.[5] Fewer children were born, and there were fewer mothers bearing children in their late thirties and early forties. Restrictions in the employment of child labour from mid-century in both factory and field and, following the 1870 Education Act, compulsory education progressively prevented working class children from earning, while employment for women may have been a further disincentive to prolonged years of child-bearing. Whatever the cause, the average size of family fell from nearly 7 in 1860 to 3·5 in 1910 for women marrying young, although there are regional and class differences which would repay further investigation.

The general growth of population would have been faster in the mid and late nineteenth century had it not been for a small net loss by migration, which varied from 0·05 to 0·23% per annum between 1841 and 1910. Half the mid-Victorian emigrants were unskilled labourers, but by the late nineteenth century the proportion had dropped to one-third or less.[6] Indeed four out of five emigrants from late-Victorian Britain came from large towns and industrial areas and included a considerable and increasing proportion of skilled workers.[7]

These various demographic and structural changes led, first to changes in the age structure and, secondly, in the growth potential and size of the workforce. While lowering of mortality rates produced more people in the older age groups, a relatively high birthrate maintained a structure favourable to population growth.[8] Despite the national increase, patterns of demographic development and the structure of population varied considerably between regions due partly to differing rates of natural change, but more particularly to differential migration. From the 1830s population was increasingly drawn to the major towns and industrial regions, draining the countryside of their younger and more enterprising people and reshaping the population map of Britain.

The broad outlines of regional population change in nineteenth-century England are dominated by two main features. First, a relative and from mid-century absolute loss of population from the rural areas was accompanied by movement to the towns and industrial areas. These migrants provided much of the stock which produced high rates of natural growth up to the First World War and significantly shaped the demographic and social structure of our towns. Secondly, population shifted from the rural peripheries of Britain to the core of economic and demographic growth in the highly urbanized region from industrial south Lancashire-west Yorkshire through the industrial Midlands to Greater London and to industrial outliers such as South Wales and north-east England. These areas accounted for the bulk of England's population growth in the Victorian and Edwardian era and provided the framework for many of the regional population problems of the earlier twentieth century.

Early nineteenth-century England was still mainly rural, with over one-third of its population dependent on agriculture and spread throughout the country, the remoter uplands apart, at moderately high population densities of 405–805 per km² (100–199 per 1000 acres). By 1851, while some 50% of the population still lived in rural areas at densities of 809–1615 km² (200–399 per 1000 acres) throughout lowland England, only around one-fifth were engaged in farming. The 1851 census marked the peak of population for most rural communities in

Table 1 Urban and rural populations in England and Wales, 1801-1911

Census year	Total		Residual			Urban						
									Percentage of total in towns of			
	Million	Per-centage change	Million	Per-centage change	Per-centage of total	Million	Per-centage change	Per-centage of total	<10 000	10-50 000	50-100 000	>100 000
1801	8·9		5·9		66·2	3·0		33·8	9·9	9·5	3·5	11·0
1811	10·2	14·0	6·4	9·5	63·4	3·7	23·7	36·6	10·8	8·4	3·7	13·7
1821	12·0	18·1	7·2	11·7	60·0	4·8	29·1	40·0	11·0	9·2	4·3	15·6
1831	13·9	15·8	7·7	7·8	55·7	6·2	28·0	44·3	10·6	11·1	4·0	18·6
1841	15·9	14·3	8·2	6·2	51·7	7·7	25·0	48·3	10·0	12·1	5·5	20·7
1851	17·9	12·6	8·2	1·4	46·0	9·7	25·9	54·0	9·9	13·4	5·8	24·8
1861	20·1	11·9	8·3	0·5	41·3	11·8	21·6	58·7	9·8	14·1	6·1	28·8
1871	22·7	13·2	7·9	−4·5	34·8	14·8	25·6	65·2	10·8	16·2	5·6	32·6
1881	25·9	14·7	7·8	−1·5	30·0	18·2	22·8	70·0	10·5	16·0	7·3	36·2
1891	29·0	11·6	7·4	−5·0	25·5	21·6	18·8	74·5	10·2	16·2	8·6	39·4
1901	32·5	12·2	7·2	−3·3	22·0	25·4	17·5	78·0	8·9	18·0	7·4	43·6
1911	36·1	10·9	7·6	6·2	21·1	28·5	12·2	78·9	8·8	18·3	8·0	43·8

Based on Law, *The growth of urban population* (1967), Tables V, VI and XI. The urban category is based on three criteria: minimum size, density and degree of nucleation. Hence the "residual" category is not confined to purely agricultural rural areas. Estimates of the truly rural vary, some arguing that it was as low as one-third in 1841 and one-eighth by 1911: for a summary see Lawton, *Rural depopulation in nineteenth-century England* (1967).

England, though parts of upland Wales, south-west England and the
Pennines had begun to experience a fall in numbers in the 1840s. By
1911 massive depopulation had reduced rural densities often to below
their early nineteenth-century level and to less than 405 per km² (100 per
1000 acres) in peripheral regions. Moreover, only 8% worked on the

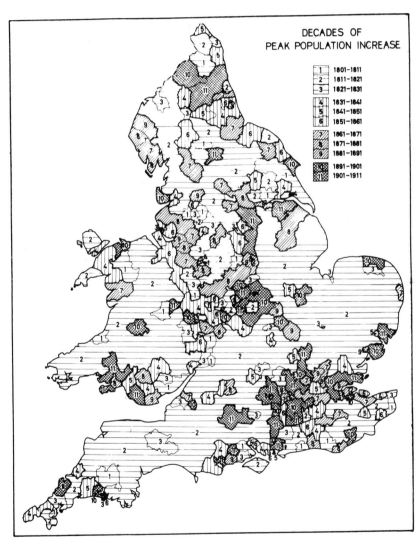

Fig. 1 Decades of peak percentage population increase in registration districts of
England and Wales, 1801-1911

land, many rural crafts and most rurally located industries of the mid-Victorian period had been lost to urban workshops and factories, and the trade which they generated was absorbed into growing urban areas.[10]

In the early nineteenth century rural areas grew almost at the national rate, but by the 1820s their population increase was scarcely half that level and little over one-quarter of that in the towns (Table 1). Moreover, rural increments fell to virtually nothing in the 1840s and 1850s. Despite often substantial natural increase the rural population of England and Wales fell by over one million between the 1861 and 1901 censuses, an inexorable process of depopulation partially arrested only with growing overspill from the large towns of Edwardian Britain. In contrast all size categories of towns recorded substantial and virtually uninterrupted increases between 1801 and 1911. The lion's share of that growth was in towns of over 100 000 population, leading to a progressive increase in the population: truly the Victorian era was "the age of great cities".[11] In contrast, the proportion of small-town dwellers fell in the late nineteenth and early twentieth centuries, whereas those in the middle ranges increased fairly sharply.

The pattern and timing of this progressive urbanization are reflected in the pattern of population increases in the various registration districts of England and Wales, 1801-1911 (Fig. 1). Population growth in most rural areas peaked in the decade 1811-1821. Except around the larger towns, where suburban expansion later extended into hitherto rural districts, and in some coastal areas, rural England was in demographic decline after 1831. The growing concentration of employment in urban areas and greater mobility aided by the railways, led to declining increments in agricultural areas from the 1830s and increasing out-migration led to a general fall in the population of the countryside after 1851.

In contrast, most of the larger cities—inner London, Birmingham, Bristol, Liverpool and Manchester for example—grew very rapidly in the late eighteenth and early nineteenth centuries to a peak of population increase in 1821-31, though successive cycles of suburban growth in the early and mid-Victorian period led to expansion into adjacent areas. The northern industrial cities peaked early, and their population expansion was limited after the 1880s. But in parts of the Midlands and south-east England city growth continued unabated in late Victorian and Edwardian times, especially in Greater London where the acceleration of suburban growth and the development of new-style industries attracted considerable migration from the growth areas of the early and mid-nineteenth century. These differing patterns of growth reflect a considerable shift in economic activity and substantial adjustments of population.

URBAN POPULATION TRENDS

The precise numbers of the urban population of nineteenth century England are difficult to estimate. Census definitions depend upon administrative status, which was subject to considerable change.[12] Hence it is impossible to give strictly comparable estimates of urban population trends. This problem has been approached in two main ways. First, in a series of studies of population changes in the nineteenth century Thomas Welton distinguished not only between urban and rural populations but also between "progressive" and "unprogressive" towns, "populous" districts (similarly sub-divided), and "sparsely peopled" and "other" rural areas.[13] A later analysis of the structure and components of change of population in registration districts of England and Wales yielded an elaborate classification of 14 categories of town, together with 5 divisions of the rural residues.[14] Slightly modified, this latter classification provided the framework for A. K. Cairncross's classic paper on internal migration in Victorian England, essentially an analysis of natural and migrational components of population trends in six types of town, in colliery districts and in the rural residues.[15]

A second approach partly rejects the purely legal, administrative definition of urban and rural populations in favour of one based mainly on the criterion of population size. The classic study of comparative nineteenth-century urbanization by A. F. Weber adopted a threshold of 5000 people within an administrative area for the calculation of English urban populations.[16] A modern estimate of urban population by C. M. Law is based on three criteria—population size, density and degree of nucleation—and is probably the most satisfactory yet devised.[17] Even so, this may well understate the size of the urban-focused populations in the growing rural-urban fringes of the large cities and conurbations of England and Wales in the late nineteenth and early twentieth centuries. Indeed in this, the most urbanized country in the world, one early twentieth-century estimate of the population of truly rural registration districts, excluding those at what were deemed to be urban densities (of over 300 per 1000 acres or 1215 per km²), was as low as 4·6 million or 12·7% of the 1911 total.[18]

Robson's comprehensive statistical analysis of the pattern and progress of urban growth in nineteenth-century England and Wales[19] uses a number of size-groups of towns based on Law's data. Robson shows that except in the smallest towns (under 5000 population) growth was general throughout the urban hierarchy, although it slackened in the largest towns after 1881. While there was individual movement up and down between size-categories and a growing concentration in larger centres, these trends did not significantly change the slope of the rank-size diagram. Nevertheless the patterns of change over time point to a series of regional systems of urban growth, rather than a single national system, though London came to dominate urban and population development from the turn of the nineteenth and twentieth centuries. These regional systems reflect distinctive phases of expansion in the British economy which are reflected in changing patterns of population development[20] and, especially, of inter-regional migration. The earlier decades of the nineteenth century were dominated by the northern textile towns and the Black Country; after mid century towns of south Yorkshire, Derby and Nottinghamshire grew rapidly, together with newly industrialized areas such as Teesside; by the late nineteenth century the towns and districts of South Wales and North East England were areas of prominent population growth but the major feature was the growth of metropolitan south-east England.[21]

Such shifts in the timing, location and relative strength of urban population movements are among the most powerful forces in regional demographic trends, both natural and migrational, in nineteenth-century Britain. Hence, the degree and pattern of urbanization is of particular significance to an understanding of regional population patterns and their underlying economic and social forces.

Robson's analysis shows in both cartographic and statistical terms that regional complexity in the timing and pattern of urban development precludes large-scale generalization: "At the national scale, it appears not to be the case that there were regions (or spatial sub systems) which underwent uniformly rapid growth during the nineteenth century".[22]

However, the *temporal* pattern of urbanization, with its distinctive regional and intra-regional contrasts in rates of population change in urban areas is of considerable importance to an understanding of regional demographic change. Friedlander's study of the spread of urbanization in England and Wales between 1851 and 1951 stresses the importance of the stage at which town-dwellers become dominant for changes in

Table 2 Levels of urbanization in England and Wales, 1851–1911

Census Year	Total population (000s)	Percentage urban according to:			Friedlander "urban counties"	
		Census[a]	T. A. Welton[b]	C. M. Law	Percentage population	No. of counties
(1801)	8893	24·2	39·1	33·8	—	—
1851	17 928	50·2	57·4	54·0	25·5	3
1861	20 066	54·6	60·7	58·7	32·5	5
1871	22 712	61·8	65·0	65·2	37·8	7
1881	25 974	67·9	67·1	70·0	52·7	11
1891	29 003	72·0	68·8	74·5	65·2	12
1901	32 528	77·0	79·4[c]	78·0	63·8	13
1911	36 070	78·1	80·7[c]	78·9	75·4	18

[a]*Census*, 1851 and 1911
[b]*J. Roy. Stat. Soc.* **63** (1900)
[c]*J. Roy. Stat. Soc.* **76** (1913)
[d]*Trans. Inst. Brit. Geogr.* **41** (1967)
[e]*Pop. Stud.* **24** (1970)

industry and in terms of the socio-economic consequences of urbanization.[23] He identified "predominantly urban" counties in which less than
the following proportion of the male workforce was engaged in
agriculture: 1851-81, 15%; 1891-1921, 12·5%; 1931-51, 10%. This
coarse measure undoubtedly understates both the national level and the
intra-county incidence of urban population (Table 2), but it underlines

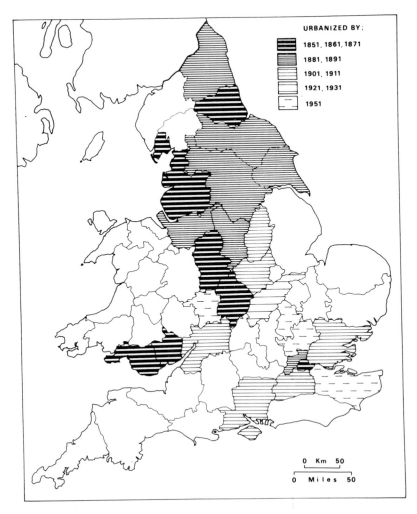

Fig. 2   Spread of urbanization by counties of England and Wales, 1851-1951

the relatively early urbanization of the industrial north, the Midlands and south Wales as compared with the slower and later urban dominance of south-eastern England (south of the Severn to the Wash) outside the Metropolitan region, and the continuing predominantly rural character of Cumbria and the majority of the Welsh counties (Fig. 2).

Regardless of the degree of urbanization, regional trends were consistently towards greater concentration of population. Welton's analysis of population progress between 1801 and 91 designated five types of district, using criteria of area (adjusted to the several census dates), population size and density.[24] The proportion of people living in towns of over 4000 increased nationally from 31·4% in 1801 to 50·5% in 1891, while those in small towns and populous areas grew from 13·4% to 18·2% and 9·1% to 12·2%, respectively. Most of his "northern" regions (that is north of the heavy boundary line in Fig. 4) were dominated by urban and populous areas, except for Cumbria and (in 1801) Wales and the Borders. In contrast, except for London the "southern" areas had large and, until the late nineteenth century, predominantly rural populations.

During the course of the century the proportion of the population living in towns, especially the larger ones, increased in all regions. According to Welton the rate of growth in urban and populous areas was above the national average throughout the northern area, except in Cumbria and north and east Yorkshire. But in all southern regions the equivalent increases were below the national level, even in the Metropolitan Circle, where the full impact of the spread of Greater London was largely experienced from the 1890s. Most of the urban increments were in areas described by Welton as "progressive", that is, sustaining substantial growth throughout this period, particularly in the larger towns and the many "new" towns and populous areas which grew rapidly after mid-century. These included mining communities in north-east England and south Wales, new industrial towns in the north-west, Yorkshire and the Midlands, and above all residential towns around London and the major provincial cities. In contrast over half the towns of less than 4000 population and a substantial number of older county towns labelled as "unprogressive" experienced relatively slow growth after the early nineteenth century. As a result, despite the "vast change in the territorial distribution . . . of our population since 1801", in the late nineteenth century consistent population growth was relatively restricted even in urban areas, as Welton correctly observed.

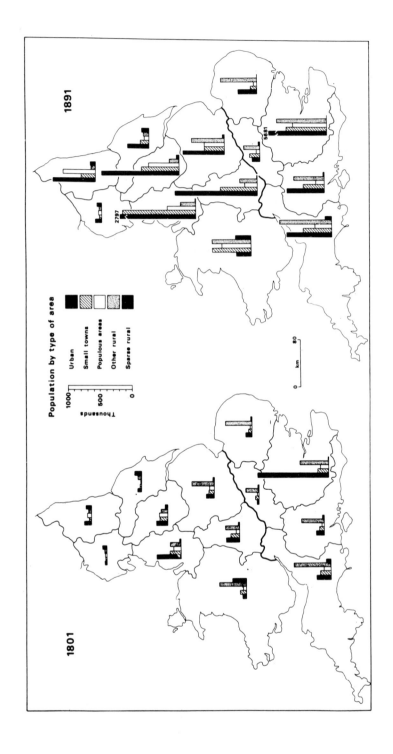

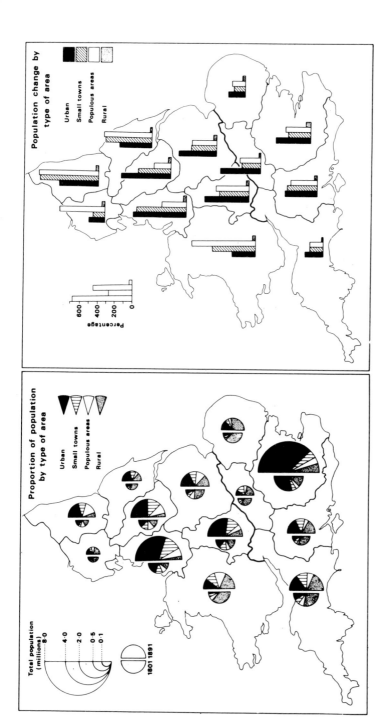

Fig. 3   Regional population trends in England and Wales by type area, 1801–1891

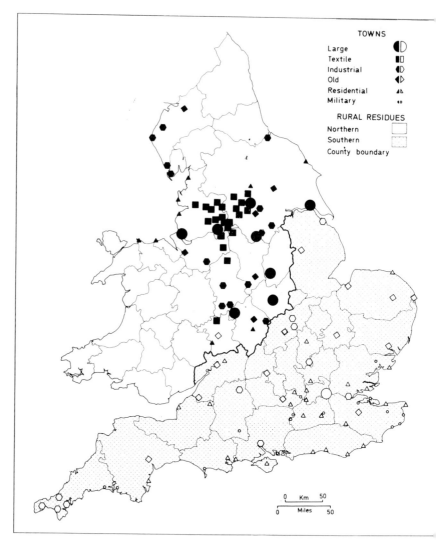

Fig. 4   Urban, industrial, residential and residual areas of England and Wales, 1891

Components of Urban Population Change

The differential levels of urbanization reflected in the broad regional trends outlined above betoken considerable shifts in population at both local and regional level. The extent to which these were the outcome of differences in levels of natural growth, whether due to fertility, mortality or differential migration, is a matter of continuing debate. The response of people to changing social and economic circumstances is complex. It affects marriage and family formation, standards of living, and exposure to ill-health and disease, and the propensity to migrate and the composition of migration streams. Migration is age- and sex-selective and also differs between occupations and social classes, thus producing a complex interplay between natural and migrational components of change.

Unfortunately there is little direct information on population migration in England and Wales prior to the first census question on place of birth in the 1841 Census of Britain and especially the greater detail from the 1851 Census. Moreover, the quality of parochial registration deteriorated in the early nineteenth century, especially in the large towns and industrial areas. Thus, despite the remarkable calculations of baptisms and burials by John Rickman published in the Parish Register Abstracts of the 1801–1841 Censuses and his retrospective calculations of eighteenth-century trends, the data for the study of regional birth and death rates are very unreliable before the 1840s. The techniques of back-projection developed by the Cambridge Group for the History of Population and Social Structure combined with their detailed estimates of birth and death rates for a large number of English parishes afford hope for more accurate analyses of regional demographic change in and prior to the early nineteenth century.[25]

However, the Deane and Cole tables of birth and death rates for the counties of England, which are based on the Rickman figures, give some idea of the components of regional population change in the early nineteenth century.[26] Much of the direct impact of early industrialization was on the countryside and was based on water power, handicraft and the family productive unit. From the 1780s, however, the pull of London, always strong, and especially of the major provincial capitals and seaports increased rapidly. Liverpool, for example, experienced an explosive period of growth from 34 407 people in 1773 to 53 853 in 1790 and 77 653 by the Census of 1801. Perhaps two-thirds of the 1790s increase was due to migration much of it from distant areas of Britain and from overseas. The rapidly growing textile areas of Lancashire and Yorkshire and of industrial Staffordshire attracted considerable numbers of migrants, mostly in a short-distance "wave-like motion" setting towards the towns.[27] Moreover, in the industrial towns and districts of the North and Midlands, early nineteenth-century prosperity may well have promoted more marriage, reduced the average age of marriage, and led to higher birth rates not least in the areas surrounding the major labour markets. Deane and Cole argue that while London and the inner areas of the large provincial towns depended on high in-migration to sustain their growth, much of the urban population growth in the industrial areas depended on relatively high rates of natural increase to which increased births and, perhaps, falling deaths both contributed. Nevertheless, net inward migration contributed substantially to urban growth in the West Midlands, the north-west, the West Riding and the north-east.

The systematic return of births and deaths under the Civil Registration Act of 1837 permits fuller analysis of the components of population change in England and Wales. Under-registration of births remained a problem up to the 1874 Act and may have been as high as 7% of the whole in the 1840s,[28] but in combination with fuller censuses from 1841, especially after the first really detailed census of 1851, civil registration permits reasonably accurate estimates of natural and migrational trends in some 623 registration districts. Unfortunately these administrative divisions, which cover areas served by Superintendent Registrars, do not easily permit separation of urban and rural populations. A number of large cities were served by more than one Superintendent Registrar and were often separated from suburbs which were returned in large, only partly urban registration districts. Many "new towns" of the mid nineteenth century were not separated from the larger districts in which they were embedded until mid or late Victorian times: Middlesbrough became a separate registration district only in the 1870s and Grimsby in the 1890s. Moreover, many smaller county towns such as Cambridge and Shrewsbury remained in or were amalgamated with their surrounding countryside. Welton has provided a suitable framework for analysis based on "an elaborate typology related to the 1891 registration district boundaries".[29] He allocated 133 registration districts to 13 types of urban area; the remaining districts were placed in 24 rural groups divided between a "residential" category and four regional categories (Fig. 4). This framework, slightly modified, provided the basis for A. K. Cairncross's calculations of the natural and migrational components of growth 1841–1911.[30]

Cairncross showed that despite fluctuations from region to region and town to town, urban growth dominated population trends in Victorian England (Table 3). Between 1841 and 1911 the towns accounted for over three-quarters of the total population increase in England and Wales.

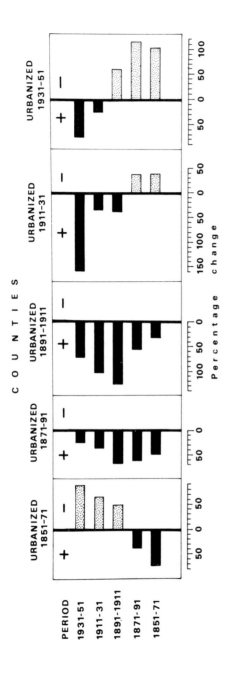

Fig. 5   Net migration in urbanized counties, 1851–1951

Table 3 Population trends by type-area in England and Wales, 1841–1911

Type of area	Total population (000s)		Components of change, 1841–1911						migrational change/natural change (%)	Percentage of total national change 1841–1911		
	1841	1911	natural total	natural %	migrational total	migrational %	total total	total %		natural	migration	total
1. TOWNS												
London	2261·5	7314·7	3802·3	168·1	+1250·5	+55·2	5053·2	223·4	+32·9	18·9	+6·2	25·1
8 large	1551·1	5191·8	2747·3	177·1	+893·3	+57·7	3640·7	234·7	+32·5	13·6	+4·4	18·1
22 textile	1386·7	3182·4	1705·8	123·0	+89·9	+6·5	1795·7	129·5	+5·3	8·5	+0·4	8·9
25 industrial	899·2	2520·9	1790·4	199·1	−168·6	−18·8	1621·7	180·3	−9·4	8·9	−0·8	8·0
20 old	954·6	2024·3	1076·0	112·7	6·1	−0·6	1069·7	112·1	−0·6	5·3	−0·0	5·3
35 residential	899·1	2329·1	962·4	107·0	+467·6	+52·0	1430·0	159·0	+48·6	4·8	+2·3	7·1
16 military	470·8	1212·4	616·6	131·0	+124·9	+26·5	741·6	157·5	+20·3	3·1	+0·6	3·7
Northern towns	4037·7	11 394·1	6370·0	157·8	+986·3	+24·4	7356·3	182·2	+15·5	31·6	+4·9	36·5
Southern towns	4385·3	12 381·5	6330·7	144·4	+1665·1	+38·0	7996·2	182·3	+26·3	31·4	+8·3	39·7
ALL TOWNS	8423·0	23 775·6	12 700·8	150·8	+2651·5	+31·5	15 352·5	182·3	+20·9	63·0	+13·2	76·1
2. COLLIERY DISTRICTS												
9 northern	1320·3	5334·0	3363·1	254·7	+650·5	+49·3	4013·7	304·0	+19·3	16·7	+3·2	19·9
3. RURAL RESIDUES	6165·8	6960·8	5302·0	86·0	−4507·0	−73·1	795·0	12·9	−85·0	26·3	−22·4	3·9
12 northern	2425·6	2875·1	2093·3	86·3	−1643·8	−67·8	449·5	18·5	−78·6	10·4	−8·2	2·2
12 southern	3740·2	4085·7	3208·7	85·8	−2863·3	−76·6	345·5	9·2	−89·2	15·9	−14·2	1·7
ALL AREAS												
northern	7783·6	19 602·9	11 826·4	151·9	−7·0	−0·1	11 819·4	151·9	−0·1	58·7	−0·0	58·6
southern	8125·6	16 467·2	9539·7	117·4	−1198·1	−14·7	8341·6	102·7	−12·6	47·3	−5·9	41·4
TOTAL	15 909·2	36 070·2	21 366·1	134·3	−1205·1	−7·6	20 161·0	126·7	−5·6	106·0	−6·0	100·0

The classifications in the table are T. A. Welton's groupings of registration districts as modified by A. K. Cairncross. 'The main change from Welton's classification is the division of the country into north and south, the dividing line being drawn roughly between the Severn and the Humber' (Cairncross, 1953, p.66).

The classifications used in the tables are as follows:

1. *Towns* (Cairncross, 1953, Table 13, p.67)

London

8 Large Northern: Birmingham, Hull, Leeds, Leicester, Liverpool, Manchester, Nottingham, Sheffield.

Textile towns

22 Northern: Ashton-under-Lyne, Blackburn, Bolton, Bradford, Burnley, Bury, Dewsbury, Glossop, Halifax, Haslingden, Huddersfield, Keighley, Kidderminster, Leek, Macclesfield, Oldham, Preston, Rochdale, Saddleworth, Stockport, Todmorden, Wharfedale.

Industrial towns

14 Northern: Barrow, Burton, Cockermouth, Crewe, Doncaster, Middlesbrough, Millom, Potteries, Rotherham, Rugby, Stafford, Walsall, Whitehaven, Wolverhampton.
11 Southern: Falmouth, Grimsby, Helston, Kettering, Luton, Penzance, Redruth, Southampton, Swindon, Tilbury, Wellingborough.

Old towns

7 Northern: Carlisle, Chester, Coventry, Derby, Northampton, Wakefield, York.
13 Southern: Bristol, Cambridge, Exeter, Gloucester, Ipswich, King's Lynn, Lincoln, Maidstone, Norwich, Oxford, Reading, Worcester, Yarmouth.

Residential towns

9 Northern: Blackpool, Harrogate, Leamington, Llandudno, Malvern, Morecambe, Rhyl, Scarborough, Southport.
26 Southern: Bath, Bedford, Bournemouth, Brentwood, Brighton, Cheltenham, Clacton, Cromer, Eastbourne, Easthamstead, Guildford, Hastings, Herne Bay, Isle of Wight, Maidenhead, Poole, Reigate, Southend, Staines, Thanet, Torquay, Tunbridge, Watford, Weston-super-Mare, Worthing, Uxbridge.

Military towns

16 Southern: Aldershot, Canterbury, Chatham, Colchester, Deal, Dover, Farnham, Folkestone, Godstone, Plymouth, Portsmouth, Salisbury, Sheerness, St. Germans, Weymouth, Windsor.

2. *Rural residues*: Counties are grouped into 12 Southern and 12 Northern, divided as follows (Cairncross, 1953, Table 18):

(a) Southern — Bedford, Berkshire, Buckingham, Cambridge, Cornwall, Devon, Dorset, Essex, Gloucester, Hampshire, Hertford, Huntingdon, Kent, Lincoln, Norfolk, Northampton, Oxford, Rutland, Somerset, Suffolk, Surrey, Sussex, Wiltshire;

(b) Northern — Anglesey, Brecon, Cardigan, Carmarthen, Caernarvon, Denbigh, Flint, Merioneth, Monmouth, Montgomery, Pembroke, Radnor, Cheshire, Cumberland, Durham, Hereford, Lancashire, Leicester, Northumberland, Nottingham, Salop, Stafford, Warwick, Worcester, Westmorland, Yorkshire.

The single biggest growth was that of London, with one-quarter of the national increase, which attracted 47% of the total urban net migrational gain. But the eight large provincial towns distinguished in the table — all of them northern — absorbed 18% of the national increase and 34% of urban net migration. Between them, London and the large provincial cities dominated the broad pattern of demographic change in Victorian England.

The development of other industrial towns was less spectacular. Indeed, in the group of textile towns identified by Welton, population grew only at around the national average, and over the period as a whole gains by migration were small. Following very rapid increases in the late eighteenth and earlier nineteenth centuries, many of the textile towns were net exporters of population from the 1880s, while some older-established heavy industrial towns, for example those of the Black Country, had passed their peak of growth by 1870 and thereafter experienced net migrational losses. However, without exception these "growth towns" of the industrial revolution continued to progress much more quickly than the twenty "old towns" (all older ports and county towns), the overall increases in which were below the national level, mainly owing to a relatively low rate of natural increase. In contrast, the overall growth of "residential towns", which include both older spas and watering places and newer seaside resorts, was some 25% above the national rate despite a relatively low natural growth. In these, as in the "military towns", it was migrational gain which accounted for their increasing share of the national population in the Victorian period. The fastest-growing areas of the late nineteenth century were by far the towns and mining communities of Welton's "colliery districts", in which very high natural increase of nearly twice the national level and substantial migrational gain combined to produce growth at 2·4 times the national level.

Two interesting aspects of demographic development suggested in Table 3 are the varied relationships between natural and migrational change in different *types* of area and the similarity of levels of population growth in the "northern" and "southern" areas defined by Welton and slightly modified by Cairncross (Fig. 4). Despite the commonly held view that — as in the eighteenth and early nineteenth centuries — population continued to shift progressively to the northern towns, there were almost identical figures of both urban and rural change in the two regions between 1841 and 1911. It was the rapid rise of the colliery districts which gave the north somewhat more rapid growth at this time. The dominance of London was a major factor in the south's urban growth, more than counterbalancing the continuing pull of the large provincial cities and newer centres.

The pattern of population growth in London and the large Victorian cities was determined by relatively high levels of natural growth and substantial migrational gains. However, in many other types of town— the textile centres, the old, the residential and the military towns— natural growth was relatively modest and below the national level, and the contrasts in their overall rate of increase was due essentially to varying migrational experience. One useful index of this relationship is the rate of migration to natural growth expressed as a percentage in Table 3. In contrast to heavy and persistent migrational losses which removed over four-fifths of the natural increment of the rural areas, the towns added a further one-fifth to their natural growth from net inward migration: indeed 70% of the above-average level of urban over national growth was due to migration as against only 30% from higher natural increase. Looked at in relation to the overall national increment 1841–1911, natural growth in rural areas accounted for 26·3% of the total compared with 63% in the towns and 16·7% in colliery districts: urban migrational gain contributed 13·2% of natural growth as against 3·2% in the colliery districts, but the level of loss in rural areas was 22·4% of the national increment.

These relationships varied a good deal from town to town and from time to time during the Victorian era. Table 4 summarizes my recalculations of the components of population change in some of the major types of town identified by Welton. They differ from those used by Cairncross and in Table 3 in a number of respects. First, the figures are for 1851–1911, because the under-registration of births seriously impairs the data in national change for 1841–51 and must inflate the figures of net migration which are derived from a comparison of natural and total increase in individual registration districts. Secondly, my classification differs from that used by Cairncross in several respects (see notes to Table 4).

Many of the main features of Table 4 are those identified by Cairncross: the similar rate of growth of northern and southern towns; the dominant role of large cities and the increasing relative importance of Greater London; the slow growth and low natural increase of old towns, especially in southern England. It also underlines the considerable range

Table 4 Demographic trends in selected groups of town 1851–1911

Type of town[a]	No. of registration districts	Population in 1851 (000s)	Components of change (nos in 000s)					
			Total	(%)	Natural	(%)	Migrational	(%)
London (Regn. County)	(14)	2708·8	4604·7	170·0	3634·0	134·2	+970·4	+35·8
9 large[b]	(35)	2156·1	3477·2	161·3	2839·7	131·7	+637·7	+29·6
22 textile	(24)	1643·4	1556·1	94·7	1529·1	93·0	+27·0	+1·6
14 northern industrial	(18)	747·2	1077·5	144·2	1282·1	171·6	−204·7	−27·4
8 southern industrial	(9)	230·8	395·1	171·2	335·3	145·3	+60·4	+26·2
15 in selected colliery districts	(15)	695·5	1488·3	214·0	1327·3	190·8	+161·3	+23·2
RESIDENTIAL[d]								
7 Greater London	(8)	135·3	258·6	191·1	146·3	108·1	+112·2	+82·9
6 spas	(6)	218·0	122·2	56·1	120·6	55·3	+1·5	+0·7
6 northern seaside resorts	(6)	156·5	282·0	180·2	150·0	95·8	+131·7	+84·2
14 southern seaside resorts	(17)	443·6	638·0	143·8	413·2	93·1	+224·8	+50·7
6 old northern	(6)	281·5	304·9	108·3	298·7	106·0	+6·2	+2·2
13 old southern	(19)	539·3	425·3	78·9	463·2	85·9	−38·1	−7·1
TOTALS								
Northern (73 towns)		5534·2	8006·6	144·7	7225·9	130·6	+780·6	+14·1
Southern (London + 47 towns)		4421·8	6623·3	149·8	5313·6	120·2	+1309·8	+29·6
OVERALL		9956·0	14 629·9	146·9	12 539·5	125·9	+2090·4	+21·0

[a]Based on the classification devised by T. A. Welton (1911)

[b]The 9 large towns include Bristol. The southern industrial towns exclude Falmouth, Helston and Penzance from those listed under Table 3

[c]The 15 towns selected from 3 colliery districts are varied in character and many could have been classified as industrial. They are: *North East coalfield* Newcastle upon Tyne, Tynemouth, South Shields, Gateshead, Sunderland, Durham, Hartlepool, Stockton, Darlington; *South Lancashire* Prescot, Wigan, Warrington, Leigh, Chorley; *South Staffs* Cannock

[d]Excluding Bedford

of natural growth between different types of town. In general, natural growth in London and the large cities was close to the overall urban rate: other types of town diverged considerably from it. The significantly lower level of natural growth in the textile areas contrasts markedly with the high rates in the northern industrial and colliery towns. Residential towns, especially the spas, had relatively low rates as did the older towns, particularly those of southern England.

Greater London, especially its residential towns, also had a substantial level of net in-migration. But the northern industrial towns, apart from those of the colliery districts, unable to retain all their high natural increment, experienced considerable migrational losses especially towards the end of the nineteenth century. In London and the large provincial cities most of the natural and migrational increase was focused on the suburbs. The rapid growth of seaside resorts, due mainly to migration, placed them among the fastest-growing towns of the later nineteenth century and reflects increasing accessibility to leisure facilities for a growing proportion of the urban middle classes and the more prosperous artisans.

Thus, while in the late eighteenth and earlier nineteenth centuries the north dominated urban growth in England and (London apart) received most of the rural-urban migrants, in the later nineteenth century many older northern industrial towns were exporting population, some overseas and some to southern towns, particularly in the Greater London area. Because natural increase in urban areas remained highest in the heavy industrial and coalfield areas of the north, the acceleration of urban growth in the south was to a considerable extent due to the changing pattern of net migration.

The details of decadal population change in individual towns (which are too bulky to reproduce here) show many interesting variations both between and within the major categories of towns in Table 4. Within the large cities the 1851–1911 natural growth ranged from 107% Manchester-Salford to 182% in Sheffield. While natural growth in Manchester and Liverpool (109%) was depressed by high mortality, Birmingham (176%), Hull (155%) and Leicester (151%) had a much better record. Except in Bristol, which lost 7·9% by net migration over this period, the range of migrational change in London and the larger provincial cities was relatively small (20·1 to 39·2%) except for Hull (56·5%). The dependence on high levels of migrational gain to sustain population growth which characterized the rapid urbanization of the early nineteenth century became less marked. Indeed, in the larger towns redistribution of population through residential movement to the suburbs produced greater internal contrasts in both vital and migrational rates than those between towns.

The significantly lower natural increase in textile towns as compared with other industrial centres may partly be attributed to their rapid growth in the early industrial revolution. However, much of the explanation lies in lower birth rates, especially in cotton-spinning towns in which there was a substantial dependence on female mill-hands. In older textile areas whose growth dates from the development of water powered mills Macclesfield (43%), Saddleworth (66%) and Todmorden (57%) had particularly low levels of natural increase. Moreover, in a number of larger textile towns (including Preston, Bury, Ashton-under-Lyne, Halifax and Huddersfield) there was a net loss by migration over the period as a whole, while in others, such as Blackburn and Bolton where natural increase was higher, the relative decline of textiles is reflected in migrational losses in the last two decades of the nineteenth century.

In contrast, the heavy industrial and mining towns were dominated by male employment and all had rapid natural increase due primarily to high birth rates. Middlesbrough, with only 40 inhabitants in 1829, and 2000 in 1862, when Gladstone described it as "an infant . . . but an infant Hercules", was exceptional. By 1911 there were 180 000 people in the area, with an increase of 558% in natural, and 204% in migrational growth since 1851. Moreover the natural growth in other towns in this group ranged from 130 to 269% between 1851 and 1911. The more recently developed—Rotherham, Doncaster, Hartlepool, South Shields and Gateshead for example—also had substantial net migrational gains (up to 97% over the period).

In contrast, older industrial towns such as those of the West Midlands, south Lancashire and west Cumberland experienced substantial migrational losses in the later nineteenth century: in the Potteries net out-migration between 1851 and 1911 was 26%, in Wolverhampton and Walsall 79% and 24%, respectively; in five urban areas of the south Lancashire coalfield there was an overall loss of 10·2% by net migration ranging from −23% in Wigan to +22·9% in Warrington, a reflection of the declining cotton industry of the former and the more varied metal-working and chemicals industries of the latter area.

In the later nineteenth century the southern industrial towns attracted newer industries and population moved to these new employment opportunities. With the exception of the declining Cornish mining centre of Camborne-Redruth, where natural increase was low and net migrational losses heavy, all towns in this group grew substantially, with migrational gains ranging up to 91% between 1851 and 1911. Moreover, this stimulated natural increase to levels comparable with those in the northern industrial areas: for example, 156% in Southampton, around 170% in mid-Northamptonshire towns and 239% in the railway town of Swindon.

Thus while general and large-scale movement, primarily of young adults, transferred much of the country's fertility potential to the towns, the individual urban experience varied in relation to the level and demographic and social structure of migrants. Increasing urbanization in Victorian Britain and a shifting balance of regional prosperity led to the progressive dominance of urban–urban migration and rural–urban movement and underlies the slowing down of migration to and growth of textile and older industrial towns and the increasing role of the colliery districts and the southern towns in English urban growth.

The extent to which cities grow principally by in-migration or by their own natural increase has been a question of continuing interest to demographers. Süssmilch believed that high urban mortality made migration essential for the growth of European cities in early modern times,[31] a view restated by Davis in 1965.[32] However, as urban mortality fell in the later nineteenth century, natural increase came to dominate except over short periods of very rapid increase. Migration is highly age-selective, so high levels of in-migration added considerably to natural growth potential, especially as health controls began to improve the mortality experience of English towns in the later nineteenth century. Nathan Keyfitz has recently calculated that with natural increase everywhere the same the role of migration in population growth progressively declines: the greater the level of migration the faster will be the fall in the migrational component of growth.[33] He showed that the predicted crossover point from dominant migrational to dominant natural increase, given particular levels of urban population growth and rates of natural change and net in-migration, are close to the actual experience at a macro-level: for example in a rural population of 10 million with a natural increase of 3% per annum and a net rural–urban migration of 2% per annum the crossover point would be achieved in 25 to 30 years.

Although it is impossible to apply Keyfitz's formula directly to the

Table 5 Crossover from dominant migrational to dominant natural increase in categories of urban area in nineteenth century England

Type of town	No. of registration districts	Crossover in decade[a]															
		Pre-1851		1851-61		1861-71		1871-81		1881-91		1891-1901		1901-11		Post-1911	
		No.	%	No.	%	No.	%	No.	%	No.	%	No.	%	No.	%	No.	%
London	52	16	8·4	6	3·1	6	3·1	1	0·5	7	3·7	1	0·5	6	3·1	9	4·7
Large cities	26	5	2·6	6	3·1	6	3·1	3	1·6	4	2·1	—		1	0·5	1	0·5
Old cities	8	6	3·1	—		1	0·5	—		—		—		—		1	0·5
Dockyard towns	6	—		—		6	3·1	—		—		—		—		—	
Resorts	18	10	5·2	1	0·5	—		—		—		1	0·5	—		6	3·1
Other towns	14	7	3·7	3	1·6	2	1·0	1	0·5	—		—		1	0·5	—	
Textile & potteries	24	19	9·9	2	1·0	1	0·5	1	0·5	—		1	0·5	—		—	
Heavy industrial	17	11	5·8	1	0·5	—		1	0·5	3	1·6	—		1	0·5	—	
Mining	26	15	7·9	4	2·1	2	1·0	2	1·0	—		2	1·0	—		1	0·5
TOTAL	191	89		23		24		9		14		5		9		18	
Percentage of districts		46·6		12·0		12·6		4·7		7·3		2·6		4·7		9·4	

[a]The crossover point is the decade during which natural growth began consistently to exceed migrational increase in the registration districts of the several types of town identified by T. A. Welton (1911). These categories are not directly comparable with those in Table 4, but are similarly defined.

more complex situation of nineteenth century England where natural rates varied considerably from area to area and patterns of internal migration were complex, the concept is useful in dating the phase at which dominant migrational growth gave way to dominant natural growth in the population growth of various types of town (Table 5). By mid-Victorian times the growth of most towns was already dominated by natural growth. In nearly half the registration districts defined as urban by Welton natural increase exceeded migrational gain before 1851. In the absence of precise vital statistics before 1837 we do not know exactly when this occurred, but in many industrial towns, including the textile towns, natural growth exceeded migrational increase by the 1840s. In London and the large cities the unhealthiness of the inner areas delayed their crossover to the 1860s or 1870s, by which time there were heavy losses of population to the residential suburbs. Here and in the residential towns, especially around London (in 30 out of 51 districts) a high level of net in-migration dominated growth into the twentieth century. Similarly in the suburban districts of the large cities, 15 out of the total 26 districts were largely supported by migration up to the later nineteenth century, while seaside resorts, especially of Wales and northern England, depended more on migration than on their generally modest natural growth up to the early twentieth century.

NATURAL TRENDS

The question thus arises as to the extent to which the level of natural change (which differed considerably from one type of town to another) was caused by variations in mortality, or in fertility, or in a combination of vital trends. Secondly, to what extent was the trend towards greater demographic self-sufficiency in many towns of Victorian England due to reduction in death rate, especially in large industrial towns?

Fertility

Despite high urban mortality, which did not begin to fall substantially until the 1880s, natural growth was above average in most large cities and industrial towns. Selective migration of younger adults provided the potential for high birth rates in "progressive towns" of continuous and rapid growth. However, the vital experience of towns varied considerably, both regionally and between different types of town: moreover, birth rates often varied more between different areas and social classes of individual towns than between towns. For example, in the highly urbanized county of Staffordshire the ratio of decadal increase from births to the national rate was substantially higher than that for deaths, ranging between 6·27 percentage points in 1841–51 and 11·29 (1871–81). Even Liverpool, where death rates were commonly 50 to 100% higher than the national level and held back natural growth, birth rates were usually above the national average: in the suburban registration district of West Derby, though the ratio of deaths to national levels exceeded that of births by 11·47 percentage points in 1841–51, by the late nineteenth century birth ratios (reflecting high birth rates) exceeded death ratios. Thus, though in most large cities high mortality was "the major factor in differential natural growth until the late nineteenth century",[34] urban fertility differentials repay close examination.

Robert Woods has recently shown that there are substantial variations in levels of standardized marital fertility between registration districts of England and Wales.[35] In 1861 the highest levels were found in both semi-rural and urban areas, especially in mining and heavy industrial districts. In contrast many textile towns, the higher class suburbs of large cities (notably West London) and smaller towns especially in southern England had low marital fertility. Local contrasts often exceeded regional and, though the rural/urban fertility differential widened with the fall of rural births in the later nineteenth century, considerable variation in fertility remained between rural areas and between different types of town and the major urban/industrial regions of England.

Woods's analysis bears out A. F. Weber's belief that the level of births was "almost universally higher in city than in country"[36] by the mid nineteenth century. This he ascribed to a more youthful population and generally higher marriage rates. Welton also pointed to the urbanward flow of young adults and families reflected in the migrational gain of the 20- to 30-year-old male age groups and 15- to 30-year-old women in the large towns, of 20- to 35-year-olds in mining areas and of 25- to 35-year-olds in the industrial districts. Another aspect of this question, the higher marriage rates of towns and industrial districts and the earlier marriage in colliery and heavy industrial areas, was reflected in the transfer of women of marriageable age to London and the Home Counties, to mining districts, and to the East Midlands and Yorkshire and—to a lesser extent —the West Midlands and north-west.[37]

In the later nineteenth century, fertility differentials were partly due to patterns of nuptiality, partly to family size. From the 1870s the latter was increasingly influenced by family limitation. Although the social and economic forces underlying this led to earlier fertility decline in Greater London and the south than in mining and heavy industrial regions, they did not fundamentally change the contrasts in fertility between different regions and types of locality over the transition period from the 1870s to the late 1920s.[38] Thus Welton could point to a clear urban/rural contrast in fertility ratios (births per 1000 women under 45) in the 1880s and 1890s and to considerable variations both within individual towns and between different types of town.

In the major survey of changes in fertility in England and Wales from 1851 to 1931 carried out by the Population Investigation Committee, David Glass showed that the gross reproduction rate (female children born to women of 15-49) varied substantially over space and time, both regionally and between and within rural and urban areas.[39] The highest rates throughout the decades from 1851-1911 were in the mining and heavy industrial counties, with Durham, Monmouth, Glamorgan and Staffordshire consistently in the upper quartile of values. A second group of counties consistently above the median for each decade and sometimes in the upper quartile were among those identified by Friedlander as urbanized by 1891: Northumberland, North Riding, Derby, Nottinghamshire and Warwickshire, together with Flint (Fig. 2); only four "rural" counties—Brecon, Radnor, Huntingdon and Leicester—appear in this relatively high fertility group. In contrast, some "urbanized" industrial counties such as Lancashire, Cheshire, London and the Home Counties had consistently moderate or low fertility. While this group also contained most rural counties, especially of southern and south-west England and mid Wales, there were some eastern (Cambridge, Norfolk and Suffolk) and south Midlands (Bedford, Buckingham, Berkshire) counties where fertility fell sharply from relatively high levels up to 1871 as their potential was diminished by heavy and persistent out-migration.

Reproduction rates in urban areas ranged even more widely than between counties. The highest were in the colliery and heavy industrial areas: such county boroughs as Gateshead, South Shields, Sunderland, West Hartlepool, Middlesbrough, St Helens, Warrington, Barnsley, Dudley, Walsall, Smethwick, West Bromwich, Merthyr, and Swansea were in the highest urban fertility group from 1871 to 1911. The large towns showed considerable contrasts: Liverpool and Bootle, Stoke and

Hull had high reproduction rates, but Bristol, Leicester and Leeds were among the lowest. However, most suburban satellites (for example, Wallasey and, especially, around Greater London) were in the low fertility group, along with the textile towns of East Lancashire and West Yorkshire, most "old" towns (for example, Norwich, Worcester, Oxford and Exeter) and residential and resort towns, old and new and in both the south and the north.

Mortality

Many areas of high fertility also had high mortality, notoriously so the large cities. In contrast, the mortality rates in most rural areas and small towns, were below the national average. Despite the general decline in mortality from 22·50 in the 1860s to 15·38 in the 1900s, the urban black spots in London, the industrial north and Midlands, and many of the colliery districts remained until the late nineteenth century. Moreover, the mortality of the older urban dweller and of infants did not decline until the turn of the century.[40] Consequently, mortality contributed more than fertility to contrasts in regional and inter-urban patterns of national change.

William Farr estimated that in the 1820s mortality rates ranged from 17·8 per thousand in Suffolk to 30·3 in Middlesex for men and 17·9 (Sussex) to 25·3 for women. The worst figures were for London and a number of industrial counties—Durham, Lancashire, Cheshire, Staffordshire and (for women) Worcestershire. The worst levels for urban mortality, 1813–30 in six large towns, greatly exceeded the county levels. However, as general mortality began to fall from mid Victorian times, mainly due to improvements among children of 5-10 years and younger adults (10-25 years), the gap between best and worst widened considerably, particularly due to very high infant mortality and deaths of older people in the urban black spots.

McKeown has demonstrated that 92% of the mortality decline between 1848 and 1901 came from the fall in disease carried by micro-organisms, principally airborne disease (44%) and from infected water and food (33%).[42] This points to the significance of environmental factors (sanitation, water supply, housing, etc.) and social factors linked to these and to living standards in mortality decline in the nineteenth century rather than medical and scientific advances. The larger industrial towns in particular lagged behind in health improvement. Despite the gathering momentum of the Sanitary Reform movement following Edwin Chadwick's report on the *Sanitary Condition of the Labouring Population* (1842), the Royal Commission on the health of towns (1843) and the Public Health Act of 1845, it was not until the systematic development of public health areas under the 1872 Act that significant general improvements were made in health and living conditions in urban areas.

The gap between the "Healthy Districts" and the "Poor Districts" was reflected in successive Annual Reports of the Registrar-General. Even in the 1880s average expectation of life for males was only 28·8 years at birth in Manchester, compared with the national average of 43·7 and 51·5 in healthy areas. David Glass has pointed out a similar gap in male life expectation in the 1840s between Liverpool (25 years) and Surrey (44 years), while even in 1911-12 there was a gap of nearly nine years between the county boroughs (47·5) and the rural districts (56·3), with London (49·5) and other urban districts (51·9) also relatively adversely placed.[43]

Specific mortality rates for all ages and both sexes expressed as ratios of the national rates ranged widely between urban and "county" registration districts: 139·5-58·0 for male children, 0-4 years and 144·0-55·7 for female; 157·1-61·5 and 159·6-66·9, respectively, in ages 45-54 years, the widest differences; and 122·7-74·7, and 124·2-78·0, respectively, for the 'best' age group of 15-24 years.[44] Moreover, then and throughout the Victorian era the levels of mortality at virtually every age were higher and the decline in death rate slower in the northern industrial towns than in the rural areas, especially of the south. In a study of life insurance records for 1846-1848 (a sample of 266 633 persons and 2243 deaths), Henry Ratcliffe showed that expectation of life varied by 13·7% at age 20 years between rural and city areas over 30 000 population, the gap increasing to 23·7% at 56 years and 36·5% at 70 years.[45] He also stated that "the worst vitality" for those aged 20 years and older was in Glasgow and Liverpool, followed by Sheffield, north London and Birmingham. Lancashire towns were worse than urban areas in general and, with the exception of West Yorkshire, selected "rural areas" were better than any town. Similarly E. H. Greenhow's study of mortality in 105 of the 623 registration districts of England and Wales, 1848-54, confirms the bad record of large towns which he attributed to poor sanitation and water supply and to overcrowding.[46] Death rate varied between 36 per thousand in Liverpool to 15 per thousand in Glendale, Northumberland, while the upper quartile of the range included the registration districts of Liverpool, Manchester–Salford, Leeds, Newcastle upon Tyne, Hull, Sheffield, the Potteries, Wolverhampton, Birmingham, Nottingham, Leicester, Bristol and London, and a few smaller industrial towns, such as Wigan, Macclesfield, Coventry and Merthyr. With the exception of North Witchford (Cambridgeshire) all were urban and were statistically associated by Greenhow with high population density, the proportion in industrial occupations and—at a county level—the percentage of urban-dwellers.

In his analysis of comparative mortality in the 1880s Welton argued that migration of mainly young adults of 15–35 from country to town partly concealed the full range of the rural/urban mortality gap: for example, the most favourable age-specific mortality ratios for men were in the 15–24 year age group, 124 in Manchester to 90 in healthy areas; but these increased to 134–74 in ages 0–4 years and 157–62 for ages 45–54 years. In this and his subsequent analysis of the 1880s and 1890s Welton stressed the comparatively high death rates of large cities, some northern industrial areas such as the Potteries, the textile towns, and the heavy industrial centres of the north and Midlands. However, in many older towns, large southern towns and, especially, in resorts and residential places mortality was around or below the national average. Nevertheless, despite clear contrasts between different types of town and the remarkable gap between mortality in the large cities in which, up to the 1880s, life expectancy was little over half that of the healthy districts for men and around 60% for women, the regional patterns of mortality were complex. Woods has recently shown that the high mortality and low life expectancy in London and the large cities and mining towns was not typical of many smaller industrial towns (for example in the textile areas) or of suburban and residential districts.[47] Nor was there a universal rural/urban gap, for mortality in some rural areas was relatively high up to mid-Victorian times. By the late nineteenth century despite some reduction in the large cities, improvements lagged behind those in rural, small-town and suburban areas. Hence there were marked local variations in mortality, reflecting sharp contrasts in social, economic and environmental conditions.

These are highlighted by contrasts in child and infant mortality which was slower to respond to improvements in health, especially in the urban areas. Welton's mortality ratios for ages 0–4 years in the 1880s show a wider range than in most other age groups, ranging from 139·5–58·0 for boys and 144·0–55·7 for girls in 23 types of urban and industrial area and

14 county rural remainders. The highest rates, up to twice and seldom less than one and a half times those of the rural districts, were in large towns, colliery and northern industrial districts. The range of infant mortality was even wider and the general rate remained almost unchanged up to the 1880s. A precondition to this was, in the view of one contemporary, an improvement in "social conditions of people and their sanitary surroundings".[48] In 1890 the ratio between infant mortality between Liverpool registration district (one of the worst in the country) and "healthy districts" increased progressively from 150·3 in the first month of life to 492 between 9 and 12 months, for which the Liverpool ratio was nearly three times the national level. Housing and social conditions were the main factors in the very high mortality from respiratory and zymotic diseases. Indeed in the 1880s infant mortality in Peabody Trust housing was 14% below the general London level. However, poor care and feeding of infants were perhaps a major factor in zymotic disease and were also reflected in the high level of violent deaths among infants associated with drunkenness in Liverpool, Birmingham, Newcastle upon Tyne, Manchester, and some of the northern industrial towns. Neglect, often associated with poverty, illegitimacy and early marriage, were associated with the many social factors behind these adverse urban statistics.

MIGRATION

Although migration contributed significantly to urban population growth, its effects varied considerably in space and time. The ratio between natural and migrational change in all urban areas and colliery districts, 1841–1911 (Table 3) was 4·1:1 ranging between 4·8:1 for London and the large cities, which together accounted for 80·9% of the total urban migrational gain, and −10·6:1, involving a net migrational loss, in industrial towns. The high ratio of 2·1:1 in the residential towns was due principally to their rapid late nineteenth-century growth. Such relationships varied considerably from decade to decade, though there were few places where migration exceeded natural growth for periods of over twenty or thirty years. Thus, while natural trends were the major force in long-term urban trends, short-term fluctuations in migration reflect inter- and intra-regional fluctuations in economic and urban growth.

In broad terms the curve of migrational change in counties classified by decades of urbanization (Fig. 2) suggests that, while net gains persisted over a century, phases of relatively rapid gain (that is over 2·5% per annum) were confined to 40- or 50-year periods (Fig. 5). For example, the counties of early urbanization included London and many of the large cities where decadal growth peaked between 1821 and '31: by the 1870s these were losing population to their suburbs and satellite towns. Over the period 1851-1911 (Table 4) in no one group of towns did migration exceed natural growth. In the 121 towns studied migration dominated growth in only 20 of their 204 registration districts over the period as a whole, 15 in suburban London and 5 in provincial cities. Most textile towns lost by migration, only Oldham, Burnley, Blackburn and Stockport having substantial migrational gains, while the northern industrial towns were mainly areas of out-migration. Even though migrants continued to move to such "new towns" of the industrial north as Middlesbrough and Rotherham and to the new industries of southern towns, there were few in which migration was dominant by the later nineteenth century. Colliery districts, characterized by early marriage and large families, owed their rapid growth principally to natural increase though in the north-east coalfield (as in South Wales) towns grew rapidly up to the First World War.

The ratio of natural to migrational growth in the types of town summarized in Table 4, and in individual centres is instructive. The ratio for all towns of 6:1 agrees closely with that from the Welton-Cairncross analysis, but ranged from 1·6:1, a high proportion of migrant to natural increase, in residential towns to 80·4:1 in spas, a very low proportion, while despite low natural increase the decline of attraction to textile towns is reflected in a ratio of 56·4:1. Moreover, some major groups had quite large negative ratios usually arising from substantial migration losses: for example −6·26 for northern industrial towns and the very high −121·6:1 in old southern towns.

The major reason for these varied relationships between natural and migrational growth was that despite the enormous growth of urban population during Victorian and Edwardian times natural increase provided the main component of growth except for relatively short periods of time when new towns or suburbs would be nurtured by in-migration of young adults. As urban mortality improved in the later nineteenth century, the previous need for migrants to replace those lost by excessive mortality gradually disappeared and populations became largely self-sustaining. Moreover, the local impact of economic cycles

Table 6 Migrational trends in registration districts in England and Wales, 1851-1911

Decadal migration trends	All districts		Urban areas (as listed in Table 4)						All towns	
	No.	Percentage	Large towns	Textile	Industrial	Colliery	Residential and resort	Old	No.	Percentage
Gain throughout	53	8·5	24	1	3	—	7	—	35	19·9
Loss throughout	316	50·9	2	5	3	—	1	4	15	8·5
Gain followed by loss	63	10·3	12	3	5	8	3	7	38	21·6
Loss followed by gain	92	14·8	5	2	4	—	11	5	27	15·3
Fluctuating	96	15·5	6	12	12	7	15	9	61	34·7
TOTAL	620	100	49	23	27	15	37	25	176	100

and changes in the fortune of key industries contributed to substantial fluctuations in net migration.

Brinley Thomas has argued that overseas migration is a sensitive index of British economic conditions.[49] Internal migration similarly reflects local responses to national conditions and is a good indicator of long-term shifts in regional growth. In decades generally of economic growth (for example 1861-1880 and 1890-1901) levels of internal migration were high but when growth was relatively weak (as in 1881-1890 and 1901-1910) internal migration slackened and emigration particularly to North America increased. As the growth of many older industrial towns slackened, migrational gain was replaced by loss, for example in the Black Country, in east Lancashire and west Yorkshire, and in the older mining areas (Table 6). In contrast the "new industries" of Greater London, the East Midlands and some older towns (for example Coventry) and many residential towns and resorts moved into migrational gain in the late nineteenth and early twentieth centuries. Only in London and the large cities was net in-movement continuous throughout Victorian times, although this was associated with large-scale losses from city centre to suburb. The complexity and responsiveness of population to changing circumstances, however, is reflected in the fact that in over one-third of the registration districts analysed in Table 6 migration fluctuated between net gain and loss, often with wide swings in numbers.

This complex ebb and flow of movement and the relative briefness of phases of migrational dominance are reflected in two aspects of mobility. A qualitative analysis of the number of decades in which migration exceeded natural increment in the 204 registration districts of the urban areas analysed in Table 6 suggests, on the one hand, the relative fewness of such periods and, on the other, the limited number of towns involved (Table 7). Because the 1880s mark a distinct change in national and regional population trends in England and Wales (see above), these are classified for two periods: mid Victorian (1851-81) and late Victorian and Edwardian (1881-1911). Up to the 1870s London and the large provincial cities grew mainly by migration, but thereafter this was confined to their suburbs. In contrast very few districts in the textile and northern industrial towns were dominated by migration, especially in the later nineteenth century. By then the areas of predominant migration were mainly in the newer resorts and residential towns, and despite a considerable *volume* of migration to the large northern towns, the main

Table 7   Decadal dominance of migrational growth in urban areas, 1851-1911

| Type of town | No. of registration districts | Decades during which migration exceeds decadal natural growth in registration districts | | | |
| | | 1851-1861 | | 1881-1911 | |
		No.	%	No.	%
London[a]	43	53	41·1	29	22·5
Large[b]	34	23	22·5	12	11·8
Textile[c]	23	4	5·8	1	1·4
Industrial northern	18	6	11·1	1	1·9
Industrial southern	9	1	3·7	3	11·1
Colliery[c]	15	6	13·3	0	—
Residential and resort northern	8	4	16·7	12	50·0
Residential and resort southern	29	15	17·2	26	29·9
Old northern	6	1	5·6	1	5·6
Old southern	19	2	3·5	3	5·3
Total northern	100	43	14·3	27	9·0
Total southern	104	72	23·1	61	19·6
TOTAL	204	115	18·8	88	14·4

[a]Includes 29 in London registration county and 14 in adjacent districts of Middlesex, Surrey, Kent and Essex.
[b]Includes one "southern", Bristol with 4 districts.
[c]All textile and colliery towns are "northern".
Percentages are related to the total number of decades in the 204 districts studied (i.e. 612 for each period) and similarly for each of the several types of area.

targets of inter-regional movement were Greater London and the towns of southern England.

Net migration is a resultant of a complex of movements on which the only information for the nineteenth century comes from census birthplace tables which show only lifetime migration—the place of residence for those born in various counties and, for 1911, towns—at particular censuses but not the actual migration between censuses.[50] By the mid nineteenth century over one-quarter of the population of London and all large provincial towns had been born outside the county in which they were enumerated; in Birmingham and Manchester it was over one-third and in Liverpool nearly one-half. Moreover in most towns the proportion of in-migrants was relatively high, apart from some old towns and, in particular, the textile towns most of which were in the 15–25% bracket. In the 1911 census birthplaces are also given for county and municipal boroughs and urban districts of over 50 000 population for most of which non-local lifetime migration was over one-third of the enumerated population. However, there were wide differences between the relatively lower level of non-natives in London and the big cities and many older industrial towns (particularly in the Black Country and the textile areas) and the very high proportion of 50 to over 80% in newer resorts and the rapidly growing residential towns in the conurbations, particularly around Greater London.

Although much of this high level of lifetime migration resulted from suburban overspill from overcrowded early Victorian cities aided by growing mass transit systems, it also reflected significant changes in regional prosperity. Indeed in London, Birmingham and a number of northern industrial towns the proportion born in those towns living elsewhere exceeded in-migration. Estimates of county inter-censal migration, taking into account mortality and re-migration among lifetime migrants,[51] shows marked changes in the areas and level of net gain (Fig. 6). The areas of high and persistent gain were limited to Greater London and the South Wales coalfield. Lancashire and Yorkshire, with a mix of large cities, textile and heavy industrial towns, had moderate but fluctuating gains though this was reversed in Lancashire in 1901–11. The west Midland counties lost by migration almost consistently from 1861, partly owing to high urban natural growth, but also reflecting relative economic decline and a progressive shift of industrial and population growth to the south-east.

The changing pattern of such movements are extremely complex. Up to mid Victorian times much internal migration was a short-range "displacement of the population, which produces 'currents of migration' setting in the direction of the great centres of commerce and industry".[52] By the late nineteenth century the emphasis was switching towards inter- and intra-urban migration, and much of the latter was short-range, residential movement. Excluding migration between non-adjacent counties, the most important migration streams between 1851 and 1911 were towards Glamorgan and Monmouth, and to London and the Home Counties.[53] Hence, despite intermittently significant streams—to Nottingham and Derby from the rural east Midlands, to Warwick and Stafford in the 1850s, to Flint in the 1850s and 1900s, and to Durham—the targets for major long-distance movement were few.

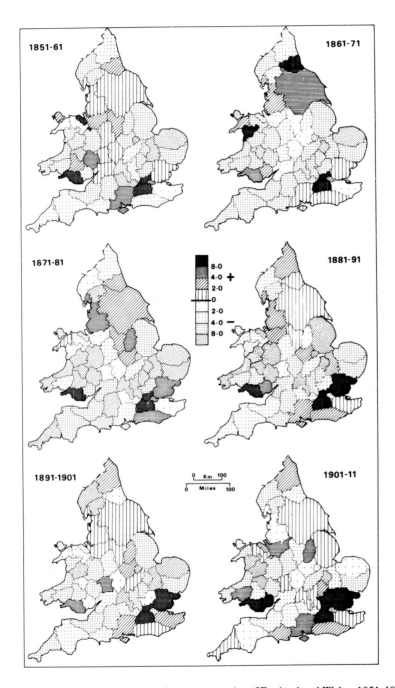

Figure 6 Decadal net migrational change in counties of England and Wales, 1851–1911

Nevertheless, in addition to its influence on fluctuations in growth, differential migration had a considerable impact on both population structure and vital trends. Weber commented on the higher level of female migration to larger towns, much of it short-range, which was reflected in the F:M ratio per 1000 of 1116 for London and 1090 for all urban sanitary districts as compared with the national ratio of 1064.[54] Evidence on age-selective migration is limited. Tabulations for lifetime migrants between selected counties in the 1911 census shows that few of those who had moved to London were under 20 years of age but there were substantially higher proportions than in the population as a whole especially in ages 25–44 years both in the county of London, and in Essex and Hertfordshire.

Welton's estimates of net migrational change by age for urban areas listed in Table 3 show considerable gains in 1881–1900 in the 15–34 year and over-65 year groups. In the old towns the gains were mainly of young women and in all older ages. In heavy industrial and coalfield towns the largest gains were of men under 35 years and of women 25–40 years. In residential towns the major gains were of younger women, 15–24 years (many no doubt in domestic service) and of older people. However, as Brinley Thomas has shown, by the later nineteenth century the attraction of many older industrial towns for younger adults (20–44 years) was diminishing.[55] The extent to which the towns continued to attract young adults at an active phase of family formation was vital to both their short-term growth and their longer-term growth potential.

In different types of town and in individual districts within large towns in particular, the level and nature of migration influenced not only the occupational, social and cultural character. An understanding of the demographic processes shaping nineteenth century urban growth depends on detailed studies of particular localities to aid interpretation of the general trends outlined in this essay.[56] These must be built up from local information on health, mortality and family patterns contained in contemporary social surveys, such as Charles Booth's classic account of *Life and Labour of the People of London*, reports of Medical Officers of Health, and the associated ward and registration sub-district statistics.[57] In addition these must be matched with the variables on age, household structure, occupation and birthplace available for individuals from enumerators' books of the 1841–1881 censuses.

A brief example from nineteenth-century Liverpool must suffice.[58] The parish registers of the late eighteenth and early nineteenth centuries reveal one of the most explosive phases of growth in any modern British city. In the 1790s the population of Liverpool grew by 40% (some 22 000), perhaps two-thirds of which was due to migration.[59] From 77 653 in 1801 the Borough's population increased to 286 487 in 1841, due principally to rapid in-migration. Despite a high birth rate, increasing mortality kept natural increase to moderate levels in the crowded inner city and dockside wards where, from the 1840s, death rates were twice those of the suburbs even in "healthy" years and not uncommonly were three to four times as great. This was reflected in one of the highest mortality rates in England, ranging from 31 per 1000 in the 1830s and 1840s to 71 per 1000 in the Irish famine and typhus epidemic year of 1847. Despite better sanitation and improving public health from the 1870s, mortality was consistently one-quarter to one-third above the national rate throughout the years 1850–1910 and the gap between healthier suburb and crowded slum often two and a half times. In epidemic and intestinal disease Liverpool's mortality was one and a half times the national rate and in chest diseases 60% higher. Both were reflected in very high child and infant mortality which accounted for 40 to 60% of deaths in mid Victorian times.

Thus the rapid growth of population to 493 405 in 1871 owed more to migration than natural growth, a migration gain of 211 685 in Liverpool's three registration districts as compared with 96 992 natural increase. Despite very high mortality among many of the poorest immigrants, it was their large growth potential which between 1871 and 1911 raised the borough's population to 746 421, with a natural increase in the three registration districts of 138 330, compared with a migrational loss of 14 950, most of which was accounted for by dispersion of population from city centre and older suburbs to the outer residential areas. Birthplace statistics, adjusted for mortality, suggest a migrant flow of almost 60 000 to Liverpool in every decade between 1851 and 1911 except the depressed 1880s.

In 1851, when 49·4% of Liverpool's population was born outside Lancashire, there were already large culturally, economically and socially distinctive migrant groups within the city: Irish-born formed 22·3% of the borough's population, Welsh 5·4% and Scots 3·7%. A 10% sample of households from the 1871 census enumerators' books confirms the demographic, occupational and social distinctiveness of different migrant groups. The Irish, dominated by semi-skilled and unskilled workers, were strongly clustered on dockside areas and experienced high fertility and mortality rates. The Welsh and Scots tended to have smaller families and were relatively more numerous in skilled manual and non-manual work. A number of groups of long-distance migrants from other parts of England seem to be associated with particular skills: for example those from Birmingham and the Black Country with metal manufacturing and dealing or machine manufacture. Such occupationally selective migration provided an important feature of inter-urban movement often associated with residential clustering, especially among culturally or socially distinctive groups of migrants which left a lasting impression on the social make-up of many English towns.

CONCLUSIONS

In nineteenth-century England urbanization was a major force in demographic, economic and social change. Although urban population trends had much in common and contrasted markedly with those in rural areas, they exhibit a wide range of responses to national economic and social change. Thus there are marked and persistent contrasts in fertility between regions and between different types of town, which in combination with mortality differentials, also persisting over long time periods, produced very different levels of national change. The broader the scale of analysis, both temporally and spatially, the more important seems the contribution of natural trends to population change. Both at regional and sub-regional level and between different individual towns and types of town, migration was often the dominant element in short-term fluctuations in population trends as individuals and localities responded differently to changing economic social or environmental conditions. Moreover, the selective nature of migration shaped future population trends.

Despite long-standing interest in the nature of the British demographic transition and the impact of industrial and urban development on demographic and social change, there remain many unanswered questions on their precise inter-relationships. From the late eighteenth to the early twentieth century urban growth in England and Wales broadly follows Gibbs's five-stage model of population concentration.[60] His second stage, the more rapid growth of urban than rural population, was reached in the early nineteenth century; from mid century rural population declined (Stage 3), followed by the decline of small towns and continuing movement to large cities (Stage 4); Stage 5, a move to more even spatial distribution, is reflected in late nineteenth/early twentieth-century dispersal of population from large cities to residential suburbs and satellite towns of expanding city regions, a process which may still be active in the so-called "de-urbanization" of the 1960s and 1970s.

However, within this general framework there are substantial differences in the time scale over which the stages operate and in the levels of vital and migrational change, regionally and between different types of town.

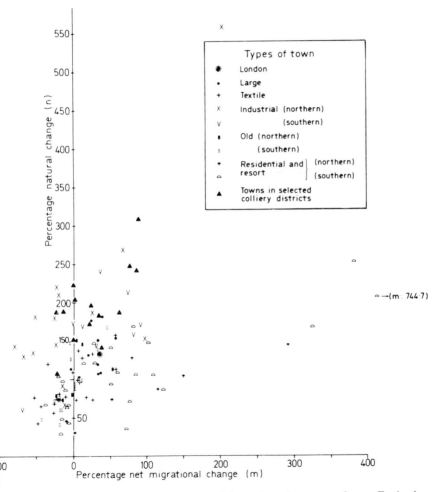

Fig. 7   Natural and migrational components of change in various types of town, England and Wales, 1851-1911

In this study, based mainly on registration and census data from the 1840s, we capture only part of the story, and much basic research on the vital period from the late eighteenth century remains to be done. Nevertheless, the varying patterns for 1851-1911 are suggestive (Fig. 7). There were only a few towns—mainly residential and newer resorts—where migration exceeded natural growth over this period. The steep angle of the grouping of industrial and colliery towns indicates their dependence mainly on natural change, some of which in older towns of high natural growth was being shed by out-migration. The modest overall increase in many textile towns was more closely balanced between natural gain and migration loss, while older towns too rarely experienced migrational gain and, with low natural growth, their increases were generally low.

Within those distinctive groupings there were, moreover, substantial differences in population trends between and within individual towns, reflecting economic, social and class differences. Explanation of differing demographic responses to similar *general* factors requires not only the application of more sophisticated demographic analyses and better classifications of the components of population change but also a fuller appreciation of the impact of economic, social and behavioural processes on population behaviour in particular localities. The studies essential for this are still very few, despite the lead given by nineteenth-century medical officers of health, social investigators, and government enquiries, but are essential for a better understanding of urban population trends and behaviour than that offered in this broad and somewhat speculative review.

REFERENCES

1. Robson, B. T. (1973). "Urban Growth: an approach." Methuen, London.
2. Wrigley, E. A. and Schofield, R. S. (1981). "The Population History of England 1541-1871. A reconstruction." Edward Arnold, London.
3. Habakkuk, H. J. (1971). "Population Growth and Economic Development since 1750." Leicester University Press, Leicester.
4. McKeown, T. (1976). "The Modern Rise of Population." Edward Arnold, London.
5. Banks, J. A. (1954). "Prosperity and Parenthood." Routledge and Kegan Paul, London.
6. Thomas, B. (1972). "Migration and Urban Development." Methuen, London.

7. Erickson, C. J. (1972). In "Population and Social Change" (D. V. Glass and R. Revelle, ed.). Edward Arnold, London. 347-81.

8. Marsh, D. C. (1965). "The Changing Social Structure of England and Wales 1871-1961" (revised edn.). Routledge and Kegan Paul, London.

9. Lawton, R. (1977). In "Regional Demographic Development" (J. Hobcraft and P. Rees, ed.). Croom Helm, London. 29-70.

10. Graham, P. A. (1892). "The Rural Exodus." Methuen, London.

11. Vaughan, R. (1843). "The Age of Great Cities, or Modern Society viewed in relation to Intelligence, Morals and Religion." Jackson and Walford, London.

12. Lawton, R. (1978). In "The Census and Social Structure" (R. Lawton, ed.), Frank Cass, London. 82-141.

13. Welton, T. (1900). *J. Roy. Stat. Soc.* **63**, 527-89.

14. Welton, T. (1911). "England's Recent Progress." Chapman and Hall, London.

15. Cairncross, A. K. (1949). *The Manchester School* **17**, 67-87: Reprinted in "Home and Foreign Investment 1870-1913" (1953), 65-83.

16. Weber, A. F. (1899). "The Growth of Cities in the Nineteenth Century. A Study in Statistics." The Macmillan Company, New York.

17. Law, C. M. (1967). *Trans. Inst. Brit. Geogr.* **41**, 125-43.

18. Bowley, A. L. (1914). *J. Roy. Stat. Soc.* **77**, 597-652.

19. Robson, B. T. (1973).

20. Deane, Phyllis and Cole, W. A. (1967). "British Economic Growth 1688-1959" (2nd edn.). Cambridge University Press, Cambridge.

21. Lawton, R. (1978). In "An Historical Geography of England and Wales" (R. A. Butlin and R. A. Dodgshon, ed.). Academic Press, New York and London. 313-66.

22. Robson, B. T. (1973). op. cit. 126-7.

23. Friedlander, D. (1970). *Pop. Stud.* **24**, 423-43.

24. Welton, T. A. (1900). *J. Roy. Stat. Soc.* **63**, 527-89.

25. Wrigley, E. A. and Schofield, R. S. (1981). op. cit.

26. Lawton, R. (1977). op. cit.

27. Redford, A. (1976). "Labour Migration in England 1800-1850." (3rd edn. ed. and rev. W. H. Chaloner). Manchester University Press, Manchester.

28. Glass, D. V. (1973). "Numbering the People." D. C. Heath Ltd., Saxon House, Farnborough.

29. Welton, T. A. (1911). op.cit.

30. Cairncross, A. K. (1949). op.cit.

31. Süssmilch, J. (1740). "Die göttliche Ordung. Berlin.

32. Davis, K. (1965). *The Scientific American* 213.

33. Keyfitz, N. (1980). *Geogl. Analysis* **12**, 142-156.

34. Lawton, R. (1978). op.cit., 349.

35. Woods, R. (1982). "Theoretical Population Geography." 112-30. Longman, London.

36. Weber, A. F. (1899). op.cit. 331.
37. Welton, T. A. (1911). op.cit.
38. Brass, W. and Kabir, M. (1977). *In* Hobcraft, J. and Rees, P. (ed.), op.cit., 71-88.
39. Glass, D. (1938). *In* Hogben, L. (ed.). "Political Arithmetic. A symposium of population studies. Allen and Unwin, London. 161-212.
40. Woods, R. (1979). "Population Analysis in Geography." Longman, London. Ch. 4.
41. Farr, W. (1837). "Vital Statistics" *In* J. R. McCulloch (ed.) "A Statistical Account of the British Empire." London. Ch. 4.
42. McKeown, J. (1976). "The Modern Rise of Population." Edward Arnold, London.
43. Glass, D. V. (1964). *In* J. Ferguson (ed.). "Public Health and Urban Growth." Centre for Urban Studies, University College London. Report No. 4.
44. Welton, T. A. (1897). *J. Roy. Stat. Soc.* **60**, 33-80.
45. Ratcliffe, H. (1850). "Observations on the rate of Mortality and Sickness existing amongst Friendly Societies." George Faulkner, Manchester.
46. Greenhow, E. H. (1858). "Papers Relating to the Sanitary State of the People of England." General Board of Health, HMSO, London.
47. Woods, R. (1982). *J. Hist. Geog.* **8**, 373-94.
48. Jones, H. R. (1894). *J. Roy. Stat. Soc.* **57**, 1-103.
49. Thomas, B. (1972). *"Migration and Urban Development."* Methuen London.
50. Baines, D. E. (1978). *In* "Census and Social Structure" (R. Lawton, ed.). 146-64.
51. Friedlander, D. and Roshier, R. J. (1966). *Population Studies* **19**, 239-78.
52. Ravenstein, E. G. (1885). *J. Stat. Soc. of London* **48**, pp.167-227.
53. Friedlander, D. and Roshier, R. J. (1966). op.cit.
54. Weber, A. F. (1899). op.cit.
55. Thomas, B. (1972). op.cit., Ch. 2, App. B.
56. Lawton, R. (forthcoming) in A. M. D. Phillips (ed.) "Victorian Staffordshire" offers a detailed study of population trends and migration.
57. *For example* Woods, R. (1978). A study of mortality in Birmingham. *J. Hist. Geog.* **4**, 35-56 and his ongoing work on local variations in fertility and mortality in England and Wales.
58. Lawton, R. and Pooley, C. G. (1976). "The Social Geography of Merseyside in the Nineteenth Century: Final Report to the SSRC." Mimeo, Liverpool.
59. Laxton, P. *Trans. Hist. Soc. Lancs. and Cheshire* **130**, 73-113.
60. Gibbs, J. P. (1963). *Economic Geog.* **39**, 119-29.

Chapter Eight

Conserving the Heritage: Anglo-American Comparisons

DAVID LOWENTHAL

Preserving the tangible inheritance has become an increasingly popular cause. On both sides of the Atlantic, older buildings attract growing appreciation. Devotion to historic ancient buildings—as distinct from concerted protection of them—emerged sooner among the British, enamoured of their ancient cultural heritage, than among Americans impatient of the shackles of tradition and the dead hand of the past. And Britain is justly renowned for scrupulous stewardship of its patrimony. A humid, temperate climate, religious iconoclasm, and the Industrial Revolution have all been inimical to the survival of physical artefacts, yet the remains of Britain's earthworks and castles and abbeys are "probably more solicitously cared for and elaborately displayed than anywhere else in the world", in one professional's view.[1] Together with historic houses and churches, this legacy comprises what has been termed England's most important contribution to European culture, and the income that legacy generates from visitors, native and foreign, who come to see history on the ground, is crucial to the British economy.[2] Yet recent conservation efforts in Britain have commanded less support and achieved less success than in America.

These and other disparities in heritage care stem from historical, geographical, economic, and cultural differences, some of them of such magnitude as to vitiate comparisons. One is the division of attention between urban and rural relics. A much greater proportion of the treasured British heritage lies in the countryside. Although four out of five Britons now live in towns, a traditional rural bias, exemplified in upper-class residential preferences, places major emphasis on the conservation of parish churches, country houses, and village buildings. By comparison, urban centres are neglected. A study in 1965 identified 324 British towns whose historic quality required urgent attention in the face of threatened redevelopment, but the only resulting action was four exemplary case studies.[3] The gutting of city centres for redevelopment and motorways went on without effective opposition from 1950 until the early 1970s. Except for parts of London and a handful of small tourist-oriented historic centres — Bath, York, Chester, Oxford, Cambridge — little has been done to secure the historic fabric of most British cities, and virtually nothing in such major urban centres as Manchester, Liverpool, and Birmingham, until quite recently not even thought of as "historic". Only in the late 1970s did the risk of demolition to Liverpool's Lyceum and Albert Docks make people aware that these cities had anything historically worth saving. Although it is the official and widely held view that protection of rural buildings has lagged behind that in towns because redevelopment pressures made urban priorities imperative, conservation in many ways systematically discriminates against British cities. Most of the redundant churches saved by grants or by conversion to new uses, for example, are in rural or historic town parishes; in London and Manchester, Liverpool and Leeds, demolition has been their more usual fate.[4]

Pro-rural sentiment in Britain is a consequence of urbanization and urban rootlessness. The parental or grandparental roots of a high proportion of city-dwellers are in the countryside. Massive displacement has intensified the commonly professed revulsion for urban forms and institutions and the nostalgia for countryside locale and community. Most Britons consider the countryside their rightful heritage. The "return to a rural place" has been seen as the appropriate reward for successful service in urban industrial England. In Raymond Williams's words: "The birds and trees and rivers of England; the natives speaking, more or less, one's own language: these were the terms of many imagined and actual settlements. The country, now, was a place to retire to." Williams's *The Country and the City* exposes the Arcadian fallacies that have led generations of Britons to idealize the rural scene. Yet even Williams congratulates his compatriates on helping to keep Britain "still in so many places a beautiful country", with much of its cultivated land better kept and its wild land made more accessible than ever before.[5]

Americans too have a history of anti-urban sentiment. Cities were traditionally viewed as seats of sin and corruption; to keep state legislators pure, many state capitols were located in small towns. But Americans have more generally sought and celebrated city life, and few great dwellings or showplaces embellish their countryside.[6]

In neither Britain nor America has rural nostalgia helped to preserve the landscape itself, as distinct from its wild life and artefacts. Birds and flowers on the one hand, tools and furnishings on the other, largely enlist British countryside activism. Landscape features like ancient hedgerows and ridge-and-furrow field patterns are eligible neither for historic listing nor for protection. The 1947 Town and Country Planning Act uniquely exempts farmers and foresters from planning controls on the use of their land, and hence leaves them free to destroy historic landscape features. And despite Williams's rosy portrait of a well cared for and accessible countryside, modern agricultural technology and government financial incentives have within the past two decades replaced much of lowland Britain's variegated patchwork quilt of small fields and pastures, interlaced by hedgerows, with an uninterrupted and featureless prairie landscape devoid of traces of the past.[7]

Landscape protection in the United States remains outside the mainstream of historic preservation for quite different reasons. The National Parks system, Wilderness Areas, and Wild and Scenic Rivers Act protect sizeable tracts, although extractive mining and forestry remain potent threats and over-crowding in many places makes the concept of "wilderness" a mockery. But concern for wild country extends only marginally to non-virgin lands valued simply because they are open (that is, undeveloped) and hardly at all to landscapes valued for the legacy of human history. Devotees of wilderness, of open space, and of historic landscape features represent three separate constituencies.[8]

Landscape preservation is, however, beyond the compass of this chapter. The special circumstances that cause Britons and Americans to neglect or cherish their countrysides involve considerations quite distinct from those that apply to the built environment. They can be touched on here only where they cast light on preservation attitudes in general.

How then does preservation in these two nations differ? In Britain, an inherited emphasis on country houses, the prolonged endurance of an ancient heritage, a more extensive and hence burdensome stock of older buildings, and tax structures that penalize rehabilitation alike animate and qualify conservation. In America, modern revulsion against earlier rejection of the past, public participation in neighbourhood rehabilitation, a widespread awareness that preservation saves energy and materials and helps create jobs, and tax benefits that favour adaptive use all generate exuberant support for preservation and shape the character it takes.

This chapter explores what these circumstances imply for conservation problems, strategies and results. I begin by surveying the recent growth of preservationist sentiment, go on to examine transatlantic differences in the selection and use of what is conserved, and conclude by considering the traits that Britain and America share. Neither country is homogeneous, to be sure; but regional and local differences are here discounted so as to focus on larger national differences. Moreover, I sometimes use "America" as a short-hand for the United States and "British" to signify preponderantly English traits and legislation.

One common trait the two countries lack is an accordant terminology. By and large Americans use "preservation" to mean what the British refer to as "conservation"—although in both countries "conservation" also commonly involves natural resources. "Preservation" in Britain is a restricted term, meaning to stabilize a structure at a point in time; in America "preservation" covers the broad spectrum of attitudes and actions toward stability *and* change usually termed "conservation" in Britain.[9]

Even more than words, concepts of what is "old" and "historic" divide the two countries. With their much shorter history (as distinct from pre-history), Americans view both nature and the very recent past—a past within their own remembered lifetimes—as "historic". For most Britons, "historic" refers neither to nature nor to events within living memory.

THE RISE OF PRESERVATION SENTIMENT

One of the most striking phenomena of modern times is the attention devoted to the tangible heritage, notably to buildings. In the United States the number of local preservation groups has doubled within the past decade and now exceeds five thousand. Less than a generation ago, preservation was a labour of love among a few rich *cognoscenti*; although still disproportionately genteel, the cause now seeks ardently to enlist blue-collar Americans and ethnic minorities.[10] Rehabilitation accounted for 54% of all United States construction activity in 1980, and four years previously the editor of *Progressive Architecture* judged "work with older buildings perhaps the most rapidly expanding area of activity within the profession today"; few architectural firms lack preservation projects.[11] Almost two-thirds of a recent Harvard College alumni class were engaged in restoring old houses—an avocation that graduates twenty-five years previously had deemed highly eccentric.[12]

In Britain buildings officially listed as of "special architectural or historic interest" numbered over 300 000 in 1982, a figure projected to double by about 1985, when they will comprise more than 3% of the total building stock. England also has 5100 Conservation Areas, implying some measure of protection for a large proportion of historic cities and villages. Britain's 1500 ancient monuments, old churches and cathedrals, and historic houses and gardens regularly open to the public rank first in visitor popularity; receipts from the foreign 28% of 49·5 million paid visits (some £66 million in revenue) contribute substantially to the UK balance of payments.[13] Preservation sentiment and legislation have stimulated the training of craftsmen in old vernacular skills and located supplies of compatible materials for use in repair and renovation.

The reasons for this upsurge of interest in the tangible past I have elsewhere explored at length and can only summarize here.[14] We need the familiar; without reminders from the past we could not function in the present. Old structures and artefacts affirm our sense of identity through continuity with forebears, enrich our life by making memory and history vivid, and provide a desirable contrast with, if not a refuge from, the new.

Although popular concern with preservation is largely a post-war phenomenon, it is rooted in Renaissance admiration of classical precepts, in the search for origins and heritage of early nineteenth century nation-states, and in a medley of contemporaneous perspectives that profoundly altered individual consciousness—intense curiosity about newly re-discovered ancient sites and artefacts, romanticism and the cult of ruins, the rise of the historical novel, the perception of life as a career and awareness of childhood, the older view of people of the past as essentially like today's being replaced by an awareness of and an emphasis on the precious uniqueness of each epoch and culture. All this transformed old buildings, previously valuable mainly as exemplars and ready sources of materials for new structures, into monuments to be preserved for symbolic or aesthetic reasons. Protective legislation, first introduced in

Germany in 1818, had spread to most European countries by the end of the nineteenth century.[15]

Widespread public involvement in preservation, however, stems from the post-war pace of technological and social change and rising apprehension about the present and the future. The impact of rapid change is no new phenomenon; witnesses of the French Revolution saw history proceeding at a dizzying pace, and the environmental effects of the Industrial Revolution alarmed many Victorian observers. But the visible alteration of the environment in recent decades brooks few comparisons with earlier times. War and technology have left many urban landscapes quite unrecognizable, and the pressure of development, together with the mania for modernization, has devastated more historic structures than ever before, partly because it is now mechanically easy to demolish even the sturdiest buildings.

The artefacts of everyday life vanish along with the building fabric of the past. Modern machines and material abundance make clothing and crockery, cars and computers, ever more quickly obsolete and disposable. The things we use, like the buildings around us, pass through our lives at an accelerating pace. Social change and migration likewise deprive us of familiar environments; few older Britons or Americans inhabit environments that look much like those of their childhood.

Change is not only swift and comprehensive, it is now often seen as unfortunate or ominous. The old have always looked back with regretful fondness on the days of their youth, but the current malaise goes beyond valetudinarian grumbling. Doubts about what lies ahead seem pervasive. It is hard to recall that less than a generation ago the idea of progress was taken for granted in both Britain and America. Science and technology, democracy and limitless resources, would yield the promised land. And faith in the future led many to dismiss the past as backward or negligible. The overwhelming emphasis at the 1876 Centennial celebration in America was on new machines, inventions, ideas; Americans were obsessed with the glorious progress made since the bad old days. By contrast, every celebration at the 1976 Bicentennial looked back with nostalgia, seeking to re-enact or recreate a land of lost content.[16]

Loss of faith in the future has shed new lustre on the past. Beyond the depletion of resources, the spread of pollution, the decline of industrial might, the rise of social unrest, the erosion of moral values loom fears of ultimate ecological or nuclear disaster. Not least have modern architecture and planning appeared to let us down. The Brave New World on both sides of the Atlantic has left high-rise slums, urban deserts and showpiece buildings less livable, for all their vaunted functional efficiency, than their highly decorated precursors. Disillusionment with modernism was the more intense in Britain, where post-war planners promised a phoenix from the ashes and where modern architecture proved singularly unprepossessing. In the United States, the conspicuous failure of grandiose urban-renewal schemes coalesced with public outcries against environmental degradation, with fuel and energy crises, and with the nostalgic advent of the Bicentennial.[17]

Those disillusioned by the present now take comfort in older structures—even in structures associated with less agreeable aspects of the past, such as slave quarters in the American South and nineteenth-century factories in the north of England. "This affection for the symbols of earlier and unpopular progress" arises, suggests the chairman of Britain's Central Electricity Generating Board, because

> we are living in an acutely uncertain age . . . Because of rapidly advancing technology and social and other trends, we are experiencing perpetual change in almost every aspect of our daily lives. . . . People's capacity to absorb [such change], particularly in an age of international uncertainty and tension, is becoming strained. Does their regard for old buildings, therefore, denote not simply nostalgia but a rational hunger for some degree of permanence? . . . reassurance from solid, everyday, familiar things?[18]

Nowhere is approval of the past and aversion to the present stronger than in England. As recently as 1957, William Holford's judgement that "it would be a sad day for this island if the preservation of the past were to be regarded as more important than building for the future" typified his generation's faith in progress; "seldom", comments a journalist, "has there been a more complete, or a more rapid, reversal in public attitudes".[19]

The view is reiterated that "old buildings are all fine, sound, sensible, full of character; new buildings ugly, shoddy, unfit for purpose and anonymous". Selwyn Lloyd complained he could not "think of a single modern building I like"; Bernard Levin called London's modern architecture "hopeless", "completely devoid of distinction", "strenuously vile".[20]

Attachment to an idealized past merges with English chauvinism. Back in a Suffolk pub after an American sojourn, two English writers met "an affable old countryman" who

> had never in his life been more than five miles away from the village. Nevertheless, "Back home again, eh?" he cried. "Ah, you got to go a long way to beat old England, eh?" and his words set up in our minds a train of thought that culminated in the concept of 'phogy', . . . that stout spirit of British phlegm in which the artificial stands superior to the real, the traditional to the new . . . The phogy is half fogy, half phony — phony because there is a structure of tradition and pretense in the phogy. . . . Add a touch of the word 'foggy' and you have our meaning. It was natural enough to be nineteenth century in the nineteenth century, and anyone could do it, but in the twentieth it takes quite a lot of toil.[21]

Outdated scenes and artefacts are treasured no less for demanding effort. "I've got fond of it", explains the owner of a nineteenth-century mangle in Penelope Lively's novel, *Treasures of Time*.[22] "If a thing is nice to look at *and* reasonably functional — *and* old — then isn't it worth sacrificing a bit of convenience?" "It's posh to like old things", says a knowing youngster in the same writer's *Road to Lichfield*.[23] "Antique furniture and houses with beams everywhere, and vintage cars. And old maps. Dead posh. It shows you've got nice taste". Belief in the superiority of the past, nostalgic affection for the old, have become deep-seated and influential English traits.[24]

The English are not alone in preferring olde England; foreign visitors also venerate its antique flavour. "The *prime* reason we come", one American explains, "is to experience what is left of the Past".[25] Trekking from the Tower of London and Westminster Abbey to Windsor, Stratford, and Oxbridge, York, Canterbury, and Bath, they seek out an England devoid of the twentieth century or even the nineteenth. England, as Henry James said, is full of places to "lie down on the grass in forever, in the happy faith that life is all a vast old English garden, and time an endless English afternoon".[26] James was referring to Oxford undergraduates, but he wrote from an American perspective.

American visitors are one key to the vital distinction between English and American appreciation of the past. The English are fundamentally attached mainly to the past of their own country (though this includes many relics and borrowings conceived in Greek, Egyptian, Chinese and other styles). No less nationalistic about their heritage Americans long rejected rather than revered the English past; up to and even beyond the end of the nineteenth century English relics of antiquity aroused painful ambivalence at best.[27] But much of the past that Americans now revere is *in England*. Whether or not of British extraction, they all claim roots there. Shakespeare's Stratford may be an especially American place of pilgrimage, but the whole pre-industrial English cultural landscape in fact forms part of the American heritage.

PRESERVATION AIMS AND ACHIEVEMENTS

Britain's wealth of historical relics is both a benefit and a burden. To be in Britain is to feel saturated by time, the present resonating with a long human past; many people, native and foreign, gladly pay to experience this sense of continuity and of return to roots. But income from tourism hardly begins to maintain the immense stock of antique structures; and British residents resent their role as heritage honeypot hosts. They also suspect that emphasis on the past, glorious or quaint, may deter modern innovation; "the image of history and Beefeaters", a government spokesman told SAVE Britain's Heritage, "was making it difficult for British exporters to sell our goods abroad".[28] Veneration of the past might ultimately lead to preserving an England valueless save as a relic.

Tourism's compensatory worth is only rarely appreciated. "Shudder as we may, perhaps the creation of a living history book in this clutch of islands is not so bad a prospect", the MP Andrew Faulds suggested. He envisaged Britain's future as

> a sort of Switzerland with monuments in place of mountains . . . to provide the haven, heavy with history, for those millions . . . who will come seeking peace in a place away from the pulsating pressures and the grit and grievances of their own industrial societies. . . . Already millions of visitors flood in . . . to gape and marvel at our heritage. Should we not be doing our utmost to enhance it?[29]

But few in Britain seem to concur with him, or to relish the prospect of becoming a nation of museum attendants.[30]

American appropriation of the British heritage helps to compensate for the fact that relatively little of the past survives in America. When Americans want to experience the past they come to England; at home, aside from occasional excursions to the never-never lands of Williamsburg and Disney World, they live emphatically in the present. To cite a theatrical analogy, a British actor asked to play a Shakespearian role steps back into the past with ease, whereas an American actor feels at home only in a present-day role and is self-conscious in the past. "The one society relates best to the past," concludes a critic; "the other only to its living present."[31] The tendency to locate the past in England and the present in America partly explains why the American historical landscape is both more scanty and more recent than the English. Not even the mania for "earlying up" residential neighbourhoods and Main Streets affects the prevalent view that what Americans live with is—and should be—mostly "new".

Yet the paucity of structures felt to be historically valuable helps to account for America's recent success in preservation. The British heritage is an omnipresent burden: ancient streets, buildings and precincts everywhere need care. Whereas Britain's voluminous heritage involves huge maintenance costs, America has practically no structures extant from before the eighteenth century and relatively few before the nineteenth, of which only a small proportion rank as "historic" by any criteria other than age. Up to 1941, the Historic American Buildings Survey, focusing mainly on pre-Civil War structures, had included fewer than 6400 buildings for the whole US; by 1963 about 2000 of these had been demolished or ruined.[32] More buildings were listed when criteria for historical significance were broadened, and the US National Register of Historic Places now contains 26 000 designations (including 1500 Historic Districts). This is less than one-tenth of the historic listings in Britain, with only one-fourth the population of the US. A recent compilation of "Britain's Best Buildings" enumerates more than 5000 Grade I structures (not including Anglican churches) in England alone.[33]

Until 1982 roughly equivalent government grants help to maintain these disparate heritages, although American levels of federal assistance, which once far exceeded British levels, have been drastically cut by the Reagan Administration. US Federal preservation grants amounted to $25·4 million for fiscal year 1982, while Department of the Environment (DoE) grants to British listed buildings and Conservation Areas in 1981-82 were £12·9 million. DoE grants in England and Wales are supplemented by local authority funding (£27·4 million for conservation-related expenses in 1981-82), the National Trust (£15 million), the Redundant Churches Fund and the Friends of Friendless Churches, numerous private trusts, and the new National Heritage Fund (£1·8 million in 1981-82 in grants for purchase and repairs).[34] Home improvement and repair grants in Housing Action and General Improvement Areas greatly exceed grants made for specific historical purposes, though how much they aid conservation is hard to estimate. A recent study of the Yorkshire town of Beverley concludes that improvement grants have been used to "ruin" many listed cottages.[35] In America grants from states, cities, and private foundations, notably the National Trust, have likewise supplemented and now substantially exceed Federal preservation funding.

An attempt to produce comparative totals would mean little, for only a fraction of these sums go to repair and rehabilitation; the residue is spent on investigation, survey, recording, staff salaries, negotiation, and litigation. However, one difference is clear: a larger proportion of certified historical structures in the United States get *some* aid than in Britain, where DoE grants equally divided among all listed buildings would mean only £40 for each, and only a tiny proportion of listed buildings qualify for any assistance.[36]

Conservation in Britain is necessarily more restricted in scope than in America. Not only are British funds scarcer, they are less equitably allocated. Less money for more buildings constrains Britain to concentrate on truly outstanding monuments; a few major projects pre-empt funding. To save from the bulldozer and put in reasonable repair only the most spectacular gems from the past takes most of the money the Department of the Environment can grant—two-thirds of it to top-rank listed buildings (Grades I and II*) and churches. Indeed according to a former DoE chief investigator of Historic Buildings the mere knowledge of a list of less-important recognized structures (Grades II and III) "became almost an advertisement that here was a set of buildings the Minister would never do anything about."[37] The remaining one-third of DoE grant money goes mainly to Conservation Areas, but much of this, too, is spent on individual listed buildings, and relatively little on unlisted vernacular structures or on neighbourhoods. A new DoE-funded focus on long-term, coordinated conservation projects in some 16 towns has recently begun to operate.[38]

Priorities given to splendid monuments generally accord with British selection and evaluation procedures that emphasize high quality. A few public appeals for immense sums for such famous buildings as Westminster Abbey, York Minster, and St Paul's Cathedral, Harvey noted, "exhaust the greater part of the public money that can be subscribed for purposes of conservation [and] have a disastrous effect upon the conservation of almost all other buildings."[39]

Preservation in America is differently slanted. The United States, as noted, has few spectacular structures to match Britain's prime thousands. Measured by high-style criteria, little American architecture of the eighteenth century is of comparable quality, and relatively little even of the nineteenth. Even if the merits of early American architecture are disputable, there is no gainsaying the traditional lack of concern for this heritage, barring a few patriotic shrines. Until quite recently, the finest buildings in American cities were regularly torn down by a speculative, impatient and profoundly anti-traditionalist society. "The very bones of our ancestors are not permitted to lie quiet a quarter of a century," wrote a Mayor of New York in 1845, "and one generation of men seems studious to remove all relics of those which preceded them. . . . Overturn, overturn, overturn! is the maxim of New York."[40] Returning from Europe in 1904, Henry James was appalled at the breathless speed with which his boyhood home near Boston was demolished. "I had often seen how fast history could be made" but had "never felt that it could be unmade still faster"; what was taking place, he reflected in New York, "was a perpetual repudiation of the past."[41] The guiding American maxim was to pull down and build over again; some old buildings gained more fame for being demolished than for having existed.[42] Whether present American devotion to preservation represents a permanent change of heart cannot yet be judged. "The miracle of New York is not that we have so many historic structures," wrote one critic, "but that we have any at all in a city that lives for the moment."[43]

With fewer great monuments to worry about, American preservation efforts have encompassed a wider range of structures. They extend not only to buildings so architecturally commonplace or historically inconsequential they would not merit even passing mention in Britain, but to structures valued solely for their associational and neighbourhood contexts. Spreading preservation efforts and funds far beyond the masterpieces on which the British have concentrated their attention, Americans preserve fewer exceptional buildings, but perhaps more representative ones.

Compensating for the lack of man-made antiquity, American likewise accord historical status to artefacts from a more recent past than most British people take seriously. The rehabilitation of any structure more than 50 years old qualifies for substantial tax incentives under legislation passed since 1976. The Economic Recovery Tax Act of 1981 offsets such costs for certified historic buildings with 25% investment tax credits, and 20% and 15% credits respectively for commercial buildings 40 and 30 years old. State Historic Preservation Offices inventory even younger buildings to qualify for grants as soon as they come of age. The Society for Commercial Archeology (founded 1976) celebrates anonymous roadside structures from the 1920s through the 1950s.[44] Thanks to the speed with which the present recedes into the past, Americans view with rueful detachment such post-war relics as Stanley Marsh's Cadillac Ranch, a "monument to the tail-fin" made of ten half-buried Cadillacs from vintage years of the 1940s and 1950s.

By contrast, Britain's new 1930s Society (founded 1979) half-apologetically combats the received image of Auden's "low dishonest decade" whose Depression and hunger marches made them for many the "sad, wasted years, whose artifacts are best forgotten". "The people who knew the period hate it," says the Society's chairman, and its secretary acknowledged the irony of looking back on it when a major principle of the period was not to look back at all.[46] They emphasize the craftsmanship and romantic individuality of a small number of inter-war masterworks, from Lutyens viceregal to steamship moderne and dream-palace Odeons, and their exemplary inter-war list features buildings by the principal architects of the time, the high and mighty rather than anonymous vernacular structures.[47] To be sure, American roadside architecture from the 1920s on has been much more pervasive and inventive than in Britain.

With so much of their venerated heritage built within living memory, American historic preservation is apt to be intensely self-conscious. "The West behaves like a pioneer country which knows it is present at its own birth," T. H. White remarked: "if William Rufus had already begun to preserve the site of the Battle of Hastings" that would be the English parallel to restoring the 1870s Front Street saloon in Dodge City, Kansas.[48] To add insult to injury, the new Front Street saloon was no reconstruction, but a wooden replica of the TV version, located several blocks from the original site on what is now Wyatt Earp Boulevard.[49]

The mechanisms of government aid likewise foster British concentration on the greatest and the best, American on the typical and the everyday. Preservation initiative in Britain is highly centralized; in the US it is widely dispersed. UK listed-building and Conservation Area grants are made directly by the DoE on advice from its Historic

Buildings Council in accordance with professionally determined national standards, not for their importance as neighbourhood landmarks. In the US, State Historic Preservation Offices (SHPOs) have dispensed federal matching funds for preservation in response to applications from localities and community action groups. Conservation criteria in most local programmes depend less on formal standards of architectural worth than on the role structures play in the local scene. Besides government grants (with Federal sources now severely curtailed), local preservation groups rely heavily on such devices as revolving funds—low-interest loans for renovation which can be re-used many times over[50]—a device copied in recent years by some British amenity groups. However, few local British communities have much say in funding what they think important, let alone the self-confidence to articulate their own goals in defiance of the deference traditionally accorded to experts.

Preservation interest in both countries has moved beyond individual structures to groups of buildings and the townscape as a whole, beyond architectural merit narrowly defined to environmental quality broadly conceived. Historic Districts in the US have powers that depend on the localities that created them. Many of Britain's Conservation Areas are paper tigers, however, rather than effective or creative guardians of environmental heritage. Government improvement grants to Conservation Areas are often ineffectual because they are too small, too restrictive, or thought too burdensome by local councils reluctant to match such grants.

Established to stem the tidal wave of development that threatened to engulf Britain in the 1960s, the main enemy of Conservation Areas in the 1980s is lack of cash.[51] Local councillors and planning officers often neglect the general ambience of Conservation Areas, and I have met some who seemed unaware that any demolition in a Conservation Area required listed building consent. Lacking any power, Conservation Area Advisory Committees (CAACs) are wholly at the mercy of local authorities at liberty to disregard their advice—or to terminate their existence. Thus the London Borough of Greenwich, the first Greater London council to appoint an Advisory Committee, in 1981 proposed its abolition to save £250 a year in officers' overtime; the committee was temporarily reprieved only when members agreed to meet for a trial period without officers, but in 1982 both of Greenwich's CAACs were terminated. (The Council ignored the Blackheath Society's no-strings offer to pay the officers' overtime costs.) Representatives of neighbourhood amenity groups serve on most CAACs, but professionals designated by architectural, town planning, and the major national conservation organizations usually predominate. Hence some CAACs are as remote from local public opinion as they are impotent to sway local councils.[52]

Area conservation in Britain is thus less a reality than a pious hope. "It is not enough to protect a building while permitting its setting to be destroyed," according to the chairman of England's Historic Buildings Council.[53] And the HBC's 1979-80 Annual Report asserts that "most impact can be made by repairing all decaying buildings within a single street or district rather than by dispersing grants over widely scattered areas."[54] But few economic incentives fuel these admirable precepts. Even the small sums the Council allocated for environmental work— paving, pedestrianization, landscaping—in 1978-79 were cut off in 1980 to give priority to important buildings that might otherwise have been lost.[55] Just as the Hollywood star system denigrates the indispensable role of the supporting cast, observed the HBC's chairman, so does British hierarchical grading of listed buildings jeopardize the integrity of the architectural canvas as a whole.[56]

By contrast, public and private American agencies offer substantial aid to area conservation, notably for neighbourhood preservation schemes and Main Street rehabilitation programmes. Grass-roots projects initially funded by the National Endowment for the Arts now receive funds from half a dozen major private foundations and low-interest loans from local banks. The Main Street renewal programme fostered by the American National Trust has begun to transform tacky and chaotic downtowns into well-cared-for and harmonious environments. The do-it-yourself approaches that mark these American efforts contrast strikingly with the improvement machinery for commercial areas sanctioned by the Urban Areas Act in Britain, and with minuscule grants for improvement schemes under the avuncular sponsorship of the British Civic Trust.[57]

FINANCING PRESERVATION

American preservation taps greater resources than British because it is funded in a wider variety of ways. Government grants have provided significant seed money, but American preservation mainly depends on tax-incentive schemes generated by the federal Tax Reform Act of 1976 and subsequent revisions. These acts enable localities, owners, and developers of historic properties to write off the costs of commercial rehabilitation.[58] Well-publicized practical preservation guides and National Trust seminars have made these benefits familiar to the business community, detailing how commercial buyers can set purchase and rehabilitation costs against taxes and accelerate depreciation rates. A typical title is *New Profits from Old Buildings: Private Enterprise Approaches to Making Preservation Pay*.[59] Owners of American historic houses also use private preservation easements for long-term protection. Such easements can prohibit not only demolition but alteration, change of use, and sub-division—and do so in perpetuity. And by reducing the assessed values of properties they carry significant federal income, local real estate, gift, and inheritance tax benefits. Because easements are recorded among local land records, they are virtually self-enforcing in fending off development pressures that threaten historic sites.[60] Historic District designation for a 14 000-acre tract in Virginia based on such restrictive easements proved legally binding against a 1981 court challenge brought by strip-mine operators.[61]

By late 1981 an estimated 125 000 American structures were eligible for historical tax concessions, and SHPOs had approved 1500 million dollars' worth of tax-benefit rehabilitation work for older income-producing properties. "Tax inventives have the ability to reach far more buildings worthy of preservation," concluded US National Trust President Michael Ainslie, "and to do so more efficiently and effectively than grants and other forms of direct government assistance."[62]

In American preservation, as in American society generally, money talks. Realtors and bankers see that renovation often costs less and yields higher profits than re-building. In the early 1940s, realtors and businessmen in Charleston, South Carolina, found that down-town preservation raised property values and increased profits;[63] their experience has been repeated again and again across the country. Within just two years (1977-79) the National Trust's Main Street renewal programme increased sales-tax revenue by 25% in Hot Springs, South Dakota, raised the occupancy rate from 75% to 95% in Galesburg, Illinois, and spurred businessmen to invest 11 dollars for every Trust dollar spent.[64] Re-cycled buildings prove highly marketable; the renovation of Seattle's Pioneer Square has raised the tax base 1000%.[65]

American tax incentives do have some drawbacks. One is their focus on rehabilitation for commercial use, to the detriment of non-profit domestic maintenance and repair. It is therefore more profitable to sell historic residential structures for conversion than to keep their use unchanged. Nor is such conversion always carefully undertaken, despite tax act inspection requirements. Tax incentives attract developers who pay lip service to preservation, but whose projects may not respect nor enhance the past. The viability of many American programmes requires "improvements" unrelated or even antithetical to historic fabric. "We were telling cities about Victorian cornices when what they wanted to know about was survival," explained the National Trust's Main Street programme director. "The lion and the lamb may lie down together," Baltimore's housing commissioner warned preservationists, "but the lamb won't sleep much." Referring to the 1981 accelerated depreciation allowances, one preservationist wrote, "We all love the tax breaks, but . . . so do the glass-panel people and the aluminum-grill people."[66] Self-professed conversion to historic preservation is not always convincing. "My partners were mildly interested in old buildings but very interested in the tax benefits," stated a Texas tax lawyer newly into rehabilitation. But since then, he claimed, his views had changed. "Maybe my heart wasn't completely pure when I joined the Heritage Society, but it's been purified a whole lot."[67]

None the less, many heritage-conscious Britons would gladly adopt at least some of these tax incentives. "If the American experience is anything to go by, and we see no reason why it should be peculiar to the United States, comparatively small central Government funds channelled through the tax system can result in considerable private capital being injected," urged the Historic Buildings Council, thus far in vain.[68] Tax allowances to acquire and convert empty listed buildings would be especially desirable. The few tax incentives now available in Britain are of dubious value and seldom utilized. Exemption from Capital Transfer Tax and Capital Gains Tax for privately-owned historic buildings, for example, has been given to only 90 applicants in five years.[69]

However, other British observers, including Treasury officials, deplore these American methods. Tax incentives are felt to be unselective, to allow developers rather than conservationists to choose which buildings to conserve and how to do it, and to encourage often undesirable conversion. Beyond this antipathy to broad-based tax incentives lurks a general bias against realtors and developers as socially inappropriate agents of conservation. Whereas American preservationists habitually sit down with the construction industry to find out how to meet its needs, their British counterparts appear to regard such contacts as unnecessary and unseemly—much as nineteenth-century British architects felt it beneath their dignity to discuss craftsmanship or aesthetics with the stone masons and technicians who realized their designs.[70]

Not only is the British Treasury reluctant to offer tax incentives, it penalizes preservation with serious disincentives. For example, empty listed buildings may be exempted from local rates—ostensibly to encourage their repair, but actually an inducement not to find tenants for them. But the greatest impediment to British preservation is the imposition of value-added tax (VAT), now 15% on all repairs, whereas new construction is tax free. The result is a built-in bias in favour of tearing down buildings and replacing them with new ones. "VAT is a blight on our architectural heritage", according to SAVE Britain's Heritage. "It discriminates relentlessly against historic buildings." Fifteen per cent is "a really sizeable margin militating against conservation in many decisions on whether to repair or redevelop". Nor does VAT "just encourage neglect and destruction of historic buildings: it positively fosters their mutilation and disfigurement" by favouring the replacement of original features with new ones; repairing old fixtures is taxed, but "faking, fudging and botching are tax-exempt".[71] VAT collected on historic building repairs far exceeds total government aid in conservation grants. The absurdity of penalizing conservation in a country hard-pressed to repair even its greatest buildings and where history-hungry visitors swell tax revenues and local receipts is evident to all, but nothing is done about it.

The rigorous application of modern public health and safety legislation likewise penalizes the use of older buildings. To install fire-proofing that meets twentieth-century British standards without unsightly excrescences, for example, would bankrupt many historic house owners. Adhering to the letter of such regulations puts in jeopardy most surviving Victorian and Edwardian architecture, saved from the Scylla of fire only to succumb to the Charybdis of cost.[72]

Financial bias against preservation in Britain is not confined to government. It is shared, and indeed promoted, by powerful private interests. Building societies lend less, levy higher interest rates, and impose stricter condition for mortgages on old than new houses—on the mistaken assumption that older buildings are shorter-lived and riddled with maintenance problems, even when modernized. Almost one-third of Britain's housing stock was built before 1919, and 22% between the two world wars; many of these older houses are soundly built, more spacious and flexible than newer buildings, with intrinsic character and townscape value. Millions of intending house buyers would prefer roomy, gracious older houses but cannot obtain them owing to the prejudices of banks, estate agents, and building societies. One building society survey shows that three-quarters of first-time buyers wanted older houses than they got; fewer than one-fourth of those who sought Victorian houses could get them. Lending associations view listed buildings with particular antipathy, fearing that their historic importance "may attract restrictive conditions that render them unattractive as a marketable proposition". A well-known chartered surveyor considered listed buildings in the Bedminster area of Bristol worthless even if put in good repair "because no mortgage would be available".[73] Yet despite all these disincentives, pre-1919 period dwellings are holding their price far better than any other property today.[74]

MATERIAL BENEFITS OF PRESERVATION

Preservationists on both sides of the Atlantic know that saving and re-using historic buildings makes economic sense; it conserves energy and materials, creates job, and takes up less money for shorter periods of time than new buildings do. Adapted older buildings with superior structures and energy-conserving shells provide lower-cost space, hence higher profits.

> Re-using older buildings requires less capital in the beginning and takes less time to complete than new buildings, so that money is tied up for shorter periods before rents begin to repay loans. . . . Labour appreciates that preservation and remodeling efforts require more workers and craftsmen than do new buildings. . . . The revitalization of sound structures and viable neighbourhoods is both less expensive and less socially disorganizing than new construction.[75]

The social benefits of preservation are legion. Because existing bricks, windows and floors need not be taken down and hauled away and new materials brought in to put up in their place, preservation is "faster and creates less dust, debris and noise. . . . Utilities don't have to be relocated, streets remain intact and . . . patterns of life continue essentially as before."[76] In Britain, conserving buildings also saves time and effort otherwise needed to gain planning permission for new structures.

Resource conservation arguments often buttress preservation sentiment in America, but seldom in Britain. Economic recession and fuel shortages have alerted Americans to the need to save energy and materials, and even if this awareness is seldom acted on, it has created a climate favouring rehabilitation that preservationists effectively exploit. Elaborate analyses are made to show just how many units of energy are saved by refurbishing old buildings, and how much less heat and air conditioning the substantial structures of yesteryear require than flimsy or environmentally sealed modern buildings. Recent conversion of a Seattle hotel into shops and offices, for example, required only 15% of the energy that new buildings would have taken. As the building industry consumes one-third of all U.S. energy needs, such savings are vital to the economy. Urban rehabilitation consumes up to 45% less energy, 50% less land, and 55% less capital than building anew. So much energy is embodied in old buildings that preservation is said to be synonymous with energy conservation.[77] . Preservation thus promises Americans ecological thrift along with heritage and aesthetic satisfaction.

The British, by contrast, have only begun to advance energy and materials saving as rationales for preservation. The public is left to infer that except for the not unmixed gains of tourism, heritage benefits are wholly uneconomic—hence sentimental, and dispensable in stringent times. A variety of spokesmen deplore the "tyranny" of sentimentalists who supposedly seek to preserve at any price—so long as someone else pays—and block modern architecture in the process.[78] But recent British studies show that re-using old buildings saves capital costs, and also that a well-maintained historic ambience can be an incentive for industrial location, enabling firms to recruit staff attracted by livable milieus.[79] Yet local councillors are flabbergasted when they are told that preservation makes economic sense.

Private owners of historic houses likewise tend to be entrepreneurial in America, sentimental in Britain. When William Cecil inherited Biltmore, the Vanderbilt estate in North Carolina, he re-organized it as a successful showplace on strict business lines, moving his own family out to another house. By contrast many British period home owners give up ownership to the National Trust or some other charity for the privilege of staying in it. Not all owners act in these ways, but the instances cited point to profoundly differing perspectives. An American treats his house as a productive enterprise and goes off to live elsewhere; a Briton dispossesses himself of his estate so that he can go on inhabiting it. For many Americans, possession matters most; for many English, residence is all-important. Indeed, continuing family residence is a prime attraction for visitors too; according to Chamberlin it is "precisely this subtle link between the house, and the same genetic group who have inhabited it for centuries that saves the English country houses from being mausolea, like so many of the chateaux of France."[80]

The compulsory nature of listing in Britain and its present voluntary character in the United States reflect analogous proprietorial emphases. The traditional view of an Englishman's home as his castle long delayed British conservation legislation, and Ministry investigators seeking to document historic listing in the late 1940s were often rebuffed as the "advance-guard of the Gestapo".[81] But while morally outraged that property could be listed without their consent, few home owners were then concerned about the financial implications of historic designation, and the obligations that listing actually imposed were then virtually negligible; only after 1968 was listed-building consent made a condition of demolition. Some owners resent that they have no right of appeal from DoE listing decisions and decry the sacrifices listing may entail (a few stoop to arson to avoid them),[82] but the principle that historic designation should be independent of ownership is generally accepted.

In the United States matters are otherwise. National Register listing was at first by government fiat, but compulsory listing, with its attendant financial burdens and loss of property value, was repugnant to property owners. Pressure from developers and commercial interests in concert with home owners amended the Historic Preservation Act in 1980 to require formal notification of intent to list on the National Register; properties are not listed if owners object.[83] Thus the status of "history" in the United States may depend on who owns it.

PRESERVATION EDUCATION AND ADVOCACY

The growth of preservation and conservation has engendered acute needs for qualified personnel in both countries. Britain has concentrated on technical skills; since 1913 the Ancient Monuments Service has recruited a permanent corps of masons, carpenters and other craftsmen to protect and display its 20 000 structures, and workshops at fourteen cathedrals train and employ cadres of stone masons, glaziers, and conservators of stained glass wall paintings and sculptures. These crafts programmes give British conservation a high degree of continuity and a renown for technical mastery.[84]

Americans have emphasized broad-based, academic, and largely non-technical training, starting with the Winterthur Program in Early American Culture from 1952 and the historic preservation programme in Columbia University's School of Architecture in 1964. Because historic preservation in the United States is intimately linked with urban rehabilitation, downtown renewal, resource conservation, neighbourhood participation, and tax legislation, expertise in all these areas is in demand. The job market for preservation has begun to attract academics—notably historians and social scientists—who until recently deprecated it as "applied" rather than "pure". The *Harvard Guide for American History* still relegates the historic preservation movement to a brief article on "Non-Documentary Sources", and the American Historical Association has held no session on preservation since 1963.[85] Yet by 1981 45 universities offered undergraduate and graduate degree programmes in historic preservation, embracing social and economic history along with art and architectural history, environmental and planning law, architecture and landscape, economics, anthropology, sociology, geography and psychology, and there were preservation-linked courses at at least eighty more universities.[86]

Historic preservation in Britain has had no such impact on higher education. Conservation plays little part in architecture and planning degree programmes, partly owing to the lack of historical training and the ignorance of traditional construction methods that now afflicts those disciplines.[87] The post-graduate conservation courses at York and the Architectural Association have overwhelmingly architectural curricula. Even undergraduates are commonly trained as specialists in one field alone, leaving them ill-equipped for the multi-disciplinary perspectives that historic preservation now needs. The bent of these training programmes thus mirrors the national character of historic preservation: free-wheeling pragmatism and public participation in America, painstaking craftsmanship and narrow professionalism in Britain.

As with education, so with politics: American preservationists are more keenly concerned with the arts of persuasion than their British counterparts. Students in American preservation programmes learn how to convince a neighbourhood association, a city council or a banker that their recommendations are economically feasible and socially desirable. Political lobbying is second nature to them. The 1981 convocation of Columbia University's preservation alumni featured a panel discussion between key government agency representatives and leading preservationists, orchestrated by Preservation Action, the movement's national lobbying group, on the impact of impending federal budget cuts. Legislative timetables and names on key committees in the House of Representatives were circulated among the audience, which was told how to urge congressmen to support preservation appropriations and how to spur mayors and other influential local officials into action. Beyond the significant tax incentives such lobbying helped to secure, preservationists built bridges with Congress and the Treasury Department.[88]

British conservation seeks to influence national decision-makers through SAVE Britain's Heritage (founded 1975), an informal and highly effective committee of professionals and journalists, and a joint committee representing the principal national amenity groups (Society for the Protection of Ancient Buildings (SPAB), 1877; Ancient Monuments Society (AMS), 1924; Georgian Group, 1936; Victorian Society, 1958; and on occasion the Council for British Archaeology, the Civic Trust and the National Trust). But grass-roots political activism is rare in British preservation. The million-member British National Trust (1895) devotes virtually all its energies and £31·6 million income to maintaining and displaying its extensive properties (156 historic houses, 20 castles, 30 churches, 88 gardens, 17 villages, 420 miles of coast for 6·2 million visitors in 1981), but takes no formal stand on preservation issues, and influences policy mainly by setting high standards of conservation and display. The American National Trust (1949) by contrast, has fewer than 150 000 members and keeps only 19 historic house museums and other properties, but engages in extensive educational and advisory work, programme promotion and lobbying for preservation. The dynamic tone of debate at the American National Trust meeting of 1980 struck a British conservation reporter as in striking contrast to the seemly and placid discussions in British amenity groups.[89]

Political activism conforms with American convictions that—if only to consolidate its recent success—historic preservation must be a mass rather than a class-based movement. Away with the image of little old ladies in tennis shoes who fought to save old buildings twenty years ago; preservation today is espoused by the young—and it may be significant, thinks the editor of an architectural journal, "that today's youth wear tennis shoes for everything". In order to make historic preservation relevant for all, and not, as it has been accused, "to just save landmarks and create lily-white neighborhoods" the National Trust's new Inner-Cities Ventures Fund gives preferential awards to minority and low-income groups.[90]

Preservationists' main function, one spokesman maintains, is to help communities articulate their own architectural values. To do this, they need to show that "they are not fusty antedeluvians [sic] busily pre-occupied with genealogy or misty events of the past [but] committed citizens who want a healthy, interesting, useful, and pleasing environment". Emphasis on the vernacular and the recent rather than the ancient and aristocratic is both a cause and a consequence of this image. But the image itself requires continual re-vamping. Threatened federal cuts in 1981 showed that "preservationists must rehabilitate their public image", according to a state official:

> Preservationists cannot afford to ignore public opinion. We have done a bad job of public education because we appear not to have convinced people that we are acting in their best interests. . . . We should present ourselves not as cranky, intransigent opponents of progress, but as concerned Americans anxious to join our fellow countrymen in shaping a better future.[91]

In this spirit, no doubt, the American National Trust's 1981 annual meeting advertised a session on "Reaching the Unsympathetic Property Owner".

By contrast, national amenity societies in Britain are prototypically middle class. The largest of the four, the Society for the Protection of Ancient Buildings, has only 5000 members. If the sprinkling of blue-jeaned youth in the Victorian Society contrasts with the tweedy ante-diluvians of the Georgian Group, the members of both, along with the SPAB and the AMS, make up a clearly recognizable and professional élite. Outsiders' impression of the SPAB as "a society of mediaevalists and lovers of crucks" is certainly too narrow, but it is noteworthy that a Civic Trust spokesman, stung by SPAB's Secretary calling the Trust "very middle class", recently retorted that by comparison SPAB was *upper* class. The counterparts of American rank-and-file preservationists in Britain are less likely to be concerned with old buildings than with old trains; steam railway outings at Quainton in Buckinghamshire attract a blue-collar following no-one could mistake for devotees of nearby Waddesdon Manor.[92]

In America, historic preservation has begun to involve people of all backgrounds and ethnic origins, poor as well as rich, unlettered as well as learned. In Britain, safeguarding historic buildings tends to be left to a small minority; the rest of the population, beyond occasional outings to the Tower of London, Woburn, Beaulieu and Longleat, reserves active participation for non-architectural aspects of the heritage.

HERITAGE AS SHRINE, MUSEUM OR PROFITABLE CONVERSION

Attitudes toward the re-use of historic structures reflect the social differences and reinforce the economic considerations I have outlined. Preservation in Britain is traditionally purist: the essential feeling is that old buildings ought not to be touched or changed; neither restorations nor replicas are countenanced. This strictness stems from the reaction to nineteenth-century mutilation of English churches under the guise of restoration. Against George Gilbert Scott and other Victorian "improvers", Ruskin and later Morris issued the famous "anti-scrape" denunciations still enshrined in British conservation.

> It is *impossible*, as impossible as to raise the dead, to restore anything that has ever been great or beautiful in architecture. . . . Do not let us then talk of restoration. The thing is a Lie from beginning to end. You may make a model of building as you may of a corpse, and your model may have the shell of old walls within it; . . . but the old building is destroyed, and that more totally and mercilessly than if it had sunk into a heap of dust, or melted into a mass of clay.[93]

Ruskin's abjuration had little immediate effect. A quarter of a century later, in 1877, when Scott was about to "destroy" Tewkesbury Abbey, William Morris wrote the letter that brought into being the Society for the Protection of Ancient Buildings and its anti-scrape manifesto:

> The Restoration of ancient buildings [is] a strange and most fatal idea, which by its very name implies that it is possible to strip from a building this, that, and the other part of its history . . . and leave it still historical, living, and even as it once was . . . In the course of this double process of destruction and addition the whole surface of the building is necessarily

tampered with; so that the appearance of antiquity is taken away from such old parts of the fabric as are left; . . . a feeble and lifeless forgery is the final result.

Morris's new society sought to

resist all tampering with either the fabric or ornament of the building as it stands; . . . in fine to treat our ancient buildings as monuments of a bygone art, created by bygone manners, that modern art cannot meddle with without destroying. Thus, and only thus . . . can we protect our ancient buildings, and hand them down instructive and venerable to those that come after us.

Over the past century Morris's anti-scrape manifesto has become infallible dogma, a sacramental text with which aspiring SPAB members must still pledge their concurrence.[94]

Strictly adhered to, this dictum would result in the speedy disintegration of some ancient buildings and the grotesque deformation of others. "Take proper care of your monuments, and you will not need to restore them," Ruskin had advised. "Bind [a building] together with iron where it loosens; stay it with timber where it declines; do not care about the unsightliness of the aid; better a crutch than a lost limb. . . . Its evil day must come at last; but let it come declaredly and openly."[95] Morris's insistence on visual honesty in repairs "to prop a perilous wall or mend a leaky roof by such means as are obviously meant for support or covering, and show no pretense of other art", would, John Harvey notes, deface old buildings with crude buttressing masses or pillars and drill-hall roofs. Architect-members of the SPAB who had already diverged from the original manifesto in practice amended it in 1924 to permit additions to ancient structures provided "the new work is in the natural manner of today, subordinate to the old, and that the addition be permanently required and will not" be rendered "inadequate and superfluous" by "future events"—though how to guarantee such a future was not specified.[96] Likewise, where extreme purism once forbade the Ancient Monuments Service to re-erect even a single fallen stone—according to the 1913 Inspector's Report, restoration was "the most heinous offence making a foreman liable to 'instant dismissal' "[97]—time has mellowed the Morris orthodoxy, allowing fragments to be restored and fallen colonnades re-erected on sites of ruins.

Scrupulous anti-scrape regard for the continuity of history has made Britain an outstanding custodian of its heritage. But the integrity of old buildings is apt to be respected at the cost of their present use. New life is seldom possible for structures so faithfully maintained; they can only become shrines or museums, unmodified and unmodernized. This is, to be sure, just what Morris and his followers intended: buildings no longer usable for their original purpose should not be altered to suit new uses, but preserved as monuments of bygone art. But far more buildings become obsolete than can be kept as museums; if not adapted, they become derelict.

The anti-scrape image, however modified in practice, remains potent in Britain today. The mutilations which often passed for restoration in the nineteenth century justified Morris's strictures, but "much of the disrepute in which 'Preservationists' are held in some official quarters and by large bodies of the general public", in Harvey's view, "is directly due to the extreme form in which Morris's protest was cast".[98] The notion of treating the past with hands-off reverence reinforces the spectre of historic buildings as a useless and crippling burden.

In the United States, preservation is both less scrupulous and less exacting. Americans freely and often gleefully adapt old buildings, returning them to some "original" appearance, converting them to modern convenience, or conforming them with present-day views of how old buildings should look. Some buildings are "earlied up", others modernized, still others converted into a pastiche of old and new; few Americans mind that history is revised in the process. What people do with the relics of the past they preserve or replicate is considered to a large extent their own affair. Thus Walter Knott copied structures from the old California ghost town of Calico as an historical backdrop for his Chicken Dinner Restaurant; the brochure advertising Knott's Berry Farm notes that he built "as authentically as possible" and, no less commendable, that "needless to say, he also added a few whimsical touches of his own".

Americans are not merely willing to alter old buildings; they deliberately choose to renovate them. Far from admiring the appearance of age, they prefer their historic structures to seem as new and fresh as when they were first put up. To prove their present worth, old buildings should be devoid of cobwebs, spick and span, in perfect repair. Signs of age are marks of failure; like old people, old things need rejuvenation. Hence historic artefacts, original or reconstructed, are made bright and shiny. They must also be clean, which explains the failure of a scheme to export bags of "historic" Thames mud as souvenirs to the United States:

the Americans insisted the mud first be sterilized. "I couldn't have done that," said the Southend entrepreneur. "It would have cooked all the history out of it."[99]

Not only did every machine in Henry Ford's Greenfield Village have to be in working order, but Ford actually brought Thomas Edison there to perform experiments in an exact replica of the aged inventor's Menlo Park laboratory. The Smithsonian Institution's 1976 revival of the 1876 Philadelphia Centennial Exposition exhibited a similar modernizing zeal. As modernity was the guiding spirit of the original exhibition, almost everything in the historical replay had to be new as well. The 1976 show excluded original 1876 artefacts marked by age and use or decay in favour of newly minted replicas.[100]

Every preserved structure is either appreciated as a relic or converted for modern use, and most historic buildings serve both functions in some measure. But the balance between these aims differs strikingly between the two countries. The British emphasize keeping the past as it is; Americans emphasize re-use for present-day purposes.

These emphases reflect the relative capacity of what survives to attract lucrative attention. Whereas visitor receipts keep hundreds of British ancient monuments and historic houses solvent and in adequate repair, few historic house museums in the United States show a profit. But Americans nowadays deprecate preservation for display not simply because historic house museums seldom pay their way, but because they seem elitist. Rare and sumptuous relics are apt to be isolated amidst mean or unsympathetic structures. The museum house

> is too often surrounded by a degenerating neighbourhood—tenements, taprooms, loft buildings, warehouses, vacant lots, and general filth. Visitors make their way through this squalor to the preserved monument; they enter a house where nobody lives, look across rope barriers at chairs that nobody is allowed to occupy and at glasses forever empty, then file out again into the sordid neighborhood.[101]

American distaste for historic house museums goes beyond environmental aesthetics; to juxtapose latter-day grandeur with modern squalor is considered anti-social. Antiquarians in nineteenth-century England hoped their descendants would not have to view Stonehenge in the midst of a turnip field;[102] Americans would be dismayed less by a turnip field than by farm labourers' hovels.

Americans readily accept the changes that conversion and re-use inevitably require. They welcome new uses as evidence that old buildings need not be pickled to be saved but can fend for themselves in the modern scene—and in today's marketplace. Do-it-yourself manuals laud successful conversions in terms that make the past itself seem the better for being altered to suit the present. Mundane and unremarkable old workshops and meeting halls, for example, are refitted for various modern uses. By contrast with British towns such as Burnley, Lancashire, which evince active hostility to using old mills for any other purpose, American cities such as Worcester, Massachusetts, and Troy and Cohoes, New York, capitalize on their industrial past without becoming museums in the process.[103]

In Britain the original use of a building is sacrosanct, conversion to any other function a second-best solution. A recent essay terming architectural salvage "a misuse of conservation resources" exemplifies British uneasiness with altering, moving or changing the use of their heritage. "New uses for old objects imply debasement and a loss of meaning", as in cutting and refitting the carved reredos of Birmingham's Church of the Messiah for the centrepiece of a wine bar, or in advertising a "Georgian door suitable for a garage". Materials salvaged from one epoch should not be transplanted to structures of another, nor old materials be assembled in modern ways, nor the splendid fireplaces of yesteryear's fine buildings adorn newly fashionable artisan's dwellings.[104] Even Lord Montagu's working party, which was convened to promote the adaptation of old buildings to new uses, felt "unequivocally that . . . the best use in most cases is the use for which it was originally designed and intended, or a use approximating closely to it".[105]

British conversion of old buildings is by no means rare; indeed, the re-use of historic structures may be more pervasive than in the United States, where buildings are habitually torn down as soon as they outlive their original purpose, if not before. Of eight hundred Anglican churches declared redundant in Britain from 1968 to 1981, almost half have been altered for other denominations or converted[106] into libraries, old people's centres, auditoriums, museums, bookshops, offices, warehouses, factories, even into restaurants and private homes. Redundant chapels are converted on an even greater scale, partly because fewer conditions are usually attached to their re-use.[107]

However, many Anglican transfers arouse great resistance. Some parishioners balk at handing over Church of England buildings to Muslims or Sikhs. Conversion of the medieval church of St Lawrence,

Evesham, Worcestershire, into the town library was rejected as "not in keeping with the concept of a modern public library service".[108] Moralists oppose the re-use of churches as community centres for fear of desecration by bingo or other forms of gambling. Some conservationists worry that alternative use may result in irreparable mutilation and that private owners may lose interest or, daunted by the unremitting task of repair and maintenance, simply abandon churches to decay.[109]

But "the surest way to arouse agitated local opinion against re-use of a country church", reports Patrick Brown, "is to suggest that it might become a house". Some think it wrong that the parish church should become private property, others deplore the loss of sanctity for recent churchyard burials, still others resent the secularization of church fittings.[110] "That a font where the sacred mystery of Christian baptism has been practised for generations should grace someone's 'chic' living room . . . most Christians will regard as offensive." It seems obnoxious to have "stained glass in the kitchen window, and the dead of two World Wars recorded in the bathroom".[111] The Friends of Friendless Churches are scarcely less opposed to residential conversion than to demolition; their president, Lord Anglesey, would prefer to leave redundant churches vacant as perpetual reminders of the spiritual faith England once had.[112] And many parish churches stand for values beyond that faith: they play a crucial role as townscape elements and village landmarks; their unique longevity, spanning the many generations baptised, married and buried there, make them tangible emblems of an enduring community. There is something mean-spirited about selling such a village church and closing it to the public. But symbolic values pay no maintenance or repair bills. Empty churches are rapidly vandalized and subject to arson, and must sooner or later be lost to communities too small or poor to care for them.

A general plea for re-use, citing notable foreign examples of conversion, animates the Montagu Report on *Alternative Uses of Britain's Historic Buildings*. In the past, Britain focused on conserving very old, rare and ruined monuments and great country houses as shrines and showplaces. Present-day concern with a wider range of potentially convertible structures requires a different strategy, yet "the case for re-use has never been considered at all". Adaptations of historic buildings could meet urgent needs for community facilities and housing. But the inflexible application of regulations meant for new buildings and the "marked reluctance among building societies, insurance companies and pension funds to invest in older buildings" impedes conversion prospects.[113] Developers and local authorities who see cleared sites as more profitable and less troublesome than old buildings in need of repair and adaptation likewise discourage alternative uses.

The lack of apparent demand for certain kinds of older buildings, especially large nineteenth century factories and warehouses in the north of England, poses another serious obstacle to conversion. "Some local authorities, particularly in the Lancashire/Yorkshire textile area, were almost in despair about the possibility of finding new uses for industrial buildings", owing in part to their sheer scale. Out of 917 working factories surveyed in Lancashire in 1951, barely 213 remained even partly in textile use in 1978. Many of these mills are in remote rural areas devoid of employment opportunities or housing needs comparable to the inspiring examples of conversion cited from Lille and Boston.[114]

British devotees of the past view askance still other alterations which are blithely accepted in America. Historic structures in both countries are often removed from their original sites—in Britain with reluctance at the loss of the authentic ambience, and usually as a last recourse to avoid imminent destruction; in the United States with scarcely a qualm, and often with pride in the technical feat. "We have literally moved tons of history," said the director of the Pioneer Arizona Foundation of her success in transporting remote abandoned cabins to a "living museum" north of Phoenix.[115]

American landmarks are frequently to be found, as I have noted previously not where history happened but where they are least in the way. High land values in built-up areas militate against retention of historic structures there; when relics of the past on valuable real estate are saved from demolition they are as a rule moved elsewhere.[116] Old buildings are often gathered together in "historic" districts, the authentic structures in restored villages come from some distance away. Protests against the removal of a courthouse made famous by Abraham Lincoln from Illinois to Henry Ford's museum village in Dearborn, Michigan, were overridden by the argument that millions would visit it in its new location as opposed to the few thousand who saw it *in situ*.[117]

Strict preservationists may deplore historic removals, but the American public, long accustomed to shifting buildings by road, rail, water and air, takes the process for granted. Federal guidelines provide technical advice and spell out the implications of moving historic structures for preservation and tax breaks.[118] And British qualms about re-use or removal of the heritage work to the advantage of dealers and American buyers who import quantities of British antiques, including entire oak-beamed cottages and barns into American settings as outré as London Bridge in the Arizona desert.

Transplanting historic features suggests a lack of sensitivity to the milieu often belied by the facts. Americans often choose new sites expressly to restore to relics the ambience now lost in their original locales; other relics are returned to their original locations. Plymouth Rock, the supposed 1620 Massachusetts landing place, split in two when moved from the waterfront in 1774; the top half was moved again in 1834 for display purposes. Brought back together in 1880, the recemented fragments were returned near the Rock's original site in 1921 "so that the high tide might surround it, and the winter storms break over it as they did in 1620".[119]

Setting is seen as no less essential to the integrity of structures in America than in Britain, but is apt to be sacrificed to the exigencies of preservation itself. For example, owners are often tempted to pull down historic buildings on prime urban sites because new buildings there could be much larger, hence more profitable. To recompense owners for the loss of development potential, New York City's zoning code permits unused development space above and around certified historic landmarks to be transferred to adjacent sites, to an equivalent bulk beyond the local height and setback restrictions for the area. But such transfers further maroon landmark buildings, already lower and smaller in scale than their modern neighbours.

Excess development rights above the old US Customs House in lower Manhattan, for example, amount to 800 000 square feet, the equivalent of a 60-storey skyscraper; redistributed to adjacent lots, this would "create intolerable congestion, and inundate the diminutive building in a sea of superdensity".[120] Nearby skyscrapers now swamp McKim, Mead and White's elegant Italianate Villard Houses in midtown Manhattan. Strictly speaking, the Villard Houses misfit results from the merging of building lots of which the other part was intensively developed, but the effect is analogous to the transfer of development rights.[121] UK "planning gains" similar to such transfers have helped preserve some historic structures, as at Spitalfields in London.

USES AND ABUSES OF TANGIBLE HISTORY

Americans tend to be free and easy even with the past they save for display. Where the British aim to leave the past alone, Americans explain it, interpret it, alter it, sell it, and when desired invent it. Interpretation, let alone animation, is sometimes felt inappropriate in Britain because the heritage is both ubiquitous and sacred, not to be tampered with. Only the ignorant need to be told what they are seeing; anyone intelligent will already know, or can read it up in a guidebook. Hence visitors to the National Trust's segment of Hadrian's Wall at Housesteads (unlike sections in the care of the Department of the Environment) can experience the Roman remains unencumbered by explanatory signs and obviously refurbished stonework, though the National Trust would draw the line at "pleasing decay" along the lines of admirers lampooned by John Harvey, who suggested that "the holy ruins of England, ivy and all, should have been left to crumble gradually away, haunted by their ghosts and visible at rare intervals (by gracious permission of the noble proprietor) by poets of sensibility".[122]

The need to cater for masses of less refined or well-prepared sight-seers has in recent years promoted such interpretive activities as town trails and heritage centres, yet Britain's interpreters are told that "the visitor is often sold short". His being there "implies a question not often formulated, and which the visit often fails to answer". Colin Ward has attributed this failure to the elitist assumption that "when we go somewhere it is because we're scholars or members of an esthetically aware elite; others are merely trippers."[123]

To bring the tangible past alive, Americans now not only interpret but animate it. A generation ago, admiring a costumed girl playing 1860s tunes on a piano in the Curtis-Lee mansion near Washington, National Parks official Freeman Tilden "noted with pleasure that most of the visitors were not curious about it, a sure sign that it was in perfect harmony and accepted as part of the recreation".[124] Today, historic-site curators animate exhibits to stimulate interaction; actors playing historical roles converse with visitors in the dialect and supposed mental set of the chosen time. "Character imposture", as Plimoth Planta-tion's chief interpreter terms the staffing of restored or replica houses with replica people, advances historical presentation from the material realm to the social to induce in visitors a sense of suspended disbelief.[125]

Populism as well as dramatic impact are held to justify such animation:
since the 1960s, people "are not interested in seeing only how the rich
lived," asserts a "Colonial farm" curator, "they want to see how their
own counterparts lived, the dirt farmer, the working man."[126] Visitors
who seek to identify with their own past find verisimulitude in the
portrayals of humble, everyday folk activities. Hence "we seek 20th
century counterparts to the people we wish to portray," explains
Plimoth's interpreter: "house-wives portray house-wives, truck drivers
farmers of yeoman stock, etc."[127] But commercial viability as much as
populism accounts for the increase of historical animation; from
Williamsburg to Old Sturbridge Village and beyond, actors (or
"impostors") have taken to historic streets to depict everyday life in the
past, because marketing surveys show that gate receipts respond more to
relic people than to relic artefacts.[128]

A US National Park Service study of interpretation at Tatton Park,
Cheshire, the National Trust's second most popular historic house,
underscores British–American differences. The Americans felt that the
Tatton Park attendants functioned more as guards than interpreters.
Instead, costumed butlers and ladies' maids should demonstrate and talk
about their duties. Period newspapers, not those of today, should appear
in the rooms. The kitchen needed a "worked-in" look; the meat model
should be "a more realistic replica, or, on occasion, the real thing".
Guides should eschew dates and facts about objects to establish "the
humaness of the participants in Tatton's evolutionary story. . . . The
factor of a common humanity shared by today's visitor and Tatton's
medieval residents should be inherent in . . . all interpretation". Finally,
an "authentic medieval house" should be moved into the village, peopled
by a hypothetical peasant family (mother, father, children, livestock).
Both the house and a self-guided medieval village trail have proved
highly successful.[129]

The pressure of popularity has induced some American-style re-
enactment and animation in England. At Blickling Hall, Norfolk,
National Trust re-enactments for children featured the Earl of
Buckinghamshire in eighteenth-century costume and required a vicar in
period garb to baptize the same village infant several times a week.[130]
Theatrical re-enactments in 1981 at Clandon Park, Beningbrough Hall,
Buckland Abbey, and Little Moreton Hall transported some 35 000
pupils back to Tudor days as "time-travellers in the best Tom Baker
tradition," in a Cheshire headmaster's words; as an eleven-year-old said

after being immersed in 16th century Buckland Abbey, "I knew it was now but thought it was then."[131]

Britain has plenty of re-enactors seeking historical roles: the Jousting Association runs the world's only Knights Training School and offers medieval entertainment as an historic-house attraction; the Practical History Society involves entire communities in recreation of the past; the British Civil War Society, professedly disenchanted with Hollywood showmanship and "inauthentic" cavaliers, re-enacts not only battles but "hangings" and camp-follower "wenching".[132]

Yet many consider such dressing up and make-believe vulgar or embarrassing, not to say unnecessary, in a country so well endowed with an actual past. And few who manage Britain's heritage are eager to supply the needed verisimilitude. Imagine historic house owners having to "sit around all day creaking in armour with swords dripping in blood or in wigs and crinolines armed with smoking warming pans", scoffs the Duke of Bedford, whose Woburn Abbey is one of England's most popular heritage honey-pots. Sir Francis Dashwood might draw vast crowds by re-enacting his eighteenth century forebear's porno orgies at Hell Fire Caves, but the Duke wondered whether modern High Wycombe could supply enough virgins to meet the demand.[133]

The very notion of re-living history seems somehow absurd in British eyes. British reluctance to popularize the past is evident in the glacial pace of a Heritage Interpretation programme funded by the Carnegie Foundation; in over a year, only 44 applied for grants, of whom 25 received less than one-quarter of the £100 000 available; most applications lacked innovative appeal.[134]

The past is entertainment on both sides of the Atlantic. Elizabethan banquets, jousting tournaments, Madame Tussaud's and the Tower of London are no less a feature of the English scene than re-enactments of Revolutionary battles, daily shoot-outs in Western ghost towns, and history à la Disney in the United States. But they play quite different roles. In England, where historical fun and games are truly common, in the sense of being vulgar, they have little bearing on the appreciation of actual relics and historical structures. The "fun" to be found at Longleat and Beaulieu is not their history, but their adventitious lions and antique cars. "My Home [Blenheim Palace] is an education, not an entertainment," says the Duke of Marlborough. "If you inherit an historical place from your ancestors, it is a pity to turn it into a fun-fair."[135] In the United States, history itself is entertainment. Outdoor-museum curators should become "user satisfaction managers", in Janiskee's words, seeking to "make site users go away happier and remember these places more fondly".[136]

Precinct restorations in the two countries exhibit analogous differences. San Francisco's Ghirardelli Square, Boston's Quincy Market, and their ubiquitous and unabashedly commercial counterparts heed the spirit rather than the letter of architectural restoration, freely revamping the past to attract maximum numbers of visitors. And notwithstanding accusations of purveying "kitsch for the rich", they are enormously popular.[137] In London, Covent Garden's prize-winning faithful restoration keeps tourist tat resolutely at bay, with baked beans and hamburgers banned in the interest of high quality and earnest tidiness—an epitome of ghastly good taste set against lively American vulgarity.[138]

One reason why the built heritage in Britain is taken so seriously is that an influential minority, linked by family or tradition with historic houses and locales, strongly identifies with their enduring continuity. As one period home owner expressed it, "the house has been here for so long it makes me conscious of my own relative insignificance. I don't feel that I own it, rather that it has been lent to me for a time, and that I have an obligation to care for it". Not all historic home owners share this concept of their stewardship role—indeed, a recent survey showed that many were ignoring or side-stepping public access rights statutorily conditional on HBC repair grants.[139] But Ruskin's view that we are simply stewards of the ancient buildings handed down to us, and to be handed on by us in turn, is generally compatible with the English sense of history as an embedding flow.[140] It conflicts with the American view of history as a set of remote and static scenes and as private property.

In the United States, history is a material commodity bought and sold in pieces of various sizes, taken like vitamins to make people healthy and happy. Americans treat history as if it were geography, stepping back at will into the past of their choice, as Spender put it.[141] And when they tire of the past they abandon it; history is a specific and delimited experience, rather than a presence infusing the whole of life. This perspective makes preservation only one of several options for a valued heritage: imitation or invention is sometimes preferred. "If our attachment is only to the unique place once experienced," writes a landscape architect, then preservation and enhancement are called for. But where surrogates are acceptable, the essential features of the historic object or scene can be extracted and replicated.[142]

Replicas are considered appropriate rewards for helping to save originals. Donors of ten dollars toward preserving San Francisco's cable cars receive an "Honorary Cable Car Gripman" certificate signed by the Major of San Francisco, donors of thousand dollars get a "handcrafted walnut cable car music box that plays "I Left my Heart in San Francisco", and for ten thousand dollars one gets a "certified . . . authentic bell that has been rung on a San Francisco Cable Car".[143] Beyond the gradation from humorous testimonial to miniature replica to actual relic, the point is that money buys all these attributes of the past. Britain, too, sells historic plaques, plastic Anne Hathaway cottages, and actual Mentmores. The popular magazine *Everything Has a Value* stresses the profits to be made out of relics, from heirlooms to any kind of old rubbish.[144] But the British continue to believe that the real past is beyond price.

CONVERGING ANGLO-AMERICAN ATTITUDES

British and American views and treatment of their building heritage do differ substantially. But the similarities are no less striking. Public interest has made historic preservation increasingly popular on both sides of the Atlantic, and the patterns of growth are largely parallel. If some differences are fundamental or ingrained, others are trivial or ephemeral. Britain has led the way in safeguarding its great architectural monuments and in appreciating the interplay of buildings and milieu; America has pioneered in protecting its vernacular, everyday, commonplace structures; but the two countries share a common pool of ideas and exhibit convergent general trends.

The exchange of people as well as ideas strengthens this mutuality. Just as the work of the Massachusetts Trustees of Public Reservations helped to stimulate the foundation of the British National Trust, so the British Trust served as a model for the American, and the Royal Oak Foundation enables Americans to participate in British preservation.[145] Summer-school programmes at Attingham and West Dean introduce scores of American professionals to British conservation problems and techniques; a smaller but significant stream of British visitors has sampled American preservation know-how. British conservationists now cite American instances of how to adapt historic structures to new uses, and of how re-use saves energy and materials. Anglo-American symposia alert preservation leaders to problems of mutual concern. Exchanges and conferences in particular arenas of conservation, from blacksmithing and thatching to legislation and mortgaging, familiarize craftsmen and technicians with circumstances across the ocean.

A single enthusiast can be of inestimable significance in transfers of ideas. For example, the evocative photographs of Randolph Langenbach, a pioneer celebrant of the magnificent factory complexes at Lowell, Massachusetts, and Harrisville, New Hampshire, have helped to reverse the ostracism, as unsavoury symbols of the Industrial Revolution, long suffered by the great textile mills of the Pennines, enabling Britons to see them not only as fine architectural structures but as living memories for those who worked in them.[146]

British and American resemblances are more apparent when contrasted with preservation elsewhere. With a longer history of protective legislation, France, for example, has none the less adopted for conservation only 31 000 buildings in a century and a half—less than one-tenth the number in Britain. French preservationists carry out the limited objectives they aim at supremely well, but public opinion in Britain, let alone in America, would hardly be content to protect so few buildings or be happy with their centralized uniformity.[147]

The rapid growth of preservation interest has also burdened both Anglophone countries with similar problems. Pressures to certify and protect historic buildings have outrun government resources. Further listings in the US National Register, estimated as only 10 to 25% complete,[148] are jeopardized by the curtailment of federal grants to the State Historic Preservation Offices charged with initiating Register nominations and with processing those prepared at local levels. Shortages of funds and personnel have likewise seriously slowed Britain's relisting programme. Whereas 24 000 buildings were added to the list in 1974, fewer than 7000 were added in 1981, largely because the Department of the Environment's resurvey staff for the whole of Britain was cut from 18 inspectors to only six and a half.[149]

The first survey of England and Wales, completed in 1969, took 23 years; the resurvey now under way is unlikely to be finished by the 1984–85 target date, although DoE staff is to be augmented by architects in private practice under country and local authority supervision.[150] How feasible this devolution of listing is remains to be seen, but American experience suggests that it is almost certain to introduce widely varying standards of historical worth.

Additions to the heritage tally in both countries reflect not simply completion of unfinished inventories, but broader and vaguer criteria for architectural and historical significance. Structures of more recent periods, of wider substantive scope, of local and regional as well as national import, and of environmental as well as architectural context all now potentially qualify. As tastes and motives change, the broadening of criteria makes it more difficult to choose which structures should be saved. Less than a generation ago, American preservation efforts emphasized battlefields and statesmen's birthplaces; today the homes of labour leaders and sites that hold significance for ethnic minorities are eagerly sought for inclusion on the National Register.[151]

Indeed, so much is worth saving for so many different reasons that no steadfast criteria can guide their selection or use. "It is not easy to identify a national historic landmark," notes the American architectural historian Richard Longstreth, "if one considers eligibility to extend beyond the widely known examples contained in standard texts". Lacking a coherent rationale, preservation may come to rely too much on evanescent economic conditions and on fickle current taste for the old as a backlash against the deficiencies of the new. "If preservation has made such factors its principal foundation", Longstreth warned in 1980, "it will be vulnerable on all fronts when conditions change".[152]

Conditions have already changed dramatically since Longstreth's warning; the inadequacy of public funding has forced preservationists in both countries to seek support in the business world. In their zeal to demonstrate economic utility and social responsibility, they risk trivializing, if not selling, the common birthright for a mess of pottage. They renovate and revitalize the heritage, some critics charge, less by saving history than by scuttling it.[153] But as we have seen, "history" takes on new dimensions all the time, and today's trash may become tomorrow's treasured heritage.

NOTES AND REFERENCES

I am indebted to the following for corrections and helpful comments: in Britain, Judith Anthony, Max Hanna, Peter J. Fowler, Bernard Kaukas, Penelope Lively, David Pearce, Hugh Prince, Matthew Saunders; in the United States, Frank Gilbert, Antoinette J. Lee, Robert Z . Melnick and Richard Longstreth.

1. M. W. Thompson, *Ruins: Their Preservation and Display* (London, British Museum Publications Ltd., 1981) p. 10.

2. Marcus Binney and Max Hanna *Preservation Pays: Tourism and the Economic Benefits of Conserving Historic Buildings* (London, SAVE Britain's Heritage, 1978).

3. Council for British Archaeology, *Historic Towns* (London, 1965). The four conservation studies were of Bath, Chester (by Donald W. Insall *et al.*), Chichester (by G. S. Burrows), and York (by Lionel Brett) (all London, HMSO, 1968). See also Alan Dobby, *Conservation and Planning* (London, Hutchinson, 1978) pp.54-55; Wayland Kennet, *Preservation* (London, Temple Smith, 1972) pp.68-98; Larry R. Ford, "Continuity and Change in Historic Cities: Bath, Chester and Norwich", *Geographical Review*, Vol. 68, 1978, pp.253-73.

4. Historic Buildings Council for England, *Annual Report 1980-81* (London, HMSO, 1982), p.3; *Period Home*, Vol. 3, No. 3, Oct.-Nov. 1982, p.1; Ken Powell, *The Fall of Zion: Northern Chapel Architecture and Its Future* (London, SAVE Britain's Heritage, 1980); Ken Powell, *The New Iconoclasts* (London, SAVE Britain's Heritage, 1981).

5. Raymond Williams, *The Country and the City* (London, Chatto & Windus, 1973), pp.282, 301. The conventional view is that a "desperate need . . . to relate to something with deep roots in the past" animates city dwellers to seek out the countryside (Earl of March, in The Georgian Group *News*, London, December 1979).

6. *See* Morton G. White and Lucia White, *Intellectuals Versus the City* (Cambridge, Mass: MIT Press and Harvard University Press, 1962); Anselm L. Strauss, ed., *The American City: A Sourcebook of Urban Imagery* (Chicago, Aldine, 1968).

7. Marion Shoard, *The Theft of the Countryside* (London, Temple Smith, 1980); Marion Shoard, "Why landscapes are harder to protect than buildings", *in* David Lowenthal and Marcus Binney, ed., *Our Past Before Us: Why Do We Save It?* (London, Temple Smith, 1981), pp.83-108.

8. *New Directions in Rural Preservation* (Washington, D.C.: U.S. Dept. of Interior, Heritage Conservation and Recreation Service, Publication No. 45, 1980); Robert M. Newcomb, *Planning the Past: Historical Landscape Resources and Recreation* (Hamden, Conn., Archon Books, and Folkestone, Kent, Dawson, 1979); special landscape issue, *Bulletin of the Association for Preservation Technology*, Vol. 11, No. 4, 1979.

9. P. A. Faulkner, "A philosophy for the preservation of our historic heritage", *Journal of the Royal Society of Arts*, Vol. 126, 452-80, 1978.

10. Local history and preservation groups together increased from less than 2500 in 1966 to more than 6000 in 1975 (Advisory Council on Historic

Preservation, *The National Historic Preservation Program Today* [Washington, D.C., USGPO, 1976], p.3).

11. John Fidler, "The economics of conservation", *Building Conservation*, Vol. 3, No. 3, March 1981, p.10; David Morton, "Looking forward to the past", *Progressive Architecture*, Vol. 35, No. 5, Nov. 1976, p.45. In 1977-8, remodelling projects accounted for an estimated one third of the work of U.S. architectural firms (David Morton, "Is preservation progress?" *Progressive Architecture*, Vol. 37, No. 5, Nov. 1977, pp.51-52).

12. John Lukacs, "Obsolete historians", *Harper's*, Vol. 261, Nov. 1980, pp.80-84.

13. *English Heritage Monitor* 1982 (London, English Tourist Board), pp.7-8, 21, 26-27.

14. David Lowenthal, *The Past is a Foreign Country* (Cambridge, Cambridge University Press, in press); Lowenthal and Binney, ed., *Our Past Before Us*.

15. John Harvey, *Conservation of Buildings* (London, John Baker, 1972); pp.157ff.; Michael Hunter, "The preconditions of preservation: a historical perspective", *in* Lowenthal and Binney, ed., *Our Past Before Us*. The theft from historic buildings of old bricks whose tones cannot be matched today shows that relics continue to serve as sources of supply for raw materials ("Chicago brick pickers demolish old buildings", *Kansas State Collegian*, Sept. 9, 1981, p.10). I am indebted to Robert Melnick for this nugget of continuity.

16. John Maass, *The Glorious Enterprise: The Centennial Exhibition of 1876 and H. J. Schwartzmann, Architect-in-Chief* (Watkins Glen, N.Y., American Life Foundation, 1973), pp.89-90; John Brinckerhoff Jackson, *American Space: The Centennial Years, 1865-76* (New York, W. W. Norton, 1972), pp.104-5; David Lowenthal, "The bicentennial landscape: a mirror held up to the past", *Geographical Review*, Vol. 67, 1977, pp.253-67, ref. on pp.265-66.

17. On planning blight and the failure of redevelopment see, for example, "The concrete Jerusalem", *New Society*, Vol. 38, 23-30 Dec. 1976; Peter Blake, *Form Follows Fiasco: Why Modern Architecture Hasn't Worked* (Boston: Little, Brown, 1977); Alison Ravetz, *Remaking Cities: Contradictions of the Recent Urban Environment* (London, Croom Helm, 1980).

18. Glyn England, press release, Feb. 17, 1981, quoted in Marcus Binney, "Oppression to Obsession", *in* Lowenthal and Binney, ed., *Our Past Before Us*, p.210.

19. Deyen Sudjic, "Monuments to twenty-five years of muddle", *Sunday Times* (London), April 25, 1982, p.23.

20. Tony Aldous, "Buildings old and new", *The Times*, Oct. 18, 1973; Selwyn Lloyd, quoted in *Daily Express* (London), May 9, 1964, p.3;

Bernard Levin, "Something old, something new", *The Times*, Oct. 18, 1973, p.18.

21. Malcolm Bradbury and Michael Oursler, "Department of amplification", *New Yorker*, Vol. 35, July 21, 1960, pp.58-62.

22. Penelope Lively, *Treasures of Time* (London, Heinemann, 1979), pp.80-81.

23. Penelope Lively, *The Road to Lichfield* (London, Heinemann, 1977), p.7.

24. Martin J. Wiener, *English Culture and the Decline of the Industrial Spirit, 1850-1980* (Cambridge, Cambridge University Press, 1981).

25. M.T., "An American looks on London", *Journal of the London Society*, No. 403, Oct. 1978, p.7.

26. Henry James, *A Passionate Pilgrim, and Other Tales* (Boston, James R. Osgood, 1875), p.104.

27. David Lowenthal, "The place of the past in the American landscape", *in* David Lowenthal and Martyn J. Bowden, ed. *Geographies of the Mind: Essays in Historical Geography in Honor of John Kirtland Wright* (New York, Oxford University Press, 1976), pp.89-117.

28. Quoted in Binney, "Oppression to Obsession", p.205.

29. Andrew Faulds, "The ancient assets that may be our salvation", *The Times*, 1976, reprinted in Society for the Interpretation of Britain's Heritage, *Newsletter* 3, Spring 1976. On the problems tourism brings in its wake, see *English Tourism and Cathedrals: Problems and Opportunities* (English Tourist Board, London, 1979); Max Hanna, "Cathedrals at saturation point?" in Lowenthal and Binney, ed., *Our Past Before Us*, pp.193-202; *Economics of Historic Country Houses* (London: Policy Studies Institute, 1981). Cambridge, Oxford, Chester, Stratford and Windsor in 1980 set up a Historic Towns Tourism and Management Group to monitor these problems.

30. Hywel Francis, quoted in Robert Merrill, "Cefn Coed coal and steam centre: the interpretation of a mining community", *Interpretation*, No. 17, Spring 1981, p.13.

31. John Heilpern, "Another victory for Joseph Papp, and New York theatre lives again", *The Times*, Oct. 7, 1981, p.7.

32. Charles E. Peterson, "Thirty years of HABS", *Journal of the American Institute of Architects*, Vol. 40, No. 5, 1963, pp.83-85; Helen Duprey Bullock, "Death mask or living image?" in *With Heritage So Rich* (New York, Random House, 1966), pp.139-156.

33. Steve Weinberg, "Super list: The 16-year-old National Register of Historic Places faces its toughest challenge", *Historic Preservation*, Vol. 34, No. 4, July-Aug. 1982, pp.10-17; *The Best Buildings in Britain* (London: SAVE Britain's Heritage, 1980).

34. *English Heritage Monitor* 1981, pp.14-17; 1982, pp.13-16; *Preservation News*, Oct. 1981, March and June 1982.

35. Ken Powell, *Beverley: Will Housing Sprawl Engulf Minster?* (London, SAVE Britain's Heritage, 1981).

36. In 1980-81, 884 grants totalling £8·6 million were made for listed buildings and places of worship (Historic Buildings Council for England, *Annual Report* 1980-81 [London, HMSO, 1982], pp.7, 11).

37. Antony Dale, "Thirty-five years of listing: a personal view", *Period Home*, Vol. 2, No. 3, Oct.-Nov. 1981, pp.32-35, ref. on p.32.

38. H.B.C. *Annual Report* 1980-81, pp.14-19.

39. Harvey, *Conservation of Buildings*, p.199.

40. Philip Hone, *The Diary of Philip Hone 1828-1851*, ed. Allan Nevins, 2nd edit. (New York, Dodd, Mead, 1936), p.730.

41. Henry James, *The American Scene* (1907), (Bloomington, Indiana University Press, 1968), pp.53, 229.

42. See, for example, Ada Louise Huxtable, *Kicked a Building Lately?* (New York Times/Quadrangle Books, 1976), p.256.

43. Richard F. Shepard, "Standing up", *New York Times*, July 16, 1981, p.C18.

44. Society for Commercial Archeology *News Journal* (Boston, Mass., Museum of Transportation). In 1980 the Society offered members an "All Night All-Night Diner Tour" of southeastern New England. featuring a Kullman, a Musi, a Fodero, a Sterling and several Worcester Diners, "pure" roadside forms from 1925 through the 1960s.

45. Bill Marvel, "The ideas of Marsh", *TWA Ambassador*, April 1981, pp.37-42.

46. *Unlocking the Thirties*, RIBA Heinz Gallery Exhibition notes, London Aug. 17, 1979; Thirties Society leaflet; Bevis Hillier quoted and Clive Aslet cited in Mary Blume, "Saving Buildings of the '20s and '30s", *International Herald Tribune*, April 29, 1980; Bevis Hillier, "The voice of the Thirties", *Sunday Times*, Jan. 25, 1981, p.51; The Thirties Society, *Journal* No. 1, 1980, list compiled by Timothy Thomas, pp.30-39.

47. *Historic Building and Conservation Areas*, Department of the Environment Circular 12/81.

48. T. H. White, *America at Last: The American Journal of T. H. White* (New York: Putnam, 1965), p.112.

49. Robert Z. Melnick, personal communication, Sept. 10 1981.

50. Arthur P. Ziegler, Jr, Leopold Adler II, and Walter, C. Kidney, *Revolving Funds for Historic Preservation: A Manual of Practice* (Pittsburgh, Pa., Ober Park Associates, 1975).

51. Wendy Le-Las, "Conservation Areas", *Heritage Outlook*, Vol. 1, 1981, pp.116-17.

52. David Gamston, *The Designation of Conservation Areas*, Research Paper No. 7, Institute of Advanced Architectural Studies, University of York,

1979; Alan Dobby, *Conservation and Planning* (London, Hutchinson, 1978), pp.67-8; Patricia Ray, *Conservation Area Advisory Committees* (London, Civic Trust, 1978); "Budget Threat to Conservation", *Heritage Outlook*, Vol. 1, 1981, p.113. Other local authorities, forced by lack of funds to cut planning staffs, increasingly view CAACs as expendable (David Warren, "Are advisory committees under threat?" *SPAB News*, Vol. 3, 1982, p.59).

53. Jennifer Jenkins, quoted in "Conservation of settings is just as important as protecting fine buildings", *Building Conservation*, Vol. 3, No. 9, Sept. 1981, p.25.

54. H.B.C. *Annual Report* 1979-80, p.12.

55. Ibid., pp.10-11.

56. Jenkins, quoted in "Conservation of settings", *op.cit.*

57. Tony Aldous, "Conservation in the New World", *Heritage Outlook*, Vol. 1, 1981, pp.40-43; Katherine Ann Oliver, "The Care of Streets" London University Ph.D. Thesis; Arthur P. Ziegler, Jr, and Walter C. Kidney, *Historic Preservation in Small Towns: A Manual of Practice* (Nashville, Tenn., American Association for State and Local History, 1980); *Neighborhood Preservation: A Catalog of Local Programs* (Washington, D.C., US Dept. of Housing and Urban Development, 1975) pp.125-48.

58. Gregory E. Andrews, ed., *Tax Incentives for Historic Preservation* (Washington, D. C., National Trust for Historic Preservation/Preservation Press, 1980).

59. By Raynor N. Warner, Sybil M. Groff and Ranne P. Warner (New York, McGraw Hill, 1978).

60. Thomas Coughlin, *Easements and Other Legal Techniques to Protect Historic Houses in Private Ownership* (Washington, D.C. Historic House Association of America, 1981), Russell L. Brenneman and Gregory E. Andrews, "Preservation easements and their tax consequences", *In* Andrews, ed., *Tax Incentives for Historic Preservation*, pp.147-55.

61. Ben A. Franklin, "Judge backs down in face of changes in preservation law", *New York Times*, July 25, 1981, p.11.

62. *Preservation News* March 1982, p.3; Ainslie in National Trust for Historic Preservation (U.S.), *Annual Report* 1980, pp.11-12.

63. Samual Gaillard Stoney, *This is Charleston* (Charleston, S.C., Carolina Art Association, 1944); Charles B. Hosmer, Jr, "'The broadening view of the historical preservation movement", *In* Ian M. G. Quimby, ed., *Material Culture and the Study of American Life* (New York, W. W. Norton for the Winterthur Museum, 1978), p.128. See also Charles B. Hosmer, Jr, *Preservation Comes of Age: From Williamsburg to the National Trust, 1926-1949*, 2 Vols. (Charlottesville, Va., University Press of Virginia for the Preservation Press, 1981) II, 232-74.

64. National Trust (U.S.) *Annual Report* 1980, pp.5-6.
65. Arthur M. Skolnik, "A history of Pioneer Square", in *Economic Benefits of Preserving Old Buildings* (Washington, D.C., Preservation Press for the National Trust for Historic Preservation, 1976), pp.15-20, ref. on p.19.
66. Mary C. Means, quoted in Jonathan Walters, "Main Street turns the corner", *Historic Preservation*, Vol. 33, No. 6, Nov.-Dec. 1981, p.37; Jay Brodie quoted in Neil R. Peirce, "Energy conservation — preservation's windfall", *In* National Trust for Historic Preservation, *New Energy from Old Buildings* (Washington, D.C., Preservation Press, 1981), p.42; Donald L. Dworsky, "Bureaucracy — the real enemy", *Historic Preservation*, Vol. 33, No. 5, Sept.-Oct. 1981, p.11. See Paul J. Goldberger, "The dangers of preservation success", in *Economic Benefits of Preservation*, pp.159-60.
67. Bruce Reich, quoted in Carrie Johnson, "Preservation in the 1980s: A dynamic movement looks at itself" *Historic Preservation*, Vol. 32, No. 6, Nov.-Dec. 1980, pp.33-39, ref. on p.38.
68. H.B.C. *Annual Report* 1979-80, p.2.
69. Ibid., 1980-81, p.12.
70. Harvey, *Conservation of Buildings*, p.9. Generally negative British responses to substituting for or augmenting grants by means of tax incentives were voiced at a joint US/UK conference on The Preservation of the Heritage: New Directions, New Incentives, New Initiatives, held under ICOMOS auspices at Leeds Castle, Kent, October 23-26, 1980.
71. Marcus Binney and Laura Grenfell, *Drowning in V.A.T.* (London, SAVE Britain's Heritage, 1980), p.3.
72. Dobby, *Conservation and Planning*, pp.152-53; Patricia Brown, "Safety in older buildings", *The Times*, April 8, 1978, p.15; Lord James of Rusholme, "Fire regulations in historic buildings", *The Times*, Sept. 8, 1978, p.15.
73. Jenny Freeman, "Mortgage myopia", *Chartered Surveyor*, March 1980, pp.291-98, with citations from Alliance Building Society, West Bromwich Building Society, and Bristol Visual and Environmental Group.
74. Robert Langton, "Property: The period house still attracting the right price", *Period Home*, Vol. 2, No. 3, Oct.-Nov. 1981, pp.36-37.
75. Morton, "Looking forward to the past" [see note 11]. For similar savings of time and money at Harrisville Mills, see Terence Maitland, "Corporate takeovers", *Historic Preservation*, Vol. 33, No. 5, Sept.-Oct. 1981, pp.42-48.
76. Arthur P. Ziegler, Jr, *Historic Preservation in the Inner City: A Manual of Practice* (Pittsburgh, Pa, Ober Park Associates, 1974), p.11.
77. *Preservation and Energy Conservation*, Advisory Council on Historic Preservation, *Annual Report* 1979 (Washington, D.C., US GPO,

1980); Richard H. Jenrette, "Chairman's message", Advisory Council on Historic Preservation, Annual Report, 1980; *New Energy from Old Buildings*, pp.16, 23, 27, 119.

78. Owen Luder, cited in Deyan Sudjic, "The case for the bulldozer", *Sunday Times*, Nov. 1, 1981, p.21; Roy Worskett, "New buildings in Conservation Areas: I. Conservation: the missing ethic", *Monumentum*, Vol. 25, 1982, pp.29-54.

79. Max Hanna and Marcus Binney, *Preserve and Prosper* (London, SAVE Britain's Heritage, in preparation).

80. William A. V. Cecil, "Problems of the historic house owner and their solution", paper presented at the US/UK conference on the Preservation of the Heritage, Leeds Castle, 1980; E. R. Chamberlin, "Living with history", *Daily Telegraph*, June 7, 1982, p.10.

81. Dale, "Thirty-five Years of Listing", p.33; see also Harvey, *Conservation of Buildings*, p.185; Thompson, *Ruins*, p.11.

82. Neglect and dereliction until repair is impossible or public safety is endangered, under-reporting intended alteration and extension, bulldozer "mistakes" like the one that knocked down Monkspath Hall in 1980, and outright local authority vandalism to avoid an impending preservation order, as in the 1982 demolition of Kensington Town Hall, are equally serious and increasingly pervasive threats to listed buildings (David Peace, *Historic Buildings and Planning Policies* [London: Council for British Archaeology, 1979]); George Allan, "When an alteration is 'demolition'", *Period Home*, Vol. 2, No. 3, Oct.-Nov. 1981, p.26; *Period Home* Vol. 3, No. 1, June-July 1982, p.3; Marcus Binney, "Introduction", in Michael Dillon, *West Midlands: Historic Buildings at Risk* (London, SAVE Britain's Heritage, and Birmingham, The Victorian Society, 1981).

83. See Evelyn R. Moore, "Preservationists must learn the art of compromise", *Historic Illinois*, Vol. 3, No. 6, April 1981, p.6.

84. Thompson, *Ruins*, p.11; Harvey, *Conservation of Buildings*, p.187; Peter Burman, "The care and protection of churches and cathedrals", *Journal of the Royal Society of Arts*, Vol. 129, 1981, pp.210-29. A British Register of Conservation Skills lists 168 thatchers, 32 timber-framed building specialists, and 17 stained-glass experts (*Heritage Outlook*, Vol. 12, Jan.-Feb. 1982, p.8).

85. Hosmer, "Broadening view of the historical preservation movement", p.13.

86. *Guide to Degree Programs in Historic Preservation*, 3rd ed., (Washington, D.C.: National Trust for Historic Preservation, 1980); Higher Education, *Preservation News Supplements*, October 1980 and 1981. I am indebted to Antoinette J. Lee then educational coordinator of the US National Trust for up-to-date data on US college programmes.

87. Harvey, *Conservation of Buildings*, p.217. Surveys of UK schools of architecture in 1973 and 1976 showed that three-quarters of their curricula contained some element of conservation, but for most this was very little (Derek Linstrum, "Education for conservation", *In* International Council on Monuments and Sites, *Nessun futuro senza passato*, Atti 6th Genl. Assembly, Rome, 1981, pp.679-89).

88. The Economics of Historic Preservation in the 1980s, Columbia University, New York, April 10-11, 1981; Steve Weinberg, "Lobbying Congress . . . the inside story", *Historic Preservation*, Vol. 34, No. 1, Jan.-Feb. 1982, pp.17-24.

89. Aldous, "Conservation in the New World", p.40. Sponsorship of ten conferences on Preservation Tax Incentives across the U.S. during 1981-82 (jointly with the National Park Service and the National Conference of SHPOs) to explain the opportunities generated by the 1981 tax act is characteristic of the American National Trust's role. But Trust meetings strike some American observers as self-congratulatory rather than dynamic (Sam Hall Kaplan, "Preservationists at odds", *Washington Post*, Oct. 17, 1981, p.E-24).

90. John Morris Dixon, "What's in it for the architects?" *Progressive Architecture*, Vol. 59, No. 5, Nov. 1978, p.7; Thomas J. Colin, "A promise kept", *Historic Preservation*, Vol. 33, No. 5, Sept.-Oct. 1981, p.64. However, many blacks remain more suspicious of the unhappy consequences of preservation than attracted by its potential benefits. See Henry W. McGee, "Historic preservation and displacement: regeneration or resegregation", UCLA Center for Afro-American Studies Newsletter, Vol. 6, No. 1, Nov. 1981, pp.11-16; Richard K. Dozier, "From humble beginnings to national shrine: Tuskegee Institute", *Historical Preservation*, Vol. 33, No. 1, Jan.-Feb. 1981, pp.41-45.

91. Ziegler, *Inner City Areas*, p.9. William G. Farrar, "A new direction for historic preservation", *Historic Illinois*, Vol. 3, No. 6, April 1981, p.13.

92. John Cornforth, "Where Morris's ideals live" *Country Life*, Mar. 24, 1977, p.711; *Heritage Outlook*, Vol. 2, No. 4, July-Aug. 1982, p.115. See also Timothy Cantell, "The 'eyes' have it", *Period Home*, Vol. 3, No. 2, Aug.-Sept. 1982, pp.28-30.

93. John Ruskin, *The Seven Lamps of Architecture* (1849) (New York, Farrar, Straus and Cudahy, Noonday Press, 1961), pp.184-5. See Nikolaus Pevsner, "Scrape and anti-scrape", in Jane Fawcett, ed., *The Future of the Past: Attitudes to Conservation 1174-1974* (London, Thames and Hudson, 1976), pp.35-53.

94. Morris's Manifesto forms part of the SPAB prospectus.

95. Ruskin, *Seven Lamps of Architecture*, p.186.

96. Harvey, *Conservation of Buildings*, pp.179-82, 189.

97. Thompson, *Ruins*, p.20.

98. Harvey, *Conservation of Buildings*, p.178. See also Hugh Prince, "Revival, restoration, preservation: changing views about antique landscape features", *In* Lowenthal and Binney, ed. *Our Past Before Us*, pp.47-48.
99. *Sunday Times*, Feb. 14, 1982, p.5.
100. Hosmer, "Broadening view of the historical preservation movement", pp.127-8; Hosmer, *Preservation Comes of Age*, I, 86-91; II, 988-92; Robert C. Post, ed., *1876: A Centennial Exhibition* (Washington, D.C., Smithsonian Institution, 1976) p.25.
101. Ziegler *et al.*, *Revolving Funds*, p.7.
102. William Long, *Stonehenge and its Barrows* (*Wiltshire Archaeological and Natural History Magazine*, Vol. 16, 1876), p.186.
103. Ken Powell, *Burnley: Mill-Town Image: Burden or Asset?* (London, SAVE Britain's Heritage 1980). See Walter C. Kidney, *Working Places: The Adaptive Use of Industrial Buildings* (Pittsburgh, Pa., Ober Park Associates, 1976). American animus against pickling the past informs Barbaralee Diamonstein, *Buildings Reborn: New Uses, Old Places* (New York, Harper and Row, 1978): "Successful revitalization demonstrates that the forms and materials devised in the past are still valid when properly adapted to the functions of today's life" (p.13). See also Roland Jacopetti and Ben VanMeter, *Rescued Buildings: The art of living in former schoolhouses, skating rinks, fire stations, churches, barns, summer camps and cabooses* (Santa Barbara, Calif., Capra Press, 1977).
104. Robert F. Walker, "Architectural salvage—A misuse of conservation resources", *Building Conservation*, Vol. 3, No. 5, May 1981, pp.11-14.
105. *Britain's Historic Buildings: A Policy for Their Future Use* (London, British Tourist Authority, 1980), p.7. The point is emphasized with a plea for multiple residential occupancy in Christopher Buxton, "Preserving— and living in—historic houses", *Journal of the Royal Society of Arts*, Vol. 129, 1981, pp.245-58.
106. Powell, *The New Iconoclasts*, p.3.
107. Powell, *Fall of Zion*.
108. Marcus Binney and Peter Burman, ed. *Change and Decay: The Future of Our Churches* (London, Studio Vista, 1977), p.37.
109. Marcus Binney and Peter Burman, *Chapels and Churches: Who Cares?* (London, British Tourist Authority, 1977), pp.165-69, 188-204; Burman, "Care and protection of churches and cathedrals", p.220.
110. Patrick Brown, "New uses for churches", in Binney and Burman, ed., *Change and Decay*, p.169.
111. Letters in *The Times*, summer 1976, quoted in Binney and Burman, *Chapels and Churches*, p.198.
112. Lord Anglesey, Address at Friends of Friendless Churches Society annual meeting, 1978. This is hardly a viable solution in counties like Norfolk,

more than half of whose places of worship are now redundant (*The Times*, Apr. 13, 1982, p.5).

113. *Britain's Historic Buildings*, pp.3, 5, 6; Binney, in *West Midlands: Historic Buildings at Risk*.

114. *Britain's Historic Buildings*, pp.18-19. See also Marcus Binney *et al.*, *Satanic Mills: Industrial Architecture in the Pennines* (London, SAVE Britain's Heritage, 1978).

115. Jo Ann Graham, quoted in "Youth Corps helps build Pioneer Arizona", *Preservation News*, Vol. 10, No. 11, Nov. 1970, p.7. See Shaaron Cosner, "Melting pot at Pioneer", *Americana*, Vol. 8, No. 3, Aug. 1980, pp.68-73.

116. David Lowenthal, "The American way of history", *Columbia University Forum*, Vol. 9, No. 3, summer 1966, pp.27-32.

117. Erik Robinson, "Henry Ford and the Postville courthouse", *Historic Illinois*, Vol. 3, No. 3, Oct. 1980, pp.1-3, 13-15. See also Hosmer, *Preservation Comes of Age*, I, 88-90.

118. John Obed Curtis, *Moving Historic Buildings* (Washington, D.C., U.S. Dept of the Interior, Heritage Conservation and Recreation Service, Publication No. 9, 1979).

119. Rose T. Briggs, *Plymouth Rock: History and Significance* (Boston, Mass., Pilgrim Society, 1968) ref. on p.18.

120. John J. Costonis, *Space Adrift: Landmark Preservation and the Marketplace* (Urbana, University of Illinois Press for the National Trust for Historic Preservation, 1974), pp.54-61. See also Harmon H. Goldstone and Martha Dalrymple, *History Preserved: A Guide to New York City Landmarks and Historic Districts* (New York: Schocken Books, 1976), p.25.

121. Huxtable, *Kicked a Building Lately?* pp.269-72.

122. Harvey, *Conservation of Buildings*, p.188. On current maintenance differences at Hadrian's Wall, see Chris Tighe, "The wall that defied the Celts falls to ramblers", *Sunday Times*, Apr. 11, 1982, p.5.

123. Colin Ward, "Goals for Interpreters", *Interpretation* (Society for the Interpretation of Britain's Heritage), No. 16, Summer 1980, pp.7-11. See also *English Heritage Monitor* 1981, p.26.

124. Freeman Tilden, *Interpreting Our Heritage: Principles and Practices for Visitor Services in Parks, Museums, and Historic Places* (Chapel Hill, University of North Carolina Press, 1967), p.76.

125. Robert Marten, personal communication, September 1981.

126. Jay Anderson, quoted in Cary Carson, "Living museums of everyman's history", *Harvard Magazine*, July-Aug. 1981, pp.22-32, ref. on p.23. See also Linda Lvestik, "Living history—isn't", *History News*, Vol. 37, No. 5, May 1982, pp.28-29.

274 DAVID LOWENTHAL

127. Marten, personal communication.
128. "History stumbles", *Wall Street Journal*, June 27, 1980, reprinted in *Landscape*, Vol. 25, No. 1, 1981, p.35. I am indebted to Darwin P. Kelsey, Jr., for material on visitor motivation from *Old Sturbridge Village: An Exploration of the Motivations and Experiences of Visitors and Potential Visitors* (New York, Fine, Travis and Levine, July 1979).
129. United States National Park Service, *Tatton Park Interpretive Survey*, (Cheltenham, Glos., Countryside Commission [1975]), pp.31, 33-4, App. II pp.ii, x; Jane Camp, Tatton Park Mediaeval Village Trail: Critique (Cheshire County Council, Countryside and Recreation Division, July 1979), summarized in *Interpretation*, No. 13, Summer 1979, p.11; Dolly Pile, "Interpreting Old Hall, Tatton Park, *Interpretation*, No. 17, Spring 1981, pp.3-5. Tatton Park is owned by the National Trust but held on lease and managed by Cheshire County Council.
130. Philip Howard, "Blickling's ghosts dramatise our heritage", *The Times*, April 27, 1978, p.6.
131. Lawrence Rich, "Ten thousand children in need of a sponsor", *National Trust*, No. 35, Spring 1981, pp.8-9.
132. "The Jousting Association of Great Britain", *Historic Houses Association Journal*, Vol. 3, No. 3, Summer 1979, pp.13-15; Charles Kightly, "17th century fun", *Interpretation*, No. 15, Spring 1980, pp.10-12; Tom Forester, "Weekend warriors", *New Society*, Sept. 10, 1981, pp.417-18. For comparable American re-enactments, see Lowenthal, "Bicentennial landscape", pp.259-261; Betty Doak Elder, "War games: recruits and their critics draw battle lines over authenticity", *History News*, Vol. 36, No. 8, Aug. 1981, pp.8-12.
133. Duke of Bedford, "Historic homes", *The Times*, Sept. 9, 1976, p.15.
134. Civic Trust, *Report for 1980* [p.2]; "Understanding our surroundings: grant for two more years" (interview with Geoffrey Lord, Carnegie UK Trust), *Heritage Outlook*, Vol. I, 1981, pp.96-8.
135. Quoted by Atticus, *Sunday Times*, April 14, 1963, p.9. See David Lowenthal and Hugh C. Prince, "English landscape tastes", *Geographical Review*, Vol. 55, 1965, pp.182-222, ref. on p.210.
136. R. L. Janiskee, "Recreational user research and historic preservation", paper presented at meeting of the Association of American Geographers, Atlanta, Georgia, April 1973, p.2. See David Lowenthal, "Environmental perception: preserving the past", *Progress in Human Geography*, Vol. 3, 1979, pp.549-59.
137. *Marketplace Life*, No. 2, Spring/Summer 1977, acknowledges brickbats from "romantics incensed [*sic*] by the fast food phalanx" (p.2); see also Diamonstein, *Buildings Reborn*, pp.32-34.
138. Robert Thorne, *Covent Garden Market: Its History and Restoration*

(London, Architectural Press, 1980); John M. Hall, "Covent Garden newly marketed", *London Journal*, Vol. 6, 1980, pp.215-24; Terry Christensen, "A sort of victory: Covent Garden renewed", *Landscape*, Vol. 26, No. 2, 1982, pp.21-28.

139. Quote from Horsham Society Newsletter, in *Period Home*, Vol. 1, No. 1, May 1980, p.1; Neil Burton, cited in Deyan Sudjic, "Public: no entry", *Sunday Times*, Apr. 25, 1982, p.13.

140. Ruskin, *Seven Lamps of Architecture*, p.140.

141. Stephen Spender, *Love-Hate Relations: A Study of Anglo-American Sensibilities* (London, Hamish Hamilton, 1974), p.121.

142. Robert Riley, "Reflections on landscape and memory", *Landscape*, Vol. 23, No. 2, 1979, pp.11-15.

143. "Endangered Species", advertisement in *Preservation News*, Vol. 20, No. 13, Dec. 1980, p.3.

144. *Everything Has a Value* began in 1980. Its commercial pitch is by no means unique even in Britain. "There's no present like the past, and when everything from the past is worth cash, what better present could there be than Miller's Antiques Prices Guide?" (advertisement in *Period Home*, Vol. 1, No. 4, Dec.-Jan. 1980-81, p.10).

145. Hosmer, *Preservation Comes of Age*, II, 814-16, 822, 840. "To preserve and protect'; A short history of the trustees", Trustees of Reservation, *7th Annual Report*, 1966, pp.8-9.

146. Tamara K. Hareven and Randolph Langenbach, *Amoskeag: Life and Work in an American Factory City* (New York, Pantheon Books, 1978); Binney *et al.*, *Satanic Mills*; Tamara K. Hareven and Randolph Langenbach, "Living places, work places and historical identity", *In* Lowenthal and Binney, ed., *Our Past Before Us*, pp.109-29. A Pennine Heritage Trust was launched in 1981-82. Citizens of Bradford, whose mill-town relics from the basis of nascent tourism, are said to "show no sense of envy or discomfiture about their new status as quaint relics of a vanishing industrial civilization" (*The Times*, Mar. 13, 1982, p.6).

147. Antony Dale, "France: The great chateaux", *Period Home*, Vol. 2, No. 1, June-July 1981, pp.11-15. The "charming diversity" of English restoration work was contrasted with French "cast-iron rigidity and sameness" at the turn of the century (G. Baldwin Brown, *The Care of Ancient Monuments* [Cambridge: University Press, 1905] p.82).

148. John M. Fowler, "Federal legislation for the protection of historic resources", paper presented at the US/UK Conference on the Preservation of the Heritage, Leeds Castle, 1980; National Trust for Historic Preservation, "Afterword", in Hosmer, *Preservation Comes of Age*, II, 1067.

149. H.B.C. *Annual Report* 1979-80, p.4; Dale, "Thirty-five years of listing".
150. *English Heritage Monitor* 1982, p.7. Tony Aldous, "Incentives for quality" (interview with Michael Heseltine), *Heritage Outlook*, Vol. 1, 1981, pp.86-7; Department of the Environment, *Organisation of Ancient Monuments and Historic Buildings in England* (London, HMSO, 1981), and *The Way Forward* (London, HMSO, 1982).
151. Robin Winks, "Conservation in America: national character as revealed by preservation", in Fawcett, ed., *Future of the Past*, pp.141-46.
152. Richard W. Longstreth, "Preservation's exposed flank", *Historic Preservation*, Vol. 32, No. 6, Nov.-Dec. 1980, pp.54-5.
153. Larry E. Tise, cited in Charles Phillips, "The missing link: can interpretation find a home in restored neighborhoods?" *History News*, Vol. 36, No. 10, Oct. 1981, pp.9-12. See also Weinberg, "Super list" (see note 33).

Chapter Nine

The Dissolution and Growth of Ethnic Areas in American Cities

CERI PEACH

This chapter sets out to show how the geographical view of ethnicity in American cities has changed during this century. Ethnicity began as "noise" in the economic models of Burgess and Hoyt, but has ended with race as perhaps the most fundamental divide in the American urban structure. This revolution in view came about first through a re-assessment of the degree of spatial segregation of blacks, then through comparisons with the position of Puerto Ricans, which was much more favourable to the Puerto Ricans than it should have been if the original explanations of black segregation were true. Finally it has led to a re-assessment of the apparent melting of the European ethnic groups. From this it appears that even the European ethnic areas may not have disappeared. This chapter points to the early contribution which Gottmann made in the re-assessment of ethnicity in American cities. The dissolution and growth to which the title of the chapter refers is less a physical process at work in American cities than an abstract development apparent in the literature.

The classical models of Burgess, Hoyt, Harris and Ullman which dominated geographical thinking on urban land use conceived of class in economic terms. Yet although social class is linked to the economic structure, it is by no means fully congruent with it. Economic class has to do with employment and earnings; social class has to do with living and spending. Economic class is to do with producing; social class with life style and consumption. In the United States ethnic groups are integrated

THE EXPANDING CITY
ISBN 0 12 547250 1

into the economy but they are divided both from one another and internally by social differences.

In the United States it is argued that the major divisions of both the nation and the cities are racial rather than economic (Pettigrew, 1981). However, such as been the dominance of the economic model that until the 1960s race was seen as a temporary division that would, with the economic progress of blacks, follow the same path of dissolution as that of European ethnics in the United States. The paradox is that not only have the black ghettos not dissolved but the ethnic areas of the European precursors may not have done so either.

THE MELTING POT VIEW OF BLACK ETHNICITY

Up to the 1960s American geographical literature on ethnic groups had the melting pot, or a modification of it, as its basic model. The spatial concomitant of that model was the spatial dispersal of ethnic groups. In the 1950s blacks were portrayed as the last of the ethnic groups, and the resistance of black ghettos to dispersal was accounted for by their relative recency. The explanation of black ethnic areas at this time was optimistic and cast in the mould of European ethnic areas. In other words the black ghetto was regarded as a temporary phenomenon, the last of a series of ethnic areas which had been characteristic of American growth.

European immigrants had come to the city, formed distinctive areas and then gradually dispersed. Evidence for the break-up of the spatial concentrations of immigrant European groups came from a wide variety of sources. Cressey (1938), Ford (1950), and Kiang (1968) showed the dispersal of the groups by measuring their outward movement from the centre of Chicago over time. Writing of the Germans, Cressey stated: "The great majority of the group has ceased to live in specific German communities and is scattered through more or less cosmopolitan residential areas. This widespread dispersion is an index of the decline of social unity among the Germans and of their gradual absorption into the general life of the city" (Cressey 1938, 65). Of the Irish he stated: "The Irish are even more widely dispersed through the city than the Germans, a fact which reflects the more complete disintegration of their group life and a greater degree of cultural assimilation" (Cressey, 1938, 66). Later workers using indices of dissimilarity were able to demonstrate the spatial dispersion of immigrant groups more convincingly. Lieberson,

Table 1 Indices of dissimilarity of selected foreign-born white groups, native-white and black population, Chicago[a] 1930 and 1950

Country of Origin	1	2	3	4	5	6	7	8	9	10	11	12
1 England & Wales	—	28·5	29·7	29·5	58·4	55·9	26·3	38·3	56·8	45·7	77·8	18·9
2 Eire	24·7	—	40·2	43·9	66·7	63·2	38·3	54·2	59·8	52·0	81·4	31·8
3 Sweden	30·7	42·4	—	32·3	67·8	66·0	38·8	54·0	66·2	60·9	85·5	33·2
4 Germany	35·0	44·1	35·1	—	55·9	47·2	21·3	47·2	54·3	54·3	85·4	27·2
5 Poland	64·6	68·3	73·5	57·7	—	43·5	47·3	58·3	50·8	52·6	90·8	45·2
6 Czechoslovakia	60·0	63·7	68·8	58·6	47·2	—	47·8	61·4	50·5	55·9	89·2	48·8
7 Austria	34·3	43·9	45·3	22·3	49·4	49·1	—	45·6	53·8	45·6	82·5	18·1
8 USSR	50·1	59·5	65·5	56·4	56·7	62·5	48·2	—	67·5	57·5	87·1	44·0
9 Lithuania	62·5	62·2	72·8	65·5	51·2	49·9	57·1	68·6	—	61·6	84·7	51·5
10 Italy	53·4	56·6	66·9	57·4	58·8	63·6	52·2	56·7	66·4	—	69·6	40·5
11 Negro	83·6	84·3	90·1	88·6	93·2	92·7	88·4	89·8	90·9	79·2	—	NA
12 Native whites	19·1	31·8	34·0	26·0	50·8	51·9	25·0	49·8	57·0	48·3	NA	—

[a]For the 75 community areas.
[b]Above diagonal, 1950 figures, below 1930, numbers at head of columns refer to countries numbered on stub
Source: Compiled from tables 1, 2 and 3, pp.366–368, Duncan and Lieberson (1959).

for example, was able to show that decrease in segregation of European ethnic groups in relation to the native white population of the ten cities which he studied for the period 1910 to 1950 (1963, 122, table 38). However, the very detailed study carried out by Duncan and Lieberson (1959) for Chicago alone for the period 1930 to 1950 showed not only how the degree of segregation of the ethnic groups decreased in relation to the native white population but also how it broke down between the ethnic groups (see Table 1). Thus, according to the 1950s traditional argument, the black population was acting spatially in the same way as other white immigrant groups, but at a later date.

> The Negro migrant to the central city will, without question, follow the same patterns of social mobility blazed by the successive waves of immigrants who settled in our central cities. Just as the immigrant underwent a process of "Americanization" the in-migrant Negro is undergoing a process of "urbanization". The Negro is already rising and will continue to rise on the social-economic scale as measured by education, occuation, income and the amenities of urban existence. Furthermore, the Negro, in time, will diffuse through the metropolitan area and occupy outlying suburban as well as central city areas. (Hauser, 1958, 65; see also Handlin, 1959, 2, 92 and 118; Park, 1950, 149-50; and Calef and Nelson, 1956)

This optimistic view of the future was reinforced by historical hindsight, in which blacks were seen as having experienced under certain circumstances, a much more dispersed distribution within American cities in the past. This view also allowed a historical explanation for the degree to which blacks became concentrated. It was a product of the scale and speed of the northward movement of blacks during and after the First World War.

This view can be clearly seen in Gunnar Myrdal's massive account of race relations in the United States, *An American Dilemma* (Myrdal, 1944).

THE HISTORICAL VIEW OF BLACK GHETTO FORMATION

Myrdal argued that inside American cities before the great migration to the North and to the cities, there had been, generally speaking, two patterns of black distribution: one scattered and one concentrated. In old, Southern cities, where the black population was the successor to the former slave population which had acted as servants to the white population, the pattern was scattered. The black population generally lived in side streets or along alleys at the back of white houses. Although the pattern was scattered, it was nevertheless segregated, depending on ceremonial, rather than spatial distance (Myrdal, 1944, 618–619, 621). Similarly, in Northern cities with a small black population, the pattern of their settlement was scattered. However, in Northern cities with a large number of blacks and in Southern cities which received the bulk of their black population after the Civil War, there tended to be large areas in which the black population lived separated geographically from the whites. After the urbanization of the black population had gained momentum, all cities, in both the North and South, became segregated. Northern cities, which before the First World War migration had experienced small and scattered distributions of their black population, witnessed a rapid change to segregated conditions in the wake of that migration. Other authors supported Myrdal's general argument.

Duncan and Duncan (1957) illustrated the tightening noose of the Chicago ghetto with a series of Lorenz curves from which it could be shown that in 1920 60% of the black population were living in census tracts which were over 50% black and 45% were living in tracts that were between 75 and 89·9% black (Duncan and Duncan, 1957, fig. 5, 92). By 1930, just under 80% of the black population was living in areas that were over 75% black (Duncan and Duncan, 1957, fig. 6, 92), and 19% were living in areas that were almost exclusively black (Duncan and Duncan, 1957, 95).

Thus, the degree of black segregation and concentration rose to a severe intensity during the first half of the twentieth century, far greater than that experienced by European ethnics, and has remained there with little variation since. From an analysis of ten northern cities from 1910 to 1950, Lieberson (1963, 132) concluded:

> In summarizing the findings about Negro-European immigrant housing patterns, we may observe that although at one time certain specific immigrant groups in a city have been somewhat less segregated from Negroes than from native whites or more segregated than Negroes were from native whites, the general summary figures indicate that Negroes and immigrant groups have moved in opposite directions, i.e., declining segregation for immigrants and increasing segregation for Negroes. In terms of sheer magnitude, the Negroes are far more highly segregated than are the immigrant groups (Lieberson, 1963, 132).

Table 2 "Ghettoization" of ethnic groups, 1930

Group	Group's city population	Group's "ghetto" population	Total "ghetto" population	Percentage of group "ghettoized"	Group's percentage of "ghetto" population
Irish	169 568	4993	14 595	2·9	33·8
German	377 975	53 821	169 649	14·2	31·7
Swedish	140 913	21 581	88 749	15·3	24·3
Russian	169 736	63 416	149 208	37·4	42·5
Czech	122 089	53 301	169 550	43·7	31·4
Italian	181 861	90 407	195 736	49·7	46·2
Polish	401 316	248 024	457 146	61·0	54·3
Negro	233 903	216 846	266 051	92·7	81·5

Source: Philpott (1978, 141, table 7)

Introducing their conclusion from a later study of 207 cities, the Taeubers stated that:

systematic study of the block by block patterns of residential segregation reveals little difference among cities. A high degree of racial residential segregation is universal in American cities. Whether a city is a metropolitan center or a suburb; whether it is in the North or South; whether the Negro population is large or small — in every case, white and Negro households are highly segregated residentially than are Orientals, Mexican Americans, Puerto Ricans or any other nationality group. In fact, Negroes are by far the most residentially segregated urban minority group in recent American history (Taeuber and Taeuber, 1965, 2, see also pp. 35, 36).

The Taeubers constructed indices of segregation for the non-white population of 207 cities of the coterminous United States for which census block data were available in the 1960 census. Virtually all the large cities of the country (those of more than 50 000 population) were included as well as a large but non-random selection of smaller cities (Taeuber and Taeuber, 31). The lowest value for any of the cities was 60·4. The index value ranged from this figure to 98·1, with very few cities in the lower part of the range. Eight cities had values below 70 and 31 had values below 79; half of the cities had values above 87·8 and a quarter above 91·7 (Taeuber and Taeuber, 34).

Philpott's work (1978) and that of Ward (1971, 1982) has shown that

European ethnic areas in American cities even at the time of the most intense immigration did not achieve the intensity and completeness of the black ghetto (see Table 2).

RE-APPRAISALS OF THE TRADITIONAL VIEW OF THE TRADITIONAL VIEW OF THE BLACK GHETTO

By the 1960s the fiction of the newness of the blacks as an immigrant group to explain the lack of dissolution of the black ghettos could no longer be maintained. Gottmann (1961) was one of the earliest to doubt the optimistic view of the black ghetto as yet another ethnic area on the European model. Having quoted Handlin (1959, 118), who saw racial prejudice to blacks and Puerto Ricans as only a temporary brake to their spatial, social and economic freedom of movement, Gottmann (1961, 720–722) argued that the problem was more complex and that those faced with racial discrimination were presented with a situation that was different in kind rather than degree from that of earlier ethnic groups.

The critical attack on the conventional explanation of black segregation came from two directions. The first was the demonstration that income differentials between black and white households explained very little of the degree of black segregation. The second was the demonstration that Puerto Ricans, who were newer than blacks as an immigrant group and poorer, were nevertheless more dispersed.

In 1964, an article written by Taeuber and Taeuber demonstrated that family income differences between blacks and whites contributed little to the explanation of the degree of geographical segregation of blacks from whites. They demonstrated this by a technique of indirect standardization. The percentage that non-whites formed of each income band for the city as a whole was calculated. For example, 40% of families with incomes from $2000 to $2999 in Chicago in 1960 were non-white; 44% of families with incomes from $1000 to $1999 were non-white, and so on. The appropriate percentage for the city was then applied to the number of families in each income band in each of the Chicago 75 community areas. If there were 1000 householders with an income of $2000-$2999 in a sub-area, 400 of them would be "expected" to be non-white, 600 white, and so on. This yielded the number of non-white and white households in each community area of the city that would be "expected" if their representation in each were directly related to income alone. An index of residential segregation

(Peach, 1975) was then calculated between the expected number of non-whites and white families for the city as a whole across all the community areas. For 1960 the expected index was 12 while the observed index was 83. In 1950 the expected index had been 11 and the observed index 79. Thus not only did income 'explain' only 12% of black segregation from white in Chicago in 1960 but the explanatory force of income differentials had decreased from the already low 14% explanation of 10 years earlier. Blacks were segregated not because they were poor but because they were black.

These findings were ignored by the new wave of marxist geographers writing about the ghetto. For Harvey (1973) and Castells (1977) the explanation of the ghetto was entirely economic. Indeed, at the heart of Harvey's chapter on ghetto formation, which is the crucial chapter of *Social Justice and the City*, there is a *léger de main*. Harvey tells the reader that he is going to show how the capitalist state, working through the market mechanism of the bid rent curve, creates the ghetto. But Harvey does not do this. He demonstrates instead how the poor are segregated from the rich. As we have seen from the Taeubers' work cited above, segregation of the poor from the rich explains little of the segregation of black from white.

PUERTO RICANS AND BLACKS IN NEW YORK

The analysis of Puerto Rican and black distributions in New York and Chicago further opened the way to a reappraisal of European ethnic areas in American cities.

Gottmann again was one of the first to show that Puerto Ricans, despite arriving later than blacks, had an advantage over them:

> In New York City the Puerto Ricans have for some time provided a transition between white and non-white groups — not because there is much association between them and the American Negroes, with whom they do not wish to be linked, but because of their own racial composition. Seven per cent are classified as Negro, and many more have some Negro blood, but a large proportion of them are white. By virtue of the latter, the Puerto Ricans, white and colored together, gain access to housing in deteriorating tenements that are still closed to American Negroes. Thus, the Puerto Ricans have been able to spread out more widely than Negroes (Gottmann, 1961, 705).

In their 1964 article on Chicago, Taeuber and Taeuber were able to extend the argument. They showed that Puerto Ricans and other

Table 3 Indices of dissimilarity for various ethnicities (foreign stock), Negro and Puerto Rican for the New York Standard Metropolitan Statistical Area (SMSA) 1960 and 1970

	1	2	3	4	5	6	7	8	9	10	11	12	13	14	15	16	17
1 UK	—	33·0	*ᵃ	40·3	27·9	45·3	43·8	40·6	43·0	48·4	44·8	30·6	72·8	64·8	66·5	81·3	79·8
2 Eire	28·1	—	*	47·9	36·6	53·0	49·7	48·3	49·8	57·6	46·1	42·5	75·3	64·4	68·0	82·8	79·3
3 Norway	51·4	58·7	—	*	*	*	*	*	*	*	*	*	*	*	*	*	*
4 Sweden	31·8	41·3	45·8	—	43·9	60·5	56·8	56·5	58·1	63·3	54·2	43·6	77·8	74·9	75·4	85·8	85·5
5 Germany	25·6	33·3	56·4	38·2	—	44·8	42·0	39·0	42·1	49·3	43·4	36·1	73·9	64·7	66·8	82·7	80·6
6 Poland	45·0	51·7	67·9	57·9	47·1	—	45·2	24·1	36·8	22·3	52·5	49·6	76·2	66·9	66·7	81·0	77·9
7 Czechoslovakia	39·5	44·5	65·6	51·1	39·5	41·7	—	43·3	40·6	51·3	53·4	48·7	76·2	65·2	69·9	84·6	81·5
8 Austria	40·2	47·1	68·0	54·2	40·4	20·3	39·9	—	31·9	21·3	52·3	46·1	74·2	64·5	66·5	81·9	79·1
9 Hungary	39·1	44·2	68·3	52·9	38·7	31·3	33·9	24·7	—	37·9	55·1	46·7	75·4	65·4	68·1	83·6	79·7
10 USSR	50·2	57·1	72·9	62·2	52·1	20·0	49·0	19·0	32·7	—	59·6	51·8	76·3	67·9	68·1	82·2	80·3
11 Italy	44·9	48·0	60·2	51·9	45·6	52·7	51·6	53·0	53·9	60·5	—	47·9	78·2	70·3	70·7	83·1	79·4
12 Canada	*	*	*	*	*	*	*	*	*	*	*	—	74·4	67·6	68·8	82·1	80·6
13 Mexico	*	*	*	*	*	*	*	*	*	*	*	*	—	70·9	72·8	80·4	71·7
14 Cuba	*	*	*	*	*	*	*	*	*	*	*	*	*	—	52·0	72·8	68·3
15 Other America	*	*	*	*	*	*	*	*	*	*	*	*	*	*	—	42·1	56·4
16 Negro	80·3	80·3	88·4	83·7	80·6	79·7	81·9	81·1	80·4	81·8	80·5	*	*	*	*	—	55·9
17 Puerto Rico	79·8	76·5	88·2	83·9	79·7	75·5	78·6	76·6	76·3	78·1	77·8	*	*	*	*	63·8	—

ᵃ* = not available

Above the diagonal, 1970, Below the diagonal, 1960 (source: Kantrowitz, 1969a, table 6).

Source: Jackson (1981).

Hispanics, despite their more recent arrival than the blacks, despite their lack of English, and despite their lack of education and lower median income than the blacks, were nevertheless less segregated from the white population of Chicago than were the blacks.

In a series of cartographic essays, Kantrowitz (1969b) showed that Puerto Rican distributions in New York City in 1960 encircled the major black ghettos: "Puerto Rican settlements appear almost without exception as foothills to Negro mountains" (Kantrowitz, 1969b, 1). Kantrowitz also demonstrated that the blacker Puerto Ricans were tucked into the black edge of the ghetto while lighter Puerto Ricans were found at the outer edge (Kantrowitz, 1969b, 3). Kantrowitz saw in this distribution a possibility that Puerto Ricans were acting as a bridge between black and white populations. However, while Kantrowitz thought that Puerto Rican dispersal would depend on prior black dispersal (Kantrowitz, 1969a), Gottmann as we have seen, viewed the Puerto Ricans as the pioneers.

Thus, by the middle 1960s it became apparent that although the *effects* of the black ghetto and those of other ethnic or linguistic areas might be similar, their *causes* were significantly different. It was inevitable, given chain migration and the linkage of migration cycles to economic cycles (Jerome, 1926; Thomas, 1954) that new immigrants would move to areas in which their contacts had settled. In this way they would have friendly contacts and be able to feel their way into their host society.

The distinctive quality of the black belt was that, while other such colonies seemed to break up with time, the black area maintained or increased its degree of segregation. Although the formation of foreign immigrant colonies was understandable in the needs for a friendly milieu in which to adapt to American conditions, in the case of the black American it was not. For many foreign born persons, language was an obvious difference between themselves and the host population, and it might take two generations before the children of immigrants became indistinguishable linguistically from the mass. Cultural customs might take at least as long a period to become adapted. Although many of the black migrants had to adapt from the life of the rural South to the urban North, this did not explain the continuing spatial contrast between black and white ethnic groups.

TRADITIONAL VIEWS OF THE
DECLINE OF EUROPEAN ETHNICITY

Traditional views make the distinction between culture race and ethnicity. *Race*, although its biological basis may be difficult to define, is taken as that group of physical characteristics, such as skin colour, hair texture, mouth and lip shape etc., which can be genetically transmitted and which is thought to be characteristic of a group of people. *Culture* is defined, rather loosely, as that group of institutions such as language, literature and social values, which is maintained by a population. *Ethnicity* is defined as the union of a particular racial group with a particular culture. Race and culture are thus separate and distinct structures. A Chinese child, brought up from birth by English parents in England would be Chinese racially and English culturally. He would not belong to either the English or the Chinese ethnic group. There are enormous pressures in society for a culture to maintain its racial composition and for racial groups to maintain their cultural links.

The dominant element differentiating European immigrants in the United States from the rest of society, it was argued, was the cultural part of their ethnic character. Thus, broadly speaking, the European immigrants were similar racially to the majority of American society but different culturally. The cultural element in ethnicity is that part that is assimilated environmentally, unlike the racial element, which is transmitted genetically.

The dominant element in the ethnicity of the black population, however, was racial; in cultural terms, the black Americans spoke the same language as the majority, had lived in the country for generations and knew its *mores*. Cultural accommodation had been made, but racial difference persisted. Thus, because the ethnic distinctiveness of the Europeans was essentially cultural, it was capable of vanishing within a few generations; because the ethnic distinctiveness of the black Americans was genetic, it was not susceptible to elimination. The language of the European ethnic groups eroded; the blackness of the Afro-Americans remained. The audibility of the Europeans declined; the visibility of the black Americans persisted. The successors of the European immigrants became, it was argued, more spatially dispersed; as they became more like the rest of society, so their spatial patterns resembled that of the rest more closely. Black Americans, who had previously been only one of a multitude of ethnic groups, now became the dominant ethnic group within what was represented as a progressively more homogeneous white population. As black ethnic distinctiveness became highlighted, so their spatial pattern became more segregated.

By the 1960s, therefore, the situation had been reached in the literature, in which the segregation of Afro-Americans was seen as different in kind rather than different in degree from that experienced by European ethnics. Blacks had experienced degrees of segregation very much higher than that of white ethnic groups and had remained highly segregated despite economic progress. Thus, it was argued, that while whites converged, blacks diverged.

THE WHITE MELTING POT?

In the late 1960s and early 1970s the convergence of white groups began to be seriously questioned. As early as the 1940s, Kennedy (1944) had written a highly influential paper in which she argued that whites were not merging in a single pool. Kennedy (1944, 1952) put forward the hypothesis and evidence for a triple melting pot, with national and ethnic divisions among the white population slowly breaking down but religious boundaries between Jews, Protestants and Catholics being maintained. In this system, the British-Americans, Germans and Scandinavians were seen as forming a Protestant pool, the Irish, Italians and Poles as forming an endogamous Catholic pool, and the Jews as forming a third pool. Glazer and Moynihan (1963, 315) supported this idea from their New York evidence, adding the (white) Puerto Ricans to the Catholic pool and the black population as a fourth, separate pool. However, both Kennedy's argument and that of Glazer and Moynihan were broadly in favour of the convergence of European ethnics.

A contrary view on the convergence of European ethnics was put by Kantrowitz (1969b), who argued that although ethnic segregation had weakened, reports of its demise were exaggerated. His study is interesting from a methodological viewpoint, because his ethnic groups included both foreign born and their descendants. Most earlier studies had compared the foreign born with each other or had compared the foreign born and their descendants with the white population in some aggregated form; Kantrowitz compared groups of foreign born and their descendants with other groups of foreign born and their descendants.

Kantrowitz demonstrated that even culturally similar groups such as the Norwegians and Swedes in New York City showed considerable degrees of segregation from one another (Kantrowitz, 1973, 27). Under such circumstances, he doubted whether less similar groups such as the Irish, the Poles and the Italians would ever have merged spatially, let alone maritally (see Table 3).

Peach (1980, 1981) applied Kantrowitz's argument to Kennedy's New Haven data and showed that Kantrowitz was correct. There was little intermarriage of Poles, Irish and Italians. Marital patterns, in fact, reflected spatial distributions, and the Irish intermarried more with the northern European ethnics among whom they were residentially mixed than with their Catholic co-religious nationalities from whom they were more segregated.

Kantrowitz argued therefore that the segregation of blacks in the United States should be seen not simply as segregation of black from white, but black from British, Irish, German, Italians, Poles and so on and therefore also in the context of continuing segregation of European groups from one another. Ethnic stock, however, stops for US Census purposes at the second generation.

THE TAUTOLOGY OF EUROPEAN ASSIMILATION

What Kantrowitz's argument demonstrates is that the thesis of European assimilation is circular. The argument runs: European groups become more dispersed over time; marriage with Native Americans becomes more common over time; marriage and dispersal are behavioural measures of assimilation; therefore European groups are becoming more assimilated over time.

The key factors in this analysis depend upon census data. Ethnicity of Europeans has to be inferred from birthplace. With a flow of population much below the nineteenth and early twentieth century peaks, European birthplaces are a decreasing element in the United States population (Thernstrom et al., 1980, 480). The ageing foreign born could be progressively surrounded by their Native born children. Thus within three generations an ethnic group which maintained its identity and followed strict rules of ethnic endogamy would be recorded as Native Americans born of Native Americans marrying Native Americans and living in Native American areas. The passage of time and generations would carry the group past the reach of the Census question on birthplace and parental birthplace, and since assimilation is defined in terms of relations with Native Americans of Native American parentage they would, by definition, have become assimilated even if ethnically they remained distinct.

The importance of the point becomes apparent if it is contrasted with the measurement of race. Race is a self-attributable directly questioned matter in the US Census. Race therefore remains a permanently and directly measurable variable in the US Census, while ethnicity, because it is an inferred characteristic and dependent on birthplace inevitably erodes over time even if the reality which it is sought to capture from this method remains alive. The importance of this difference between ethnic and racial measurement can be seen if it were attempted to measure black ethnicity in the way in which white ethnicity is measured. On this basis American blacks would have been assimilated into the American population in the nineteenth century before many of the apparently disappearing European groups had arrived.

CONCLUSIONS

In the late 1970s and 1980s it seems that the geographical view of ethnicity in the United States is more one of structural pluralism than of the melting pot—American society has more the consistency of chunky marmalade than mayonnaise. The deepest fissures in American society seem, from the outside at least, to run along ethnic and particularly along racial lines rather than along economic lines.

The two major spatial structural re-alignments of the US urban system seem likely to intensify rather than to bind this ethnic wound. The first re-alignment is that of population redistribution in cities. This has acted in two ways. In the first place black expansion and white flight have created hostile interfaces in the racial transition zones. Black urbanization during the twentieth century lagged behind that of the whites. White urbanization had already peaked and turned into suburbanization and exurbanization, while urbanization of the blacks continued. These trends were most marked in relation to the central cities of large Standard Metropolitan Statistical Areas (SMSAs). The areas of racial succession and transition were, therefore, the narrow interface between two very large-scale movements with different directions. The black population was continuing to urbanize while the white population was decentralizing. Thus, an alternative to the view of black penetration, invasion, and succession is that of white withdrawal with black replacement (Rose, 1969). In the second place, the situation was made more acute by the political underbounding of cities, so that decentralization of whites meant also the transfer of wealth from the central cities to the functionally integrated but politically independent control of the suburbs. The simultaneous decay of retail activity and employment in the central cities and the growth of such activities in the suburbs have increased the political polarization between rich white suburbs and poor and increasingly black cores. The zone of transition now seems to eat both inward into the CBD and outwards into the inner residential zones.

The second major structural re-alignment is perhaps the relative decline of Gottmann's Megalopolis as part of what is popularly seen as the rise of the Sunbelt at the expense of the Snowbelt (Berry, 1980). In the dynamic areas of population growth, however, race still seems indelibly etched into the urban fabric. Even in the affluent and apparently more tolerant Californian environment, Rabinovitz and Siembieda (1977) reported pessimistically on black suburbanization. On the whole, it seemed, black suburbanization was the expansion of the central city ghetto across the suburban political line.

Perhaps the most chilling evidence for the triumph of race over other forms of ethnicity comes from Jackson's work on Puerto Ricans in New York City. Jackson's review of the Puerto Rican situation confirmed Gottmann's pessimistic analysis. He showed the Puerto Rican population being "pulled apart, with white Puerto Ricans being able to disperse while the darker-skinned Puerto Ricans resided more with blacks than with other Puerto Ricans or with non-Hispanic whites" (Jackson, 1981, 117-120).

REFERENCES

Berry, B. J. L. (1969). Monitoring trends, forecasting change and evaluating goal achievements: the ghetto v. desegregation issue in Chicago as a case study. *In* Chisholm, M., Frey, A. E., and Haggett, P. (ed.). "Regional Forecasting." London, Butterworths. Also reprinted in Peach (1975).

Berry, B. J. L. (1980). Inner city futures: an American dilemma revisited. *Transactions of the Institute of British Geographers* 5, 1, 1-28.

Calef, W. C., and Nelson, Howard, J. (1956). Distribution of Negro population in the United States. *Geographical Review* 46, 82-97.

Castells, M. (1977). "The Urban Question: A Marxist Approach." London, Arnold.

Cressey, P. F. (1938). Population succession in Chicago. *American Journal of Sociology* **44**, 56-59.

Drake, St Clair and Cayton, H. (1945). "Black Metropolis", New York, Harcourt, Brace.

Dollard, J. (1949). "Caste and Class in a Southern Town", (2nd edit.) New York, Harper and Brothers.

Duncan, O. D. and Duncan, B. (1955). Residential distribution and occupational stratification. *American Journal of Sociology* **60**, 493-503.

Duncan, O. Dudley and Duncan, B. (1957). "The Negro Population of Chicago." Chicago, University of Chicago Press.

Duncan, O. Dudley and Lieberson, S. (1959). Ethnic segregation and assimilation. *American Journal of Sociology* **64**, 364-374.

Ford, R. G. (1950). Population succession in Chicago. *American Journal of Sociology* **56**, 156-60.

Frazier, E. F. (1947). Sociological theory and race relations. *American Sociological Review* **12**, 265-271.

Gordon, M. M. (1964). "Assimilation in American Life." New York, O.U.P.

Gottmann, J. (1961). "Megalopolis: The Urbanized Northeastern Seaboard of the United States." New York, The Twentieth Century Fund.

Glazer, N. and Moynihan, D. P. (1963). "Beyond the Melting Pot, The Negroes, Puerto Ricans, Jews, Italians and Irish of New York City." Cambridge Mass., The MIT Press and Harvard University Press.

Grozier, E. and Grozier, G. (1960). "Privately Developed Interracial Housing" Special Report to the Commission on Race and Housing. Berkeley, University of California Press.

Handlin, O. (1959). "The Newcomers: Negroes and Puerto Ricans in a Changing Metropolis." Cambridge, Mass., Harvard University Press.

Harvey, D. (1973). "Social Justice and the City." London, Arnold.

Hauser, P. M. (1958). On the impact of urbanism on social organization, human nature and the political order, *Confluence* **7**.

Jackson, P. (1981). Paradoxes of Puerto Rican segregation in New York. *In* "Ethnic Segregation in Cities" (C. Peach, V. Robinson and S. Smith, ed.) London, Croom Helm. 109-126.

Jerome, H. (1926). "Migration and Business Cycles." New York, National Bureau of Economic Research.

Kantrowitz, N. (1969a). "Negro and Puerto Rican Population of New York City the Twentieth Century." New York, American Geographical Association.

Kantrowitz, N. (1969b). Ethnic and racial segregation in the New York Metropolis, 1960. *American Journal of Sociology* **74**, 685-695.

Kantrowitz, N. (1973). "Ethnic and Racial Segregation in the New York

Metropolis: Residential Patterns among White Ethnic Groups, Blacks and Puerto Ricans." New York, Praeger.

Kennedy, R. J. R. (1943). Premarital residential propinquity and ethnic endogamy. *American Journal of Sociology* **48**, 580-584.

Kennedy, R. J. R. (1944). Single or triple melting pot? Intermarriage trends in New Haven, 1870-1940. *American Journal of Sociology* **49**, 331-339.

Kennedy, R. J. R. (1952). Single or triple melting pot? Intermarriage in New Haven, 1870-1950. *American Journal of Sociology* **58**, 56-59.

Lieberson, S. (1963). "Ethnic Patterns in American Cities." New York, The Free Press of Glencoe.

McEntire, D. (1960). "Residence and Race, Final and Comprehensive Report to the Commission on Race and Housing." Berkeley, University of California Press.

Morrill, R. L. (1965). The Negro ghetto: problems and alternatives. *Geographical Review* **55**, 339-61.

Myrdal, G. (1944) (with assistance of Sterner, Richard and Rose, Arnold). "An American Dilemma: The Negro Problem and Modern Democracy." New York, Harper.

Northwood, L. K. and Barth, E. A. T. (1965). "Urban Desegregation: Negro Pioneers and their White Neighbors." Seattle, University of Washington Press.

Park, R. E. (1950). "Race and Culture." Glencoe Ill., Free Press.

Peach, C. (ed.) (1975). "Urban Social Segregation." London, Longman.

Peach, C. (1980). Ethnic segregation and intermarriage. *Annals of the Association of American Geographers* **70**, 371-381.

Peach, C., Robinson, V. and Smith, S. (ed.) (1981). "Ethnic Segregation in Cities." London, Croom Helm.

Pettigrew, T. F. (1981). Race and class in the 1980s: An interactive view. *Daedalus (Proceedings of the American Academy of Arts and Sciences)* **110**, 233-255.

Philpott, T. L. (1978). "The Slum and the Ghetto: Neighborhood Deterioration and Middle Class Reform, Chicago, 1880-1930." New York, Oxford University Press.

Rapkin, C. and Grigsby, W. G. (1960). "The Demand for Housing in Racially Mixed Areas: A Study of the Nature of Community Change" Special Report to the Commission on Race and Housing and the Philadelphia Redevelopment Authority, Berkeley, University of California Press.

Spear, A. H. (1967). "Black Chicago." Chicago, Chicago University Press.

Taeuber, K. E. and Taeuber, A. F. (1964). The Negro as an immigrant group: recent trends in racial and ethnic segregation. *American Journal of Sociology* **69**, 374-382.

Taeuber, K. E. and Taeuber, A. F. (1965). "Negroes in Cities, Residential Segregation and Neighborhood Change." Chicago, Aldine.

Thernstrom, S., Orlov, A. and Handlin, O. (1980). "Harvard Encyclopaedia of American Ethnic Groups." Cambridge, Mass. Belknap Press.

Thomas, B. (1954). "Migration and Economic Growth." Cambridge, Cambridge University Press and National Institute of Economic and Social Research.

Ward, D. (1971). "Cities and Immigrants." New York, Oxford University Press.

Ward, D. (1982). The ethnic ghetto in the United States: Past and Present. *Transactions, Institute of British Geographers* **7**, 257-275.

Wilson, W. J. (1978). "The Declining Significance of Race." Chicago, Chicago University Press.

Chapter Ten

Geographers and the City
A Contribution to the History
of Urban Geography in France

PHILIPPE PINCHEMEL
in collaboration with Geneviève Pinchemel

If one casts a glance over the shelves of a library or consults bibliographical compilations, it is clear that innumerable articles dealing with the city are the work of geographers. Is not the city at the centre of our civilization, of our spaces, and also of the problems of contemporary societies? Does it not therefore seem natural that contemporary human geography should be very largely urban geography? Over the past thirty years the contributions of geographers — textbooks of urban geography, theses on cities or urban systems, specialist reviews run by geographers, urban atlases and plates dealing with cities in regional and general atlases, works on urban research — have been producing a feeling of identification between the city and geography. And does not this book offer a double proof of it — in the high proportion of the studies treating an urban theme — and the geographer in whose honour it is published, whose contributions to the knowledge of cities and to thinking on the characteristics of contemporary urbanization are fundamental?

THE ENTRY OF THE TOWN INTO THE GEOGRAPHICAL FIELD

A look back at the last century of French geography makes it easier to understand the origins and the roots of urban geography, indicating the

THE EXPANDING CITY
ISBN 0 12 547250 1

conditions under which this domain of geographical knowledge has developed and drawing attention to facts and to currents of thought that may point the way to a less simplistic assessment of the present components of urban geography and its important contemporary developments.

Bringing together geography and the city gives rise to a number of questions. How did the city gain access to geography? What view did the geographer first take of the urban fact, and how did this view evolve? Was there at the outset one single way, or were there several ways, of studying the town geographically?

Once urban geography had become a constituent part of human geography what was its content and how was this sub-divided? How are the contents to be defined and situated in the general evolution of human geography? What have been the reciprocal influences of geography on urban analysis and of urban geography on geography?

The history of urban geography has still to be written. Works of general, human, or urban geography rarely speak of it. An exception is Harold Carter who, in his classic work, *The Study of Urban Geography*, devotes fifteen pages to it. He acknowledges that "urban geography is a comparatively young branch of the subject [general field of geography]".[8]

This opinion is confirmed by Paul Claval's assertion: "The geographers are latecomers . . . For a long time they avoided analysing the town as a general category"[18] (p.5).

If the papers presented at the International Congresses of Geography accurately reflect the interests of the geographers of the period, one can only conclude that they were not greatly drawn to the urban phenomenon. In the recent bibliography of the Congresses published by Georges Kish,[31] the subject index "Urban Geography" gives no reference for the first eight congresses, only three for the ninth, none for the tenth and eleventh, and only one for the twelfth. It is not until the thirteenth congress (Paris, 1931) that urban geography features quite strongly (nine references). There was a real division between geography and the city, a state of affairs that seems to have continued for a long period.

We shall attempt to discover the reasons for this by an examination of the French school of geography.

URBAN GEOGRAPHY AND THE
FRENCH SCHOOL OF GEOGRAPHY

This failure to give much attention to towns may seem surprising on the part of German and British geographers, whose territories were undergoing intense urbanization during the last decades of the nineteenth century. In 1969 André Meynier wrote: "strangely enough, the first [French] geographers did not immediately grasp the significance of this transformation [the growth of towns], and did not highlight the real importance of towns in the contemporary world".[43] Anne Buttimer went further still in her assertion: "For two generations of French geography, however, cities were somehow anathema, unwelcome intrusions in the neatly ordered landscape"[7] (p.118).

In point of fact French geography was to develop from the 1870s onwards, in a way that diverted its interest from the urban phenomenon. This geography, established by Paul Vidal de La Blache and institutionalized, by his own efforts and those of his pupils, in the Faculties and great university establishments, was taking root in the natural sciences; it saw itself as the science of the relations between natural environments and human civilizations; its basic concern was the study of relations between human societies and natural environments.

The town is the least natural and the most artificially produced of geographical phenomena. One can clearly see, as one reads the geographers of this period, that the town presented them with a serious problem. When dealing, in *Le Tableau de la Géographie de la France*, with the development of Paris, Vidal de La Blache wrote: "We are not called upon to trace its historical development . . . this development is linked ever more closely with the actual history of France. *Geography certainly does not dissociate itself from this, but no longer plays the leading role*".[59] The wording here leaves no room for argument and the positions are very clear.

In 1936, that is to say roughly twenty years after the first contributions, Pierre Lavedan, in his *Géographie des Villes*, wrote, with a touch of humour: "A town exists when man dominates nature and succeeds in freeing himself from it. The town is a thing that escapes from its physical environment. *It would surely be the very negation of any sort of urban geography* if that science consisted solely in investigating the effect that nature has on man; but every problem has two aspects; nature is in charge in the village, the opposite is the case with the town"[35] (p.195).

If one bears in mind that university research work reflects the dominant interests of a period, the study of titles of theses presented in France may be significant. With the exception of the thesis of Paul Meuriot, to which we shall return, the first theses dealing with cities were not presented until the 1930s — on Bône by Lespès in 1930, on Grenoble by Jouanny in 1931, on Marseilles by Rambert in 1934, on Cairo by Clerget in 1934. Raymond Quenedey's thesis on Rouen Housing is unique of its kind for the period.[47]

Raoul Blanchard is generally regarded as one of the founders of urban geography in France; he owes this reputation to his monographs on towns — Grenoble in 1911, Annecy in 1916 — and to an article, "Une méthode de géographie urbaine", which appeared in 1922 in *La Vie Urbaine*. The preface of the book on Grenoble states clearly: "The essential idea of the study is that the origin and development of the town are explicable in terms of the physical conditions of its site"[3] (p.5).

At the heart of this urban geography are the concepts of site and, at a subsidiary level, situation. The geographers excelled in the analysis, description, and typology of sites and in the dialectic interaction of site and situation, with the conditions favourable to both or conflicting.

To regard the site as the explanation of the town is not very far from regarding it as the cause: "Grenoble came into being as a town at a confluence — one of rivers much more than one of valleys. If the valley-junction later brought the town prosperity, it was the junction of the rivers that brought it into being, by providing at this unique spot within the depression of the Isère a permanent crossing-point"[3] (p.53).

Urban geography was thus developing in a "determinist" current of thought, since the geographer's role was to look at urban phenomena within the context of the natural-environment data, and Blanchard wrote accordingly: "In spite of human changes, nature always asserts her rights, even on an organism as complex as a town"[3] (p.159).

This trend and this causal relationship were leading urban geography into an impasse. For the geographical analysis of the town could not be restricted to relations with the natural environment, which were only marginal compared with the components of the town: population, functions, landscapes...

Raoul Blanchard himself showed awareness of this in his article in 1922, when he wrote: "urban geography which is the most human there is, since here everything is constructed by men who, when they found and develop a town, are intent on masking nature, transforming nature's elements to the point of distorting them, pursuing adaptation to nature in such a complex fashion that nature is no longer immediately visible. Hence the task is not an easy one [for the geographer]" he adds! "A sound method is thus all the more imperative..."[5] (p.302).

There really was a lack of balance between the two causal relationships; the problem of geographical determinism was indeed hampering the development of urban geography. Lucien Febvre made it his business to show that this was so: Les Villes is the title of the last chapter of *La Terre et l'Évolution Humaine*. It is known that this book, published in 1922, had been conceived just before the 1914 war. In the first paragraphs of that chapter Lucien Febvre lets fly a volley of criticism aimed at Jean Brunhes:

> But really, with the best will in the world, what can one discover that is "geographical" in the resemblances between these various quarters of towns? To compare the water-mills district of Strasbourg to Venice would surely be regarded as carrying a joke a bit too far. If what you mean is that, within our area of western civilization, urban landscapes by the waterside resemble each other, in the sense that they comprise a sky, houses, and water, I am very willing to agree. But if you want to label this brilliant advance in knowledge "geographical", I must say that I don't follow you—unless perhaps "geographical" covers everything, in which case we have to conclude that the word is meaningless[27] (p.413).

And on the next page he continues: "Actually it was Vidal de La Blache, once again, who formulated, and at the same time solved, the real geographical problem of the town on the day when he wrote: 'nature prepares the site, and man organizes it in such a way that it fits in with his desires and his needs'. That is self-evident"[27] (p.414).

Lucien Febvre develops his ideas further in the following section, which deals with fortress towns:" To none of these towns has geographical predestination ever been applicable. They were not brought into being by a rock, a loop of a river, a belt of water or marshland. But essentially by a human will"[27] (p.420).

In 1936 P. Lavedan hammered home the point made by Lucien Febvre: "The human factor is the primary one. Formulae such as 'that site was bound to attract men' or 'the town grew out of that site' seem to us totally inaccurate. The way to put it is: 'that site *may* attract men'; but in any case the human will, human caprice, human skill remain in complete control of men's choice".[35]

However, the debate goes beyond the problem of determinism. Two texts of Lucien Febvre and Raoul Blanchard, both published in 1922, reveal the wide range of the discussions between historians and geographers on the subject of towns.

Raoul Blanchard, in his "Méthode de Géographie Urbaine", when introducing the theme of Urban Evolution (the second of the three themes), writes: "It is the life of the town explained geographically. Hence history has a leading role to play here; yet it must all the same be said, without any disrespect to history, that it figures in an auxiliary capacity. The main concern is not the consideration of historical events in themselves, but in their relations with the town and the geographical conditions of its existence; it is these last that remain for us the basis of the study . . . and that not only because the specific subject of our studies is the geography of towns, but also because we believe that man cannot, in fact, free himself from these conditions"[5] (p.313).

Now, Lucien Febvre, basing himself on the analysis of Annecy by Raoul Blanchard (1916) and works by Camille Jullian, concludes a long exposition by statements that eliminate all doubt:

> We say to the historians: it is certainly no desire of ours to impair goodwill or to provoke one of those wretched "shop" disputes that are the shame, if not of scholarship, at least all too often of scholars. But the fact is that research of this sort has so completely ceased to have any real connection with geography that, when reading accounts of work carried out on certain towns by qualified geographers, one sometimes begins to think that, after all, a certain type of "human geography" is perhaps nothing but history with its sources revitalized, its methods rejuvenated, and its subjects beneficially renewed[27] (pp.427 and 428).

OTHER CURRENTS OF URBAN ANALYSIS

This account of the birth of urban geography in France is in accordance with "Vidalian" geography in the form in which it became established at the École Normale Supérieure, in the Facultés des Lettres, and in a whole collection of publications, reviews, and theses.

It is certain that a geographical view of the town on these lines set the tone, but it was not in a position of total monopoly. There exist other currents, other schools of geographical thought, less powerful and hence less well known, which looked at the urban phenomenon in quite different ways.

The most important of these currents is that of Emile Levasseur

(1828-1911), who held the chair of Géographie-Histoire et Statistiques Economiques at the Collège de France (1868-98). He was the author of several school textbooks and was responsible in 1871 with Himly for a report on the teaching of geography.

Levasseur's geography is based on an analysis of the distribution of populations derived from statistical data and on explanation of the inequality of densities. In 1886 he gave an account of the attraction exerted by towns, proportionately to their size, on rural populations. But Levasseur (1886) was also interested in urban environments and their "pathology", in so far as inquiries and statistics made it possible to work out densities and distributions.

Paul Meuriot's doctoral thesis *Les Agglomérations Urbaines dans l'Europe contemporaine*, appeared in 1897. The sub-title is more specific: "Essai sur les causes, les conditions, les conséquences de leur développement". The author, Professeur Agrégé d'Histoire, dedicates his work "à mon Maître, M. Emile Levasseur" (Paul Meuriot also thanks a professor of geography: "M. Marcel Dubois, our Maître en Sorbonne, who has on occasion kindly given us helpful advice"[42] (pp.10-11)), and he presents his research as "a work on comparative statistics and demography".[42]

A summary of the book would certainly not be repudiated by a geographer of our own day: study of urban populations and their movements; definition of the agglomeration; migrations, their causes and nature; consequences of the development of urban agglomerations; suburbs; demographic, hygienic, political, economic, and social consequences (role of the towns as consumer centres—role of the social classes of urban agglomerations). And many of Paul Meuriot's reflections and observations express a sensibility that is very modern.

Nevertheless, when he gives his third chapter the title "De l'influence de la géographie sur la situation des villes", Paul Meuriot expounds ideas that are in keeping with the naturalist content of the geography of the period:

Before proceeding to examine urban groups in Europe, we would like to indicate, in a general way, the part played by geography in their formation. The position of towns is, indeed, not the result of pure chance nor of the arbitrary decision of some celebrated founder. Their situation is attributable to nature itself; and a person studying the map of a region still uninhabited could work out in advance where the towns would be sited once the region had attained a certain population density. It is natural influences that are the most powerful force in bringing men together in groups—whether it be the sea, facilitating communications, or the direction of the course of a river, or the juxtaposition of plain and mountain regions, or differences in geological formations, etc."[42] (p.59).

And when Paul Meuriot asks the question: "Does the expansion of large agglomerations come about in accordance with certain geographical laws?" it is in connection with the often observed spread of towns towards the west[42] (p.276).

As well as Levasseur, the urban question was also taken up by economists and sociologists: Adolphe Coste,[22] who, in "Les Principes d'une Sociologie Objective", reveals some notions of the hierarchy of towns and of urban networks; R. Maunier, who was to deal with "L'Origine et la Fonction Économique des Villes".

But for decades the geographers had not been restricting themselves to Vidal de La Blache's genetic view of geography. Elisée Reclus had published, in 1895, an article on "The Evolution of Cities".[50]

When at the beginning of the twentieth century the geographers tried to go beyond this naturalist urban geography they turned to the formula of the regional monograph and applied that to the town. Thus Antoine Vacher, whose thesis dealt with Berry, published in 1904 a "model for a local monograph", on the lines laid down by Albert Demangeon, on Montluçon;[58] in 1913 came Levainville's "Rouen, Étude d'une Agglomération Urbaine".[38]

But the currents of thought of statisticians, sociologists, economists, even of certain geographers, were accepted neither by the precursors of Vidal nor by Vidal and his pupils. In fact Himly's report on the oral examination of Meuriot's thesis expressed serious reservations.

It thus seems hard to deny that there were uncertainties and ambiguity in academic geography's attitude to the urban phenomenon. It had great difficulty in extricating itself from a naturalist "geographical" framework. Apart from their analysis of situations and sites, the geographers took into consideration only minor aspects of the urban question. Enclosed within the narrow circles of natural environments, they did not realize the importance of the town.

It is paradoxical that what was regarded by scholars holding their views as geographical led to a dead end, whereas what they were writing on side-issues is seen by many of today's geographers as belonging to the category of urban geography.

At the same time, one should add some important qualifications and distinctions. There can be found already, in this transition period of the history of geography, from the pen of geographers as well known as Vidal de La Blache, observations that show a very "modern" perception of urbanization and of the role of towns. It is easy to collect from Vidal de La Blache a series of quotations tending in that direction; for example, in one article, written in 1910, dealing with the Regions of France, we find: "Every town represents a nodal point of relationships." Then again: "Towns and roads are great initiators of unity; they create solidarity in regions".[60]

But these remarks come from a geographer; and consequently are not intended by him as statements of the geographical approach to the problem; the content of the article as a whole bears witness to this.

FROM THE GEOGRAPHICAL CONDITIONS OF THE TOWN TO THE TOWN AS A GEOGRAPHICAL OBJECT

Conscious as they certainly were of the epistemological obstacle that the introduction of the urban phenomenon represented, geographers sought other approaches which would enable them to make of the town a geographical phenomenon.

In 1922 Raoul Blanchard was actively working at this by identifying, for urban geography,

> three orders of problems, and hence three of research . . . First, the study of geographical factor, an element of a physical or human order, under the influence of which the urban nucleus was constituted and became established. Then the examination of the reactions that the organism produced by these geographical elements manifests under the impact of historical events. Finally, the detailed study of the present forms of urban activity as affected by geographical and political factors[5] (p.302).

This text is interesting; it shows the efforts of the Grenoble professor to go beyond the naturalist "geographical" content, and to extend the scope of the geographer's intervention in urban analysis.

The town becomes a geographical phenomenon because it exists as a visible fact and is a component of the landscape. Jean Brunhes, in his *Géographie Humaine*,[6] expresses the same ideas as Blanchard, but using "geographical" in this sense of "visible fact" and no longer of "natural cause": "The town . . . must be treated as a sort of natural being, to which the comparative methods of the observational sciences are applicable." The layout of a town, the physiognomy, that is to say, the forms of the built-up environment, and the situation are "the three essential factors which combine to make the town a geographical phenomenon".[6] One passes thus from the geographical conditions of the town to the town as a geographical fact in its own right.

During the period that follows, the books on urban geography by P. Lavedan (1936), G. Chabot (1948), P. George (1952) and Max Sorre (1952) reflect these major orientations of the French school of geography. The emphasis is on layout, landscape, functions, zones of influence, and relations between towns and rural areas.

When Max Sorre writes: "it is incontestable that the town is a geographical fact; it forms part of the landscape, contributes to its character . . . But this geographical fact is a fact of human geography",[54] he is describing unerringly the way this current was going; one is thus enabled to assess how the meaning given to urban geography had evolved since the beginning of the century.

It is significant that, in his first work on the town, in 1952, Pierre George presents the theme of the urban landscape as a new one: "M. Roger Dion has introduced the rural landscape into the vocabulary and into the inventory of facts of human geography. A strictly symmetrical system would call for the study of the urban landscape . . . It actually is possible to describe an urban landscape by assembling observable facts and their infrastructures"[28] (p.11).

This remark clearly confirms that geographers were much more at ease when observing rural landscapes, the product of nature and of man, than when dealing with urban landscapes. The emphasis on the rural in French geography at that time is undeniable: it is very apparent in the theses on regional geography, it asserted itself even more markedly in the works of Albert Demangeon and Roger Dion, and in the great rural theses of the 1950s there was an outburst of it. On the other hand, there was no thesis on urban geography. As well as the essential paradigm of Nature-Society relationships, geographers found in the countryside vast expanses; one must not overlook this difference in scale, and hence in impact, between the rural and the urban. The difference in scale affected also the availability of maps.

Furthermore, it is necessary to have a clear idea of what the notion of "urban landscape" covers. One finds grouped together a number of themes: layout, differentiation of intra-urban spaces, ranging from the

Question 102 was worded thus: "What are the natural, economic, and historical laws that govern the coming into being, the distribution on the ground, the expansion, and the decline of towns?" Léon Lalanne did not provide an answer to that question, which was obvious, but the seventh, in the "Mathematics" section, was one for which his training had equipped him: "Synthetic study of the occurrence of natural alignments, observations that may reveal the existence of alignments, apart from those already to be found on mountain-chains, hydrographic troughs and contours. Pentagonal network. Application of these studies."

At a general session, on 2 August 1875, Lalanne read a paper: "A Note on the Occurrence of Natural Alignments in relation to the laws that govern the distribution of centres of population on the earth's surface".[34]

The author recalled, moreover, that "these mutual distances (that separate agglomerations of a similar order) appear not to have been the subject of any research since the time when the exposition of the laws governing them was submitted to the Académie des Sciences". Foreseeing the reservations which his speech would encounter and the difficulties he would have in getting his ideas accepted, Lalanne emphasized that "since the statement setting forth these new laws . . . has never yet been published in any form, the author is not unaware that at first sight they may produce an impression strange enough to necessitate his making an appeal to the assembly's indulgence . . . and begging it to wait for the justifications that he will very shortly produce".

Lalanne formulates and demonstrates two laws: the Law of the Equilateral Triangle and the Law of Multiple Distances. The first states the equality of distances between two agglomerations of the same order; the second states that "the mean distance separating two neighbouring agglomerations of the same order is an exact multiple of the mean distance relative to each of the lesser orders". These results are proved correct by a study of the triangulations carried out at each administrative level. The author lays stress, as the wording of the title indicates, on the rectilinear alignments of the town sited at the apexes of equilateral triangles, and, showing a rare "geographical" sense of proportion, he writes: "no doubt the irregularities of the earth's surface, rivers, lakes, mountains, forests, mere variations in the productive quality of the soil, in a word disparities of whatever nature, have played a considerable role and have many times upset the law of the equilateral triangle, without either the power or the number of these disruptive causes preventing its main characteristics from manifesting themselves".

To say that these ideas were not accepted by geographers is to put it mildly, yet they had been expounded to members of a geographical congress and printed in the proceedings of that congress! Not an echo or trace of them can be found, and not even any criticism of them in the works of geographers!

One has to wait for 1952 and the extraordinary intellectual acuity of Max Sorre to find any further mention of Lalanne. It was not until 1952 that he made his entry into the world of French geographers. Max Sorre devotes a long paragraph to him in the third volume of his *Fondements*: "However, in 1863 a French engineer, Lalanne, thought he could prove that, in a region where the population was balanced, the development of a road network of which towns were the nodal points would finally produce a geometrical figure whose centres of attraction of equal value would be equidistant. This would be a system made up of triangles grouped round a central point." A note at the end of the chapter is more specific: "In this system the territory of each urban centre forms a hexagon, and the centres (apexes of equilateral triangles) are equidistant from each other". But Max Sorre's final assessment is harsh: "All this geometry is far removed from the true spirit of geography"[54] (pp.206, 216-17).

Lalanne's ideas were to be rediscovered, developed, and formalized by Walter Christaller, in the three publications[15,16,17] of 1933, 1938, and 1950. In fact these have never been the subject of any review in France; the 1950 work was merely mentioned in the "Books Received" list of the Annales de Géographie.

The historical circumstances no doubt explain to a large extent this non-diffusion of the ideas of the German geographer. What came out of Nazi Germany was not received in the same way as the ideas of the nineteenth-century German geographers had been, even after the French defeat of 1870.

It is not surprising that it was Georges Chabot who presented the ideas of W. Christaller to the French-speaking geographers. Chabot had read, at the Congrès de Géographie of 1931, an important paper on zones of influence of towns.[9] He was the best qualified to understand the contribution of the German geographer.

However, he gives only a somewhat toned-down version of the hierarchy of the centres, although also stating clearly that: "without wanting to confine ourselves within a rigid over-simplification, we must recognize that each town does appear to be a grade in a complex hierarchy where it can be at the same time vassal and suzerain. The towns are linked by a whole system of relationships, close or remote, indirect or direct, that in each country weave the network of the towns"[10] (p.195). Georges Chabot makes no reference to the hexagonal arrangement, any more than he does to the nature of the different categories of relationships.

Four years after Georges Chabot's book came out, Max Sorre referred very briefly to Christaller, in conjunction with Kant and Ahlmann: "With the search for theoretical or empirical formulae . . . a spirit of rigorous precision is introduced into geographical analysis".[54] He goes no further into the matter than this. Similarly, Christaller is merely mentioned in Pierre George's *La Ville* (1952).[28]

It is significant that the most important presentation of Christaller's theories appeared in 1954, in a duplicated course of lectures given by Jean Tricart, who had become Professor at Strasbourg a few years earlier. The chapter on *"semis urbains"* analyses Christaller's diagrams in great detail. Tricart's final view is more qualified: "thus we may criticize Christaller's theory for its geometrical rigidity. It is, however, not without value; there really does exist, as a result of the competition between towns, a tendency for them to be arranged in a more or less regular pattern, and to be spaced out in accordance with a certain rhythm"[55] (p.260).

The Tricart-Christaller connection allows one to suggest the hypothesis that perhaps the German language formed a barrier to the diffusion of Christaller's ideas. All his books and articles were first published in German. The English translation of his book was published in 1966 and it was not until that year that his ideas were disseminated worldwide. A first breakthrough occurred at the Stockholm Congress, on the occasion of the Lund symposium (1960).

But it should not be forgotten that, besides Christaller, there were other geographers, English-speaking ones, who were pursuing very similar research. Robert E. Dickinson had published several very interesting articles as early as 1929 and 1934. During the war French geographers undoubtedly had excuses for not obtaining direct and speedy access to the articles of Edward L. Ullman (1941) and Arthur E. Smailes (1944); the obstacle then was no longer of a linguistic order but geo-strategic!

Quite soon after the Second World War this line of research broadened out. In 1946 Arthur E. Smailes published *The Urban Mesh of*

England and Wales, and, in 1947, Robert E. Dickinson's *City Region and Regionalism* came out. This same author, in *The Scope and Status of Urban Geography* (1948), cited Christaller, Bobeck, and the researches in English. So the linguistic-barrier excuse does not stand up to investigation.

Making an assessment, in 1957,[11] of French urban geography in the middle of the twentieth century, Georges Chabot gives a good summary of the evolution the situation in this field of knowledge: "Studies of towns were formerly often found acting as a sort of appendix to regional monographs; today the practice seems to be to start with the town and then construct the region round it." And, speaking of the relations between town and country, he explains that "it is the whole region that now comes within the orbit of the town, and the region is defined more and more in relation to the town upon which it depends"; the terms *réseau, trame, armature* (network, web, framework) nowhere appear.

It was surely between the mid 1950s and mid 1960s that the turning-point of French urban geography came. Detailed analysis of that transformation is outside the scope of this chapter. It is known that French geographers have been devoting works of increasing importance to studies of networks, of urban systems, within a regional or national framework. However, it must be stated that reservations have always been expressed as soon as they have gone beyond the areas that have become classic—networks, levels of functions, hierarchies—to those of interlocking hexagons, of the regular patterning of space.

Twenty-five years later the novelty of the content of Tricart's work still appears just as strange. The textbooks of geography most recently published in France still allot very little space to Christaller's ideas. The reason is that this corpus of ideas—whose components are logic, regularity, ordered spacing, division into hexagons—clashes with decades of thinking on the part of geographers who had been trained to give accounts of personalities, stress contingent data, and look for the distinctive character of each situation.

In 1963 George Chabot, actuated by his strong intellectual honesty, could not help expressing reservations about Christaller's models, while acknowledging that "the theories of W. Christaller have had great success" (J. Beaujeu-Garnier and G. Chabot[2]). Two years later, in a review of an Italian book on the theory of centrality, Georges Chabot wrote: "The author takes as his starting-point the now classic theory of W. Christaller, initiated by his paper of 1933. We know the mathematical structure of W. Christaller, who assumes a homogeneous population, but deserves great credit for having formulated the urban hierarchy" [12] (p.331).

The situation of French urban geography in the 1960s was thus complex and ambiguous. It was well acquainted with the ideas of Christaller, Loesch, and Zipf; it had for a long time been carrying out research and developing fresh ideas on the relations between towns and rural areas; the concepts of the urban network, of hierarchy, were familiar to it. This was the period when the theses were being worked on which, in that decade and under the influence of Pierre George in particular, were to constitute the first university research on urban networks.

All the same, Christaller's theory was not easily incorporated into this research. The concept of geometric regularity, the idea of units of space polarized by towns, was not accepted. Just as Jean Tricart's university post at Strasbourg had facilitated the discovery of Christaller, a period of residence in Strasbourg, and some research on the urban network of Alsace, brought Michel Rochefort into contact with German geographical work.

But the duality of the geographical thought appears on one page only. Michel Rochefort does indeed write

In the Strasbourg network we are struck . . . by the geometric pattern of the distribution of the key-towns; around the big Rhine port that acts as regional centre, the three sub-regional centres are arranged in a semi-hexagon, in apparent conformity with Christaller's diagram, which is cut in two by the frontier on which the regional centre is sited.

Yet, after pointing out a number of exceptions, the author adds:

It is our opinion, after this brief, general examination, that the historical factors that have influenced the coming into being of the Strasbourg network are more important, for an understanding of its present physiognomy, than some hypothetical geometric distribution. Is not this latter a fortuitous coincidence rather than a real consequence of a network structure? [51] (p.127).

And in Jean Labasse's great work W. Christaller and E. L. Ullman are accorded no more than seven lines, in a section dealing with the measurement of urban spheres of influence. A diagram taken from the *Economie Géographique* of Courtin and Maillet (1962) entitled "Vocations urbaines en espace abstrait", although based on equilateral triangles and hexagons, has only a very indirect connection with W. Christaller's system (1). However, Jean Labasse, like Georges Chabot some years earlier, cites Christaller who "gave in 1933 his famous paper on 'tributary areas' arranged in a hexagonal pattern".[32]

Again, in 1969 André Meynier was to write: "German researchers, such as Christaller, had believed that they had found evidence there of fairly regular polygonal patterns. But the arbitrary factor in all this was too great . . . The French are on the whole disinclined to adopt abstractions of this sort"[43] (p.165).

One would arrive at a similar conclusion is one looked at the matter from the view-points of the statistical hierarchy of towns and the rank-size rule. George K. Zipf's first book was published in 1941; the second in 1949. In 1958 the first applications and discussions appeared in American geographical reviews: articles by Brian J. L. Berry and William L. Garrison appeared in the *Annals of the Association of American Geographers* and by Charles T. Stewart Jr in the *Geographical Review*. But in France the first mention and the first application by geographers date from 1964.[1]

French-speaking economists were quicker to grasp the novelty and interest of these new insights into the systems of towns. English, American, German, and Swedish researchers were, in the 1950s and 1960s, beginning to take note of a conceptual and theoretical field opened up by F. Perroux, J. R. Boudeville, and A. Piatier. The thesis of Marie Andrée Prost, presented in 1963 and published in 1965, makes it possible to assess the difference in interests and orientations—especially since the bibliography contains a very large number of French and foreign geographical references.[48] Whereas the economists were inclined, as a result of their intellectual training, to think abstractly, to theorize, the geographers, on the other hand, were conditioned by their empirical education, on the actual ground, and had been trained in France to look for the contingent and the exceptional.

However, it was not merely a matter for the French geographers to be able to understand and accept these ideas, of their passing from induction to deduction, from the ideographic to the nomothetic. It was necessary for them to undergo a basic transformation of concept and paradigm, to pass from the idea of environment and the problematic of the relations between environments and societies to the concept of space and the problems of the organization of space by societies.

The beginning of the 1960s and perhaps the year 1963 mark the turning-point for the rise of a new French urban geography concerned with its inter-urban aspects. This brief incursion into the history of French urban geography may promote a better understanding of its evolution and its various aspects, strengths and weaknesses. The stages such as we have noted, with their strengths and weaknesses, mark the continuous appraisal with which men, whether geographers or not, subject towns, considered in relation both to their environments and to the spatial patterns that they impose on these settings.

REFERENCES

1. Adam, H. and Ioos, A. (1964). Hiérarchie urbaine: une application de la règle de la taille suivant le rang, à l'étude des villes de la région du Nord. *Hommes et Terres du Nord* **2**, 77-83.

2. Beaujeu Garnier, J. and Chabot, G. (1963). "Traité de Géographie urbaine." Armand Colin, Paris.

3. Blanchard, R. (1911). "Grenoble: Etude de géographie urbaine." Armand Colin, Paris (3ème édit., 1935).

4. Blanchard, R. (1916). Annecy, Esquisse de géographie urbaine. *Recueil Travaux Institut de Géographie alpine* **4**, 369-463.

5. Blanchard, R. (1922). Une méthode de géographie urbaine. *La vie urbaine*, **16**, 301-319; *R. Géog. alpine* **16**, 1928, 193-214.

6. Brunhes, J. (1910). "La Géographie humaine." Alcan, Paris.

7. Buttimer, A. (1971). Society and Milieu in the French geographical tradition, Rand McNally, Chicago. Assoc. Amer. Geog. Monograph Series, 6.

8. Carter, H. (1972). "The Study of Urban Geography." London, Arnold.

9. Chabot, G. (1931). Les zones d'influence d'une ville. *Comptes rendus du Congrès International de Géographie de Paris*. Colin, Paris, Vol. III, 432-437.

10. Chabot, G. (1948). "Les Villes, Aperçu de Géographie humaine." Armand Colin, Paris.

11. Chabot, G. (1957). La Géographie urbaine. In "La Géographie française au milieu du vingtième siècle." J. B. Baillière, Paris.

12. Chabot, G. (1965). La théorie de la centralité d'après Eliseo Bonetti. *Annales de Géographie* **403**, 331-335.

13. Chastel, A. et Boudon, F. (1977). "Système de l'architecture urbaine, I. Le quartier des Halles." CNRS, Paris.

14. Chatelain, A. (1946). Cette nouvelle venue: La géographie sociale. *Annales de Géographie* **55**, 266-276.
15. Christaller, W. (1933). "Die Zentralen Orte in Süddeutschland." Verlag von Gustav Fischer, Jena.
16. Christaller, W. (1938). Rapports fonctionnels entre les agglomérations urbaines et les campagnes. *In* "Comptes rendus du Congrès International de Géographie d'Amsterdam", 123-127, Leiden.
17. Christaller, W. (1950). "Das Grundgerüst der raumlichen Ordnung in Europa: Die System der europäischen zentralen Orte." Frankfurter Geographische Hefte.
18. Claval, P. (1968). Le théorie des villes. *R. Géog. de l'Est* **1-2**, 3-56.
19. Claval, P. (1970). La géographie urbaine. *R. Géog. Montréal*, **24**, 117-141.
20. Clerget, M. (1934). "Le Caire: Etude de géographie urbaine et d'histoire économique" (2 vol.). E. & R. Schindler, Le Caire.
21. Clout, H. Z. (1977). "Themes in the Historical Geography of France." Academic Press, London and New York.
22. Coste, A. (1899). "Principes d'une Sociologie objective." Alcan, Paris.
23. Coste, A. (1902). "De l'Influence des agglomérations urbaines sur l'état matériel et moral d'un pays." Masson, Paris.
24. Dickinson, R. E. (1932). The distribution and function of the smaller urban settlements of East Anglia. *Geography* **17**, 19-31.
25. Dickinson, R. E. (1947). "City, Region and Regionalism." Routledge and Kegan Paul, London.
26. Dickinson, R. E. (1948). The scope and status of urban geography. An assessment. *Land Economics* **24**, 221-238.
27. Febvre, L. (1922). "La Terre et l'évolution humaine: Introduction géographique à l'histoire." La Renaissance du Livre, Paris.
28. George, P. (1952). "La ville, Le fait urbain à travers le monde." Presses Universitaires de France, Paris.
29. George, P. (1961). "Précis de Géographie urbaine." Presses Universitaires de France, Paris.
30. Jouanny, J. (1931). Les origines de la population de l'agglomération grenobloise. Grenoble, Imprimerie Allier. (Thèse complémentaire, Grenoble).
31. Kish, G. (1979). "Bibliography of International Geographical Congresses, 1871-1976." G. K. Hall, Boston.
32. Labasse, J. (1966). "L'Organisation de l'espace: Eléments de géographie volontaire." Editions Hermann, Paris.
33. Lalanne, L. (1863). "Essai d'une théorie des réseaux de chemin de fer fondée sur l'observation des faits et sur les lois primordiales qui président au groupement des populations." Comptes Rendus de l'Académie des Sciences, Séance du 27 juillet.

34. Lalanne, L. (1878). Note sur les faits d'alignement naturels dans leurs relations avec les lois qui président à la répartition des centres de population à la surface du globe. Deuxième Congrès International de Géographie, Paris, 1875. E. Martinet, Paris, Vol. 2, pp.45-55.

35. Lavedan, G. (1936). "Géographie des villes." Gallimard, Paris.

36. Lespes, R. (1925). "Alger, esquisse de géographie urbaine." J. Carbonel, Alger.

37. Levainville, J. (1913). "Rouen, étude d'une agglomération urbaine." Paris.

38. Levasseur, R. C. (1878-1890). "La France et ses colonies" (3 vols). Delagrave, Paris.

39. Levasseur, R. C. (1889-1892). "La Population française" (3 vols). Rousseau, Paris. Vol. 2, Chap. 17, Les populations urbaines.

40. Maunier, R. (1910). Théories sur la formation des villes, Revue d'Economique Politique, juillet et septembre.

41. Maunier, R. (1910). La fonction économique des villes, Paris, Librairie générale de droit et de jurisprudence.

42. Meuriot, P. (1897). "Des agglomérations urbaines dans l'Europe contemporaine." Paris, Thèse.

43. Meynier, A. (1969). "Histoire de la Pensée géographique en France." Presses Universitaires de France, Paris.

44. Panerai, P., Depaule, J. C., Demorgon, M., Veyrenche, M. (1980). "Eléments d'analyse urbaine." Editions des Archives d'Architecture moderne, Bruxelles.

45. Pinchemel, G. (1954). Les cours et courettes lilloises. La Vie urbaine 9, 38.

46. Ponsard, C. (1955). "Economie et Espace." SEDES, Paris.

47. Quenedey, R. (1926). "L'habitation rouennaise, étude d'histoire, de géographie et d'archéologie urbaines." Rouen, Imprimerie Lestringant (Thèse principale, Paris).

48. Prost, M. A. (1965). La hiérarchie des villes en fonction de leurs activités de commerce et de services. Gauthier-Villars, Paris, Thèse, Lyon, 1963.

49. Rambert, G. (1934). "Marseille, la formation d'une grande cité moderne", Thèse, Paris, Société anonyme du Semaphore de Marseille, Marseille.

50. Reclus, E. (1895). The Evolution of Cities, The Contemporary Review, 67, 2, 246-264.

51. Rochefort, M. (1960). L'organisation urbaine de l'Alsace, Strasbourg, Thèse.

52. Smailes, A. E. (1944). The Urban Hierarchy in England and Wales, Geography, 29, 41-51.

53. Smailes, A. E. (1946). The Urban Mesh of England and Wales, Trans. Inst. Brit. Geog. 2, 84-101.

54. Sorre, M. (1952). "Les fondements de la géographie humaine." Vol. 3: L'habitat, Paris, Armand Colin.

55. Tricart, J. (1954). "Cours de géographie humaine." Vol. 2: L'habitat urbain, Paris, Centre de documentation universitaire.
56. Tricart, J. (1950). Contribution à l'étude des structures urbaines. *R. Géog. Lyon* 145-156.
57. Ullman, E. L. (1941). A Theory of Locations for Cities, *Amer. J. of Sociol.* **46**, 86-99.
58. Vacher, A. (1904). Montluçon, essai de géographie urbaine, *Annales de Géographie* **13**, 121-137.
59. Vidal de la Blache, P. (1903). "Tableau de la géographie de la France." Hachette, Paris. Vol. 1, of E. Lavisse, "Histoire de France."
60. Vidal de la Blache, P. (1910). "Régions françaises." *R. de Paris* **17**, 821-849.
61. Vidal de la Blache, P. (1917). "La France de l'Est." Armand Colin, Paris.
62. Zipf, G. K. (1941). "National Unity and Disunity." Bloomington, Principia Press.
63. Zipf, G. K. (1946). The P1.P2/D Hypothesis on the Intercity movement of persons. *Amer. Sociol. R.* **11**, 677-687.
64. Zipf, G. K. (1949). "Human Behavior and the Principle of Least Effort." Addison-Wesley, Cambridge, Mass.

Chapter Eleven

The Ville Moyenne
A French Strategy for Town Expansion

D. I. SCARGILL

In his writings, Jean Gottmann has always stressed the functional inter-dependence of cities. Unlike Christaller, whose urban systems were inward-looking and closed, Gottmann has constantly drawn attention to those functions that bind cities together in complex transactional networks. He has demonstrated clearly the importance of looking beyond the single city to the system of cities—regional, national and increasingly international—of which it is a part. The study that follows recognizes this contribution of Jean Gottmann to urban studies by selecting for examination a component of the French urban system, the medium-sized town or *ville moyenne*.

PLANNING THE FRENCH URBAN SYSTEM

In comparison with that of Britain, the urban system of France exhibited remarkable stability during the 250 years before 1950. The main outline of the system had been established by the end of the seventeenth century and after that there were few changes in the distribution or order of towns within the system.[2] Manufacturing industry promoted a number of towns in the hierarchy—Lille and Saint-Étienne for example—but in general the urban system and the way of life that accompanied it reflected a society organized on a traditional, agricultural basis.

The one major exception to this generalization lay in the emergence of

THE EXPANDING CITY
ISBN 0 12 547250 1

Paris to a position of primacy within the system. After 1850 the political and cultural supremacy that Paris had long enjoyed was reinforced by economic growth, industrial expansion following the construction of a highly centralized main-line rail network. Population growth reflected these changes. The number of people living in the capital doubled between 1851 and 1876 to reach 2½ million. In sixty years after 1876 it increased by a further 3½ million whilst that of the rest of the country fell by 100 000. More than a sixth of the population lived in Greater Paris after the Second World War, and the city dominated the political, economic and social life of the country. The extent of this dominance and the consequences of it, both for Paris and the provinces, were demonstrated by Gravier[10] in *Paris et le Désert Français*. Whereas in 1801 only the second city, Marseille, was appreciably smaller than its rank-size "ideal", by the 1960s most of the twenty largest provincial cities of France were "too small" according to Zipf's city-size distribution (Fig. 1).[25]

Early postwar planning in France showed an awareness of the problems caused by the primacy of Paris, but attempts to redress the balance were mostly of a broad-brush nature aimed at decentralization of industry from the capital (the Petit Plan of 1950) and the promotion of regional development (*comités d'expansion économique*, 1954). It was not until 1962, following publication of the Fourth Plan (1962-1966), that significant attempts were made to manipulate the urban system as part of a coherent strategy of national development. The establishment in 1963 of DATAR (*Délégation à l'aménagement du territoire et à l'action régionale*) was most important in this respect. DATAR's role was to co-ordinate planning strategies and to ensure that a regional component was built into the National Plan. To this end CODERs (*commissions de développement économique régional*) were set up in the planning regions in 1964, the latter now being headed by a *préfet de région*. The same year saw the designation of eight *métropoles d'équilibre*, intended to assist policies of regional development by promoting growth in the larger provincial cities.

The introduction of an urban component to regional planning represented a growing awareness in the early 1960s, both of the role of the city as a focus of regional life and activity and of the possibility of utilizing this dynamic function of the city to spread economic benefits through the region. As early as 1910 Paul Vidal de la Blache had observed that, "Aujourd'hui, c'est la ville qui crée la région", and this

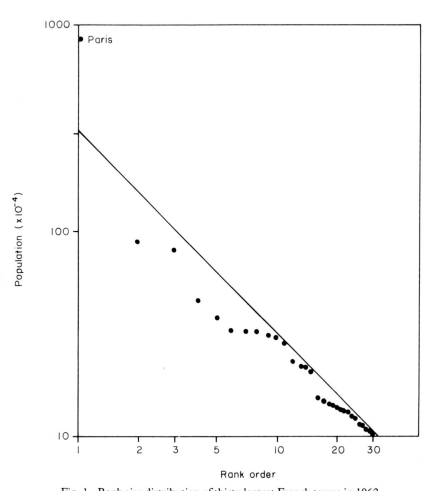

Fig. 1   Rank-size distribution of thirty largest French towns in 1962

idea had been stressed by later writers, including Jean Gottmann, who in 1952 wrote "La ville engendre en rayonnant par le jeu de la circulation une nouvelle région qui sera généralement, à cheval sur les limites entre régions naturelles".[19] Recognition that the city might act as a pole of development within this region stems from the work of such writers as Perroux[26] and, more importantly, Jacques Boudeville. Many of the latter's ideas are summarized in *L'Espace et les Pôles de Croissance* published in 1968.

The choice of cities to act as *métropoles* was limited to those which already possessed a certain level of high order functions and which exercised an obvious and extensive regional influence. Information about these activities was set out in two reports[11,12] which investigated the nature of the French urban hierarchy—what the authors described as *l'armature urbaine*—and which ranked towns according to these two basic criteria (Fig. 2). Hautreux and Rochefort distinguished three levels below Paris in the hierarchy: *métropoles régionales, centres régionaux* and *centres sous-régionaux*. Selection by the government of the *métropoles d'équilibre* was limited to the eight *métropoles régionales*, although in all but three cases the *métropoles* grouped towns which were considered to

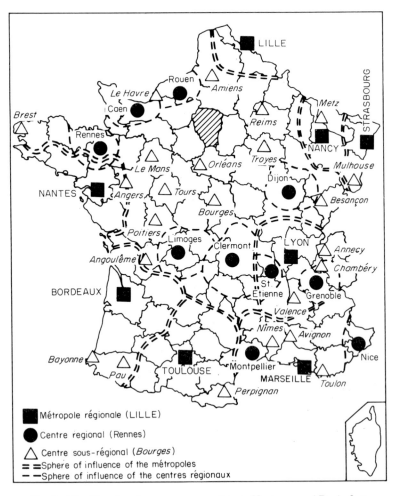

Fig. 2   The French urban system according to Hautreux and Rochefort

have strong local or regional links. The need to look beyond the municipal limits of individual cities for purposes of planning was also recognized in the setting up of OREAMs (*organismes d'étude d'aire métropolitaine*) in 1966 and the creation in 1967 of the first *communautés urbaines*.

French planning in the 1960s showed a strong preference for the *métropoles d'equilibre*. Financial institutions and centres of higher education and research, including some of the *grands écoles*, were encouraged either to move or to establish offshoots in these cities. Investment in transport and communications was directed both to improving their links with Paris and to integrating them more fully into European networks. Projects like the new airport of Satolas outside Lyon were indicative of a desire to compete on equal terms with the larger provincial cities of other EEC countries. New Towns were built (Lille-Est, L'Isle-d'Abeau) and major schemes initiated for central city renewal. Problems of traffic circulation were to be countered in the case of both Marseille and Lyon by the building of underground railway systems.

THE MEDIUM-SIZED TOWNS

The *politique des villes moyennes* that emerged in the early 1970s may be regarded as an extension of policies relating to the *métropoles d'équilibre*. Having promoted growth in the largest centres of the hierarchy it was logical to turn to the lower-order towns in the hope that benefits conferred on the former would spread through the regions as organizations which had been set up in the cities sought to expand their activities by opening branches in the surrounding towns. It was a good example of polycentric planning, taking advantage of the known tendency for certain kinds of innovation to diffuse down the urban hierarchy. Policies for the medium-sized towns were thus to complement those for the larger ones, further assisting the government in its attempts to decentralize activity from Paris.

A rather different interpretation is one that sees the emphasis on the medium-sized towns as a reaction to the earlier concentration of investment in the *métropoles*. By the 1970s the government was being accused of favouritism towards the cities, and it was pointed out that far from conferring benefits on their respective regions, the major urban centres were draining them of the most active elements in their population, creating at the regional scale the sort of problems that Gravier had highlighted in *Paris et le Désert Français*. The difficulties were particularly acute in a region such as Midi-Pyrénées where Toulouse was experiencing burgeoning growth but where there were no other towns with a population exceeding 55 000. It was suggested that diseconomies of size were already evident in the bigger cities, witness the need for *métros* in Lyon and Marseille. For a time in the late 1960s Lyon was even subjected to the kind of control on industrial expansion that had been exercised in Paris (the *agrément* requirement).

Yet another explanation of the attention given to medium-sized towns arises from changes in attitude towards the city. Large-scale, prestigious schemes that had characterized the 1960s gave way in the following decade to a preference for developments on a smaller, more human scale. *Gigantisme* of the kind that had produced the *grands ensembles* on huge housing estates like that of Le Mirail at Toulouse, was no longer fashionable. Small was beautiful, and as increasing recognition was accorded to the social problems, travel costs and pollution of the cities, corresponding stress was laid on the more ordered qualities of life that were to be experienced in the *villes moyennes*. Here it was still possible to park the car; local traders had not yet been put out of business by the hypermarkets on the urban fringe; there was space to build *pavillons* for those who preferred an individual dwelling, and the nearby countryside provided opportunities for recreation and the purchase of a *résidence secondaire*. "Par la qualité des services qu'elles offrent, leur cadre de vie, elles peuvent devenir le lieu privilégié d'un nouveau mode de développement urbain".[27]

But if the medium-sized towns were felt to offer certain social advantages, they were not without problems of their own. Population growth over the previous twenty years had strained existing services, and their employment base was often narrow, especially in manufacturing, offering limited job opportunities for young people leaving school. Their architectural legacy of fine buildings had been neglected and funds were needed to restore these and to check the progressive decay and abandonment of the towns' historic cores as population moved out to, frequently ill-planned, estates on the urban fringe. '*Les belles endormies*', as one politician (M. Chalandon) described them, were stirring but it needed the caress of an enlightened planner to revive them and awaken their hidden beauty.

The initiatives that led to the formulation of a *politique des villes moyennes* were taken in 1971 and 1972. In October 1971 M. Jérôme Monod, head of DATAR, addressed a congress in Bordeaux and spoke of a greater willingness on the part of major industrial companies to break up the production side of their organization into smaller units, of perhaps a thousand employees, which might be located in medium-sized towns where they would not be so large as to dominate the existing employment structure. He also referred to the social benefits of the *villes moyennes* where new housing could be built without recourse to the *grands ensembles* that had invited such criticism in the larger cities. These and other advantages were stressed in a number of studies published over the succeeding months by DATAR, or its research arm SESAME (*Système d'études pour un schéma d'aménagement de la France*).

In March 1972 the government announced its intention of carrying out pilot projects in up to half-a-dozen medium-sized towns, and official support for the *villes moyennes* was expressed in a speech made by M. Albin Chalandon of the Ministère de l'Equipement (quoted in *Le Monde*, 14 April 1972):

> Elles sont souvent belles, toujours riche en complexité et de singularité. En étroite relation avec leur petite région, elles sont réellement des cités. Ceux qu'elles accueillent deviennent des citadins, alors que dans les grandes métropoles ils sont des banlieusards . . . On peut espérer que le développement des villes moyennes va être un mode privilégié de dévelopment de l'économie dans les décennies qui viennent.

"Les villes moyennes, animation et développement" was the theme of the *Congrès national des économies régionales et de la productivité* (CNERP) which was held in Nice in October 1972. Opening the conference, M. Olivier Guichard, the minister responsible for planning, outlined the government proposals for the medium-sized towns but emphasized that the details of individual projects would depend on local circumstances. "Les responsables des villes moyennes devront inventer eux-mêmes les voies de leur développement." In a closing speech, the Prime Minister, M. Pierre Messmer, placed his seal of approval on the movement in favour of *villes moyennes*:

> "Je vois, enfin, dans les villes moyennes, le terrain d'élection du renouveau de notre vie locale . . . Où pourrait s'exercer, mieux que dans une ville moyenne, l'association des habitants au choix des conditions de leur vie quotidienne? Dans une collectivité humaine limitée, les hommes connaissent non seulement leurs voisins et leurs partenaires de travail,

mais aussi ceux que le hasard de la vie quotidienne leur fait côtoyer. Ils peuvent choisir en meilleure connaissance ceux d'entre eux qu'ils chargent de gérer la cité. En retour, c'est là que la communication se fait le mieux entre les élus et les électeurs" (Le Monde, 24 October 1972).

Shades of Aristotle?

Could the politicians have felt that there was political capital to be made out of support for the medium-sized towns? The thought was probably not absent from the mind of Etienne Mallet when he headed an article on the government's proposals (Le Monde, 1 November 1972) with the question: 'Les villes moyennes: thème électoral ou modèle d'urbanisme?'

POPULATION AND EMPLOYMENT

How big is a medium-sized town? The official definition is an agglomeration with a population of between 20 000 and 200 000. Defined in this way, France possessed 193 villes moyennes at the time of the 1968 Census. They housed just over 11 million people, nearly a third of the country's urban population.

Population (000s)	20-30	30-40	40-50	50-100	100-200
No. of towns	65	28	26	46	28

With such a wide range of population totals, one could hardly pretend that the concept of the ville moyenne was derived from some notion of optimum size, though broad comparisons have been made between the cost of public services in these towns and those in the biggest cities.[15] The 193 towns also differed widely in their geographical location, particularly in relation to larger centres of population, and GER (the Planning Ministry's Groupe d'études et de recherches) has distinguished five categories of ville moyenne on the basis of location.

1. Towns that form part of a larger urban region, e.g. Versailles and Saint-German-en-Laye in Greater Paris, Longwy in Lorraine, and Armentières in the northern industrial conurbation.
2. Towns that may be regarded as satellite to a larger agglomeration, e.g. Mantes and Melun in the case of Paris, Vienne and Givors near Lyon, and Elbeuf outside Rouen.
3. Free-standing towns such as Rodez, Auch, Tulle and Draguignan.
4. Towns that fall between categories 2 and 3, being influenced to

some extent by a larger city, e.g. Roanne (Lyon), Arras (Lille), Chartres (Paris), Haguenau (Strasbourg).

5. Towns owing their importance to local resources or related influences. These include resorts such as Royan and Les Sables-d'Olonne, spas (Vichy, Thonon), army towns (Rochefort), ports (Sète) and, most commonly, centres of industry or mining (Montceau-les-Mines, Forbach, Le Creusot, Carmaux, Cluses).

Support for a *politique des villes moyennes* was boosted by the findings of the 1968 Census which revealed a buoyant demographic situation. Between 1954 and 1968 the population of the 193 medium-sized towns had grown by an average of 2·2% a year. The corresponding figure for the urban centres of over 200 000 was 1·9%; that for towns of under 20 000 was 1·7%. In his Bordeaux speech (1971) M. Monod attributed the high rate of growth in the medium-sized towns largely to the drift from the land. He drew attention to the fact that rural to urban migration commonly took place in two stages, from the farm or village to the towns of the *département* or region and later, if work were unavailable or social conditions poor, to the big city. According to Monod, most French regions were nearing the end of the first stage in 1968 and "Si nous voulons donc éviter un mouvement de super-concentration urbaine, c'est maintenant et pas plus tard qu'il faut développer une politique d'emploi, de logement et d'accueil, dans les villes moyennes".

Rural to urban migration was not, however, the only cause of population growth. Michel[24] looked at population change in towns of 30-100 000 between 1954 and 1975 and in general found the most dynamic to have been the ones closest to Paris, Lyon and Marseille. He concluded that growth was a function of regional economic conditions and not of the size and other characteristics of the *ville moyenne*. There is the further suggestion, though it is not stated, that outward diffusion of activity had been taking place, not only from Paris, but also from the largest provincial centres.

Studies of several medium-sized towns in the south-west, carried out under the direction of Professor Bernard Kayser of the University of Toulouse-Le Mirail, point to a number of other reasons for population growth. These include expansion of jobs in the public service sector, the return of French families from Algeria, and the arrival of foreigners to work in unskilled manual occupations.[15] The effect of these inward migration currents is to obscure, so far as crude totals are concerned, a rather complex pattern of population change that includes a significant outward movement, especially of better-educated school-leavers.

The town of Auch, *chef-lieu* of the *département* of Gers serves as a somewhat extreme example on account both of its relative isolation and of the dependence of the surrounding area on agriculture (51% of the active population in 1968). The *département* has lost population continuously for over a century, but the pattern of loss was reversed in Auch after the First World War, and the town had almost doubled its population by 1968 (Fig. 3). Between 1962 and 1968 the annual rate of growth was 2·2%, 84% of the increase being accounted for by migration which would seem to support the argument of M Monod. However, examination of the 1968 total (21 462) reveals the presence also of 1058 repatriates from North Africa and 1286 foreigners (Algerians, Portuguese), the latter engaged mainly in construction and related occupations. A further clue to demographic change is suggested by the employment structure of the town, no less than 67·6% of the working population being engaged in the "tertiary" sector in 1968, especially in administration,

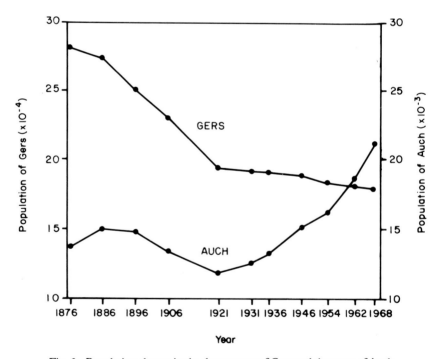

Fig. 3   Population change in the department of Gers and the town of Auch

education and other services. Lévy[21] refers to the "tertiarisation de l'économie", the national average for *villes moyennes* being 53·2%. Most of the new employment created in the 1960s was of a white-collar nature, attracting middle-aged and middle-class administrators to the town, so that Auch was becoming increasingly "une ville moyenne pour classes moyennes".

Expansion of the service sector has, without doubt, been the principle "pull" factor behind the growth of the medium-sized towns in the southwest. It has had the greatest impact in those towns that act as *chef-lieu* of their respective *départements*, for example growth in the public service sector accounted for over 1250 new jobs in Rodez between 1954 and 1968.[22] In addition to having the *préfecture* and its own *mairie*, the departmental capital is important within its region for the provision of secondary education and hospital services and together these functions constitute what has been described as "le moteur de la croissance".[30] Expansion of this sector has in turn stimulated the construction industry, banking and retail services which cater for the incoming population. Superstores, car-sale lots, and centres for the distribution of furniture and other goods have sprung up on the fringes of these towns in response to the demands of well-paid, white-collar staffs—a case of what Lévy and Poinard refer to as "l'induction du tertiaire".

Manufacturing industry has contributed very little to the growth of employment, the medium-sized towns remaining for the most part dependent on a narrow range of traditional activities. There are those who suppose that industry can be induced to follow the service sector. Such is the view of Prager,[27] who stresses the advantages to decentralized operations of the improved financial and public services. Most of the towns have laid out industrial estates in the hope of attracting such manufacturing enterprises. Others are less sanguine, however, viewing the expansion of existing services as a trend towards greater economic vulnerability despite the present veneer of prosperity. Montauban, where the population grew by 1·3% a year between 1954 and 1968 and where over 100 new jobs a year were created over the same period, mainly in services, has been referred to as "une ville à l'économie fragile".[13] The growth of Cahors has similarly been described as "croissance sans développement".[30]

A study of migratory movements lends some support to this idea of structural weakness. Montauban (1968 total: 45 895) received 11 544 migrants 1962-68, but 8358 people left the town over the same period.

(The corresponding figures for 1954-62 were 7210 and 5288.) The source of immigrants was as follows:

Tarn-et-Garonne	3032
Remainder of Midi-Pyrénées	1948
Remainder of France	3272
Repatriates from Algeria	2152
Foreign (esp. Portuguese)	1140

The migrants from Tarn-et-Garonne were mainly young, unmarried and of rural origin, but this departmental component accounted for only 26·3% of the 1962-68 total compared with 42·6% for 1954-62. Those from the "remainder of France" were older, typically civil servants and their families filling jobs in the expanding public service sector. Analysis of the 1968 population by age reveals, in fact, that 47·4% of those who were newcomers to Montauban in 1968 were aged 15-44, compared with only 41·1% of those who had been resident in the town in 1962. The outward migrant was typically young, educated in the town but compelled to seek work outside it; the total included a higher proportion of males than females.[13]

An indication of where these young migrants went is provided in a similar study of population movement to and from the town of Albi.[3] The Albi agglomeration (1968 total: 53 365) received 11 876 migrants in the years 1962-1968, but more than 7000 former residents left the town over the same period. Most of the latter were within the age group 15-34 and were moving to the cities (1176 to Toulouse). Some were students going to places of higher education, but others were seeking employment, and it is the failure of the town to provide work for its better-educated school-leavers that is most indicative of structural deficiency.

The findings quoted above suggest a migratory pattern of growing complexity in the 1960s. The rural to urban component is still present but this is dominated increasingly by inter-urban movements reflecting expansion of employment in the service sector. The medium-sized towns of the south-west may be regarded as representative of many departmental capitals, and some sous-préfectures, in other parts of France. Differences, however, arise over the role of manufacturing industry, with the larger of the villes moyennes and those that are satellite to the largest cities, having attracted overspill firms on a scale that elsewhere was still far more of a hope than a reality in 1970.

THE FIRST CONTRACTS

The *politique des villes moyennes* can be said to have been fully launched when, in February 1973, M. Guichard (Ministre de l'aménagement du territoire et de l'équipement) addressed a letter to all *préfets*, informing them that it would now be possible for *contrats d'aménagement* to be drawn up and signed between town councils and the State. At the same time he announced the setting up of a *Groupe opérationnel des villes moyennes* made up of representatives from DATAR and DAFU (*Direction de l'aménagement foncier et de l'urbanisme*), the purpose of which would be to provide local authorities with the necessary advice and technical assistance to draw up the contracts and to negotiate with the various government departments that might be involved.

Details of what might be included in these contracts were spelled out more fully in a report to the government's *Conseil économique et social* in May 1973.[17,18] Reference was made to the need to find employment for those leaving the land, "sans qu'ils soient obligés d'aller vivre dans les grandes villes et dans les zones urbaines congestionnées". Plans should include the provision of housing and related services; attention should be given to the improvement of transport and communication links with both the regional metropolis and the town's own rural hinterland; there should be concern for education and cultural facilities; and thought should be given to the role which the town might play in the revival of the local countryside. Local authorities were urged to adopt an overall approach to planning, avoiding the fragmentation of decision-making that had resulted in the slow adoption or even abandonment of many earlier plans.

An interesting example of this latter problem is to be found in a study of five medium-sized towns (Aix, Annecy, La Rochelle, Poitiers, and Valence) undertaken by the *Centre de recherche d'urbanisme* and made the subject of a conference in 1974 under the title of "Trente ans d'expérience de la planification urbaine dans cinq villes".[4] The investigation revealed that of 48 *projets d'urbanisme* no fewer than 31 had been abandoned and that the five towns had had an approved plan to guide their urban development for an average of only eight out of the past thirty years.

Government spokesmen in the early 1970s laid great stress on the quality of life experienced in the medium-sized towns. "Il est clair que la très grande majorité des Français préféreront, s'ils peuvent choisir, le cadre d'une ville mesurée. L'accès à la campagne y est plus aisé, le sentiment d'entassement moins grand, l'anonymat moins pesant" (M. Guichard, quoted in *Le Monde*, 21 October 1972). However, there was a danger that these advantages would be lost if the physical expansion of the town were uncontrolled and if suitable provision were not made for the social and cultural needs of the growing population. "Il s'agit d'une politique d'urbanisme qui cherche à réhabiliter des villes à l'échelle humaine avant qu'il ne soit trop tard" (*Le Monde*, 9 February 1973). Municipalities were thus urged to make provision for environmental improvements in their *contrats d'aménagement*. These might include the restoration of historic buildings in the "old town", the making of pedestrian streets and more open spaces, improvements to both public transport services and car parking, and the addition of sports and cultural facilities. Funds to help carry out these projects were to be provided by the government's *fonds d'intervention pour l'aménagement du territoire* (FIAT).

The first three contracts to be agreed were with the towns of Rodez (Aveyron), Angoulême (Charente) and Saint-Omer (Pas-de-Calais).

With his letter to the *préfets* in 1973, M. Guichard included a copy of the agreement already drawn up with the municipal council of Rodez (1968 population: 29 952). The economic progress achieved by Rodez in the 1960s was already well-known and the *contrat* sought to extend this story of success with a programme of urban renewal in the town centre. The latter had lost half its resident population to the suburbs over the previous thirty years.

Rodez is similar in several respects to other towns in the south-west described above. The population of Aveyron, of which it is *chef-lieu*, had fallen from 415 000 in 1886 to only 281 000 in 1968. No fewer than 68% of the town's working population were engaged in the service sector at the latter date, and the expansion of public service employment had played an important part in growth here as elsewhere. In addition to the offices of the *préfecture* and municipality, Rodez has several *lycées* and colleges, and also provides a wide range of services for the agricultural population of the *département*. Progress in this agricultural sector has been one of the more distinctive aspects of what has happened in Rodez. Under the leadership of a number of active young farmers groups, the agriculture of much of Aveyron has been modernized since the Second World War, and the town has the headquarters of unions and cooperatives as well as organizations that provide animal feedstuffs, seed and machinery, or manufacture food products. Rodez has also been fortunate in having as mayor a former Minister of Agriculture who was also Vice-President of the National Assembly between 1968 and 1972.

The success of Rodez owes much to the enterprise of its municipal leaders. It has also attracted attention for the attempts made to draw Aveyronnais living elsewhere in France back to the town, hopefully to set up factories there. In doing this, the example could always be quoted of M. Bessières who, in 1939, moved his precision engineering company from Paris. He turned to the manufacture of injection pumps after the War, and although taken over by the German company of Bosch in 1960, the enterprise has continued to grow, employing around 1000 workers. It has prospered despite the fact that Rodez is 160 km from Toulouse and 610 km from Paris, and the firm's progress is used to support the argument of those who believe that manufacturers of specialized products may now be persuaded to decentralize a part of their operations to the *villes moyennes*.

To make Rodez more attractive to industrialists, two industrial estates have been laid out, a Class C airport built, and pressure has been brought to bear on the authorities to improve the town's road links.[23] A number of small firms have come to the town as a result of the campaign. Describing how one of these came to be set up, John Ardagh stresses the importance of regional loyalty.

> The message is clear: in a country where regional attachments remain far stronger than in England, the dramatic growth of big cities and big factories over the past 30 years is now producing a counter-swing. A generation of urban ex-peasants crave a return to their local roots, not of course to the farms, but at least to smaller factories or offices in small towns near the home patch.[1]

Regional sentiment there may be, but businessmen are more likely to be influenced by the level of investment grants available from central government and Aveyron has been well-favoured in this respect. The role of development grants is most evident further north, however, in regions such as Pays de la Loire, where industrialists tend to be less conscious of the distance from Paris and where town councils have had correspondingly greater success in attracting firms. Tuppen[31] quotes the example of Cholet, where grants of up to 17% of investment costs have been available and where Michelin opened a factory in 1970 which now employs 2000 workers.

"Dix actions sur le centre" was the title of the *contrat d'aménagement* drawn up for Rodez (nine operations were, in fact, finally agreed). Among the proposals were plans to close certain streets to traffic, to widen pavements and plant trees, to restore historic buildings without dispossessing their elderly occupants, to encourage arts and crafts, to make provision for cafés, art galleries, film and theatre clubs, and to install a system of street lighting that was sympathetic to the varied character of the town centre. The programme was to be completed in five years (it has taken seven), 45% of the cost being borne by the State. (The anticipated cost of the operations in 1973 was 14·2 million francs; the actual cost has slightly exceeded 20 millions.) Ardagh recorded the following impression in 1976 when the schemes were well advanced: "The Aveyron's capital is a remarkable place . . . there on a hill-top is this towering pink granite cathedral, and in the old streets at its foot a succession of smart boutiques, modern hotels and restaurants that would not disgrace Cannes. You can buy expensive ceramics or jewellery, hear Paris pop singers in 'Le Pacha Night Club'."[1] The mayor of Rodez put the matter a little more poetically (in *Le Moniteur*, 1981): "La vieille ville se réveille, nous sentons son coeur battre et cela est fort agréable. Rodez qui est beaucoup plus qu'un ensemble de pierres, aussi belles soient-elles, a su conserver un âme".

Of the half-dozen or so originally proposed by the government in March 1972, only Angoulême was, in fact, chosen to serve as *ville moyenne pilote* and the contract with this town was signed in October 1973. That Angoulême should have been selected was seen by one observer as a gesture of compensation for losing the motorway.[8] Considerable disappointment had been expressed when the government had announced that the route of the A10 from Poitiers to Bordeaux would pass through Saintes rather than Angoulême, and there was need to restore public confidence. Interest was certainly aroused, as Comby noted: "Le journal local a ouvert une rubrique spéciale, sorte de boîte à idées; les Angoumoisins paraissent se réveiller de leur torpeur traditionnelle, le maire affiche à la télévision régionale un enthousiasme de bon aloi quant à l'avenir de la ville".

A *schéma directeur d'aménagement et d'urbanisme* (SDAU) for Angoulême and its surrounding communes had been adopted in 1972, and it was made clear by the government that the intention behind the pilot scheme was to complement existing plans rather than to initiate an entirely new set of proposals. Fourteen projects were eventually chosen as the basis of the *contrat*.[9] Half of these were concerned with roads or the provision of parking. They included a new bridge across the Charente to be built as part of an inner ringroad project, and an improved link between a major new housing area and the town centre. Prominent amongst the other proposals were plans for better social facilities on the suburban housing estates, a government minister (M. Chalandon) having been particularly critical of Angoulême's large ZUP (*zone à urbaniser en priorité*) which he had described as "conçue de manière trop traditionelle" (*Le Monde*, 14 April 1972).

The emphasis in Angoulême's *contrat d'aménagement* is different from that of Rodez. It reflects the problems of a larger town which had been under some pressure to house its growing population and which had experienced difficulties of traffic circulation, in part due to this expansion and in part to the accidented relief of Angoulême's site. The plans were in keeping with the government's intention that *contrats* should meet local needs, but it is difficult in these circumstances to appreciate why Angoulême should have been thought to provide an especially useful example, worthy of designation as *ville moyenne pilote*. A range of pilot schemes would have made sense; the selection of only one would seem to support the view of those who saw in it a measure of political expediency.

Saint-Omer was little affected by the industrial revolution despite its proximity to the northern industrial belt. Its genteel, country town atmosphere was in sharp contrast with that of the centres of coal mining such as Béthune and Bruay, only 50 km to the east. But Saint-Omer has not been able to escape the pressures resulting from changes that have taken place in the Northern Region since the 1950s. The town's population has been swelled by labour leaving agriculture and mining, and new forms of employment have been created by the growth of industry, notably glass-working and the manufacture of telephone equipment. The deep-water canal from Dunkerque follows the valley of the river Aa on which Saint-Omer stands, adding to the town's attractiveness to industry but leading to conflict over the future of the famous *hortillonnages*, areas of marshland cultivation.

A need to accommodate growth was apparent in 1962 when the first steps were taken to create a *district urbain*. This now takes in 18 communes and it has enabled plans to be prepared for the whole agglomeration. The latter's population, around 60 000 in 1962, is expected to reach 80 000 by 1985 and 100 000 by the end of the century. It was in this context of planned growth that the town decided to seek a *contrat d'aménagement* in 1973, the objects being mainly of a social and environmental nature, complementing the intentions of the SDAU. According to the mayor, "Nous avons recensé toutes les actions qualitatives susceptibles d'améliorer la physionomie de la ville; c'est-à-dire de rajeunir son habitat et de parfaire ses conditions de vie; puis celles qui pouvaient bénéficier du dynamisme de son appareil commercial; celles enfin, qui permettaient d'y maintenir un certain nombre d'équipements attractifs" (quoted in *Le Monde*, 5 December 1973). A package of thirteen measures was eventually agreed. They included the laying out of a park on the slopes of Vauban's ramparts, restoration of a seventeenth-century barracks, the establishment of a new municipal library in a disused chapel, closure of streets to traffic, and various steps to preserve 7000 hectares of marshland. Under the terms of the *contrat*, half the cost of these works was to be borne by central government.

TOWARDS A FULLER STRATEGY

Other town councils were quick to follow the examples of Rodez, Angoulême and Saint-Omer in seeking *contrats d'aménagement*. The strategy was well-publicized in the mid-1970s and it was even suggested that the formula might be applied to planning in the Paris Region. In a report to those preparing the Seventh Plan (1976–80), the *préfet* of the Paris Region drew parallels between the national strategy of *villes moyennes* and *métropoles d'équilibre* and the role which the smaller towns of the Paris Region might play in complementing the five *villes nouvelles*. A list was drawn up of 14 towns in the *grande couronne*, including such places as Coulommiers, Fontainebleau and Nemours, whose population it was thought could be doubled by 1990 without prejudice to their essential character. "L'objectif est de les traiter en villes moyennes par un développement équilibré et par le maintien d'un cadre de vie satisfaisant" (*Le Monde*, 27 February 1975). The *préfet*'s suggestion, it may be supposed, was not well received by DATAR who would regard it as another example of Parisian interests seeking to neutralize the effects of decentralization policies.

By March 1976 the list of towns seeking *contrats d'aménagement* had reached 82. Of these, 28 already had *contrats*, 23 were awaiting signature, and a further 31 were still under negotiation. From this date the government sought to discourage any further applicants, and councils were urged instead to take advantage of the newly established *fonds d'aménagement urbain* in order to fund their own improvement schemes. *Contrats*, however, continued to be signed until 1979, and the list of *villes moyennes* possessing such a *contrat* finally closed at a total of 73 (Fig. 4).

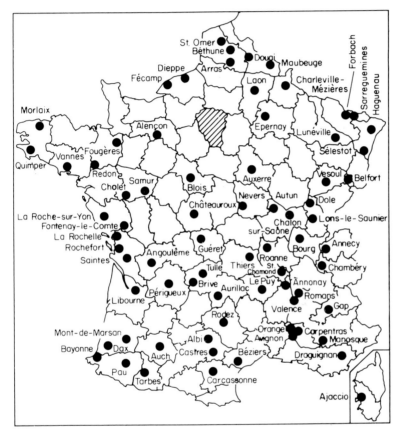

Fig. 4   Towns entering into a "contrat ville moyenne", 1973-1979

Michèle Champenois[5] carried out a study of the 82 towns that had sought *contrats* between 1972 and 1976 to see whether there had been any shift in emphasis in the strategy over these years. Since the *contrats* were tailored to local needs, this was not expected to be great, but some slight change was nevertheless discernible. Expenditure on environmental improvements, including open spaces and pedestrian streets—what critics have called the *"pots de fleurs"* approach—accounted for 46% of expenditure in the early schemes but only 27% in the later ones. There was a corresponding increase in the concern for housing and in the provision of social and cultural amenities. Funds devoted to car parking and road systems likewise fell, from 19% to 13% of the total, more being spent on traffic management schemes.

The list of places to which *contrats* were awarded shows some bias towards the smaller *villes moyennes* and away from the towns of the Paris Basin. Otherwise the distribution is fairly even. It is possible that politics played some part in determining the choice of towns to benefit from *contrats*, but it is unlikely to have been a major role. Of the 82 interested municipalities, 58 were of the same centre-right persuasion as the central government, but this apparent bias must allow for the fact that town councils unsympathetic to the government's policies are less inclined to seek favours lest they seem to be supporting those policies.

Two further examples may be quoted to illustrate the range of circumstances giving rise to the *contrats* and the variety of measures contained within them.

Few better examples could be found than the town of Manosque in the southern Alps to illustrate the problems of reconciling the old France with the new. The old town stands high above the river on a defensive site, its buildings tightly packed within the confines of the former ramparts. Many houses are built above stables, a clue to the town's traditional involvement with the seasonal movement of sheep to and from the mountains: "Manosque des Moutons". Below, in the valley of the Durance, are the modern hydro-electric power stations and, a few kilometres downstream where the Durance is joined by the Verdon, the atomic research station of Cadarache. The effect of this industrialization has been striking. The town's population has grown from 5000 to 20 000 within a generation, with the advent first of power workers, then of repatriates, and finally of immigrants. New houses, schools (one-third of the population is of school age), sports facilities and two industrial estates, have created a new town *extra-muros*: "Manosque de l'Atome".

Growth of the new town has accelerated the decay of the old as the more affluent and more mobile sections of the population have been drawn away by the attractions of modern housing and services. The old houses, expensive to maintain in good repair, have been abandoned to the elderly and poor or, increasingly, to a replacement population of immigrants. "Le vétuste menace l'ancien. Les taudis 'historiques' n'en sont pas moins taudis. Le délabré—à côté du noble—devient l'apanage d'une population vieillie ou démunie, et des migrants. C'est classique".[28] The challenge of Manosque is that of many French towns where long neglect created "*taudis historiques*", the repair and restoration of which has been made more difficult by changes in occupancy. Legislation in the early 1960s enabled *secteurs sauvegardés* to be designated and loans obtained for the repair of historic buildings. Valuable though this has proved, it was nevertheless a fragmentary approach and did not meet the need to look at town centres and their problems as a whole. Not until April 1976, when the "Loi Galley" came into effect, was it possible to treat an area comprehensively by designating it a *zone d'intervention foncière* (ZIF). Here the local authority could exercise controls over redevelopment as well as drawing on funds for schemes of environmental improvement. Before these powers became available, however, the strategy of the *ville moyenne* provided some means by which a sufficiently interested local authority could carry out a package of measures in order, as one observer put it, "préparer l'avenir sans brader le passé".

The programme agreed for Manosque contained eight sets of proposals, involving the rehabilitation of old houses and the provision of amenities, promotion of "*foyers de vie*", making a park, and various traffic measures including the widely favoured solution of pedestrian streets. *Foyers de vie* have been installed in some of the more historic buildings following their restoration. One has become the town library, another a school of music, while others have been used to house municipal offices or been re-equipped for accommodating the elderly. Physical repairs are undertaken, but the wider aim is the human one of reviving the old town and making it an attractive environment in which to live and work.

Périgueux, *chef-lieu* of the *département* of Dordogne, had a population of some 60 000 in 1975. Compared with other medium-sized towns, its growth has been steady rather than striking. Twelve thousand were added to the total between 1946 and 1968, and the total is expected to reach between 70 000 and 80 000 by 1985. Most of the new development has taken place in suburbs which follow the valley of the Isle to the west and east. The central commune of Périgueux itself now houses only 37 000, little more than half the total in the agglomeration, having lost population at an annual rate of 0·5% between 1962 and 1968 and, even faster, by 0·8% a year 1968-75.

Modern Périgueux has grown around two historic nodes, a small

Roman town—Civitas Petrocoriorum—and Puy Saint-Front, a monastic suburb which takes its name from the apostle who is said to have brought Christianity to the region. The two settlements were not united under one administration until the thirteenth century, and the old division is still apparent in the layout of Périgueux at the present time.[29] The Roman quarter, still known as *La Cité*, has some impressive monuments scattered among a mass of later building, while the medieval bourg, corresponding with what in most French towns is *"la vieille ville"*, boasts many fine "renaissance" houses of the fifteenth, sixteenth and seventeenth centuries in the narrow streets that converge on the domed cathedral of Saint-Front.

The town is a route centre and has always acted as the administrative and commercial hub of its region, first of the historic *comté* of Périgord and later of the *département*. Employment is dominated by the service sector, which accounts for 75% of the active population in the commune and two-thirds of the total in the agglomeration. Expansion of public services has been responsible for much of the growth in employment here, as in other comparable towns in the south-west. Manufacturing is largely confined to non-growth industries, railway workshops accounting for a high proportion of male employment, while a variety of small textile and food trades offer work to a predominantly female workforce. Concern for the future of manufacturing led to the equipping of a 100-hectare industrial estate in the suburb of Boulazac in the 1960s. A number of new industries have been attracted to the estate, but the outstanding "capture" has been the *Imprimerie des timbres-poste* which has 700 employees in Périgueux, 150 of whom moved from Paris, the remainder being recruited locally. The decision to decentralize *l'Imprimerie* was taken in 1968, and the printing of French and other stamps began in Périgueux in 1970. The Minister of Posts and Telecommunications in 1968 was the Mayor of Périgueux, a gaullist and supporter of the government in an otherwise largely socialist *département*.

Concern for the deterioration of its historic buildings following loss of population, prompted the town council to obtain an order in 1970 designating the whole of the "old town" of Saint-Front a *secteur sauvegardé*. Within this broader zone, work was then begun in two *secteurs opérationnels*. In one of these a programme of public works was carried out involving improvements to the water supply and drainage system, the putting underground of electricity and telephone wires that had previously disfigured the locality, and the repairing of streets in a traditional manner using pebbles from the river and stone slabs for gutters and paths. The second project involved redevelopment of an area where physical decay had been so far advanced as to require almost total clearance. A hotel and nursery school were built, and new housing erected above an underground carpark. In addition to carrying out these works in Saint-Front, the council also committed itself to a number of improvement schemes elsewhere in the town.

A description of what was happening in the late 1960s and early 1970s makes it easier to appreciate the advantages to a town such as Périgueux of a *contrat ville moyenne* with its promise of funds to extend this newly devised programme of environmental works. The council were not slow to recognize the possibilities, and early in 1975 a *dossier d'intention* was submitted to the *Groupe interministériel des villes moyennes*. However, it was not until 1977 that agreement was reached, by which time changes had been made to the original proposals. The most significant of these involved the abandonment of all plans for the outer parts of the town and a decision to concentrate investment on the centre. What is described in the *contrat* as "la consistance nouvelle du programme" probably came about as a consequence of the long-standing rivalry between *la ville* and

Table 1 Proposals for Contrat Ville Moyenne, Périgueux, 1977

	Proposal	Cost (francs)
1	New bus station in la place Francheville	5 116 000
2	Environmental work in the vicinity of the cathedral	2 237 000
3	Extension of works involving paving, removal of wires etc. in the "old town"	9 608 000
4	Creation of an open space by the removal of the old fire station	428 000
5	Restoration of historic buildings in one *îlot* of the 'old town'	547 000
6	Road-widening at one of the approaches to the "old town"	555 000
7	Extension of the Hôtel de Ville	250 000
8	Restoration of a seventeenth-century convent for use in connection with cultural activities	590 000
9	Preliminary work on the site of a former old people's home	180 000
10	Conversion of a former municipal depot	40 000
11	Establishment of a Gallo-Roman museum on the site of an excavated villa	200 000
12	Improved access to the restored convent	50 000
TOTAL COST		19 801 000

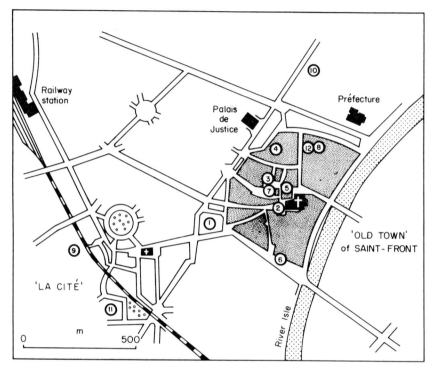

Fig. 5 Périgueux: location of the twelve projects carried out under the "contract ville moyenne"

its surrounding communes, politically supporters of the *parti communiste*.

The *contrat* finally agreed in 1977 (Table 1) contained 12 sets of proposals, all aimed at maintaining the economic role of the centre and at improving living conditions there (Figs 5-11) (Périgueux: Contrat Ville Moyenne, 1977).

The intention behind these proposals is expressed by the Mayor of Périgueux in his introduction to the *contrat*:

pour faire une cité vivante, accueillante, heureuse,

il ne suffit pas de construire et de restaurer des logements: il faut donner aux gens l'envie de les habiter,

il ne suffit pas de posséder un bon équipement commercial: il faut attirer et retenir les acheteurs,

il ne suffit pas d'être riche en chefs d'oeuvres d'architecture et témoignages du passé: il faut en faciliter l'accès aux touristes.

Telle est notre ambition pour Périgueux, VILLE MOYENNE.

Fig. 7 Périgueux Ville Moyenne. Rue Limogeanne: a historic street, pedestrianized to create a fashionable shopping precinct

Fig. 6 Périgueux Ville Moyenne. Work in progress

Fig. 8   Périgueux Ville Moyenne. Open space created by removal of the old fire station

Fig. 9   Périgueux Ville Moyenne. Restoration of the town hall square

Fig. 10   Périgueux Ville Moyenne. Small theatre created in an îlot of the old town

Fig. 11   Périgueux Ville Moyenne. Work in progress behind the museum

The programme of works was largely carried out over the three years, 1978-1980.

ASSESSMENT

In France, as in other western countries, the 1970s witnessed a growing concern for the problems of the rural environment. Decades of population loss, the contraction of services, structural changes in agriculture, and land use conflicts resulting from the spread of tourism and forestry were among the main causes of a rural malaise which is summed up in the phrase "*la France fragile*". Included in the various forms of government action which sought to offset these problems was legislation providing for *contrats de pays*. Under the terms of one of these contracts, a group of rural communes could call on government, later regional, funds in order to carry out a programme of works aimed at stimulating local employment and improving services. It was hoped in this way to reverse the steady *dévitalisation* of the countryside.

From the point of view of the present study, the key feature of the *contrat de pays* was that the communes chosen should be ones that looked to a small town (population 5-20 000) as their natural centre. "Il s'agit d'une 'formule' de coopération communal, en zone rural, qui permet en général aux villes chefs-lieux de cantons ou d'arrondissements de nouer des liens de solidarité avec les petites communes voisines" (*Le Monde*, 3 March 1980). In this emphasis which it placed on the local market town, the *politique des contrats de pays* (referred to also as *la politique des petites villes et de leur pays*) may be seen as an extension of that concerned with the *villes moyennes*, enlarging the planners' field of concern to take in the lower levels of the urban hierarchy.

The new strategy was announced by M. Michel Poniatowski of the Ministry of the Interior in 1975, and twelve schemes were launched on an experimental basis in that year. The first of these was at Loudun in Poitou, and the following observation was made five years later by the Mayor of Loudun: "Le contrat signé il y a cinq ans dans mon 'pays', englobant le sort de cinquante-deux communes, a réconcilé les citadins et les ruraux, Loudun s'étant engagée à ne bénéficier d'aucun des investissements. Ce contrat a permis aux communes rurales de retrouver l'espoir. Il a permis aussi d'affirmer la solidarité entre les Loudunais et les ruraux" (from a speech to the first *journée nationale des contrats de pays* held at Poitiers, 29 February 1980).

Fifty-one *contrats de pays* were signed in 1976 and in June of that year, DATAR published a study of the 533 towns in France having a population of 5–20 000.[16] It noted that their population had increased at an annual rate of 1·2% between 1968 and 1975. A slightly higher proportion of their active population was engaged in industry than in other towns (36% against 33%), but this often meant dependence on a single type of manufacture. Employment in services had expanded in the small towns as it had in the larger ones, but in the commercial sector the benefits of this growth risked being lost by competition from out-of-town hypermarkets. Introducing the report, M. François Essig, who had succeeded M. Monod as head of DATAR, saw the *contrat de pays* affording much-needed assistance to the small town as well as to its surrounding *pays*.

La situation des petites villes est encourageante, mais reste fragile. D'où l'intérêt de la politique contrats de pays. Celle-ci répond aux problèmes soulevés par l'évolution présente et prévisible. De meilleurs services à la population, un développement des activités apportant une meilleure qualité des emplois—objectifs majeurs de la politique des contrats de pays—, constituent des réponses directes aux besoins des petites villes à condition que ces réponses soient adaptées, cas par cas, aux situations locales particulières.

By 1980 the number of *contrats* signed had risen to more than 280, affecting 7500 communes and a population of some 5 million. During the late 1970s the responsibility for financing the agreed programmes was gradually shifted from the State to the Regions. The first of the Regions (*établissement public régional* since 1973) to sign a *contrat* with a group of communes was that of Centre, towards the end of 1975. Three others joined the scheme the following year—Poitou-Charentes, Lorraine, Pays de la Loire—and by 1978, fifteen of the EPRs were entering into *contrats régionaux d'aménagement rural* although a part of the cost continued to be borne by the State. During this same period a number of the EPRs have gone one step further and signed *contrats de villes moyennes régionales*, in effect extending to small towns the kind of planning agreement earlier reserved for the medium-sized towns under the government's *politique des villes moyennes*. A *contrat de ville moyenne régionale* may benefit the small town alone or may be combined with a *contrat de pays*.

Another town in Périgord may serve to illustrate the scope of one of these regional contracts. Ribérac (population in 1975: 3984), a small market town 35 km from Périgueux, entered into a *contrat* with the

Région of Aquitaine in 1978. Two projects were involved: extension of the market hall to serve as a place for public meetings, concerts and entertainments, and the remodelling of the central square and adjacent public garden to improve their appearance and control car parking. The cost was expected to be 2 101 540 francs, of which the Region's contribution would be 796 800 francs. Ribérac was already involved in a *contrat de pays*, and the work on the two schemes was carried out in 1979 and 1980.

Lajugie *et al.*[19] regard the term *ville moyenne régionale* as little more than a euphemism for *petite ville*, used to avoid offending the sensibilities of local politicians. A better title might be *ville d'appui*, used by the EPR of Bourgogne of those small towns thought "susceptibles de jouer un rôle d'animation et de revitalisation du pays environnant". It is not always clear how this support is to be given, however, and the *contrat de ville d'appui* signed in 1976 with the town of Decize (population in 1975: 9700) for example, is similar to a *contrat ville moyenne* in its emphasis on central area improvement and access.[7]

Whatever the terminology, it is evident that no clear-cut distinction can be made between what is a medium-sized town and what is a small one. No special meaning can be attached to a population total of 20 000, and many "small" towns have experienced growth rates similar to those of the larger ones. This is evident from the results of the 1975 Census (Table 2).

Overall, the rate of growth of French towns in the early 1970s was lower than in the preceding intercensal period, 1962-68. This is largely

Table 2   Annual population increases 1968-75

Size of agglomeration (000s) (1968)	Percentage annual population increase (1968-75)
Paris agglomeration	0·4
200-2000	1·0
100-200	1·4
50-100	1·3
20-50	1·5
10-20	1·2
5-10	1·2

Source: Recensement général de la population, 1975

explicable in terms of a slowing down in the amount of increase due to migration. It can be seen from Table 2, however, that the medium-sized towns, with the highest rates of increase, continued to be demographically buoyant. Some might find in these figures alone, a justification for the *politique des villes moyennes*.

It has already been suggested that the geographical pattern of growth amongst the medium-sized towns was an uneven one.[24] This is confirmed by P. N. Jones[14] in a study of the changes that took place between 1968 and 1975 in the urban agglomerations of more than 50 000 population. A consequence of these variations has been a certain fluidity in the rank-size distribution of the middle-sized towns, some moving up several places in rank, others falling back. Jones observes that "the French urban hierarchy in this critical (medium) size range is still undergoing considerable transformation. . . . Of the 50 000–100 000 agglomerations, almost one half were involved in rank changes of 3 or more places . . . suggesting that the impact of long-term distribution trends of economic activities and population in France is feeding back into the urban system" (p.211). He concludes: "The 'medium-sized cities' have grown particularly rapidly, continuing an established tendency to 'spread' urban growth stimuli more equitably across the national territory".

Looked at from the standpoint of population totals, it is clear that the growth over the last 20 to 30 years of France's medium-sized towns has had some impact on the nature of the urban hierarchy. But examination of the causes of this growth does not suggest that the changes have come about in response to an even redistribution of economic activity. There is limited evidence of a hierarchical diffusion or spread of growth, and it would be rash to conclude that the urban system had been restructured to display a balanced set of both vertical and horizontal linkages. The *politique des villes moyennes* has itself had little impact on such restructuring since, whatever its original intentions, it has in practice been largely concerned with physical planning in town centres. The wider objectives of national and regional planning are apparent neither in the choice of towns to which *contrats* have been awarded nor in the programmes of works which form the bases of those *contrats*. The quantitative term, *ville moyenne*, itself conveys no idea of relationship to territory.

There is no doubt that some of the medium-sized towns have attracted decentralizing industries. However, the spread effect has been far from even, benefiting mainly the towns of the Paris Basin and others close to

Lyon and Marseille. Political considerations appear to have influenced the choice of some of the towns to which firms have moved. Otherwise the principal attraction which the medium-sized towns have had to offer has been their workforce. According to Michel,[24] "La 'ville moyenne' intéresse donc les investisseurs, moins pour elle-même qu'en raison de son environnement démographique . . . l'existence d'une importante force de travail sous-employée, dans une aire suffisamment proche de la ville, crée un atout potentiel que l'économie industrielle ne peut manquer de mettre à profit". Populations swelled by migration were a welcome source of labour in the expansionist years up to the mid-1970s, especially in the larger of the *villes moyennes*. When the absolute size of the workforce was less, the attraction of the town was correspondingly reduced.

New forms of manufacturing are welcomed as a source of employment, but Michel draws attention to two sources of weakness resulting from the decentralization process. One of these relates to the attraction which labour alone has to offer to in-coming firms. Since many of the latter were looking for numbers rather than skills, the newly created jobs tend to be low in their qualification requirements. "Fonctions de production les plus banales, les plus limitées, et les moins productives, tel est le lot reservé aux 'villes moyennes'." The result has been a lowering in the overall standard of the workforce in some of those towns that have been most successful in their search for industry. "Pour l'instant, la croissance des 'villes moyennes' a conduit à leur prolétarisation." A second weakness arises from the continued concentration of decision-making in Paris, the effect of which is to orientate recipients of new industry towards the capital, at the same time loosening the economic links which the medium-sized towns have with their own region. Under these circumstances the existing national economic system is reinforced rather than changed and, far from creating a new balance within the urban system, the decentralization of industry is negative in its effects, even disruptive.

In parts of France, such as the south-west, where the larger cities are preoccupied with their own needs, there has been little spread of manufacturing industry and the medium-sized towns have become highly dependent on the tertiary sector, as we have seen. Economic balance is lacking here, too, and the provision of services, however much this may be concerned with the needs of the local population, is ultimately controlled by the ministries in Paris. Again, therefore, one hesitates to interpret growth in terms of the emergence of a more structured economic or social system.

"Il ne s'agira donc pas tant d'aider les villes moyennes à devenir plus grandes que de promouvoir un certain modèle de vie urbaine".[20] This statement of the objectives of the *politique des villes moyennes* is borne out by an examination of almost all the contracts entered into by the medium-sized towns in the 1970s. Charles[6] quotes the example of Vesoul (Haute-Saône) as an exception, the first objective in Vesoul's contract being listed as "la politique d'économie qualitative", a reflection perhaps of the town's heavy dependence in manufacturing on one firm (Peugeot). But "il est rare que les contrats de villes moyennes envisagent des actions d'ordre économique et Vesoul est la première dans ce cas". Much more typical is the example of Dole, former capital of the same region of Franche-Comté, whose *contrat* is almost wholly concerned with the core of the town, establishing walks and viewpoints, and finding new cultural uses for historic buildings.

This preoccupation with the core, observed in other towns such as Périgueux, is regarded by some as a failing of the *contrats des villes moyennes*. It divorces the problems of the "old town" from those of the modern suburbs where a majority of the population now lives, neglecting to take account of such major issues as the poverty of the ZUPs, traffic movement over the whole of the urban area, and the conflicts of land use resulting from commercial pressures on the fringe. Thus in Périgueux, for example, the *contrat* ignores completely the long-running debate over the route of an inner relief road. Others, however, argue that these wider planning matters are properly the concern of the SDAU and that the role of the *politique contractuelle* is to complement the established planning procedure, adding a cultural gloss as it were to existing *modes-de-faire*. "Le contrat de ville moyenne ajoute en quelque sorte un 'supplément d'âme' à l'aménagement prévu antérieurement".[6]

Extending this latter argument, it might be claimed that the value of the *politique des villes moyennes* lies less in its physical achievements than in the public response it has evoked to the needs of the historic town. "En fait, la préparation du contrat, dans les villes où elle a été faite avec conviction et sérieux, a parfois conduit les responsables à une prise de conscience . . . les envoyés spéciaux de l'administration parisienne ont souvent servi de catalyseurs. Venus d'ailleurs, ils ont aidé la ville à se regarder en face, à bien connaître et à mieux utiliser son capital".[5] Viewed in this way, the contribution of the *politique contractuelle* cannot be measured against any simple yardstick. Time alone may suggest whether the short-lived *politique des villes moyennes* was an electoral tool, short-circuiting for a while the existing administrative procedures, or whether it represents a turning point in French urban planning, with consequences that reach beyond the restored facades of the single city to matters affecting the whole of the urban system.

REFERENCES

1. Ardagh, J. (1976). *The Sunday Times*, 12 September.
2. Bédarida, F. (1980). *In* "Britain and France: Ten Centuries" (D. Johnson, F. Crouzet and F. Bédarida, ed.). Dawson, Folkestone.
3. Bienfait, M. (1973). *Rev. Géog. des Pyrénées et du S.-O.* **44**, 485-492.
4. Centre de Recherche d'Urbanisme (1974). "Annales", pp.17-78. CRU, Paris.
5. Champenois, M. (1976). *Le Monde*, 17 March.
6. Charles, G. (1979). *Rev. Géog. de l'Est* **19**, 365-370.
7. Charrier, J.-B. (1977). *Rev. Géog. de l'Est* **17**, 215-229.
8. Comby, J. (1973). *Norois* **20**, 647-660.
9. Comby, J. (1974). *Norois* **21**, 497-504.
10. Gravier, J.-F. (1947). "Paris et le Désert Français." Flammarion, Paris.
11. Hautreux, J., Lecourt, R. and Rochefort, M. (1963). "Le Niveau Supérieur de l'Armature Urbaine Française." Minist. de la Constr., Paris.
12. Hautreux, J. and Rochefort, M. (1964). "La Fonction Régionale dans l'Armature Urbaine Française." Minist. de la Constr., Paris.
13. Idrac, M. (1973). *Rev. Géog. des Pyrénées et du S.-O.* **44**, 397-414.
14. Jones, P. N. (1978). *Erdkunde* **32**, 198-212.
15. Kayser, B. (1973). *Rev. Géog. des Pyrénées et du S.-O.* **44**, 345-364.
16. La Documentation Française (1976). "Les Petites Villes en France: Travaux et Recherches de Prospective." Paris.
17. Lajugie, J. (1973). "Rapport au Conseil Economique et Social du 30 mai 1973: Les Villes Moyennes." Avis et Rapports du Conseil Economique et Social, no. 13, Paris.
18. Lajugie, J. (1974). "Les Villes Moyennes." Connaissances Economiques, Cujas, Paris.
19. Lajugie, J., Delfaud, P. and Lacour, C. (1979). "Espace Régional et Aménagement du Territoire." Dalloz, Paris.
20. Leruste, P. (1975). "Le Contrat d'Aménagement des Villes Moyennes." Notes et Etudes Documentaires, No. 4234, La Documentation Française, Paris.

21. Lévy, J.-P. (1973). *Rev. Géog. des Pyrénées et du S.-O.* **44**, 429-443.
22. Lévy, P. et Poinard, M. (1973). *Rev. Géog. des Pyrénées et du S.-O.* **44**, 365-382.
23. Lugan, J.-C. and Poinard, M. (1973). *Rev. Géog. des Pyrénées et du S.-O.* **44**, 415-428.
24. Michel, M. (1977). *Annales de Géog.* **86**, 641-685.
25. Noin, D. (1976). "L'Espace Français." Colin, Paris.
26. Perroux, F. (1950). *Economie Appliquée*, Archives de l'ISEA, **1**, 225-244.
27. Prager, J.-C. (1973). *Rev. Géog. des Pyrénées et du S.-O.* **44**, 383-396.
28. Rambaud, J. (1976). *Le Monde*, 17 March.
29. Scargill, D. I. (1974). "The Dordogne Region of France." David and Charles, Newton Abbot.
30. Tulet, J.-C. (1973). *Rev. Géog. des Pyrénées et du S.-O.* **44**, 445-460.
31. Tuppen, J. N. (1980). "Studies in Industrial Geography: France." Dawson, Folkestone.

Chapter Twelve

The Place of Victorian Cities in Developmental Approaches to Urbanization

DAVID WARD

For a long time a major preoccupation of urban studies has been the relationship between the acceleration in the rate of urbanization over the past two centuries and changes in the organization of urban life. First published over twenty years ago, *Megalopolis* by Jean Gottmann remains an exemplary benchmark in geographical contributions to the study of this relationship.[1] His approach revealed the potentialities of the cross-fertilization of observations about striking changes in the spatial organization of cities and discussions of those processes variously described as industrialization, modernization and the expansion of capitalism. As in many classic studies of those processes, Gottmann implies that the northeastern seaboard of the United States was the most extreme and advanced form of modern urbanization and thereby revealed the destiny of other regions of rapid urban growth. Like the cities which together formed Megalopolis in the mid-twentieth century, British industrial cities in the mid-nineteenth century were viewed as classic or prototypical examples of the kind of urban transformation that would be encountered elsewhere as the acceleration in urbanization became a world-wide phenomenon. These rapidly transformed cities and attitudes to them have been described as "Victorian" not only in Britain but also in other parts of the world where British ideas were influential in confronting this new kind of urban growth.[2]

To many Victorians, the destiny of this urban transformation was an exhilarating prospect but also one usually restrained by latent or overt

THE EXPANDING CITY
ISBN 0 12 547250 1

apprehension about the immediate urban condition. In particular, the polarization of rich and poor graphically recorded in their segregated residential patterns aroused intense social concern both at the beginning and the end of the Victorian period.[3] This concern is certainly familiar to us today as a recurring if not endemic problem of modern western urban life but the proportions of current urban populations judged to be deprived and segregated are assumed to be much smaller than in Victorian cities. Moreover, the affluent majority of cities in the developed world are internally differentiated according to socio-economic status and stage in the life cycle, and the extension of improved living conditions to progressively larger proportions of urban populations has resulted in complex patterns of suburban expansion and differentiation. These highly differentiated modern residential patterns have been contrasted with those of pre-industrial or traditional cities in which wealthy elites were concentrated around centrally located monuments of secular or ecclesiastical power and much of the remainder of urban society was differentiated on the basis of craft and kin rather than income and status.[4]

Victorian cities have for long occupied a crucial place in investigations of the origins of modern residential patterns and their relationship to earlier traditional arrangements. Interpretations of these socio-geographic changes are derived, implicitly or explicitly, from those generalizations about the transition from traditional to modern societies described as industrialization, modernization and the expansion of capitalism. Each of these sets of generalizations propose a different generic place for Victorian cities in the transformation of traditional into modern societies. Viewed as the direct consequences of the disruptive initial impacts and short run costs of the industrialization of urban employment, the Victorian city was clearly demarcated from its predecessors (Fig. 1). As the enduring effects and presumed long-term benefits of industrialization became more pronounced in the early twentieth century, a new and distinctive modern or post-industrial phase of urbanization was recognized.[5] The validity of this relationship between industrialization and phases of urbanization was, however, based upon an assumed chronological coincidence of a complex set of changes which defined this industrial transformation of urban society. Many of these changes now appear to have been neither highly synchronized nor specifically Victorian.

The identification of a second or post-industrial phase of economic

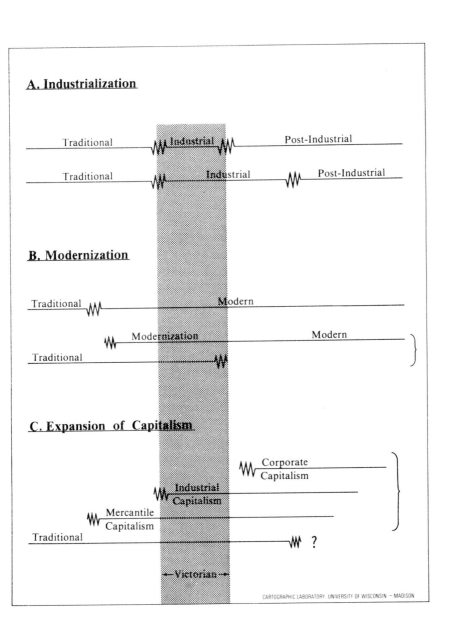

A. Industrialization

Traditional   Industrial   Post-Industrial

Traditional   Industrial   Post-Industrial

B. Modernization

Traditional   Modern

Modernization   Modern

Traditional

C. Expansion of Capitalism

Corporate Capitalism

Industrial Capitalism

Mercantile Capitalism

Traditional   ?

Victorian

Fig. 1   Development phases in urbanization

growth which extricated Victorian industrial capitalism from its late nineteenth century crisis is thought to be less decisive than our present confrontation with an uncertain future.[6] The term *post-industrial* once optimistically distinguished us from our Victorian predecessors because state intervention, industrial reorganization and adjustments in the division of labour had presumably resolved many Victorian urban problems. Recently, however, this discontinuity has become blurred, and the term post-industrial increasingly is reserved to describe still tentative adjustments to diseconomies of scale, bureaucratization and pollution which may preoccupy our immediate future (Fig. 1). While the longevity of industrialization remains a matter of debate, many changes once thought to have coincided with the initial abrupt industrialization of urban employment have been identified in earlier centuries when capitalist practices and institutions first disturbed the established patterns of life of the so-called traditional world.[7] Subsequent changes, including those associated with the beginning and end of the Victorian period, were viewed as periodic fluctuations in a long cumulative process described as modernization. From this perspective, Victorian cities were a small segment of a process which progressively if unevenly increased the scale, density and heterogeneity of urban society to levels described as modern (Fig. 1).[8]

While many attributes of modern society are now thought to have emerged before the industrialization of urban employment, some traditional patterns of life may have persisted despite the disruptive effects of that process.[9] Some descriptions of modernization are certainly sensitive to the coexistence of old and new since they argue that these relationships account for some of the differences in transitional experiences. An emphasis on the convergent consequences of modernization has, however, obscured the impact of these varied transitional conditions on enduring and perhaps generic differences amongst modern societies. Recent efforts to examine these differences have also re-opened interest in discontinuities once related to the process of industrialization.[10] While the timing and consequences of these discontinuities are quite varied, they are usually related to stressful conditions derived in part from periodic intensifications of alterations in the effects of capitalism on persisting traditional ways of life (Fig. 1). These kinds of changes certainly contributed to the social concern and instability at the beginning and the end of the Victorian period and therefore provide one basis to redefine the distinctive place of Victorian cities in the process of modern urbanization.

Over the past decade the evocative descriptions of Victorian observers have been supplemented by an abundant yield of statistical studies which have specified in considerable detail the levels and patterns of residential differentiation in Victorian cities.[11] These studies have identified social areas which are similar to those of the modern city, especially amongst the extremely affluent. The degree to which the residential patterns of the remainder of urban society were differentiated is less apparent and quite controversial. Some interpretations of these patterns have argued that Victorian cities exhibit all the characteristics of the social areas of modern cities but at a smaller scale and in different proportions.[12] Others have argued that social areas were poorly defined and that weak levels of residential differentiation resulted from a distinctive transitional phase of urbanization.[13] The former viewpoint is consistent with generalizations about modernization whereas the latter is more closely related to conceptions of a discontinuous course of change. While most studies of residential differentiation on Victorian cities relate their findings to generalizations about the social geographies of traditional and modern cities, they rarely explicitly identify the process of change which most clearly illuminates their spatial findings. Our interpretations of the developmental implications of changes in socio-geographic patterns are, nevertheless, directly or indirectly dependent upon prevailing or competing generalizations about the transitions from traditional to modern societies. In particular, our investigations of continuities and discontinuities in the urban residential differentiation need to be explicitly linked to those related processes described as industrialization, modernization and the expansion of capitalism.

Like prophecies of the degree to which our own urban future will differ from that of the past three decades, the identification of distinctive residential patterns described as Victorian in part depends upon whether the urban problems which preoccupied the second and last quarters of the nineteenth century are interpreted as major discontinuities or minor fluctuations in urban residential differentiation.

INDUSTRIALIZATION

Early Victorians had few doubts about the abrupt and recent effects of new residential patterns upon the organization and stability of urban society. Specifically, mechanized systems of production, first introduced in the late eighteenth century, created a new social group or class of industrial capitalists. Their growing wealth eventually made it possible for them to move to socially exclusive suburbs far removed from the deteriorating environment in which their employees lived and worked. These *nouveaux riches* not only isolated themselves from the remainder of urban society but also rejected those paternalistic responsibilities to their employees and the poor in general that had long been among the customary obligations of wealth and status. Under these circumstances, those whom early Victorians variously described as the poor, the labouring classes and the working classes were deprived of the influence and control of their social superiors and would, therefore, fall prey to the dangerous influences of the most radical and "depraved" amongst them. This threat of contagious religious infidelity and political rebelliousness was thought to be destroying the cohesiveness of urban society. Although these conditions were ultimately derived from industrialization, the immediate problem of growing social instability was attributed to the effects of the insensitivities and residential segregation of industrial capitalists. Indeed, some efforts to confront deteriorating social conditions were explicitly designed to reduce the impact of residential segregation.[14] Missions and schools established amongst the poor were regarded as cells of moral influence which compensated for their social isolation. The desire to act upon long-established distinctions between the worthy and unworthy poor by removing the able-bodied unemployed to workhouses had the added advantage of eliminating their negative influence upon their more worthy neighbours.

These responses to residential segregation in early Victorian cities emerged at a time when there were relatively few settlements where mechanized systems of production had stimulated the rapid growth of once small market towns or villages. Despite their small numbers, these classic industrial cities most frequently exemplified by Manchester, or more highly specialized textile factory towns, were viewed as representative of the immediate destiny of all urban settlements and accordingly were a fertile source of prophetic generalizations.[15] One common element in these generalizations was the assumption that this new urban society was too unstable to endure. It was a dynamic but temporary society which was transitional between the recently disrupted but long-established traditional world and a range of imagined worlds of an immediate future when social stability would presumably be restored by progress, reform or revolution.[16] While residential segregation was an integral part of the image of this transitional society, contemporary observers were less explicit about the spatial organization of past and future urban societies. In retrospect, the social geography of so-called pre-industrial cities have been identified as the reverse of early Victorian cities with an affluent elite clustered around centrally located civic institutions and the poor on the edge of the city.[17] Early Victorians were vague about these matters, but they did assume that the cohesiveness and stability of earlier urban societies were based upon frequent contacts between rich and poor and the sensitivities of traditional elites to the needs of the deprived. Since residential segregation was assumed to have attenuated or destroyed these relationships in the early Victorian city, retrospective visions of a more cohesive urban society certainly implied a close proximity if not interspersal of social strata.[18]

Although commentators of widely differing ideologies identified the same recent changes in the social geography of rapidly growing early Victorian cities, they certainly argued about appropriate diagnoses. Conservatives recommended the reinvigoration of neglected traditions but to liberals these same traditions were the main hindrance to unencumbered material progress which would quickly solve immediate problems. Socialists and utopians speculated on alternative principles of social organization which were closer in conception to those of conservatives than to those of liberals. In view of this range and intensity of contemporary reactions to early Victorian cities and their common interest in the dangerous social implications of their residential patterns, the more cerebral tone and vaguer interest in segregation during the third quarter of the nineteenth century are perhaps surprising. We might indeed assume that in this so called age of "equipoise", changes in the degree of residential segregation or in the frequency of social contacts with the affluent had taken the edge off the social isolation of the poor.[19] Certainly suburbanization was no longer viewed as unavoidably harmful to urban society, and there were growing if exaggerated speculations on the desirable impact of the railway and tramway systems in opening cheap land for modest housing developments.[20] If a process which had once been confined to a small affluent social strata and had been viewed as a threat to social stability was opened to a broader spectrum of social strata, then the advancing technology of movement might repair the damage for which the new technologies of production had been blamed. This optimistic vision of a technological solution to urban congestion and social isolation was, however, dimmed towards the end of the

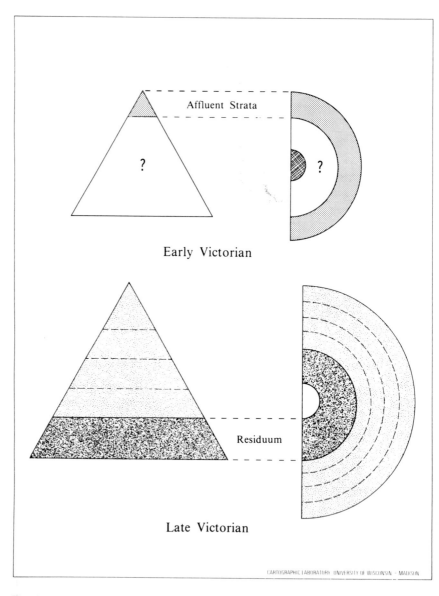

Affluent Strata

?   ?

Early Victorian

Residuum

Late Victorian

Fig. 2 Diagrammatic representations of socio-geographic patterns of early and late Victorian cities

century when anxieties about the stability of urban society were once again related to graphic images of the city.[21]

If early Victorians had been concerned about the contagious effects of the indiscriminate mixing of the worthy and unworthy poor, late Victorians were preoccupied with the size of the lowest stratum of the poor known as the residuum who were concentrated in the worst slums of the inner city (Fig. 2). This internal residential differentiation of the poor presumably eased anxieties about the damaging influence of the most depraved amongst them, but it did present problems of social control if this group formed a substantial and persistent proportion of urban society. As long as the residuum was assumed to be a diminutive strata from which escape and material advancement were possible, the social costs of residential segregation were temporary. The monumental enquiries of Charles Booth into the life and labour of London's poor, together with a host of other testimonies from settlement house workers and housing reformers, questioned these assumptions.[22] At a time when depressed economic conditions had reversed modest rates of upward mobility, subtle and small-scale patterns of internal residential far greater than had previously been thought. Moreover, many families had apparently lived under impoverished conditions for several generations, and some observers believed that this prolonged isolation had created a race apart with a well-defined appearance and culture.[23] The prospect of families, who had escaped from this stratum or from its vicinity, falling back into the social "abyss" rekindled early Victorian fears about the indiscriminate mixing of the poor. If only a small minority of the poor had actually escaped from the inner city slums and depressed economic conditions had reversed modest rates of upward mobility, subtle and small-scale patterns of internal residential differentiation amongst the lower social strata had done little to reduce the indiscriminate mixing of the poor of which early Victorians had complained.

In response to these deteriorating conditions, critics of urban society argued more forcefully than most of their predecessors that direct state intervention in not only the regulation of living conditions but also the provision of social insurance would be necessary to cure the dangerous social consequences of prolonged residential segregation.[24] Unlike early Victorians, they were more sceptical of the inevitability or immediacy of any imagined transformation of urban society, but in proposing what they believed to be radical strategies of state intervention in the solution of urban problems, they also bequeathed to us a somewhat exaggerated indictment of the negligence of earlier generations. Indeed, public intervention in urban social problems was for long spasmodic and retained much of the moralism of early Victorians, for if these new strategies failed to alleviate the problems of the poor, it was assumed that poverty was a self-inflicted condition. The role of the state in the regulation of housing conditions became more stringent and imperative, but initially the effect was to reduce the supply of low rent accommodation and to exacerbate the problem of over-crowding which it was intended to resolve. In spite of these problems, it was assumed that it was possible to reverse the attitudes and policies usually described as *laisser-faire* which had presumably created the pathological condition of urban society. This change in ideology was closely associated with the end of the Victorian period, and during the early twentieth century, the term Victorian implied negligence of human needs while new responses to this sad inheritance were perhaps piously defined as modern. The novelty, scale and consequences of residential segregation in early Victorian cities distinguished them from their immediate predecessors, while the persistence of segregation provoked reactions to the late Victorian city from which an alternative and definitively modern approach to urban problems was derived. Certainly one frequently used but possibly misleading indicator of the distance we have travelled from the Victorian city has been the reduction in the proportionate size and in the levels of residential segregation of deprived groups. This close association of the opening of the Victorian period with the full implications of the negative effects of industrialization and of its close with the decisive new commitment of the state to the removal of these effects rests on several assumptions which have since been questioned. Among these assumptions are well-defined discontinuities in the process of residential differentiation at the beginning and end of the Victorian period which coincided with the abrupt effects of industrialization and delayed responses to these effects. Subsequent interpretations have stressed incremental changes in the residential patterns of Victorian cities which resemble not only those which are familiar to us today but also those which had been recorded for at least two centuries before the Victorian period. This alternative viewpoint is either implicitly or explicitly derived from recent generalizations about modernization.

MODERNIZATION

Generalizations about modernization are primarily concerned with the convergent consequences of several distinctive transformations of the traditional world of which the industrialization of the Victorian city is but one short segment of one of several known transitional experiences.[25] The changing role of the state in the management of the British economy was for long assumed to be definitive of a major discontinuity in the process of industrialization and especially its effects on urban society. The origins of modern public intervention have been traced back into the Victorian period, and shifts in policy at the turn of the century have been viewed as incremental rather than antagonistic to established practice. Moreover, in Germany and Japan, the state was an active participant in their initial rapid industrialization and subsequently more ambitious and complete levels of state control of economic development have been established in both the Second and the Third worlds. These different trajectories of change suggest that Victorian cities should not be viewed as prototypical of a universal transformation of urban society which formed the basis of the Victorian conception of industrialization. Rather because Victorian British cities were the first to encounter this transition, they should be examined as classic but probably unique expressions of experimental pioneers. Nevertheless, those convergent elements which define the modern city have been identified in Victorian cities. Among these elements, selective suburbanization on the basis of socio-economic status and stage in the life cycle is regarded as an unambiguous indicator of patterns of residential differentiation which are described as modern.

Early Victorians feared the effects of the suburbanization of a small affluent minority on the unpredictable behaviour of the remainder of urban society, and late Victorians shared these fears because decidedly modest downward extensions of this process to less affluent strata had been suspended or reversed. Although anxieties about residential segregation and especially about the effects of the indiscriminate mixing of the poor were only temporarily alleviated during the third quarter of the nineteenth century, the massive scale of suburbanization in the twentieth century has reduced the dimensions of the problem. Segregation, social isolation and material deprivation were assumed to afflict the vast majority of the residents of Victorian cities, but segregation is now specifically associated with residual deprived minorities who have so far failed to participate in the suburban movement. The internal residential differentiation of the less affluent did, however, serve to isolate the most destitute from the remainder of urban society, and inasmuch as this group represents an adverse contagious influence, their segregation has at least alleviated one Victorian anxiety. The diverse needs of different social strata were provided by the downward filtration of housing vacated by upwardly mobile households but this process was rarely evident in neighbourhoods occupied by socially prominent families who frequently retained desirable quarters for several generations. Consequently, those sources of Victorian anxieties, which were derived from the effects of the suburban exclusivity of influential affluent families on their ability to influence the remainder of urban society have remained to this day.

This process of suburban residential differentiation is clearly closer to the optimistic vision of the Chicago School of urban ecology than it is to the pessimistic concerns of Charles Booth and his contemporaries.[26] Although an arrangement of socio-economic groups in concentric zones was common to both descriptions of the city, Booth described the diminutive dimensions and highly selective composition of the suburban movement and assumed that it had reached its limits in late nineteenth century England unless the level of social security was increased. Burgess described the rapid suburbanization of Midwestern American cities about twenty years later and envisioned a continuous incremental concentric expansion of the city. He implied that without the arrival of large numbers of impoverished immigrants to replace those leaving the inner city the slums would eventually be depopulated. Indeed, many supporters of immigration restriction assumed that their policy would alleviate and eventually remove the problems of the inner city by eliminating its apparent cause. This incremental suburban movement was attributed to individual and structural mobility rather than to state intervention and parallel developments in local transportation and the decentralization of urban employment were assumed to have accelerated the process above its more modest nineteenth century rate.

Over the past decade, the conditions upon which the suburban movement has been based have proved to be less dependable, and the traditional ecological models may no longer describe the patterns and processes of urban residential differentiation today. Nevertheless, these models are assumed to be appropriate to describe conditions not only for the period during which they were proposed but also for the preceeding

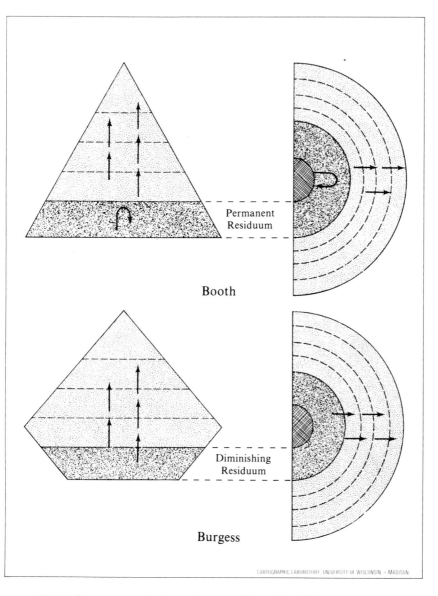

Permanent
Residuum

Booth

Diminishing
Residuum

Burgess

CARTOGRAPHIC LABORATORY, UNIVERSITY OF WISCONSIN – MADISON

Fig. 3   Some contrasts in the socio-geographic models of Booth and Bugess

Victorian generations. Booth and his contemporaries on both sides of the Atlantic described the effects of depression upon urban residential differentiation which in the absence of upward social mobility rapidly became a fixed socio-geographic pattern of segregated social groups. In contrast, Burgess and his collaborators described a period of accelerating suburbanization during a period of unprecedented prosperity (Fig. 3). In view of the slower rates and different patterns of social mobility and the immense role of municipal authorities in the suburban movement in British cities, a model based upon the American Midwest would appear to be of limited value to describe British conditions. To be sure, Burgess based his findings upon the most extensively suburbanized cities in the world, but like early Victorian industrial cities in Britain they were viewed as predictors of conditions to be expected in the future elsewhere. The assumption that modernization has convergent consequences was especially influential in interpretations of the suburban movement. Just as suburbanization was severely arrested in the United States during the Great Depression, the concerns of early and late Victorians about their cities might be viewed as similar interruptions in an incremental process rather than as major discontinuities in residential differentiation. From this perspective the differences between early and late Victorian cities recorded pauses in the cumulative process of suburbanization. Victorian suburbs were simply smaller in scale and displayed a more limited range of differentiation than more recent additions to the city.

The assumption that Victorian cities were essentially smaller and less complex versions of modern cities has been extended to include pre-Victorian cities. Patterns of residential segregation in early Victorian cities which were thought to be of recent origin and directly related to the industrialization of urban employment have been identified as early as the seventeenth century if not earlier.[27] Indeed, most classic descriptions of the industrial transformation of urban society were based upon settlements which had previously been extremely small and had retained many traditional manorial institutions. Consequently, the early Victorian period coincided with the emergence of new residential patterns. In more populous, longer-established commercial cities, however, the sub-urbanization of the aristocracy and affluent merchants had been well established for two centuries, and during the eighteenth century these developments occurred more widely in relatively small provincial towns. This movement was initiated when a land market displaced feudal customs in the assignment of people and activities to urban space.[28]

Certainly the timing of this transition from feudal to capitalist practice in the organizations of transactions in urban property varied, but in many towns it was often associated with the wealth generated when merchants organized the external markets of artisans in response to the expanding commerce of the Atlantic and Indian Oceans.

From the perspective of the process of modernization, the residential patterns of the Victorian city recorded the cumulative extension of suburbanization to progressively lower social strata. Preoccupations with residential segregation are thought to define periods of economic uncertainty when the socio-geographic boundaries between some social groups become temporarily fixed. The social implications of residential segregation were presumably exaggerated because immediate economic conditions obscured those long-term tendencies which reduced the dimensions of the problem. Periodic complaints about residential segregation should thus be identified with pauses in a more continuous process of suburban residential differentiation. Because suburbs are generally regarded as one of the most definitive indicators of modernization, Victorian cities were, to the degree that they included suburban residents, modern. The debate about the modernity of Victorian cities is precisely about this matter of the degree to which suburban residential differentiation determined their socio-geographic patterns.

THE EXPANSION OF CAPITALISM

Although efforts to relate suburbanization to modernization have increased our awareness of the longevity of the socio-geographic transition from the pre-modern world, the identification of remote and, for a long time, diminutive indicators of modernity has perhaps obscured the persisting influences of long-established patterns of life. For example, some interpretations of public intervention in the Victorian period attribute these policies to the persistence of older paternalistic traditions rather than to a precocious modernity and suggest that the debate about these issues at the turn of the century did involve some distinct and modern departures from earlier practices.[29] These relationships between established and modern practices have been most pronounced when they have confronted one another during those periodic intensifications or alterations in the effects of capitalism upon established ways of life.

These effects were limited under conditions of mercantile capitalism, greatly enlarged under industrial capitalism and almost complete under late or finance capitalism.[30] In the form of complex hybrid combinations or of well-defined dualistic segments, old and new patterns of life may coexist in prolonged stable relationships. Major disruptions to these long-standing relationships define a sequential rather than continuous pattern of change. To the degree that the anxieties at the beginning and the end of the Victorian period coincided with these kinds of disruptions, it is possible to re-open the question of the generic identity of Victorian cities. Interpret-ations of the ancestry of modern urban residential patterns which focus only on the cumulative consequences of suburbanization describe only small fragments of early Victorian cities. While these suburban develop-ments were more extensive in late Victorian cities, the precise changes in the residential differentiation of the less affluent majority of urban society remain unclear, and it was among this group that the persistence of traditional patterns of life was most pronounced.

Unlike the incremental suburbanization of the extremely wealthy, the direction of residential differentiation among the less affluent of early Victorian cities had to be reversed to create modern socio-geographic arrangements. Early Victorians complained of the indiscriminate and threatening mixing of the poor and thereby implied a weak and diminishing level of residential differentiation among them. Late Victorians were concerned about well-defined inner city concentrations of the lowest social stratum, who were now isolated from the remainder of urban society. The degree to which the remainder of society was internally differentiated is less clear, but it was scarcely firmly established because most contemporary observers feared the effects of depressed economic conditions on newly developed distinctions of status and security. These distinctions were also based upon an occupational hierarchy which was scarcely evident in early Victorian cities and hardly dominant in late Victorian cities. Victorian socio-geographic patterns are only partly smaller and less complex versions of those of modern cities. In vast sections of Victorian cities, neither the direction nor the bases of residential differentiation was strictly modern until late in the nineteenth century. This inference corresponds well with distinctions that have been made between the impact of the transition from mercantile to industrial capitalism and from industrial to corporate capitalism on the organization of the labour market.[31] The initial impact of industrializa-tion greatly diminished the security and status of many small independent producers, whereas the subsequent corporate reorganization of production created new secure strata within an increasingly hierarchical labour force.

Although early Victorians made a range of distinctions among those whom they described as the poor, they were rarely specific about their residential patterns.[32] They did, however, argue that infidelity, immorality and radicalism would spread from the least worthy amongst them once the suburbanization of the wealthy had removed their countervailing influences. Often these indices of social isolation and disorganization were associated with notoriously unsanitary sites, and there was a tendency to generalize about the poor on the basis of these extreme conditions.[33] Paradoxically, the initial impact of industrial capitalism upon the urban labour force involved the intrusion rather than removal of external influences, while the reactions provoked by these changes were most evident amongst the most articulate upper stratum of the poor rather than amongst a depraved lower stratum. Because the residential and social isolation of rich and poor or of merchant and artisan was long established under mercantile capitalism, it was the effect of new capitalist initiatives to control production which dramatically altered the social relationships rather than the socio-geographic patterns of early Victorian cities.[34] As long as merchant capitalists had relied upon independent artisans to produce their goods, the social world of the residence–workshop retained many established customs despite the increasing impact of fluctuations in market conditions on their work regimen.

Once efforts were made to substitute large-scale mechanization or small-scale sub-contracting for the labour of the artisan, the segmented relationship between merchant capitalist and independent producer was disrupted. The status and security of the independent producer and the proprietary aspirations of journeyman were undermined and destroyed, and their reactions to these losses were the sources of social instability which early Victorians attributed to residential segregation. This process was not of course instantaneous, and some artisan production persisted throughout the nineteenth century, often in quarters defined by the product manufactured there (Fig. 4).[35] Elsewhere, these older bases of residential differentiation were less pronounced, especially in newly developed housing. Indeed, the uses made of the fringes of Victorian cities and the susceptibility of these developments to speculative miscalculations suggest that the incremental suburbanization of the affluent

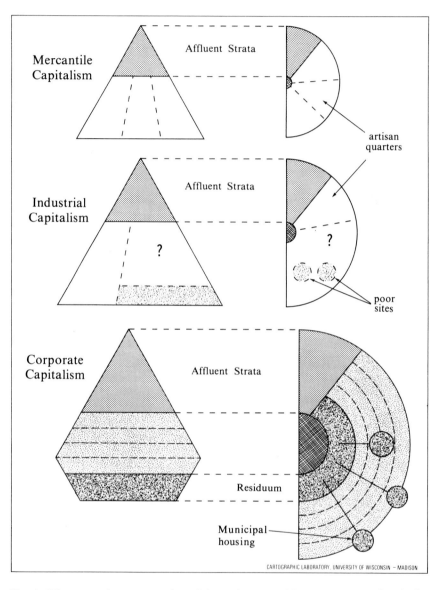

Fig. 4 Diagrammatic representation of the socio-geographic consequences of capitalist transitions

and upwardly mobile accounted for only fragments of their physical expansion.[36] Certainly residential additions which met the needs of the less affluent were far vaster in area, if more congested in design, than the suburban additions occupied by the wealthy (Fig. 4).

Patterns of residential differentiation that were once based upon local specializations in artisan production were also further weakened by the high rates of population turnover and the small-scale organization of the house-building process. Relatively few early or mid-Victorian households remained in the same neighbourhood for prolonged periods. Although their frequent moves between and within cities was structured by known distributions of relatives and friends, discrete networks of contacts rather than highly concentrated and sedentary neighbours were the basis of their social world.[37] To the degree that subtle patterns of residential differentiation occurred amongst the poor, it recorded the temporary effects of a highly mobile population, and the social characteristics of many neighbourhoods were often in flux.[38] In any event, the cottages built to serve the residential needs of the vast majority of urban residents were built in small groups, creating a patchwork of localized but modest variations in housing quality. Limited space and inadequate utilities were common to most early developments, so the recency of construction may well have been the basis of slight differences in quality. The deterioration of poorly constructed housing was also especially rapid when small-scale builders cut costs in order to rent their houses at levels which the wages of most of the poor could sustain. There were, of course, some large-scale developments which were more likely to house people of the same social strata but they were frequently the results of the strategic investments of the landed aristocracy rather than of industrial capitalists.[39] Site conditions rather than relative location within the city determined the most striking differences in neighbourhood quality. Poorly drained flood plains, filled land and low-lying slumps (from which the term slum may be derived) were not necessarily contiguous nor centrally located, so the most impoverished segment of the population was often associated with well-defined notorious sites to which Victorian sanitary engineers drew popular attention (Fig. 4). This publicity often implied that these districts were representative of living conditions as a whole.

The prosperous beneficiaries of industrial capitalism certainly increased the dimensions of the suburban movement, but for the vast majority of their employees, old craft distinctions had diminished while the new middle class of managers and supervisors remained extremely small until the late nineteenth century. There were some new distinctions based on strategic skills, and a privileged secure upper stratum of the working class known as labour aristocrats have been identified. Their identity was long dependent on their presumed political role in the mid-Victorian period when less turbulent social conditions were attributed to their conservative leadership. This mediating role has been questioned, but in any event this presumed stratum was small and probably had only a modest effect upon residential differentiation.[40] Clearly the initial industrialization of urban employment created few new social strata and greatly diminished many older distinctions based upon craft traditions. When early Victorians complained of the indiscriminate mixing of the poor, they may have exaggerated the compounding effects of sub-urbanization. They were, however, extremely sensitive to a weak and diminishing level of residential differentiation amongst the poor which was also expressed in the range of social strata who participated in "working class" movements. These developments were probably more definitive of the impact of industrial capitalism on Victorian cities than their small exclusive suburbs.

   Early Victorians not only underestimated the longevity of the exclusive residential quarters of the wealthy, some of them also exaggerated their monopoly of the urban periphery. Most early Victorian suburbs, like their Georgian predecessors, dominated one or two desirable sectors of the urban fringe rather than an entire peripheral zone (Fig. 4). In fact, the shift from polarized residential patterns to one in which there was a more complex differentiation of social strata coincided with the development of different and more definitively modern suburbs. The incremental peripheral expansion of the city to meet the needs of the highest social strata and the downward filtration of their earlier housing to upwardly mobile lower strata were not necessarily critical to the growth of prestigious wealthy suburbs. Once established, these suburbs retained their exclusivity and status and expanded outwards to form a contiguous sector rather than a circumferential zone. The apex of this sector was often anchored to locations much closer to the inner city than later developments designed for lower strata. The suburbs of the extremely wealthy were indeed the result of residential differentiation but in many respects the process itself differed from modern suburbanization. These later developments were based upon a process of filtration to which the wealthy rarely contributed in part because they yielded too small a supply of vacated housing and in part because their exclusive precincts endured for several generations.

The kinds of residential differentiation identified with modern sub-urbanization were based upon changes in the organization of the labour force associated with the transition from industrial to corporate capitalism. An increased reliance on professional services and decentralized management opened up avenues of social mobility and levels of economic security which were only rarely available to the residents of early and mid-Victorian cities. Like the transition from mercantile to industrial capitalism, the later changes in the division of labour were uneven both between industries and amongst nations. The emergence of a hierarchically differentiated labour force increasingly dominated by those described as the "new" or the "lower" middle class proceeded most rapidly in the United States where modern kinds of suburbanization clearly prevailed during the residential building boom of the late 1880s. Gradations in the income, status and security of new occupational categories supported variable consumption patterns which were clearly expressed in housing and neighbourhood choices.[41] Parallel developments in local transportation improved accessibility to these varied residential choices, but new kinds of structural social mobility were necessary to sustain the suburban movement.

This selective upward and outward mobility of new occupational strata also created more homogeneous social areas in the inner city where those who were unable to participate in this movement remained (Fig. 4). Partly because of deterministic assumptions about the negative effects of the housing environment of the inner city, its entire population was frequently judged to be impoverished and socially disorganized. Sensitive observers were, however, aware of distinctions between those who were endemically impoverished and those who were able to maintain a modest level of subsistence. The former were concentrated in the most notorious slums where pathological social conditions prevailed. The latter were usually employed in semi-skilled but increasingly unionized occupations, and the social life of their neighbourhoods are thought to resemble in some ways the traditional world of the village. Unlike the highly mobile life and dispersed social networks of early Victorians, their late Victorian descendants lived in so called "urban villages" which housed most of their relatives many of whom were to remain there for several generations.[42]

This distinction between a socially disorganized residuum and highly organized urban villagers may have been exaggerated and certainly under depressed economic conditions it may have become faded.[43] Nevertheless, the emergence of homogeneous village-like neighbourhoods was dependent upon lower levels of population turnover and a more complex organization of the labour force than prevailed in early Victorian cities. In highly specialized factory towns, however, sedentary working class communities developed earlier in the century, and certainly the effects of the transition to corporate capitalism on these towns was to destroy their economic base rather than to create a "new" middle class.[44] In larger, more diversified settlements, the residential quarters of the more secure strata of the working class and the various strata of the "new" middle class were clearly distinguished from one another and from the two extremes of wealth and poverty. At the end of the Victorian period these developments were relatively new, but they indicated a reversal those diminishing levels of residential differentiation about which early Victorians had complained. Moreover, some late Victorian observers were apprehensive about the permanence of this change and especially about the proportionate size of those who were so impoverished that they were unlikely ever to benefit from suburbanization.

Generalizations which attempt to relate the socio-geographic patterns of Victorian cities to the conditions of industrial capitalism are clearly confronted with the diverse effects of industrialization on different industries and regions. Both the timing of this process and its precise effects of social stratification, class relationships and residential differentiation remain unclear. Victorian industrial urbanization was certainly defined by divergent as well as weak levels of residential differentiation. In contrast, those changes described as the transition from industrial to corporate capitalism have had convergent effects upon patterns of urban residential differentiation. The divergent urban consequences of corporate capitalism are less apparent within the developed world than in the striking contrasts in urban life between the developed and the less developed world. Eventually, our developmental schemes of urbanization will have to be as sensitive to sectoral and regional differences as they are to continuities and discontinuities in course of residential differentiation.

Most early interpretations of Victorian cities also emphasized their distinctive transitional characteristics in relation to both preceeding traditional and succeeding modern eras. This developmental sequence was closely related to the initial negative impact of industrialization on older patterns of life which were subsequently alleviated when modern strategies of intervention were introduced. The clarity of this definition was blurred when many attributes not only of Victorian but also of modern cities were identified long before industrialization was well started. In particular, suburbanization was viewed as a long-established process which increasingly, if spasmodically, created the highly differentiated residential patterns of modern cities. A re-examination of the socio-geographic patterns which were the sources of anxiety amongst early and late Victorians suggests that the transitions from mercantile to industrial capitalism and from industrial to corporate capitalism altered the processes of residential differentiation. To read these concerns as punctuations or pauses in an essentially continuous process of modernization may encourage us to mis-read or dismiss our own anxieties about the immediate destiny of urban society as merely temporary interruptions in long-established patterns of growth. Perhaps only in Britain was there an approximate coincidence of a distinctive phase of residential differentiation and the Victorian period. Nevertheless, the term Victorian continues to be used to describe the complex effects of and reactions to industrial capitalism, and from this perspective the distinctive socio-geographic patterns of the Victorian city may have a generic validity.

REFERENCES

1. Gottmann, J. (1961). "Megalopolis: The Urbanized Northeastern Seaboard of the United States." New York, The Twentieth Century Fund.
2. Briggs, A. (1968). "Victorian Cities." Penguin, Harmondsworth. pp.11-87.
3. Coleman, B. I. (ed.) (1973). "The Idea of the City in Nineteenth Century Britain." London, Routledge and Kegan Paul; and Keating, P. (ed.) (1976). "Into Unknown England, 1866-1913: Selections from the Social Explorers." London, Fontana.
4. Sjoberg, G. (1960). "The Pre-industrial City: Past and Present." New York, The Free Press. pp.25-77.
5. Mumford, L. (1961). "The City in History." New York, Harcourt, Brace and World. 446-481; and Geddes, P. (1949) "Cities in Evolution." London, Routledge and Kegan Paul.
6. Kumar, K. (1978). "Prophecy and Progress: The Sociology of Industrial and Post-industrial Society. Penguin, Harmondsworth.
7. Wrigley, E. A. (1972). The process of modernization and industrialization in England. *J. Interdisc. Hist.* **3**, 225-59.
8. Wirth, L. (1938). Urbanism as a way of life. *Am. J. Soc.* **44**, 1-24.
9. Calhoun, C. (1981). "Before the Working Class: Tradition and Community

in English Popular Radicalism during the Industrial Revolution." Chicago: Univ. of Chicago Press.

10. Tilly, C., Tilly, L. and Tilly, R. (1975). "The Rebellious Century, 1830-1930." Cambridge, Harvard University Press.

11. e.g. Dennis, R. J. (ed.) (1979). The Victorian city. *Trans. Inst. Brit. Geog.* N.S. **4**.

12. Cannadine, D. (1977). Victorian cities: how different? *Soc. Hist.* **4**, 457-82; and Carter, H. and Wheatley, P. (1980). Residential segregation in nineteenth century cities. *Area* **12**, 57-62.

13. Ward, D. (1974). Victorian cities: how modern? *J. Hist. Geog.* **1**, 135-51.

14. Pinker, R. (1971). "Social Theory and Social Policy." London, Heinemann. 59-84.

15. Coleman, B. I. op. cit.

16. Houghton, W. E. (1957). "The Victorian Frame of Mind." New Haven, Conn., Yale University Press; and Buckley, J. E. (1966). "The Triumph of Time: A Study of the Victorian Concepts of Time, History, Progress and Decay." Cambridge, Mass. Harvard University Press; and Williams, R. (1973). "The Country and the City. New York, Oxford University Press.

17. Langton, J. (1977). Residential patterns in pre-industrial cities: some case studies from seventeenth century Britain. *Trans. Inst. Brit. Geog.* N.S. **2**, 259-77.

18. Coleman, B. I. op. cit.

19. Burn, W. L. (1964). "The Age of Equipoise. London, Allen and Unwin.

20. Kellett, J. (1969). "The Impact of Railways on Victorian Cities." Toronto, University of Toronto Press; and McKay, J. P. (1976). "Tramways and Trolleys: The Rise of Urban Mass Transport in Europe." Princeton, N.J., Princeton University Press.

21. Pfautz, H. W. (ed.) (1967). "Charles Booth On the City: Physical Pattern and Social Structure." Chicago, University of Chicago Press.

22. Booth, C. (ed.) (1902). "Life and Labour of the People in London." London, Macmillan; and Wohl, A. (1977). "The Eternal Slum." London, Arnold.

23. Stedman Jones, G. (1971). "Outcast London: A Study in the Relationship between Classes in Victorian Society." Oxford, Oxford University Press.

24. Cherry, G. E. (1979). The town planning movement and the late Victorian city. *Trans. Inst. Brit. Geog.* N.S. **4**, 306-19.

25. Tipps, D. C. (1973). Modernization theory and the comparative study of societies: a critical perspective. *Comparative Studies in Society and History* **15**, 199-226; and Caporaso, J. O. (1980). Dependency theory: continuities and discontinuities in development studies. *Int. Org.* **34**, 605-28.

26. Burgess, E. W. (1925). The growth of the city. *In* Park, R. E. (ed.) "The City." Chicago, University of Chicago Press. 47-62.

27. Clark, P. and Slack, P. (ed.) (1972). "Crisis and Order in English Towns 1580-1640." London, Routledge and Kegan Paul; and Patten, J. (1978). "English Towns: 1500-1700." Folkestone, Dawson.

28. Vance, J. E. Jr (1971). Land assignment in the pre-capitalist, capitalist and post-capitalist city. *Econ. Geog.* **47**, 110-12; and Pythian, Adams C. (1979). "Desolation of a City: Coventry and the Urban Crisis of the Late Middle Ages." Cambridge, Cambridge University Press.

29. Evans, E. J. (1977). "Social Policy 1830-1914: Individualism, Collectivism, and the Origins of the Welfare State." London, Routledge and Kegan Paul.

30. Levine, D. P. (1975). The theory of the growth of the capitalist economy. *Econ. Dev. and Cult. Ch.* **24**, 47-74; and Wright, E. O. (1980). Varieties of Marxist conceptions of class structure. *Politics and Society* **9**, 323-70.

31. Friedman, A. L. (1977). "Industry and Labour: Class Struggle at Work and Monopoly Capitalism." London, Macmillan.

32. Himmelfarb, M. G. (1971). Mayhew's poor: a problem of identity. *Vic. St.* **14**, 308-20.

33. Ward, D. (1976). The Victorian slum: an enduring myth? *Ann. Ass. Amer. Geog.* **66**, 323-36.

34. Foster, J. (1974). Class struggle and the Industrial Revolution. *In* "Early Industrial Capitalism in Three English Towns." London Weidenfeld and Nicolson; and Bythell, D. (1978). "The Sweated Trades: Outwork in Nineteenth Century Britain." London, Batsford.

35. Vance, J. E. Jr (1967). Housing the worker: determinative and contingent ties in nineteenth century Birmingham. *Econ. Geog.* **43**, 95-127.

36. Whitehand, J. W. R. (1977). The basis for an historico-geographical theory of urban form. *Trans. Inst. Brit. Geog.* N.S. **2**, 400-16.

37. Anderson, M. (1971). "Family Structure in Nineteenth Century Lancashire." Cambridge, Cambridge University Press.

38. Ward, D. (1980). Environs and neighbours in the two nations: residential differentiation in nineteenth century Leeds. *J. Hist. Geog.* **6**, 133-62.

39. Cannadine, D. (1980). "Lords and Landlords: The Aristocracy and the Towns 1774-1967." Leicester, Leicester University Press.

40. Gray, R. Q. (1976). "The Labour Aristocracy in Victorian Edinburgh." Oxford, Clarendon Press; and Grossick, G. (1978). "An Artisan Elite in Victorian Society, Kentish London 1840-1880." London, Croom Helm.

41. Crossick, G. (ed.) (1977). "The Lower Middle Class in Britain, 1870-1914." London, Croom Helm; and Pritchard, R. M. (1976). "Housing and the Spatial Structure of the City. Cambridge, Cambridge University Press.

42. Meacham, S. (1977). "A Life Apart: The English Working Class." Cambridge, Mass. Harvard University Press.

43. Roberts, R. (1971). "The Classic Slum." Manchester, Manchester University Press.

44. Joyce, P. (1980). "Work, Society and Politics: The Culture of the Factory in Later Victorian England." Brighton, Sussex, Harvester Press.

Chapter Thirteen

Centre and Periphery: The Transfer of Urban Ideas from Britain to Canada

J. WREFORD WATSON

While Professor Gottmann has stressed the great importance of urban centrality in the growth of cities and has said that we are still far from being able to acknowledge objectively a decrease in the centralizing function of large cities, nevertheless by implication the *drive into the centre* displaces people and functions that cannot compete for a central location and leads to a *flight towards the periphery*. The two forces, the drive in and the flight out, spark each other off and together create the city as we know it today.

This chapter looks at the transfer from Britain to Canada of urban ideas which, having gained strength in the Old World, were planted in the New. The flight out of town in order to make way for, or escape, the drive into the centre, was already a significant feature of town life at the time of Canada's settlement. Not unnaturally, the state of mind which in Britain led to the growing flight of the middle class from the city centre was carried across the ocean and planted itself in the Canadian scene. In so far as cities are states of mind they should be alike when governed by the same mental topography, however different they may be as a reflection of unique relief. The lay of the land increasingly takes on the myth in the mind.

British, or United Empire Loyalists devoted to British ways, started to build towns in Canada in the latter half of the eighteenth century—Halifax in 1749, Kingston in 1783, and Toronto in 1793. This was during the Georgian era when urban flight was much in vogue. In

THE EXPANDING CITY
ISBN 0 12 547250 1

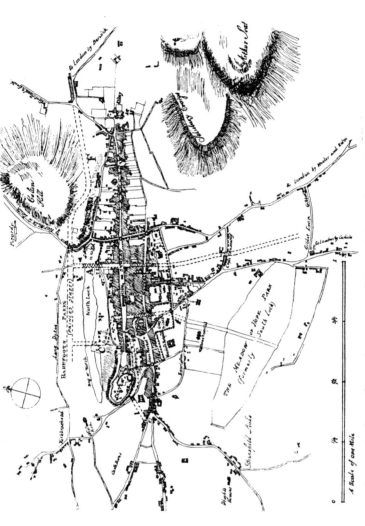

Fig. 1 This Map, based on one by James Craig of 1763, shows Edinburgh just before the Georgian Expansion. The City wall, begun in 1513, is shown in a heavy dotted line with black circles for the principal Gates. The only road from north to south is seen outside the City boundary. High Level roads begun in the reigns of George III and George IV are lettered and marked with chain lines, crosses marking the viaducts and bridges. A. North Bridge, opened for traffic 1772. B. South Bridge, opened for traffic 1788. C. The "Earthen Mound" opened for traffic about 1830. D. George IV Bridge, opened for traffic 1836. E. Western Approach (Johnston Terrace) 1836. F. Regent Bridge and Road, 1819

Britain, although a section of the upper class stayed on in the centre-city close to castle and cathedral, a larger part moved out to suburbs or satellite villages. In Edinburgh, for example, between 1725 and 1752, that is bridging the time when Halifax, Nova Scotia, was laid out, 1748-9, the then Lord Provost, Drummond, had been devising plans for a new town to take the pressure off the old. Princes Street was to be the axis of the New Town and vie with High Street, the spine of the Old (Fig. 1). As Youngson[1] recounts, the new lay-out was done along Palladian or Vitruvian lines, popular throughout Western Europe. The Palladian concept used the rectangle and the square and gave rise to a town where a grid system of rectilinear roads was punctuated by great squares. Garvan[2] has shown how effective such a mode was in Georgian New England.

Under these influences, Halifax was laid out by a Scottish engineer, Bruce, assisted by a surveyor, Morris, from New England. It is not surprising that the plan of the town, built on the east side of a peninsula jutting out between two arms of the sea, should have consisted of a Palladian grid. Long straight streets ran parallel to the Atlantic shore, and short cross roads climbed at right angles up the slope of a commanding hill, crowned by Halifax Citadel (Fig. 2a). This rectilinear pattern incorporated a large square at the centre, known as the Parade. The city on the ground was structured after the city in the mind.

There is scope for research on the training and ideas of Bruce and Morris to see to what extent and in what ways they had been imbued with the Georgian ideals of the time. Were they conscious, for instance, of the changing class patterns that were to produce changing urban forms —of what Brian Harley[3] assures us was a Britain divided into two nations, with the rise of a new élitism? To a certain extent, their work speaks for them. They designed a town for a population of owner-occupiers, who would not live in common in tenements or row-houses, but on their own, in separate homes. Halifax was plotted in terms of individual lots, 40 feet wide by 66 feet deep.

This reflected the attitude to living and property among the British well-to-do, who were in search of just such conditions. Georgian Edinburgh had been built for the élite as a town in flight; it was an escape from the medieval crowding of Edinburgh Old Town—more than that, it was a separation from the old-town mix. In the medieval city the lord, the lawyer, the artisan, and the apprentice might all inhabit a tenement in common and rub shoulders with each other going to their apartments off

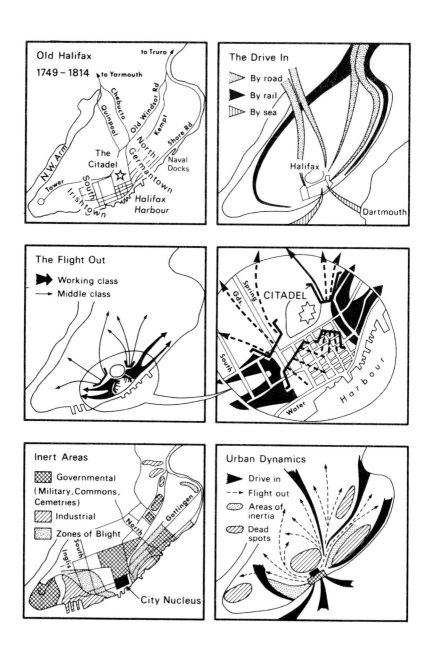

Fig. 2 Halifax, Nova Scotia

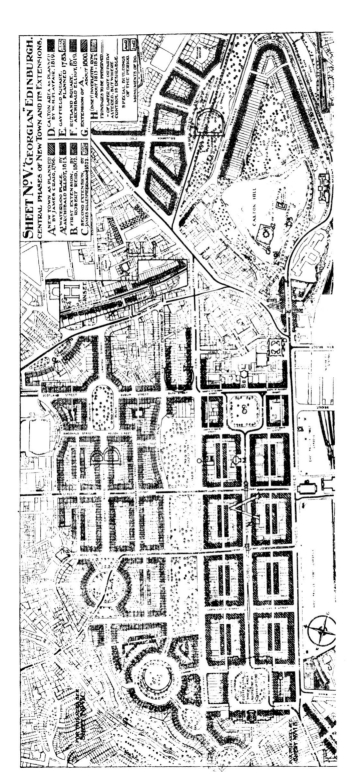

Fig. 3 Edinburgh New Town

a common stair. Edinburgh New Town had been planted "for people of fortune and a certain rank", who fled the old purlieus, too crowded and too commonplace, in search of new precincts, bathed in light and with an upper-class air (Fig. 3). The élite wanted to draw off and make themselves distinctive by living in a distinctive district. Social difference required geographical differentiation. In the New Town, as Youngson[4] points out "There were to be no shops or businesses . . . and each family was to have a house of his own". It is true that, in the course of time, the New Town did become invaded by shops and offices, but there was then a new flight, at least of "those gentlemen of taste", to what Sir Walter Scott called the new New Town, characterized by "space, order, and dignity".

Georgian Halifax (like Georgian Kingston and Georgian Toronto) had from the beginning to make room for shops and offices, yet here too the flight of the residents was in full swing. Informed of the fashion in Europe, Canadians found it fashionable to move. We must widen Wolpert's idea of the information field in intra-urban flight: that field extended from the metropolitan to the colonial situation. Here is an area of research for historical geographers interested in the transplant of cultures. Flight-minded settlers from Britain settled into still further flight in Canada.

THE WANT OF SPACE

We are dealing not only with the passion for ideas but also with the pulse of necessity that stirred Georgian man. He moved not simply to sponsor new ideals but to make room for changing realities. As towns grew with the commercial and, to a certain extent, the industrial expansion of the age, the want of space became critical. The centralizing drive into town of people and activities built up such a pressure on space that, to ease it, there grew a flight out (Fig. 2b,c). The drive in was made up of active, competitive, directional space-users, such as business, industry and transport. The flight out was of more passive, malleable, concessional space-users, like institutions and residents. What would today be called the action-spaces of these different users came into play, changing the values put upon land. How people in the late eighteenth century perceived the amount of space they needed to act out their roles is difficult to say. Their own perceptions were probably by no means clear.

Urban flight was sporadic in time and erratic in space, as though no myth of flight had been built up.

Here is another topic for the historical geographer. By using the technique of the semantic differential based not on interviews, obviously, but newspaper reports, he could measure the reaction of people to one neighbourhood or another. A rating scale created from simple word pairs such as good/bad, clean/dirty, healthy/dangerous could suggest which districts attracted and which repelled searchers after new homes or places to build their homes. A map of semantic space would show up the images beginning to appear and then entrenching themselves in the minds of urban movers. In Edinburgh images of the new town as compared with the old grew up round verbal preferences for cleanness over dirtiness, spaciousness over crowdedness, order over irregularity, security over danger, and being separate over mixing together. As images grew clearer, flight became stronger. It settled into distinct flightways.

Urban flightways are thus image corridors. They begin as mental lines, before they become geographic tracks. They result from the push of the centre-city image, and the pull of the city-margin image.

In Halifax there grew up an impression of centre-city crowdedness, even before all the lots were taken up, or buildings had grown several storeys high. The mental image was all important. People began to complain, as Akins[5] remarked, that "the want of sufficient space in the central part of the town for markets and public buildings has always been an impediment" (Fig. 2d). A mental fore-shortening of distances produced a sense of being cramped and confined that made flight out appear increasingly attractive.

These perceptual spaces had little to do with space realities since, even as late as 1870, what was thought of as a crowded down-town street, namely, Bedford Row (see Fig. 7), had only four shops, a green market, two business offices, and one public building on 45 lots.[6] The street still had 35 homes on it, and there were still two vacant lots. Nevertheless, a sense of want of space led "better" families to leave: the invasion of their street by even a few shops and offices stirred fear and warranted flight.

THE PUSH OF THE CITY-CENTRE IMAGE

Space is a relative matter. Relative space may count for more in the growth of a city than actual space. In the actual use of space, shops and offices on Bedford took up less than a quarter of the street. Indeed the old market, we are told by Miss Blakeley,[7] "was so small that goods were frequently displayed and sold along the street". Its image, however—perhaps expanded by this street-side array of produce—bulked large in the minds of the local residents. It was considered moving it uphill to the city square known as the Parade, but this was difficult "as loaded carts could not climb the hill from the ferry". Not until improvements in transport created the technological space for it near the citadel was it finally removed, but by then many people had taken themselves from its presence.

Crowding there was (images never spring from nothing), but the visual silhouette was magnified by the mental skyline. Lynch has drawn our attention to the role of landmarks in the urban image. This is only part of the matter, and much more work needs to be done on the whole mental profile of the city. In Edinburgh, the Georgian mind saw order and dignity in terms of what was not there—sheer open spaces—as well as what was there—the buildings in between. Georgian towns were built for vistas (Fig. 3). It was the space leading up to a building that gave it splendour. Hence the Edinburgh New Town skyline concentrated on sky as well as line: on long avenues going up to great squares, pierced by columns or domes. The New World was to part from this, and with a vengeance, by virtually crowding out sky with line. Streets became canyons between cliff-like buildings that practically cut out heaven's light. From that day on, parallels between Old and New World cities became increasingly difficult to establish. They had come to have very different states of mind. Nevertheless the mental heritage of earlier times produced a deep concern for space.

The feeling grew in Halifax that its public buildings were not being given room enough. They were too crowded in. Their dignity was being stripped from them. In 1872, we learn,[8] "the editor of *The Acadian Recorder* was complaining because the City Council was wasting money repairing the Town Hall—'a circumscribed, uncomfortable, dirty old hole . . .'" opposite the old city market (Fig. 7). As a result, the Council resolved on July 15, 1874, to purchase a lot extending from Lockman to Poplar along Barrington Street. This was well outside the crowded centre. In fact, it was too far outside. Urban flight could not remove from the centre, bound by a proper centrality. Access to town was as important for certain functions as flight from town was for others. Flight is not a denial of, but an attestation to, centrality. The city in flight does not—or at least should not—explode the city centre, but give it room to do a better centralizing job. In Halifax, "a public meeting condemned the new site because it was not central enough, and suggested that the new city hall should be erected on the north side of the Parade"[9] (see Fig. 7).

This helped to crystallize the issue as to what should stay in and what should move out—since the proposed location was already the site of Dalhousie College (Fig. 4). Did administration or education go with centrality? What could afford to be pushed out from the centre?

This was an issue in Edinburgh as well. The University had never been at the real centre, because it was founded (1583) long after castle (452) cathedral (821) and palace (1128), but it was within the old city wall. As the city grew, the City Chambers, the Scottish Parliament, and the Law Courts all expanded. There was even less room for the University as a central institution; together with the College of Physicians and Surgeons it expanded outside the wall. Education had to concede pride of place to administration.

Fig. 4   The original Dalhousie College 1820-1887

However, the pressures from business were even greater and constituted the real decision-making force that directed the growth of the town. To make room for the drive into the city centre of directive urban functions, the concessive functions had to move out towards the margins.

The drive into the centre of Halifax, like that into Edinburgh, was both by sea and by land (Fig. 2b). From the sea the drives were naval and mercantile. The north shore, widening out to Bedford Basin, gave room and security for naval expansion. The central and southern shores were competed for by ferries, fishing quays, freight wharves and passenger landings. Landward facilities associated with these—ships chandleries, warehouses, banks, mercantile insurance companies, ships and saloons—drove back up into town (as they did from Leith, up Leith Walk towards Edinburgh). As their pressure increased, the want of space in the town grew. From the land, road and later railroad and airway connections drove into the Halifax peninsula from the rest of the Province. They brought business with them and created a mounting need for administration that put a further premium on central space. These drives *in* quickened the flight *out*. More than that, they often controlled flight. As in Britain, where Tetlow and Goss remark on how, with the drive in of the railway, "communities were divided and segregated as never before by the steel barriers of the permanent way", so in Canada, the drive in of provincial highways and the railroad became barriers that shed urban flight to one side of them or the other (Fig. 3 Edinburgh; Fig. 2 Halifax). Their concentration at the centre created a peak of activity which, although it attracted business and administration, shed culture and town living.

In Halifax the drive in from the sea front was the most disturbing factor. It led business to move steadily uphill into streets that had been developed for family homes. Specialization in business grew, leading to business segregation and eventually to the rise of a CBD (Fig. 5). The upper streets such as Hollis, Granville, and Barrington, parallel to the waterfront (Fig. 7), became swiftly invaded by business and just as swiftly evacuated by residences. This occurred in the first four decades of the nineteenth century and exactly paralleled the business invasion of Princes Street, Edinburgh, from 1815 to 1845, which led to the flight of residents out of Edinburgh New Town to new New Town (Fig. 3). In both Canadian and British cities, both at the same time, the new mercantile mindscape came to be reflected in the new commercial landscape. While "merchants of a past generation", declares White[10] "were accustomed to deal in goods in all their multitudinous variety—cottons, pins, groceries, hardware, stationery, etc.—the advantages of classification . . . began to be recognized and merchants felt the necessity of choosing distinctive lines of business". The vogue for "classification" created specialized districts, from which business or public buildings drove out the town house. Nor was it enough to have the shop below and the dwelling above, "as was the custom of the times" when, in 1823, John Esson, lately arrived from Aberdeen, "set up for himself in a snug little shop at the corner of Duke and Barrington where he lived over his store". By the early nineteenth century specialized business architecture

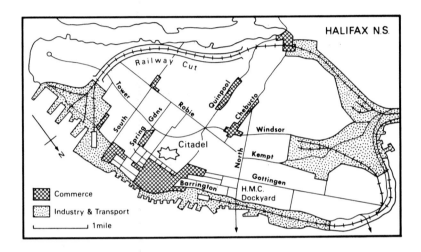

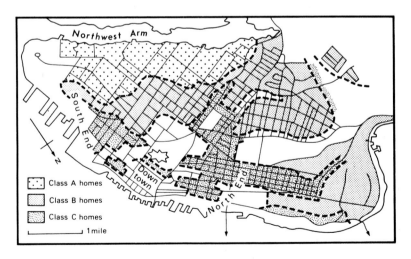

Fig. 5   The drive in from the sea front, Halifax, Nova Scotia

was beginning to mark out the business district. Thus in 1825 when the Bank of Nova Scotia was founded, that bank, together with the new Post Office, and Provincial House made the "locality of Hollis and George truly an architectural centre".[11]

Other banks moved into Hollis street, along with several insurance companies. This squeezed out the good housing, once characteristic of the area. Fears that things might get worse led to flight, even of influential people. Akins[12] has tabulated the flight of many notable families from the homes on Hollis Street, starting in the 1820s and going on through to the 1870s. Included were the town mansions of the Hon. James Black, the Hon. J. B. Uniacke, the Hon. Wm. Lawson, the Hon. H. H. Binney (all members of the Provincial Assembly), the Hon. Michael Wallace, Treasurer of the Province, J. B. Franklin, the son of Governor Franklin, the Bishop of Nova Scotia, Judge Stewart, and Chief Justice Sir Brenton Halliburton. When more than one Hon. gentleman felt it was time to leave, it became less than honourable for the rest to stay!

Specialization in finance along Hollis Street pushed shopping up-slope to the next street, Granville, which became the main retail strip (see Fig. 7). Indeed, as Blakeley[13] shows, "At the time of Confederation (1867) the best stores were located on Granville . . . Barrington not having achieved its present pre-eminence". As a result, "no part of the city has undergone greater changes (1820-94) since, from George Street northward all the old houses on both sides of Granville have been replaced by lofty buildings". Again, a state of mental fright at the effect upon house property, led to family flight. By Confederation, as McAlpine's[14] *City Directory of Halifax* shows, Granville had become well commercialized at least between Sackville and Jacob—for example: Sackville to Prince, five shops to five residences; Prince to Duke, fourteen shops to one residence; Duke to Buckingham, all shops, no residences; Buckingham to Jacob, all shops, no residences. Residential flight was well on its way.

Barrington Street, up-hill from Granville, was the next thoroughfare to experience business invasion (Fig. 5; see also Fig. 7). Almost entirely residential in Georgian times it became infiltrated by institutions, like schools and churches, in early Victorian times and then, with the advent of the tram in late Victorian years, grew to be the principal shopping street of Halifax. Once again, residences were challenged, denigrated and pushed out, either south and west, or north and west round the Citadel,

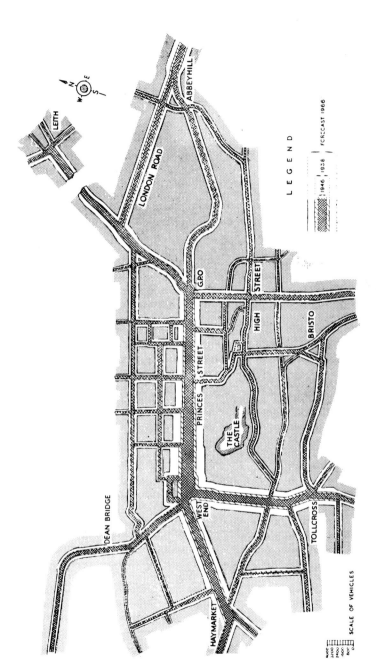

Fig. 6   Analysis of traffic flow in Central Edinburgh showing the importance of Princes Street

now a dead area in the heart of the peninsula. Many of the social institutions on Barrington had to flee. Chalmers Presbyterian Church on Barrington at Duke, seeing its members move, first started a Sunday School mission at Coburg Street and then moved there itself (Fig. 7, lower part). The minutes of November 25th, 1886 are instructive.[15] They noted: "It is very desirable in the interests of the families of our church in the S.W. part of our city, in view of the growth of the city in that direction, that we engage unitedly in organizing a Sunday School there". This subsequently became the Coburg Street Presbyterian Church, 1894 (Fig. 7, lower part).

The same years saw the same sort of movements within Georgian Edinburgh that virtually took over the first New Town and led to a flight which built up the new New Town (Fig. 3). Like Hollis, Halifax, so George Street and St Andrew's Square, Edinburgh, became a financial quarter, with a high concentration of banks and insurance companies. Like Granville, Halifax, Queen Street, Edinburgh, was invaded by doctors' consulting rooms and lawyers' chambers, though unlike Granville there were not many stores. Like Barrington, Halifax, Princes Street, Edinburgh, became the outstanding shopping thoroughfare (Fig. 6). The same forces were at work on both sides of the Atlantic, enlarging the centre city and accelerating the flight to the margins.

URBAN FLIGHT, THE ESCAPE FROM THE CENTRE

However, that flight had its difficulties. Traditionally the British well-to-do like a place with a view, either on the heights or at the outskirts of a town. In Halifax, the heights were crowned with the Citadel, and the outskirts were marked by industrial suburbs and shanty towns. There were houses high on the hill, in the lee of the fortress walls, but the residents were pimps and prostitutes. I have not yet done the research on Edinburgh that could enable me to draw for those streets close to the castle a parallel with the upper streets of Halifax, said to be full of brothels, by 1810. "The street along the base of the Citadel", according to Akins,[16] "was known as 'Knock-him-down street' in consequence of the number of frays there. No person of any character ventured to reside there, nearly all the buildings being 'houses of ill fame' for the soldiers and sailors."

Here social distance between the toffs and the tarts cancelled geographic nearness (Fig. 7). The commanding hill became a social abyss. Social

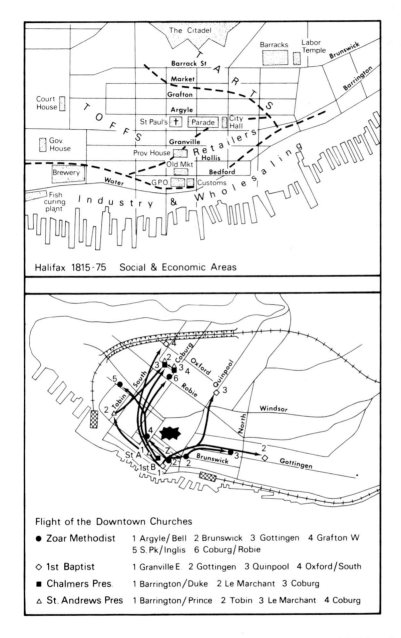

Halifax 1815-75   Social & Economic Areas

Flight of the Downtown Churches

● Zoar Methodist   1 Argyle/Bell 2 Brunswick 3 Gottingen 4 Grafton W
                   5 S.Pk/Inglis 6 Coburg/Robie

◇ 1st Baptist   1 Granville E. 2 Gottingen   3 Quinpool 4 Oxford/South

■ Chalmers Pres.   1 Barrington/Duke 2 Le Marchant 3 Coburg

△ St. Andrews Pres 1 Barrington/Prince 2 Tobin 3 Le Marchant 4 Coburg

Fig. 7   Halifax: (*upper*) Social and economic areas 1815-1875; (*lower*) Flight of the
downtown churches

space determined the path of flight. The lines of search had to follow the social contour, avoiding the status bog as much as they would the topographical swamp. Once an area was regarded as a social loss, its effect as a barrier grew stronger: reactions built up a cumulative inertia that was hard to change. Historical geography should pick out such areas and map a town in terms of its socially inert and off-putting cells. These would be found to be key points in bending the path of urban flight.

In Halifax, flight up-slope was socially frozen. But flight out of town along the shore-slope was almost equally blocked. To the south was the Irish quarter, to the north was the German (Fig. 2a): these were working-class villages that had grown up outside the wall, where squatters and tax-evaders lived, beyond the by-law limits. This reflected an old English tradition, of course. In London, for example, many squatter suburbs grew up outside the wall, occupied by people who did not want to pay city-level taxes, or to abide by the restrictions of the guilds, livery companies and other institutions with set rules of practice. Indeed, in Elizabeth's time such suburbs in London were described by Chettle[17] as "no other than dark dens for adulterers, thieves, murderers, and every mischief worker". No Halifax archivist ever waxed as eloquent as this, but both Harvey[18] and Fergusson[19] refer to the way in which the German (or Dutch) and Irish suburbs restricted town development. Here mental space came into play. It was the mental image of these lower-class and/or foreign suburbs that put them at a mental distance from middle-class flightways. Flight was bent from the natural pathways offered by flat, well-marked raised beaches to follow the mental corridors between areas of repellant mental images.

It is true that the blocking effect of the foreign community to the north was reinforced by the presence of H.M. Dockyard, which pre-empted a mile and a half of shoreline (Fig. 5). Indeed, as White[20] shows, naval property occupied valuable space "near the heart of the city itself—at the junction of Water and Hollis". Nevertheless, bearing in mind the class origin of most sailors and marines in the nineteenth century, and the saloons and brothels that clung like leeches to the edge of their district, it may be argued that mental rather than military space deflected the flight of home-seekers moving out of town. The same was true of the Citadel itself, "a great inert area"[21] and of military establishments between Windsor and Kempt streets. They were, for long, urban dead spots—at least in terms of residential growth (Fig. 2e). Although they were alive enough in that they housed soldiers and gave employment, they were as good as dead in the mental map of people seeking a nice place to live in. Again, it was the mental attitude rather than the real situation that counted. There was, so to speak, a mental anaesthetization of space which deadened areas that were feared or disliked. Such mentally dead areas deflect the course of urban flight. And though it may be difficult to reconstruct them for the past, here is a promising field for the urban geographer.

The North End of Halifax did in fact see some expansion, but not of the middle class. As H.M. Dockyards grew, they gave more employment. The working-class suburb expanded. In 1850 Zoar Methodist church, in the city centre, established a mission on Göttingen, close by the docks, for African families (Fig. 7, lower part). As these became more numerous they took it over as the African Methodist Episcopal Church. Baptists also moved north, but more to the west. The Granville Street Baptist Church, founded in the centre city in 1827, later "encouraged a few members to form the North Baptist Church, on Göttingen in 1867". Here Baptist families did establish some nice residences, but it is significant that further expansion was west, not north. The mother church on Granville "helped to establish and support the Quinpool Road mission for Baptists in that rapidly growing district, (northwest of the Citadel). In 1890 this mission became the West End Baptist Church."[22] However, it should be noted that the main congregation when Granville became invaded by business, moved south-west, along the principal flightway for the middle class, and built a new church on Spring Garden Road.

Confirming the stronger pull of the southwest was the very isolation of movement to the north. In the early 1830s a "Mr. Demolitor had built a large house at the northern extremity of Brunswick,[23] not far from the Naval Dockyards." But this, we are told, "was considered a very wild speculation" and was not followed up. Reference has already been made to the proposal by the Town Council to re-locate the first City Hall up north at Lockman. This was strongly resisted by citizen opinion, which insisted on a location at the Central Parade.

Fergusson[24] has an interesting account of the shifts of position of concert halls and theatres in Halifax. "Early plays were put on at Pontac's Coffee House on the corner of Duke and Water streets as early as 1760." Water Street soon became crowded with warehouses and workshops expanding up-slope from the harbour (Fig. 7). In 1789 the "New Grand Theatre 'especially devoted to plays' was built in Argyle

Street." This street, according to Raddall,[25] "had become the fashionable residential section" in the late eighteenth and early nineteenth century.

Blakeley[26] shows how the Temperance Hall, built in 1849, on the north end of the centre city, at Starr and Poplar, was "preferred by professional actors" because of its size. On the other hand, it had the drawback of its "distance from the South end, *where most of those with money and leisure to patronize the theatre lived* [italics added]". Consequently a final move, associated with the Lyceum theatre and with the Library and Academy of Music, was to Spring Garden Road, in the southwest of Halifax (see Fig. 9).

The blocking effect of the Naval Dockyards and the working-class suburb associated with it (tied up as all this was with the poorer areas around the north end of the Citadel) tended to turn middle-class institutions and residences to the south. Even here, flight was not free. The southerly extension of the harbour and the presence of the Irish shanty town, inhibited movement in the extreme south. When the members of Zoar central church were being pushed outward by city-centre growth, some of them made the mistake of living in and starting a mission at the South End, near Inglis Street. This was disposed of within seven years,[27] as the bulk of the congregation moved south-west.

In general, middle-class flight had to leap-frog over the nearer industrial suburbs in order to create residential suburbs further out (Fig. 2d). This occurred, to a certain extent, in Edinburgh, where a working-class suburb had grown up outside the city wall, between the West Port and Tollcross (Fig. 6, Tollcross). Later this suburb expanded round the canal turning-basin where the Union Canal ended. Many Irish, employed in the construction of the canal, lived around its terminus. Middle-class suburban expansion had to leapfrog over this whole lower-class area to find its venue on the higher ground south of the canal basin, in what is now Bruntsfield. This occurred in the 1860s to 1880s, at the very time middle-class Haligonians leap-frogged to the south west, beyond the clogged up suburbs that had housed so many of their early workers. The parallelism is remarkable, even to the extent that in both cases the Irish were involved.

Thus the squeeze in upon the centre by the old working-class districts was a reason for the burst out from the centre into the new middle-class suburbs. Social divisions became sharply marked, registering a distinct change from the old compact town, the flavour of which was its social mix.

PULL FROM THE MARGINS

Marginal attraction was as important to urban flight as central expulsion. The magnetism of more light and air with at the same time less noise kept tugging at the minds of those wanting amenity, even at the cost of access. Space-consuming users of land, like social institutions and the private-home lover, were especially moved to move out. Unable to make profits from the land, they could not keep their place at the centre where the drive in of business put land at a premium.

Churches in particular felt the attraction of the developing margins: this was where their congregations were going or had gone (Fig. 7). Only where, as in the case of metropolitan St Paul's, at the central Parade, they had the power to draw people from all over town, could they affort to remain at the centre. And one doubts whether churches could have stayed even in these circumstances had they not been made exempt from tax. Churches, other than metropolitan ones, depending less on the community as a whole and more on their discrete sub-communities, had to move if and when their group was drawn away.

Once the movement started, it snowballed. Churches carried with them the social clubs, literary and dramatic societies, and recreation associations that used their halls. Space assemblages like this became whole chains, drawing their individual links with them. *Linked space* formed a line. A flightway was developed.

Since the linkages were among non-gain users of land, they avoided profit-making land users. Since the latter were on the axes where business was driving in, flight had to take the interstices between the axial lines.

These conditions were as true of Edinburgh as they were of Halifax. When enough of the gentry and merchants had left Old Edinburgh for Edinburgh New Town, St George's and St Andrew's churches sprang up at the new margins, vying with the centre-city Cathedral. When the New Town became invaded by business, and residents fled to the new New Town, St George's West, and St Stephen's arose to satisfy their needs. In modern times as people have flown the new New Town, St George's has closed and become part of the Scottish Record Office, and churches have sprung up further west, at Murrayfield and beyond. The path of flight has been plotted by the plight of the churches: where has it been safe to stay, where most advantageous to go?

In Halifax, the history of Zoar church is typical (Fig. 7). This started as a Methodist church in 1792 at the corner of Argyle Street and Bell's Lane, at the north end of the town. Argyle north was "then a residential street with many open spaces"[28]. The Rev. Wm. Black lived up-hill from the church, and behind him, to the corner of Jacob Street, "the land was taken up in gardens [allotments]." The north part of the centre city was then a pleasant open area, attracting craftsmen and merchants. Subsequently, the district filled up, expanded beyond the line of the old wall, and impinged on the German (or Dutch) quarter along Brunswick and Göttingen Streets, behind the Naval Dockyards. In the 1830s a Methodist revival enlarged the membership beyond the capacity of the church, and it was decided to build another place of worship. Meantime the north end had lost status. Many coloured families had come to live in the vicinity, and "since the central part of the town had largely lost its residential character it was decided to follow the trend southward and build a new church on Grafton Street". The old chapel was bought out by the Anglicans in 1852, who had more members in the centre city, but the Bishop "finding himself unable to make use of the venerable old church, sold it to other parties by whom, to the great grief of those who had worshipped in its walls, it was devoted to the sale of intoxicants".[29]

The southern trend continued, but the southern extension of Halifax harbour, and acquisition of land for a southern railway terminal, deflected interest west. Another probe, started as a Sunday School mission in an outlying district in the west, proved that house-owners were moving well out of town. The horse-driven tram made this possible. We read that[30] "because of the growth of the city westward, Grafton Street ceased to be a convenient location and, as so often happens with down-town churches, the younger families tended to drift to nearby churches for the convenience of their children". By 1886 "by far the larger part of the Grafton Street congregation lived (in the district bounded by) Seymour", i.e. in the West. The Sunday school mission had become more important than the mother church! "And so, when planning a permanent church to replace the mission, a site on Coburg at Robie (in the West) was chosen [Fig. 7, lower part]. This remained under the supervision of the Grafton Street minister till 1890", after which, the principal charge was at the Coburg Road church. In 1924, Grafton Street was abandoned in favour of the suburban church at Coburg Road. "The old building still stands", it was stated in 1949 "but is now used entirely for commercial purposes."[31]

Colleges, schools, and hospitals also felt the attraction of the city margins. In Britain, these had been centre-city institutions up to Elizabethan times, but in Jacobean, and more especially in Georgian times, had either moved out or had new extensions, or counterparts, built out following the outward expansion of the middle class. In Edinburgh, George Heriot's school in 1626 and George Watson's school in 1749 moved to the then outskirts of town (Fig. 1, Heriot's Hospital, Watson's Hospital). The University, though just within the city wall when founded in 1583, built its medical school outside, and has continued to grow towards the city margins (see Fig. 8). Its medical school attracted the main hospital to move out with it, since when newer hospitals have moved still further out. George Watson's School decided in 1931 that what was outside town in 1749 was now hopelessly in: the need for larger buildings and more play space led to a new move out, well into the southern suburbs. Mary Erskine School has had a most interesting flight history. Built near the heart of the Old Town, in the Cowgate in 1696, it moved to the then south edge of the town in 1706: moving further south, to Lauriston in 1818, it was then incorporated into the New Town in 1871. Here it stayed on Queen Street (Fig. 3, at N. Castle St.) until that street became heavily commercialized. Then flight took it out to the western suburbs at Ravelston in 1966. The Edinburgh Academy also grew by going out. Built at the foot of the new New Town in 1824, it had a primary and a junior school erected far to the north in 1945 and 1960, among the stately homes of new new new suburbanites.

These trends occurred with remarkable parallelism in Halifax, Nova Scotia, where again the flight of the middle class pulled learning, science and the arts after them. Dalhousie University was originally built right in the downtown area, opposite St Paul's cathedral church at the north end of the central Parade (Figs 4 and 8). Although in the days when most students lived in the city centre and walked to college this was a fine site, the College found it very constricting. Out-of-town students increased in number. They needed accommodation, but none could be provided. Many had to live in rooms in streets that, as we have seen, were being increasingly commercialized.

Meantime, many citizens were saying that the site should have been developed for a city hall (Fig. 7, N. end of Parade). In 1869 pressure grew to build a new city hall, the outcome of which was that the city offered some of its common lands south and west of the Citadel to Dalhousie, if it would move. As Blakeley[32] shows, the College accepted the offer and on April 27th, 1887 the cornerstone of the University was laid, in the so-called Forrest campus, towards the West, between Robie and Carleton Streets (Fig. 9). The University has since then expanded still further west to the Studley Campus, which was a farm at the time of its initial flight (Fig. 8).

One institution in flight triggered off another. Most cultural institutions live by contact with others. Migration within the city is drawn into magnetic fields of institutional contacts. Universities contact libraries, research institutions, hospitals, professional associations, playhouses, restaurants, hostels, student flats, and staff homes—to mention but a few. The study of contact space is thus vital to that of urban flight. The contact field of Dalhousie drew in, first, the thought of migrating to the southwest, and then, the actual migration. Soon other institutions moved out which then evolved contact fields of their own. Eventually contacts between these contact fields developed a zone of magnetism that pulled the whole town out.

For instance, Dalhousie's outward move encouraged the migration of the Presbyterian and the Roman Catholic colleges, the city library, the city museum, and the Nova Scotia Institute—all in the same westward direction (see Fig. 9).

A year after the foundations of Dalhousie were dug, in 1819, the Pictou Academy was founded by the Presbyterian Church of Nova Scotia, in far off Pictou. It was both school and seminary. It moved to Truro in 1858. In the meanwhile the rise of the Free Presbyterian Church in Scotland led to the establishment of the Free Church Presbyterian College in Halifax. According to Falconer and Watson,[33] this "opened work at Gerrish Street" and included both Arts and Theology Departments. Although the land was cheap, this site was an unfortunate choice. It was at the north end, near the German village, close to the Naval Dockyards, and just above shore land about to be developed as the first railway terminal in the city. Few middle class families lived in the zone, though it was from the middle class that most of the students were drawn. The area was, as it were, a false creek—a pocket of low land-values in a region about to become a real pressure-point of high-demand growth.

A chance to rectify the situation came in 1878. By then, the two Presbyterian churches in Nova Scotia had united (1860). It was thought best to unite their colleges, too; in Halifax. Many of the united Presbyterians had migrated towards St Andrew's church on Robie Street, in the south-west end of the city. The Board therefore thought they

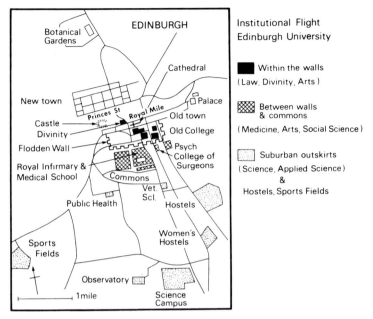

EDINBURGH

Botanical Gardens

Cathedral

New town

Princes St   Royal Mile

Castle
Divinity
Flodden Wall

Old town
Old College

Psych
College of
Surgeons

Royal Infirmary &
Medical School

Commons

Vet.
Scl.

Public Health

Hostels

Women's
Hostels

Sports
Fields

Observatory

1 mile

Science
Campus

Palace

Institutional Flight
Edinburgh University

■ Within the walls
(Law, Divinity, Arts)

▨ Between walls
& commons
(Medicine, Arts, Social Science)

▢ Suburban outskirts
(Science, Applied Science)
&
Hostels, Sports Fields

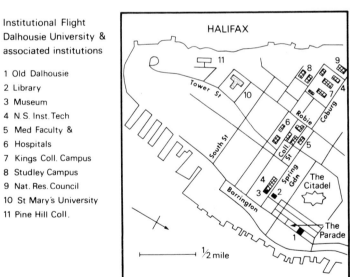

Institutional Flight
Dalhousie University &
associated institutions

1 Old Dalhousie
2 Library
3 Museum
4 N.S. Inst. Tech
5 Med Faculty &
6 Hospitals
7 Kings Coll. Campus
8 Studley Campus
9 Nat. Res. Council
10 St Mary's University
11 Pine Hill Coll.

HALIFAX

11

Tower St

10

8   9
7   4

South St

Robie

Coburg

6

Coll. St

5

Spring Gdn

4
3   2

Barrington

The
Citadel

1

The
Parade

½ mile

Fig. 8   Institutional flight in Edinburgh and Halifax

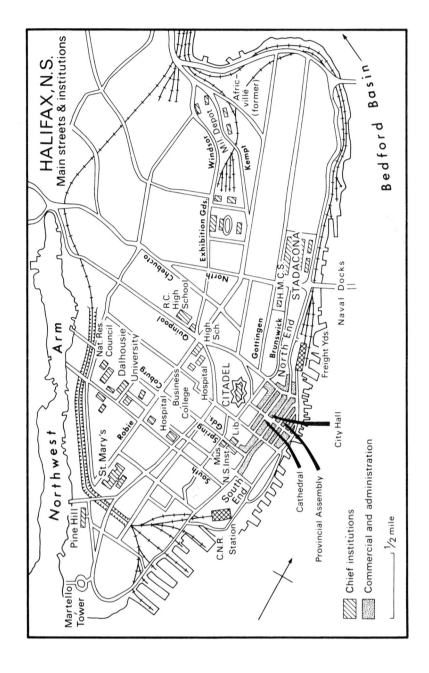

Fig. 9   Main streets and institutions in Halifax

should sell their Gerrish Street property and move to Robie Street, where the merchant and professional classes lived. (St Andrew's Church had already made several moves. It had been established in 1817 on Barrington, but Barrington became the "Princes Street" of Halifax and was rapidly commercialized in the mid-nineteenth century; therefore, as residents dwindled, the presbytery, "seeing no prospect of sustaining the church"[34] decided to move southwest to Tobin Street, in 1869. Unfortunately in this move south, they were invaded by the commercial developments associated with the southern sea and land terminals, in what was to become the international passenger harbour of Halifax. Eventually, a further move, this time towards the West, was made to Robie at Coburg (Fig. 7).) But, just as the Presbyterian College was about to accept a tender for the Robie Street site, they were offered land at Pine Hill, at the extreme western edge of the Halifax peninsula (Fig. 8). Unless their students all became residential it would be difficult for them to reach such an isolated place. Yet it was a site of extreme beauty, overlooking the sea inlet known as the Northwest Arm. If developed, the site might attract the best sort of homes and institutions to come after. By an act of faith, Pine Hill was chosen, and here, in 1878, the first session of Pine Hill College was opened.[35]

Faith more than justified itself. Houses and institutions did move west. The pull of this lovely area proved irresistible. Not long after, St Mary's College, the Roman Catholic University, set itself up at the extreme southern and western end of Robie, near Pine Hill drive—and the district was "made".

INSTITUTIONAL FLIGHT AND CULTURE BELTS

In fact a veritable "culture belt" grew up in the southwest of Halifax, with Dalhousie University on Coburg West, St Mary's on Robie south and west, and Pine Hill at the south end of the Northwest Arm. Other institutions moved into this general area (Figs 8 and 9). The Academy of Music,[36] replacing earlier music and theatrical halls in the centre city, moved to Spring Garden road in 1877, and ten years later the Halifax Conservatory of Music shifted west to Pleasant Street. The Maritime Business College,[37] which used to be on Barrington, left that commercialized street in 1907 to go up to College Street. The Museum,[38] which was begun in very small quarters in 1868, was given part of the old

Post Office building on Bedford Street in 1871. This was in the city centre, where space was at a premium. In 1899 it was moved to the Burns and Murray Building on Hollis Street, a block south and west. Today it is on Spring Garden Road, along with its child, the Nova Scotia Institute of Science, still further south and much further west.

This broad concentration of cultural institutions shows up the powerful force of functional contacts in urban flight. One educational institution draws another: together, their linkages form a broad line of attraction that then becomes an urban flightway.

The important thing here is not the physical contact, as for example in borrowing books or sharing equipment, but the mental connection. These institutions have come together because of their togetherness in thought-space. They all belong to the same universe of discourse. The fact that in terms of mental distance they are all near neighbours draws them into a neighbourhood of nearness.

Edinburgh, too, developed its lines of mutual attraction, creating an even greater flightway of cultural institutions[39] — also to the south and west (Fig. 8). The direction must be coincidental, but the force is the same. The flight has been long established; it began with the movement out beyond the original town wall — known as the King's Wall — by the Blackfriars and the Greyfriars. With the reformation the Blackfriars' school and hospital were taken over by the town school and infirmary. Here in 1625 the Surgeons' Hall was established. In the early nineteenth century this moved somewhat further south, outside the second, or Flodden Wall, to Surgeons' Place. The College of Surgeons then flanked the old quadrangle of the University. The new quadrangle, at the heart of the Medical School, was set further from town. The East of Scotland Agricultural College, in George Square, and the Royal Dick Veterinary College, at Melville Drive, represented further advances south. After the beginning of this century the University and Moray House College of Education extended their line of influence well south with the Suffolk Road hostels for women (Fig. 9). In 1924 the University took the bold move of securing land at the city's extreme south edge where it erected a science campus, known as King's Buildings, about three miles out from the original site. Meanwhile, the southern expansion of the College of Surgeons and the University was paralleled by the establishment, in their vicinity, of the Edinburgh Public Library, the extension to the National Library of Scotland, the Royal Scottish Museum, and the Edinburgh College of Art. These at first made a wave, not a line, of flight. But the

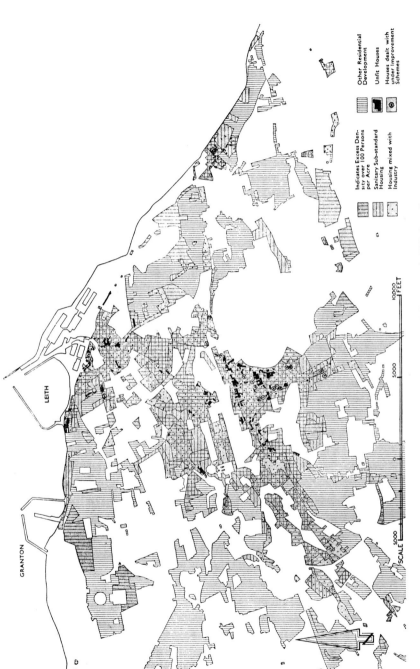

Fig. 10   Location of sub-standard living areas in Edinburgh

wave gradually became a phalanx, and was then pulled out in a line. A flightway was established. Into it have been drawn the Pollock Halls, first opened as University men's residences, though now for both sexes and, most recently (1974) the National Map Library of Scotland, and the Institute of Geological Sciences (1977).

Although urban flight continues, it is being questioned. After all, it is flight: escape. This fact now disturbs the urban state of mind. Individualism is qualified. Elitism is criticized. Segregation is opposed. The welfare state has stressed co-operation. Community is to the fore. Control is idealized. The drive into the centre is being blunted: the flight out diffused and slowed down. The planned society is concerned that the needs and rights of all should prevail over the ambitions and power of the few. In this, both Canada and Britain are still on parallel lines, though it must be said that Britain has gone somewhat further in the discipline involved: green belts are halting urban sprawl, low-cost public housing is being built cheek by jowl with private developments, the car is being inhibited, and mass transit systems are given support.

Most important, the new urban centrality is stressing central location for art, music, theatre, and convention halls and hotels. These attract people, making downtown a counter focus to the suburb. Traditionally, urban flight has been the middle-class way out of the downtown problem (Fig. 10). It is the middle-class haven from axial-route stress and centre-city conflict. A city made of driveways in and flightways out is a city increasingly at risk: it is a city growing sick at the heart and along the arteries, with its head in the air full of fond phantasies. Yet, as Higbee[40] has said, "the city is the responsibility of the total society". Escapism will have to stop. Drives have got to be controlled. The city must develop as *one world*, with all its parts contributing to the whole. Urban centrality now tries to benefit that whole, it is not only for the business sector. Therefore, there is not the same urge for flight. Cities will of course still expand—to that extent intra-urban migration must continue—but it will be in a different, more socially constrained way.

CITIES AS MENTAL SPACE

If this comparative geography of Canadian and British settlement should have any validity it suggests that (1) cities are the products of mental space; (2) mental images largely determine the use of space; (3) mental fright or frustration at the imaged conflicts of the city-centre have led to urban flight; (4) urban flight follows mental corridors; (5) these corridors lie between areas of mental deflection; and (6) they proceed along zones of mental attraction.

In the working-out of these processes relative space is more important than actual space. The relativities involved point up the value of social space, and in particular of social distances, and of contact space, and especially of mental contact.

Cities are essentially states of mind. Even if, in terms of actual space, they should be widely separated and have widely different, indeed— unique, situations, nevertheless at the level of mental space they may respond to the same images and evolve with the same forms. Thus the history of their mind has a marked influence on the pattern of their geography. Urban geographers have a great opportunity of making these relationships live and have a meaning. Their contribution is crucial to both urban history and urban ecology. As they point up change, they may affect trends, thus having a say for the future: a future in this case when the flight from problems must end, and the day for solution begin.

REFERENCES

1. Youngson, A. J. (1966). "The Making of Classical Edinburgh, 1750-1840." Edinburgh University Press, Edinburgh. 74-75.
2. Garvan, A. (1951). "Architecture and Town Planning in Colonial Connecticut." Yale University Press, New Haven.
3. Harley, J. B. (1973). England circa 1850. In Darby, H. C. (ed.) "A New Historical Geography of England." Cambridge University Press, Cambridge, 527.
4. Youngson, A. J. (1967). The city of reason and nature. In "Edinburgh in the Age of Reason: a Symposium." Edinburgh University Press, Edinburgh.
5. Akins, T. B. (1895). "History of Halifax City." Halifax, N.S., (n.p.). 126.
6. McAlpine (1870). "Halifax City Directory 1869-70." Lovell, Montreal. (See entry for Bedford Row.)
7. Blakeley, P. R. (1949). "Glimpses of Halifax." Public Archives of Nova Scotia, Pubn. No. 9, Halifax. 65.
8. Ibid., p.69.
9. Ibid., p.63, (Reference to Provincial and Dominion buildings.)
10. White, G. A. (1876). "Halifax and its Business." Nova Scotia Printing Co., Halifax. 7, 137.

11. Ibid., p.133.
12. Akins, op.cit., pp.198-200.
13. Blakeley, op.cit., p.72.
14. McAlpine, "Halifax City Directory." op.cit. (see entry for Granville St).
15. Anon. (1949). "Historical Sketches of St. Andrew's Church, Halifax." United Church of Canada pubn., Halifax. 6.
16. Akins, op.cit., p.158.
17. Chettle, H. (1916). quoted from Onions, C. T. "Shakespeare's England." London. 40.
18. Harvey, D. C. (1949). Halifax, 1749-1949. *Can. Geog. J.* **38**, 17.
19. Fergusson, C. B. (1949). "Eighteenth Century Halifax." Canadian Historical Association, Report of Annual Meeting, Halifax, 1949. University of Toronto Press, Toronto. 32-39.
20. White, op.cit. p.20.
21. Watson, J. W. (1956). Relict geography of an urban community—Halifax N.S. *In* Miller, R. and Watson, J. W. "Essays in Memory of A. G. Ogilvie." Nelson, Edinburgh. 125.
22. Blakeley, op.cit., pp.92-3.
23. Akins, op.cit., p.203.
24. Fergusson, C. B. (1950). Rise of the theatre in Halifax. *Dalhousie Rev.* **xxix**, 419-428.
25. Raddall, T. H. (1948). "Halifax, Warden of the North." McClelland and Stewart, Toronto. 68.
26. Blakeley, P. R. (1949). The theatre and music in Halifax 1787-1901. *Dalhousie Rev.* **29**, 8-20, and quote on 11-12.
27. *Historical Sketches*, op. cit., p.16.
28. Ibid., p.6.
29. Ibid., p.11.
30. Ibid., p. 27.
31. Ibid., p.49.
32. Blakeley, "Glimpses of Halifax." op. cit., p.70.
33. Falconer, J. W. and Watson, W. G. (1946). "A Brief History of Pine Hill Divinity Hall." Presbyterian Church of Canada pubn., Sackville. 13.
34. "Historical Sketches." op.cit., p.47.
35. Falconer and Watson, op.cit., p.16.
36. Blakeley, "Theatre and Music . . ." op.cit., pp.11-12.
37. Anon. (1909). "Halifax, Capital of Nova Scotia, Its Advantages and Interests." Board of Trade pubn., Halifax. 86, 82.
38. Piers, H. (1913). A brief historical account of the N.S. Institute of Science. *Proc. N.S. Inst. of Sci.* **13**, 65.

39. Watson, J. W. (1979). Edinburgh—concentration and dispersal. *In* Gottmann, J. (ed.) "Offices and Urban Growth." Special issue of *Ekistics*, **46**, 15-25.
40. Higbee, E. (1975). Centre cities in Canada and the United States. *In* Watson, J. W. and O'Riordan, T., "The American Environment: Perceptions and Policies." Wiley, London. 159.

Subject Index

413